DATE DUE

NO 29'99		
DE 18 99		
JE 1'00		
MY 7'00		
DE 5'00		
DE 1 '00		
MY 24 01		
NO 2'01		
MY 23 02		
NO		
JE 11 03		
NO 26'03		
DE 9 04		
DE 3 '05		
NO 1 5 '08		
MY 2 5 '10		

DEMCO 38-296

DRINKING PATTERNS AND THEIR CONSEQUENCES

**INTERNATIONAL CENTER FOR ALCOHOL POLICIES
SERIES ON ALCOHOL IN SOCIETY**

Grant and Litvak—*Drinking Patterns and Their Consequences*

DRINKING PATTERNS AND THEIR CONSEQUENCES

Edited by

Marcus Grant
International Center for Alcohol Policies
Washington, DC, USA
and

Jorge Litvak
International University Exchange
Washington, DC, USA
and Universidad de Chile, Santiago, Chile

Taylor & Francis
Publishers since 1798

Drinking patterns and their
consequences

Taylor & Francis
1101 Vermont Avenue, NW, Suite 200
Washington, DC 20005-3521
Tel: (202) 289-2174
Fax: (202) 289-3665

Distribution Center:

Taylor & Francis
1900 Frost Road, Suite 101
Bristol, PA 19007-1598
Tel: (215) 785-5800
Fax: (215) 785-5515

UK

Taylor & Francis Ltd.
1 Gunpowder Square
London EC4A 3DE
Tel: 171 583 0490
Fax: 171 583 0581

DRINKING PATTERNS AND THEIR CONSEQUENCES

Copyright © 1998 International Center for Alcohol Policies. All rights reserved. Printed in the United States of America. Except as permitted under the United States Copyright Act of 1976, no part of this publication may be reproduced or distributed in any form or by any means, or stored in a database or retrieval system, without prior written permission of the publisher.

1 2 3 4 5 6 7 8 9 0   B R B R   9 0 9 8 7

This book was set in Times Roman. The editors were Diane Hammond and Alison Howson. Cover design by Robb Springfield, Precision Graphics

A CIP catalog record for this book is available from the British Library.
∞ The paper in this publication meets the requirements of the ANSI Standard Z39.48-1984 (Permanence of Paper)

Library of Congress Cataloging-in-Publication Data

Drinking patterns and their consequences / edited by Marcus Grant and
    Jorge Litvak.
        p.   cm.
    ISBN 1-56032-718-9 (case : alk. paper)
    1. Drinking of alcoholic beverages—Cross-cultural studies.
    2. Alcoholism—Cross-cultural studies.   3.Drinking of alcoholic
    beverages—Government policy.   4. Alcoholism—Prevention.
    I. Grant, Marcus.   II. Litvak, Jorge.
    HV5047.D75   1997
    394.1′3—dc21   97-25113
                                                                        CIP

ISBN 1-56032-718-9

To the memory of Dan Dockery

Contents

Acknowledgments   xi

Introduction: Beyond per Capita Consumption   1
Marcus Grant and Jorge Litvak

PART 1—DRINKING PATTERNS AND OUTCOMES

CHAPTER 1   The Levels, Patterns, and Consequences of
                 Drinking   7
                 Eric Single and Victor E. Leino

CHAPTER 2   Trends in Drinking and Patterns of Drinking   25
                 Reginald G. Smart

CHAPTER 3   Individual Characteristics and Drinking Patterns   43
                 Wilson Acuda and Barton Alexander

CHAPTER 4   Health Issues and Drinking Patterns   63
                 Amelia M. Arria and Michael Gossop

CHAPTER 5   Social and Behavioral Issues Related to
                 Drinking Patterns   89
                 Nii-K Plange

CHAPTER 6   Cultural Variations among Drinking Patterns   103
                 Dwight B. Heath

PART 2—POLICIES AND PROGRAMS

CHAPTER 7   The Distribution of Alcohol Consumption   129
                 John B. Saunders and Simon de Burgh

CHAPTER 8   The Impact of Alcohol Control Measures on
                 Drinking Patterns   153
                 Stephen Whitehead

CHAPTER 9   The Social Costs of Alcohol Consumption:
                 Definitions, Measurement, and Policy
                 Implications   169
                 Richard Dubourg and David Pearce

CHAPTER 10   Alcohol Abuse: Cost Effectiveness and the
                 Economic Impact of Policies and Programs   189
                 Rhonda Galbally, Chris Borthwick, and Roy Batterham

CHAPTER 11   Community Reactions to Alcohol Policies   205
                 Dwight B. Heath and Haydée Rosovsky

PART 3—A NEW APPROACH

CHAPTER 12   The Implications for Measurement and Research   221
                 Marjana Martinic

CHAPTER 13   The Implications of Drinking Patterns for
                 Primary Prevention, Education, and Screening   243
                 Ann M. Roche and Keith R. Evans

CHAPTER 14   Public and Private Partnerships in Prevention
                 and Research   267
                     I. New Players for a New Era: How Up-To-Date Is
                     Health Promotion?   268
                 Ilona Kickbusch
                     II. Effective Partnerships Between the Public and
                     Private Sectors   272
                 Peter Mitchell
                     III. Lessons from Partnerships: The Example of the
                     United States   276
                 Yvonne Lumsden-Dill

IV. The Case of the College of Pharmacy,
University of Chile 282
Hugo Zunino, Jorge Litvak, and Yedy Israel

CHAPTER 15 Shifting the Paradigm: Reducing Harm and
Promoting Beneficial Patterns 287
Marcus Grant and Eric Single

APPENDIX Principles of Cooperation among the Beverage
Alcohol Industry, Governments, Scientific
Researchers, and the Public Health Community 299

INDEX 303

Acknowledgments

The editors wish to acknowledge the following for their help in bringing this book about: Marjana Martinic, for her coordination of the editorial process and her patient and painstaking communications with the authors; Christopher Barks, for his assistance in the final editing of the chapters; and David Thompson, for his keen eye and meticulous attention to detail in providing the technical editing. Our thanks go also to Eleni Houghton, Sally Carreiro, and Tatiana Metody for their help and advice. We would like to acknowledge the panel of independent reviewers, listed in the introduction, whose invaluable input helped us focus on the issues at hand; and the editorial advisory board, who helped birth the idea for this book and whose joint effort lent it its final shape. The members of the editorial advisory group include Wilson Acuda, Amelia Arria, René Gonzalez, Michael Gossop, Dwight Heath, Prabat Jha, Yvonne Lumsden-Dill, Enrique Madrigal, Nii-K Plange, John Saunders, Alan Simpson, Ronald Simpson, Eric Single, Reginald Smart, Henk Rijkborst, Haydée Rosovsky, and Leland Towle.

Introduction: Beyond per Capita Consumption

Marcus Grant and Jorge Litvak

For more than two decades, the basis of alcohol policy in many countries has been the assumption that there exists a direct relationship between average daily per capita alcohol consumption and the prevalence of a wide range of health and social problems associated with the misuse of alcohol. Known as either the single-distribution theory or the control-of-consumption theory, it has dominated the international debate on alcohol policies.

However, that assumption has been challenged in recent years as a result of conflicting empirical evidence and the mounting evidence regarding the beneficial health effects of moderate alcohol consumption. In particular, the theory has shown itself to be insensitive to patterns of drinking and disease in individual cultures, patterns that can be radically different from one another and from those patterns in the handful of industrialized countries that have most actively supported the per capita consumption model.

There is now broad consensus that low levels of alcohol consumption are associated with negligible health risks and probably some health benefits. Similarly, moderate alcohol consumption in appropriate circumstances is associated with possible health benefits and with levels of risk that are low enough for most to consider them within acceptable limits. On the other hand, high alcohol

Marcus Grant is from the International Center for Alcohol Policies, Washington, D.C. Jorge Litvak is from the International University Exchange, Washington, D.C., USA, and Universidad de Chile, Santiago, Chile.

consumption levels are associated with a range of health and social problems whose severity and intensity tend to increase at very high levels of consumption.

Public policy requires an understanding of the way that individual risks vary in response to changes in consumption and the differences in consumption patterns of drinkers in the population. The challenge is how best to achieve the optimum balance between population-based and individual-based approaches and between approaches that focus on consumption and harm. These need not be seen as competing approaches, since they are essentially complementary. The issue is one of emphasis. The purpose of public policy is to encourage measures that are most likely to benefit the individual and society by reducing harm and promoting an environment that enhances quality of life and is supportive of the capacity to make informed choices.

In this book, we suggest ways to reassess the propositions of Ledermann (whose statistical work has generally been used in support of the single-distribution theory) so that public policy can be targeted more effectively. In particular, by taking into account the very different drinking climates that exist around the world, the book emphasizes an integrative approach, sensitive to the wide disparity in the needs of different countries and cultures.

With these concerns in mind, the International Center for Alcohol Policies (ICAP) convened an editorial advisory group meeting in Washington, D.C., in September 1995.[1] Participants came from a wide range of countries and academic backgrounds; they included public health specialists and representatives of the beverage alcohol industry, as well as senior officials from the World Health Organization and the World Bank. The authors of the chapters in this book include many who participated in that meeting and others who did not; both groups reflect an attempt to extend the debate beyond the relatively narrow group traditionally associated with alcohol policy issues.[2]

The attempt to engage many points of view is reflected in the editorial process adopted during the preparation of the book: an editorial group within ICAP was charged with the preliminary review of the chapters as they were received, and the final manuscript was submitted for external peer review by identified experts in the alcohol field. These experts included representatives from the public health and research communities, nongovernmental organizations, and the beverage alcohol industry, all of whom have an active interest in the policy debate surrounding alcohol.[3] The external reviewers were asked for

1. Sponsoring companies of the International Center for Alcohol Policies are Allied Domecq Spirits and Wine, Bacardi-Martini, Brown-Forman, Coors Brewing Company, Foster's Brewing Group Limited, Guinness PLC, Heineken NV, International Distillers and Vintners (IDV), Miller Brewing Company, Joseph E. Seagram and Sons, and South African Breweries.

2. The opinions expressed in this book are those of the individual authors and do not necessarily reflect the views of the sponsors of ICAP. The primary goal of this book is a full discussion of the issues and a contribution to overall the body of scholarship. No effort was made to direct the individual authors.

3. Members of the external review panel were Dr. Loran Archer, Rockville, Md., U.S.; Dr. Joseph Asare, Psychiatric Hospital, Ministry of Health, Accra, Ghana; Dr. Bryan Johnstone, Uni-

their independent and unbiased opinions on the merits of the volume and on its effectiveness in providing a fresh approach to the field.

The need for a fresh approach has become increasingly apparent. The situation is summarized in the following way by Edwards et al. (1994): "For several diseases there is convincing evidence for a dose-response relation between individual consumption and individual risk. Some of these risk functions are strongly nonlinear, with more than proportionally greater risk at higher levels of intake. In other cases, J-shaped risk functions have been inferred, particularly in relation to coronary heart disease. And for several types of consequence, the exact relationship between risk and intake is not known, although it is evident that heavy consumption under certain circumstances can elevate risk" (p. 75). At the population level, the relative contribution of any consumer group to the sum of the damage varies across types of drinking problem, depending on how the risk function behaves. In other words, two populations with the same per capita consumption may have different problem rates.

Despite this, measures designed to control consumption at the population level have remained a central feature of many public health recommendations, because they are regarded as having general effectiveness. It has to be noted, however, that they attract little popular support and that they fail to differentiate among population subgroups. The composition of the drinking population has an important bearing on the population problem rate, and trends in overall per capita consumption are a poor indicator of subgroup trends in alcohol abuse.

There is now strong empirical evidence that it is more relevant to focus on heavy drinking occasions than on level of consumption per se. Such an approach is also consistent with the emerging evidence on the benefits of moderate consumption and is probably more in keeping with declining political support for rigid controls over the availability of alcohol in a world characterized by the disappearance of restrictive trade barriers.

In summary, therefore, the editors of this book take the view that the time has come to move toward a comprehensive theoretical framework that seeks to reduce harm at both the individual and societal levels without unreasonably restricting opportunities for individual choice. Average per capita consumption masks a huge variety of drinking patterns. For example, many cases of preventible harm are caused by episodic heavy drinking and not by moderate daily consumption. Equally, aggregate accounts of alcohol-related problems conceal the profound differences in the relative impact of these problems in differing socioeconomic environments.

To move forward, we need to be able to describe drinking patterns more accurately and to relate them to patterns of problems. Although this has been

versity of Kentucky, Lexington, Ky., U.S.; Dr. Enrique Madrigal, Pan American Health Organization/WHO; Dr. Stanton Peele, Lindesmith Center, Morristown, N.J., U.S.; Dr. Andrew Penman, New South Wales Health Department, Sydney, NSW, Australia; Dr. Henk Rijkborst, Heineken, Amsterdam, The Netherlands; Dr. Ronald Simpson, Seagram, Inc., White Plains, N.Y., U.S.; and Lee Towle, Burgess, Va, U.S.

widely acknowledged, little systematic effort has been made to bring together the thinking about what these patterns look like and how they might relate to each other. This book is divided into three parts, the first of which (chapters 1 through 6) addresses the central issue of the relationship between patterns of drinking and patterns of outcome. The second part (chapters 7 through 11) looks at the implications of this shift in emphasis on policies and programs at local, national, and international levels. The final part (chapters 12 through 15) proposes an approach to alcohol policy development in keeping with the complex and changing world. Each of the three sections is preceded by a short foreword that introduces the chapters and discusses the issues to be examined.

Many people have an interest in seeing alcohol policies that actually work: politicians and civil servants in the health, social affairs, trade, agriculture, and finance sectors; medical and other health practitioners and social workers; public health officials and advocates; scientists and scholars from a wide range of disciplines; those working in the production and distribution of beverage alcohol; those in the hospitality industry; and concerned individuals around the world who devote their time and energies to promoting responsible use of alcohol, fighting alcohol misuse, and seeking to improve the quality of life for all. We hope this book will encourage all these people by indicating a way forward that does not repeat the mistakes of the past but that empowers individuals and communities to find answers based on a sense of mutual responsibility.

REFERENCE

Edwards, G., et al. 1994. *Alcohol Policy and the Public Good*. Oxford: Oxford University Press, 75–106.

Part One

Drinking Patterns and Outcomes

Alcohol policies in many countries have long been based on the assumption that a wide range of health and social problems associated with the abuse of alcohol can be directly correlated with average daily *per capita* alcohol consumption. In light of increasing empirical evidence, this central hypothesis has been challenged more and more by the notion that levels of consumption are inadequate to address the global population which encompasses an array of different drinking styles, different outcomes to both the individual and society, and, not least, markedly different cultural contexts.

The first section of this book examines the general concept of drinking patterns, offering an explanation of the term and the variables to be taken into consideration when describing them. At the individual level, the authors explore biomedical and psychosocial factors which may contribute to consequences of specific drinking patterns and may serve as predictors of risks or benefits associated with drinking.

Just as individual variables may allow for the identification of those at risk for adverse consequences of drinking, so different drinking patterns can serve as predictors for particular outcomes. Measurement of drinking levels has proved inadequate in addressing the outcomes for a large segment of the drinking population, in particular for those individuals with light or moderate alcohol consumption. As recent medical evidence has demonstrated, even total abstention from alcohol may be associated with health risks, a relationship that would not have been predicted under the distribution of consumption model. Therefore, in predicting outcome, it is more important to address the fashion in which individuals drink than how much they drink.

Variations in drinking patterns are also examined as they relate to different outcomes for society. Some of these outcomes are clearly adverse, some are neutral, and still others may be beneficial and play an integral role within a particular cultural context. The role of alcohol differs widely between different societies, underscoring the need to move away from a policy paradigm which attempts to impose a uniform solution on a widely diverse world.

The policy implications of the proposed shift in paradigm are far reaching. In particular, the proposed shift in focus to patterns of drinking as predictors of outcomes emphasizes the need to address specifically harmful drinking behaviors that cannot be described solely on the basis of per capita consumption. The chapters within this section illustrate one of the central themes of this book, namely that there is no simple or uniform solution to the harm sometimes associated with drinking, but that a novel and more complex solution which extends beyond the distribution of consumption model is required.

Chapter 1

The Levels, Patterns, and Consequences of Drinking

Eric Single and Victor E. Leino

The central theme of this book is that those involved in alcohol research and prevention programs should pay greater attention to patterns of drinking, since these patterns are important determinants of both the positive and negative consequences of drinking. Indeed, preliminary evidence indicates that patterns of drinking may be more important than levels of alcohol consumption in predicting whether people will experience problems with their drinking. A logical starting point is to describe what is meant by patterns of drinking and to discuss why they are important.

Patterns of drinking may refer to several aspects of drinking behavior, including temporal variations in drinking, the number and characteristics of heavy drinking occasions, the settings where drinking takes place, the activities associated with drinking, the personal characteristics of the drinkers and their drinking confederates, the types of beverage consumed, and the clusters of drinking norms and behaviors often referred to as drinking cultures (Rehm et al. 1996). How much one drinks may also be thought of as part of a person's drinking pattern. However, we have chosen to use the term in a manner that distinguishes level of drinking from other aspects of drinking behavior. Although level of drinking is clearly an important aspect of drinking behavior, the term

Eric Single is professor of preventive medicine and biostatics, University of Toronto, Canada. Victor E. Leino is in the Department of Family Medicine, University of Maryland Medical Center, Baltimore, Md., U.S.

drinking pattern is generally used in this book to refer to these other aspects of drinking behavior. In short, pattern of drinking differs from volume of alcohol consumption. Levels of drinking refers to how much people drink, while patterns of drinking refers to how they drink and the circumstances in which they drink.

Indeed, when an individual is referred to as a light or heavy drinker, more is generally implied than habitual level of consumption. Such terms clearly encompass the level of consumption but also refer beyond level to an assessment of the individual's overall drinking pattern. Attempts have been made to quantify light, moderate, heavy, and binge drinking, but there is little cross-cultural consensus as to what an appropriate number of drinks should be for each of these terms, on either a daily or a weekly basis. Treiman and Beck's (1995) assertion that moderate drinkers exceed light drinkers in both frequency and quantity per occasion, but do not meet the criteria for heavy drinkers, is useful only in that it emphasizes that the terms are relative rather than absolute. When terms like *sensible drinking* and *binge drinking* are used in this book—as they are with some frequency—it is their relative meaning within a cultural context that is being invoked, not any fixed quantitative limits.

Thus far, alcohol epidemiology has focused mainly on levels of drinking. Research on individuals has generally measured alcohol consumption in terms of quantity-frequency scales of average consumption, and research at the societal level has focused on mean per capita consumption. Public health advocates in the field of alcohol prevention have tended to focus on the effect of alcohol control measures, such as the nature and extent of state monopolization of alcohol trade, the number and location of off-premise sales outlets, licensing regulations, restrictions on drinking age, proscribed sales to intoxicated persons, advertising and sponsorship restrictions, criminal penalties for driving while intoxicated, and alcohol taxation (Bruun et al. 1975; Moore and Gerstein 1981; Edwards et al. 1994). There are several possible explanations for this focus on alcohol control measures, the primary one being the single-distribution theory, which attempts to explain the observation that the mean level of consumption in a society is related to the number of heavy drinkers. The single-distribution theory is addressed later in this chapter.

There are reasons for focusing on levels of consumption in alcohol epidemiology. Consumption level is conceptually clear and relatively easy to standardize across time and between different societies in the developed world. The consumption of beer, wine, and spirits is readily compared by converting consumption data into volume of pure alcohol. However, consumption level is less easy to calculate in societies in which alcohol beverages are primarily home produced and in which consumption cannot be standardized easily, unless culture-free instruments are used in the collection and analysis of the data. Epidemiological research on the relative risk of various diseases and causes of death associated with alcohol consumption becomes more difficult to standardize if one attempts to take different drinking patterns into account. Thus, the predominant focus on consumption level as the key determinant of drinking problems has severely limited the effectiveness of research in predicting drinking problems. There are many heavy drinkers who do not experience problems with their drinking, and there are many moderate and light drinkers who do incur drinking problems.

This has led to what Kreitman (1986) has termed the preventive paradox. Kreitman noted that even though heavy drinkers have a higher risk of incurring alcohol problems, moderate and light drinkers constitute the majority of persons who incur problems with their drinking. Heavy drinkers are most likely to incur problems with their use of alcohol—to drive while impaired, to have a family dispute about their drinking, to have a financial problem as the result of their drinking—but these drinkers represent only a small proportion of all drinkers. Thus, heavy drinkers may not constitute the majority of persons with alcohol-related problems, because of their limited numbers, and light or moderate drinkers, who may be at lower risk of incurring a problem with their use of alcohol, may constitute the majority of persons who incur problems.

Stockwell et al. (1996) have criticized the preventive paradox on the grounds that it uses a measure of risk based solely on average consumption. When risk is measured in terms of drinking pattern (the heaviest recent drinking days) instead of mean daily consumption, the preventive paradox all but disappears: high-risk drinkers (those who overdrink on a single occasion) account for the vast majority of persons who incur acute problems as the result of their drinking. As the main purpose of Kreitman's preventive paradox is to challenge traditional concepts of risk (Single 1996), Stockwell et al. (1996) actually confirm Kreitman's main point.

In short, greater attention should be given to drinking patterns, since the temporal rhythm of drinking, and other aspects of drinking patterns, have significant impacts on alcohol-related problems quite apart from the impact of drinking levels (Bondy 1996). Indeed, the impact of heavy drinking occasions and other aspects of abusive drinking behavior on drinking patterns may be as great as or greater than the impact of levels of drinking. In the following discussion, we examine the various aspects of drinking patterns, drinking levels, and per capita consumption and the relationship of each of these to alcohol-related problems.

WHAT WE MEAN BY DRINKING PATTERNS

As noted earlier, the term *drinking patterns* is used in this book to distinguish levels of drinking from other aspects of drinking behavior, such as temporal variations in drinking, settings and activities associated with drinking, the personal characteristics of drinkers and drinking confederates, and the types of beverage consumed.

Temporal Variations in Drinking

The first major dimension of drinking patterns is temporal variation in drinking. Drinking is often associated with leisure time. As Cavan noted in her classic tavern study (1966), drinking is time-out behavior, strongly related to leisure time. Thus, drinking tends universally to be greatest during nonworking hours and on weekends, but temporal patterns of drinking vary considerably in different cultures and social groups (Dawson 1996). In Mediterranean and Latin American societies, in which wine is the predominant alcoholic beverage, drinking with meals and during the day is a common pattern. In "drier" Northern European cultures, drinking during the day is less accepted and less common.

In addition to the time of day and day of the week when drinking takes place, temporal rhythm of drinking behavior is an important dimension of drinking patterns. A mean consumption level of two drinks per day, for instance, may represent a pattern of daily moderate drinking of two drinks per day or it may represent binge drinking of fourteen drinks once a week. A number of recent studies have begun to focus on heavy drinking occasions as a key predictor of alcohol problems (Single and Wortley 1993; Midanik et al. 1994; Stockwell et al. 1994). These studies typically examine either the number of occasions when the subject consumed a large amount of drinks (e.g., five or more) in the past period of time (a week, a month, a year) or the number of drinks consumed during the subject's last drinking occasion, but there is no consensus yet on how to operationalize the temporal rhythm of drinking. Different studies use different numbers of drinks to operationalize heavy drinking occasions.

More importantly, there is no clear sense of what constitutes a drinking occasion. If a person meets someone for dinner, then goes to a show or movie, and then goes to a pub for a drink, it is not clear whether this represents one, two, or three drinking occasions. The usual solution is to let the individual concerned interpret what constitutes a drinking occasion. To our knowledge no study has examined how subjects decide what is a drinking occasion.

Settings and Activities Associated with Drinking

Another dimension of drinking patterns concerns the settings and activities associated with drinking. In many societies, drinking occurs in connection with social or religious rituals. Drinking may be related to particular work activities. Drinking patterns often vary between urban centers and rural areas. An important aspect of drinking settings is whether drinking takes place in private homes or in public places, such as bars, cafés, restaurants, or beer gardens. Public drinking occurs in an enormous variety of venues, ranging from large to small commercial establishments and to open public areas, in conjunction with eating or with religious functions, such as village festivals, or simply for its own sake. A World Health Organization study on public drinking identified a wide variety of public drinking locales in twelve participating countries but found no classification of public drinking venues that could be applied to every country (Single et al. forthcoming). The most commonly identified types of public drinking locales were bars and restaurants, which were almost universal, but clubs, nightclubs, cafés, taverns, and cultural events were also frequently mentioned.

Recently, the tavern literature on drinking settings has been supplemented by survey data on the distribution of respondents' alcohol consumption in different types of setting. For example, Single and Wortley (1993) utilized questions developed by Clark (1985) to examine the extent of drinking in various social settings uncovered in a 1989 national survey in Canada. It was found that home consumption accounted for the greatest share of total drinking, while drinking in licensed establishments accounted for approximately one-fourth of total Canadian alcohol consumption. This estimate was externally validated against sales data. The distribution of drinking was strongly related to demographic variables and individual level of consumption. In particular, drinking in bars and taverns was related to higher levels of drinking and self-reported drinking problems.

Personal Characteristics of Drinkers and Drinking Confederates

A description of the pattern of drinking in a particular country necessarily includes a discussion of the sociodemographic correlates of drinking and the sociodemographic composition of typical drinking groups. Drinking is generally associated with particular personal characteristics. For example, it is universally true that on average males drink more than females. Age is also consistently related to drinking, the highest rates of consumption occurring among young adults (from the legal drinking age to the midthirties) in most countries. Religion and religiosity are among the most powerful predictors of drinking (Bruun et al. 1975; Edwards et al. 1994; Single et al. 1997). Thus, the vast majority of persons in Moslem countries abstain from alcohol, drinking being limited mainly to foreign workers or tourists. In countries where drinking is relatively common, attendance at religious services is a powerful predictor of whether and how much a person drinks. In some countries, socioeconomic status is related to drinking or to particular drinking patterns.

At the individual level, an aspect of one's drinking pattern is the personal characteristics of one's drinking confederates, characteristics often related to sociodemographic background. One pattern may involve drinking with persons of the same gender. Low-income drinkers tend to drink in larger groups and for longer periods of time than high-income drinkers (see Single 1985).

Types of Alcohol Beverage

In developed countries there are often marked differences in the alcohol beverage most commonly consumed. Spirits have been the beverage of choice in Nordic and some Eastern European countries. Beer is the beverage of choice in many parts of Europe (e.g., Austria, Belgium, Germany, the Netherlands), the United Kingdom, North America, and Australia. Wine is the most common alcohol beverage consumed in Mediterranean countries and some South American countries. Although differences among societies with regard to beverage preference appear to be narrowing over time as drinking patterns become more international (Bruun et al. 1975; Edwards et al. 1994), it is possible to speak of beer, wine, and spirits countries. In developing countries, the pattern of drinking often involves homemade or locally produced special types of alcohol beverage.

CAN WE IDENTIFY ALCOHOL CULTURES?

In the preceding pages we argue that alcohol epidemiology has given relatively little attention to drinking patterns, such as the temporal rhythm of drinking, the settings and activities associated with drinking, the personal characteristics of drinkers and drinking confederates, and the type of alcohol beverage consumed. At issue is whether there are particular combinations of such drinking patterns that interact to influence drinking behavior and the consequences of drinking.

When clusters of particular aspects of drinking patterns occur in several countries, the term *alcohol culture* has been used to denote these similarities. Terms such as *dry* as opposed to *wet* drinking cultures refer to the relatively low or high social acceptance of drinking. It has been argued that drinking problems are manifested differently in dry cultures: fewer persons incur problems, but those who do suffer more severe individual consequences (Room 1989).

Similarly, one hears reference to the Nordic drinking pattern, typified by binge drinking, spirits as the beverage of choice, and low overall rates of consumption. This may be juxtaposed to the Mediterranean or French drinking pattern, typified by regular drinking of wine, although rarely to the point of intoxication, and high overall consumption. These terms may not apply well in developing countries, where drinking may involve a special local beverage. Thus, there is no universally recognized typology of drinking cultures applicable to all countries. A challenge for alcohol epidemiology is to analyze the major dimensions of drinking patterns in various societies and identify four or five alcohol cultures that could be universally applied.

DRINKING LEVELS AND
PER CAPITA CONSUMPTION

The Single-Distribution Theory

Until recently, the main parameter for measuring alcohol consumption has not been pattern of drinking but, rather, consumption at the per capita level. Any discussion of the relationship between per capita consumption and number of heavy drinkers needs to begin with reference to the single-distribution theory.

Several authors have noted a strong relationship between per capita consumption of alcohol and the prevalence of heavy drinking (Ledermann 1956; Bruun et al. 1975; Skog 1982a; Simpura 1987; Rose and Day 1990). This relationship has been interpreted to indicate that the mean consumption somehow causally determines the prevalence of heavy drinking.

The single-distribution theory stems from the influential and controversial work of French social scientist Ledermann (1956). Indeed, owing to his influence, the view that controls over alcohol availability can be used to prevent alcohol problems has frequently been incorrectly identified as the Ledermann theory. Other terms used to describe this theory are the single-distribution or distribution-of-consumption theory. Ledermann argued that a single function, a lognormal curve, provides an accurate estimate of the distribution of alcohol consumption in any society. Given the addictive properties of alcohol, some might have expected alcohol distribution to be bimodal, with one peak level among moderate or social drinkers and a second peak level among those who are physically dependent on alcohol. Contrary to this expectation, Ledermann found a unimodal distribution that is continuous and highly skewed.

Perhaps the most controversial aspect of Ledermann's work is the contention that the dispersion of this distribution is relatively invariate and can be estimated from the mean. The theory rests on the empirical finding that the mean level of alcohol consumption in any society tends to be closely related to the number of persons drinking at levels associated with high risk of developing alcoholism or alcohol-related problems. This implies that once the mean consumption among drinkers is known, one can predict with reasonable accuracy the number of persons consuming at any level, including the number who might be deemed to be high-risk or alcoholic. Bruun and his colleagues (1975) critically examined and extended Ledermann's analysis of the distribution of alcohol consumption, and their work gave qualified support to those conclusions.

Although the Ledermann approach helped to bring prevention issues to the forefront of policy debates, it is fundamentally flawed. The contention that the Ledermann lognormal distribution represents an accurate description of alcohol consumption in any society has been challenged by many authors (Duffy 1977; Duffy and Cohen 1978; Parker and Harman 1978; Pittman 1980; Pittman and Strickland 1981; Skog 1982a; Alanko 1992). Much of the criticism concerns the assumptions underlying the development of the Ledermann distribution function, such as that the upper limit of alcohol consumption per person is 365 liters of pure ethanol per year.

One of the most perplexing issues in the Ledermann distribution is the assumption of homogeneity, whereby the model is meant to apply only to populations in which there are no major social groups that deviate substantially from the overall mean level of consumption. This assumption would seem to eliminate the model's applicability to any known society, because all societies consist of an approximately equal number of males and females, and male mean drinking levels are invariably a good deal higher than those of females. For example, survey data indicate that Canadian males drink at least 50 percent more per capita than females (Single et al. 1994a). The Ledermann distribution would yield one estimate of the number of persons consuming at least 15 centiliters of alcohol per day, when applied to the total population of Canada but a very different and considerably higher estimate if it were applied separately to males and females. In Ledermann's original formulation, a second parameter was added to the distribution to adjust for heterogeneous populations, but this very important aspect of the distribution function was ignored or omitted in Ledermann's subsequent work and in the work of others, with the exception of Skog (1982a). Since no society meets the assumption of homogeneity, it would have been preferable for the single-parameter Ledermann function to be ignored, instead.

The basic problem with the single-distribution theory is that it is not so much a theory as an empirical generality without a firm theoretical model. A notion of "contagion" has been offered as an explanation (Bruun et al. 1975). As Rose and Day (1990) stated it: "The way most people eat, drink, and behave . . . may determine how many other, more vulnerable, persons will suffer as a consequence." Without describing the intervening processes involved in this explanation, it only takes a single empirical exception to negate the entire theory. Skog (1983) found such an exception when he compared Norwegian males to French females, groups with the same mean level of consumption. While Norwegian males are surrounded by largely abstinent Norwegian females, French females are surrounded by heavy-drinking French males. Skog noted that the distribution of consumption for these two groups is very different. Thus, it cannot be claimed that a single mathematical function can describe the distribution of alcohol consumption in any situation.

The controversy surrounding the single-distribution hypothesis continues. Skog, in particular, has carried on this line of work despite the fact that he views the Ledermann theory as "untenable" in its original form (1983, p. 1). By modifying Ledermann's work to include a number of factors that combine in a multiplicative rather than an additive fashion, as well as considering the drinker's social network, Skog has transformed a theoretically crude empirical generality into a potentially viable theory explaining major variations in rates of alcohol-related problems across societies.

Nonetheless, the single-distribution theory of alcohol consumption, as originally formulated, is scientifically untenable. There is no immutable distribution of consumption that applies to all societies and all situations. True distribution will vary over time and between societies. The single-distribution theory is only one of several possible explanations for the observation that mean levels of consumption in a society are related to the number of heavy drinkers, and this relationship is by no means the only way in which alcohol availability and alcohol-related problems are theoretically connected (Single 1984). The key underpinning for the position in favor of controls over alcohol availability is the empirical relationship between levels of drinking and adverse consequences.

Per Capita Consumption: Current Status and Change, by Country

Up to this point, the main focus of this chapter has been the variation in drinking patterns among individuals and groups. We now turn to patterns within cultures, in which variations in national-level statistics can also be used as predictors of alcohol-related problems. Levels of drinking, as measured by per capita consumption, can be used to reflect the alcohol culture within a country. For example, as mentioned earlier, consumption in dry as opposed to wet countries can be used to illustrate their respective drinking levels, patterns, and problems (Room 1989). However, the evidence suggests that while per capita consumption is an important indicator, alternative methods may exist that also allow evaluation of consumption and its relationship to problems.

Using data from *World Drink Trends, 1995,* showing countries with the highest and lowest rates of per capita consumption, it is possible to evaluate the countries studied on multiple theoretical levels. In order to standardize the results across cultures, the raw data from these countries have been subjected to met-analysis. While the data can be analyzed with respect to total per capita consumption, another question may be asked by breaking the per capita consumption down by beverage type. For example, what patterns emerge within countries when spirits, beer, and wine are evaluated separately? As the data in table 1.1 show, the pattern of spirits consumption differs from the total per capita estimates, while the beer pattern is apparently more similar to the pattern of total per capita consumption. Overall, there appears to be some specificity related to the type of beverage and per capita levels, and this is especially true at the higher end of the distribution range.

Trends in alcohol consumption can also be followed over time. Levels in some countries with high per capita consumption decreased within the interval analyzed, while in some countries with low per capita consumption, levels increased. There are both consistencies and inconsistencies in country representation across beverages. Further information can be gleaned from per capita and beverage-specific consumption when the information is broken down by gender and age groups. Unfortunately, gathering such information requires rather expensive research methodologies and can, therefore, only be estimated in some countries.

THE CONSEQUENCES OF DRINKING

Per Capita Consumption and Alcohol-Related Problems

Just as patterns emerge in the consumption of alcohol beverages, alcohol-related problems are often found in clusters. These clusters, which form problem patterns, may in turn be used as predictors of still other problems. Therefore, per

Table 1.1 Countries with highest and lowest per capita consumption, 1994

Total		Spirits[a]		Beer		Wine	
Lowest 8	Highest 8	Lowest 8	Highest 8	Lowest 8	Highest 8	Lowest 8	Highest 8
Morocco	Luxembourg	Malaysia	Russia	Morocco	Czech Rep.	Thailand	France
Malaysia	France	Thailand	China	Tunisia	Germany	China	Luxembourg
Tunisia	Portugal	Argentina	Poland	Turkey	Rep. Ireland	Mexico	Italy
Thailand	Germany	Turkey	Cyprus	Israel	Luxembourg	Singapore	Portugal
Israel	Hungary	Singapore	Hungary	Malaysia	Denmark	Peru	Switzerland
Turkey	Czech Rep.	Norway	Bulgaria	Thailand	Austria	Cuba	Argentina
Peru	Austria	Portugal	Greece	Ukraine	Slovakia	Turkey	Greece
Singapore	Denmark	Mexico	Spain	China	Hungary	Venezuela	Hungary

Source Adapted from *World Drink Trends 1995.*
[a]No statistics were available on Peru, Israel, Tunisia, and Morocco for spirits.

capita consumption may be more informative when evaluated by methodologies that incorporate three levels of analysis: macro, meso, and individual. This would allow evaluation of the relationship between per capita consumption and alcohol-related problems. Presenting per capita consumption alongside problem indicators, such as cirrhosis rates or alcohol-related death rates, provides only crude indications of a potential yet unknown relationship. For instance, per capita consumption, although a useful indicator, does not typically include the home brewing of alcohol beverages, which may vary greatly between countries and is not typically broken down by gender or age groups. Similarly, per capita consumption does not give an indication of the drinking patterns or drinking problems of a society.

Per capita consumption can better be used in an analytic evaluation by means of a predictive model in which generalized population surveys of drinking consumption, patterns, and problems are linked in time with per capita consumption rates. Such an analytic evaluation uses individual-level data (general population surveys) in conjunction with aggregate-level information in multiple countries to allow for a statistical evaluation cross-culturally.

Statistical techniques such as metanalysis, hierarchical modeling, and multilevel modeling allow for tests of significance by taking into account the differences in level between individuals and countries. For example, it is possible to ask whether per capita consumption of alcohol can be used to predict monthly frequency, quantity per occasion, monthly volume, consistency in frequency, quantity and volume over time, alcohol drinking patterns such as bingeing or chronic heavy drinking, alcohol problems, and consistency of alcohol problems.

The demonstration analysis that follows, derived from a paper presented by Leino and colleagues (1992), takes aggregate-level information from a number of countries to provide statistical relationships that can predict alcohol-related problems over time. Nineteen studies from the archive of the Collaborative Alcohol-Related Longitudinal Project (studies described in Fillmore et al. 1991; development of the archive is described in Johnstone et al. 1991) were used for each research question. Only data from drinkers were analyzed. Studies were from Canada, Czechoslovakia, Denmark, Finland, Ireland, New Zealand, Norway, the Shetland Islands, Sweden, the United Kingdom, and the United States; the periods of measurement lay between 1960 and 1986.

The studies were analyzed by means of a cross-level analytic strategy that assesses and controls for aggregate- and individual-level variables. The aggregate-level variables taken into account were (1) the normative drinking patterns of a nation, reflected by per capita consumption of alcohol, (2) societal stress (divorce, suicide, and unemployment rates), and (3) the nation in which the study occurred, which taps factors not accounted for by the two national traits explicitly evaluated. At the individual level, the factors of age and sex were regarded as important controls and predictors of the relationships under study because they have been repeatedly found to be related to drinking problems both within and across national settings (Roizen 1983).

After controlling for aggregate- and individual-level variables, one can focus on the relationships of multiple alcohol problems to the prediction of alcohol-related health problems and alcohol-related social role or social demeanor problems. Both of these dependent variables were regarded as important consequences of drinking. Groups of problems used as predictor variables were alcohol-related accidents, alcohol-related mental and existential problems, "negative" personal reasons for drinking, episodes of drunkenness, and episodes of binge drinking. The analytic strategy proceeded by testing the following questions through metanalysis:

• Are the alcohol-related predictor problems associated with alcohol-related health problems or alcohol-related social role problems?
• Is the magnitude of these associations homogeneous across studies and across age and sex groups?
• Can heterogeneity in these relationships be accounted for by contextual-level variables (per capita consumption of alcohol, suicide rates, divorce rates, unemployment rates, and country of study), controlling for age and sex groups?

Two relationships were found to be both significantly related to each other and homogeneous across studies: first, health problems were significantly predicted by both drunkenness and binge drinking; second, they remained significant when controlling for the personal characteristics of age and sex (e.g., Tuyns, Pequignot, and Esteve 1983; Skog 1982b). Of considerable importance is the fact that all relationships with either health problems or social role or demeanor problems remained significant after controlling for age and sex. However, some important patterns were observed that lend insight into the magnitude of these relationships.

For those relationships in which age was a significant predictor, the relative risk of social role or demeanor problems peaked during middle age, and binge drinking represented a progressively higher relative risk with progressive age. These relationships, particularly the homogeneous ones of drunkenness (in the middle years) and binge drinking (in the middle and late years) with social role and demeanor problems, suggest cross-sectional support for the notion that alcoholism is a clinical entity for these age groups.

The risk of accidents, on the other hand, was represented by a U-shaped curve, in which young people were homogeneously at very high risk for social role and demeanor problems. The relative risk was lowest for individuals in their twenties (homogeneous), rose in the middle years (homogeneous), and continued to rise in the later years (heterogeneous). These cross-sectional findings suggest that the relationship of accidents to social role and demeanor problems has different meanings for different age groups. A pattern emerged that suggests that either the normative drinking context or the relative stress (or perhaps both—interactions were not tested here) accounts for the strength of the associations. As has been suggested previously (Bales 1946), the stronger associations in contexts that were dry and with high societal stress indicate that stress was the critical variable in the stronger problem relationship.

The evidence reviewed suggests that the sizes of the effects evaluated are statistically significant under all conditions but that the majority of the effects are heterogeneous. Cross-study homogeneity was improved with the control of individual-level characteristics and provided insight into the social positions (designated by age and gender) of those persons in society who are at greater risk. However, the variables that eliminated heterogeneity from the associations were large contextual effects, measuring the normative drinking and the social stress of nations at the time of measurement or other traits of nations not yet evaluated. These findings strongly suggest, then, that the associations between many alcohol-related problems are in part molded by the social environments in which the problems take place. In summary, the level of consumption, although an important aspect of drinking behavior, is inadequate as an explanation for the strength of these associations.

The Impact of Drinking Patterns at the Individual Level

Much of our knowledge of both positive and adverse consequences of drinking is based on studies that examine the impact of drinking level. We know, for example, that an average intake of one or two drinks a day is associated with lower risk of coronary heart disease (see, e.g., Klatsky, Armstrong, and Friedman 1986, 1990, 1992; Moore and Pearson 1986; Stampfer et al. 1988; Poikolainen 1995). Indeed, the beneficial effect of low-level drinking on heart disease is so significant that the overall mortality of persons who consume an average of one or two drinks per day is significantly lower than the mortality of persons who abstain from alcohol altogether (Jackson, Scragg, and Beaglehole 1992; CCSA/ARF 1993; Poikolainen 1995). However, we have very limited information on whether the protective benefit of alcohol with regard to coronary heart disease is associated with particular patterns of drinking. It is very doubtful that a person who drinks heavily once a week (e.g., consuming seven to fourteen drinks in one day followed by six days of abstinence) would receive the same benefits regarding risk of coronary heart disease as someone who consumes one or two drinks every day of the week. Yet both drinkers would have an average of one or two drinks per day (CCSA/ARF 1993). Epidemiological studies on the risk of coronary heart disease and other benefits of alcohol consumption do not generally examine variations in drinking patterns.

By the same token, research on the adverse consequences of drinking has generally focused on level of drinking. Yet binge drinking (Heath 1995) and drinking to intoxication (Stockwell et al. 1996) are associated with adverse consequences and, particularly, with acute consequences. Even the time of the day when drinking takes place may be associated with consequences. Dawson (1996) analyzed survey data from the United States and found that the earlier a person drinks during the day, the higher the probability that the drinker will report adverse consequences from his or her drinking. Drinking in the morning is particularly associated with the relief of withdrawal symptoms in many societies.

Greater attention has recently been focused on the impact of heavy drinking occasions on adverse consequences. Analyses of national survey data in Australia (Stockwell et al. 1994), Canada (Single and Wortley 1993), and the United States (Midanik et al. 1994) all indicate that it may be more efficient to focus on heavy drinking occasions rather than the individual's level of consumption. In these analyses, level of consumption and number of heavy drinking occasions were related to various alcohol problems, and it was consistently found that number of heavy drinking occasions was a stronger predictor of drinking problems than level of consumption. The joint impact of number of heavy drinking occasions and level of consumption showed an important interaction effect, with particularly high rates of alcohol problems among light drinkers who occasionally drink excessively. Table 1.2 presents data from the 1993 General Social Survey in Canada on the joint impact of level of consumption and number of heavy drinking occasions on the likelihood of experiencing a drinking problem (Single et al. 1994b). It can be seen that the likelihood of experiencing drinking problems is greater for a moderate drinker who occasionally drinks to excess than for a heavy drinker who rarely or never drinks excessively.

The relatively low rates of problems among heavy drinkers who rarely or never drink immoderately may be associated with physical tolerance as well as the tendency for these drinkers to develop social supports and other mechanisms to minimize the adverse consequences of their drinking. Of course, there are limits to the extent to which heavy drinkers can control adverse consequences: over time, heavy drinking will greatly elevate the risk of chronic health consequences, such as cirrhosis. Nonetheless, for many of the more acute alcohol problems, such as impaired driving and alcohol-related family dysfunction or employment problems, relatively low-level consumers who occasionally drink immoderately contribute substantially to problem levels.

Table 1.2   Probability of experiencing a drinking problem, by heavy drinking occasions and level of consumption (percent)

Drinks per year	Number of heavy drinking occasions[a]			
	0	1	2 to 6	7 or more
1–51	2	8	7	17
52–364	2	8	10	21
> 365	7	5	14	35

Source: Statistics Canada 1993.

[a]Number of times in the previous twelve months respondent consumed five or more drinks on one occasion.

These findings indicate that prevention efforts should focus on reducing high-risk drinking patterns such as drinking to intoxication, in contrast to focusing on aggregate level of consumption. This is not to say that programs specifically targeted at heavy drinkers, such as early identification and intervention programs, should not be included in prevention programs. The available evidence indicates that such programs result in reductions in alcohol problems. However, programs focusing on reducing levels of drinking should not be adopted to the exclusion of programs that focus on high-risk drinking patterns.

CONCLUSION

Until recently, epidemiological research on the relationship between alcohol consumption and the consequences of drinking has focused largely on level of consumption. Relatively little attention has been given to temporal rhythms of drinking, the number and characteristics of heavy drinking occasions, the settings where drinking takes place, the activities associated with drinking, the characteristics of drinking confederates, and the types of beverage consumed. These aspects of drinking behavior have important influences on the incidence of both positive and negative drinking consequences. Indeed, preliminary evidence indicates that drinking patterns have an impact on drinking problems as great as, or even greater than, level of drinking.

REFERENCES

Alanko, T. 1992. Per capita consumption and rate of heavy use of alcohol: on evidence and inference in the single distribution debate. Paper presented at the Eighteenth Annual Alcohol Epidemiology Symposium of the Kettil Bruun Society, Toronto, Ontario, Canada, June 1–5.

Bales, R. F. 1946. Cultural differences in rates of alcoholism. *Quarterly Journal of Studies on Alcohol* 6:480–99.

Bondy, S. J. 1996. Overview of studies on drinking patterns and consequences. *Addiction* 91:1662–74.

Bruun, K., et al. 1975. *Alcohol Control Policies in a Public Health Perspective.* Vol. 25. Helsinki: Finnish Foundation for Alcohol Studies.

CCSA/ARF. 1993. *Moderate Drinking and Health: Report on an International Symposium.* Ottawa: Canadian Center on Substance Abuse; Toronto: Addiction Research Foundation.

Cavan, S. 1966. *Liquor Licence: An Ethnography of a Bar.* Chicago: Aldine.

Clark, W. 1985. Alcohol use in various settings. In *Public Drinking and Public Policy,* ed. E. Single and T. Storm. Toronto: Addiction Research Foundation.

Dawson, D. 1996. Temporal drinking patterns and variations in social consequences. *Addiction* 91:1623–35.

Duffy, J. C. 1977. Estimating the proportion of heavy drinkers. In *The Ledermann Curve: Report of a Symposium.* London: Alcohol Education Centre.

Duffy, J. C., and G. R. Cohen. 1978. Total alcohol consumption and excessive drinking. *British Journal of Addiction* 73:259–64.

Edwards, G., et al. 1994. *Alcohol Policy and the Public Good*. Oxford: Oxford University Press.

Fillmore, K. M., et al. 1991. The collaborative alcohol-related longitudinal project: preliminary results from a meta-analysis of drinking behavior in multiple longitudinal studies. *British Journal of Addiction* 86:1203–10.

Heath, D., ed. 1995. *International Handbook on Alcohol and Culture*. Westport, Conn.: Greenwood.

Jackson, R., R. Scragg, and R. Beaglehole. 1992. Does recent alcohol consumption reduce the risk of acute myocardial infarction and coronary death in regular drinkers? *American Journal of Epidemiology* 136:819–24.

Johnstone, B. M., et al. 1991. An integrated approach to meta-analysis in alcohol studies: the Collaborative Alcohol-Related Longitudinal Project. *British Journal of Addiction* 86:1211–20.

Klatsky, A., M. Armstrong, and G. Friedman. 1986. Relations of alcoholic beverage use to subsequent coronary artery disease hospitalization. *American Journal of Cardiology* 58:710–14.

———. 1990. Risk of cardiovascular mortality in alcohol drinkers, exdrinkers and non-drinkers. *American Journal of Cardiology* 66:1237–42.

———. 1992. Alcohol and mortality. *Annals of Internal Medicine* 117:646–54.

Kreitman, N. 1986. Alcohol consumption and the preventive paradox. *British Journal of Addiction* 81:353–64.

Ledermann, S. 1956. Alcool, alcoolisme, alcoolisation. In *Données scientifiques de caractère physiologique, économique et social*. Vol. 1. Paris: Presses Universitaires de France; Institut National d'Études Démographiques, Travaux et Documents, Cahier 29.

Leino, E. V., et al. 1992. Associations of alcohol-related health and social role problems with other alcohol-related problems: a research synthesis from the collaborative alcohol-related research project. Paper presented at the Eighteenth Annual Alcohol Epidemiology Symposium of the Kettil Bruun Society, Toronto, June 1–5.

Midanik, L., T. Tam, T. Greenfield, and R. Caetano. 1994. Risk functions for alcohol-related problems in a 1988 U.S. National Sample. Berkeley: California Pacific Medical Center Research Institute, Alcohol Research Group.

Moore, M., and D. Gerstein. 1981. *Alcohol and Public Policy: Beyond the Shadow of Prohibition*. Washington, DC: National Academy Press.

Moore, R., and T. Pearson. 1986. Moderate alcohol consumption and coronary artery disease: a review. *Medicine* 65:242–67.

Parker, D. A., and M. S. Harman. 1978. The distribution of consumption model of prevention of alcohol problems: a critical assessment. *Journal of Studies on Alcohol* 39:377–99.

Pittman, D. J. 1980. Primary prevention of alcohol abuse and alcoholism: a critical analysis of the control of consumption policy. Cardiff: International Institute for the Prevention and Treatment of Alcohol.

Pittman, D. J., and D. Strickland. 1981. A critical evaluation of the control of consumption policy. Paper presented at conference, Control Issues on Alcohol Abuse Prevention: Local, State, and National Designs for the 1980s, Charleston, S.C.

Poikolainen, K. 1995. Alcohol and mortality: a review. *Journal of Clinical Epidemiology* 48:455–65.

Rehm, J., M. J. Ashley, R. Room, E. Single, S. Bondy, R. Ferrence, and N. Giesbrecht. 1996. On the emerging paradigm of drinking patterns and their social and health consequences. *Addiction* 91:1615–36.

Roizen, R. 1983. The World Health Organization. Study of community responses to alcohol-related problems: a review of cross-cultural findings. In *Community Response to Alcohol-Related Problems, Phase 1*, ed. I. Rootman and J. Moser. Doc. MNH/83,17, Annex 41. Geneva: WHO.

Room, R. 1989. Response to alcohol-related problems in an international perspective: characterizing and explaining cultural wetness and dryness. Paper presented at conference, La ricerca Italiana sulle bevande alcoliche nel confronto internazzionale. Santo Stefano Belbo, Italy, September 22–23.

Rose, G., and S. Day. 1990. The population mean predicts the number of deviant individuals. *British Medical Journal* 301:1031–34.

Simpura, J., ed. 1987. *Finnish Drinking Habits*. Vol. 35. Helsinki: Finnish Foundation for Alcohol Studies.

Single, E. 1984. International perspectives on alcohol as a public health issue. *Journal of Public Health Policy* 5:238–56.

———. 1985. Studies of public drinking: an overview. In *Public Drinking and Public Policy*, ed. E. Single and T. Storm. Toronto: Addiction Research Foundation.

———. 1996. The sound of one hand clapping: a commentary on "Unraveling the Preventive Paradox for Acute Alcohol Problems" by T. Stockwell, D. Hawks, E. Lang, and P. Rydon. *Drug and Alcohol Review* 15:17–18.

Single, E., J. Brewster, P. MacNeil, J. Hatcher, and C. Trainor. 1994a. The 1993 General Social Survey I: alcohol use in Canada. *Canadian Journal of Public Health* 86:397–401.

———. 1994b. The 1993 General Social Survey II: alcohol problems. *Canadian Journal of Public Health* 8:402–7.

Single, E., et al. Forthcoming. Public drinking, problems, and prevention measures in twelve countries: results of the WHO project on public drinking. *Contemporary Drug Problems*.

Single, E., and S. Wortley. 1993. Drinking in various settings: findings from a national survey in Canada. *Journal of Studies on Alcohol* 54:590–99.

Skog. O.-J. 1982a. The distribution of alcohol consumption. Part 1: A critical discussion of the Ledermann model. SIFA Monograph 64. Oslo: National Institute for Alcohol Research.

———. 1982b. On the risk function of liver cirrhosis. SIFA Monograph 61. Oslo: National Institute for Alcohol Research.

———. 1983. The collectivity of drinking cultures: a theory of the distribution of alcohol consumption. SIFA Monograph 69. Oslo: National Institute for Alcohol Research.

Stampfer, M., et al. 1988. A prospective study of moderate alcohol consumption and the risk of coronary disease and stroke in women. *New England Journal of Medicine* 319:267–73.

Stockwell, T., D. Hawks, E. Lang, and P. Rydon. 1994. Unraveling the preventive paradox. Perth, Wash.: National Centre for Research into the Prevention of Drug Abuse.

————. 1996. Unraveling the preventive paradox for acute alcohol problems. *Drug and Alcohol Review* 15:7–15.

Treiman, K. A., and K. H. Beck. 1995. Alcohol problem behaviors and social contexts of drinking among adolescents. Paper presented at the International Conference on Social and Health of Different Drinking Patterns, Toronto, Ontario, Canada, November 13.

Tuyns, A., G. Pequignot, and J. Esteve. 1983. Greater risk of ascitic cirrhosis in females in relation to alcohol consumption. *International Journal of Epidemiology* 13:53–57.

World Drink Trends. 1995. *International Beverage Alcohol Consumption and Production Trends*. Henley-on-Thames: NTC Publications.

Chapter 2

Trends in Drinking and Patterns of Drinking

Reginald G. Smart

Traditionally, the field of alcohol epidemiology has concentrated on trend studies of per capita alcohol consumption, with little consideration of more complex changes in patterns of consumption. There is even less consideration of the relationship between overall consumption and patterns of how alcohol is consumed. Per capita consumption data are available for most countries from the 1970s to the present and for developed countries from much earlier than that. Such data are easy to compute, and they provide a rough way to compare countries. Unfortunately, problems with data on overall alcohol consumption and consumption patterns make the available information less than ideal. Also, they do not fully describe some important aspects of behavior, such as type of beverage consumed, amounts consumed at a sitting, and rates of heavy drinking.

However, more research attention has been given recently to how people actually drink alcohol and how variations in patterns of consumption relate to overall consumption and to problems. In this chapter, trends in consumption over the past thirty years are analyzed, with the emphasis on patterns rather than overall consumption levels. Attention is paid to changes in patterns of various demographic groups, to changes in beverage preferences, and to the main explanatory factors for such changes. Last, there is a discussion of the way that changes in drinking patterns relate to drinking problems.

Reginald G. Smart is with the Addiction Research Foundation, Toronto, Canada.

ALCOHOL CONSUMPTION DATA:
SOURCES AND PROBLEMS

Several large-scale studies have been made of alcohol consumption. The Brewer's Association of Canada (1992) produces biennial reports on consumption and patterns. Work by Smart (1989, 1991), Grant (1987), and Moser (1992) have concentrated on various aspects of the international consumption data. Holder and Edwards (1995) provide the best recent analysis of trends in per capita consumption, though they give less attention to patterns of consumption. Earlier books by Bruun et al. (1975) and Mäkelä et al. (1981) cover much the same subject areas for earlier time periods.

Most observers have noted that the published data on consumption have many shortcomings and hence may be inaccurate for trend purposes. Conversion factors transforming beverages into absolute alcohol are not up-to-date. With the appearance of low-alcohol and "near" beers in some countries, as well as lower, or "soft," alcohol spirits, older conversion factors are likely to need revision. Problems also arise from illicit and home production as well as foreign purchases in many countries. Studies by Österberg (1987) indicate that 15–50 percent of alcohol consumed in some Scandinavian countries may be unrecorded. That amount has probably been increasing in recent years.

Home production of spirits is uncommon in Canada. However, it was recently estimated that 50 percent of the spirits consumed in homes were smuggled from the United States (Smart and Ogborne 1996). In addition, home wine and beer production has increased greatly in the past few years in Canada. Several provinces now allow local microbreweries and wine clubs to produce alcoholic beverages, and they have become popular with some drinkers. Single and Giesbrecht (1979) estimated some years ago that for Ontario the unrecorded consumption was about 6 percent of the total. That figure should now be revised upward but by how much is uncertain.

It is also not clear whether recent apparent small reductions in consumption in many countries might be explained by an increase in unrecorded consumption than by an actual increase in drinking. Walsh (1989), for example, has shown that in Ireland (1978–82) per capita alcohol consumption appeared to be decreasing. However, when unrecorded consumption, especially from smuggling, was added, there was an apparent increase in alcohol consumption.

A further problem is that there are few studies of alcohol use patterns, apart from beverage preferences, that use international data. Studies by Pyörälä (1990), Hupkens, Knibbe, and Drop (1993) and Reader's Digest (1991) are exceptions. Moreover, internationally collected data on consumption do not allow for studies of patterns by age, sex, or geographic area. More surveys are needed that are national, regional, or local in scope and allow demographic variables to be used as explanatory variables. Also, surveys encounter many problems because of the low reliability of self-report data; this question is dealt with further in chapter 12.

WORLDWIDE TRENDS IN PER CAPITA ALCOHOL CONSUMPTION

The best available long-term per capita consumption data are for the developed countries of Europe and North America. Bruun et al. (1975) analyzed these data for the period 1950–70 for thirty-three countries. Their analysis showed that alcohol consumption increased in almost all countries, and in some (e.g., Canada, Hungary, Switzerland) by as much as 50 percent. Only two countries (Cuba and France) showed no increase in consumption. The World Health Organization (WHO 1988) also reported that beer consumption increased greatly in African, Asian, and South American countries between 1960 and 1981.

Smart (1989) extended the data to 1985 for the thirty-three countries selected by Bruun et al. (1975) and developed the idea that the postwar drinking binge had ended. Between 1974–76 and 1983–85, eighteen countries showed declines in drinking levels, two stayed at the same level, and the other thirteen showed increases. There was a tendency for wine-drinking countries to show more declines, and the declines were more common among countries with high initial consumption levels. The tendency for countries to have a dominant beverage was less marked, indicating that the homogenization noted by Bruun et al. (1975) continued. Countries dominated by beer and wine retained the same preferences between about 1950 and 1975, but spirit-drinking countries moved toward beer domination.

These observations have been expanded and brought up-to-date with new data by Holder and Edwards (1995), who analyzed data from eighteen developed countries for the years 1961–89. In general, they found no predominant pattern. Six countries (Australia, Canada, France, Ireland, Italy, and the United States) showed decreasing alcohol consumption, five (Austria, East Germany, Norway, Sweden, and Switzerland) showed stable consumption, and seven (Denmark, Finland, Iceland, Japan, Poland, the United Kingdom, and West Germany) showed increasing consumption. Why only those countries were included in the study is unclear, as data for other developed countries were available. Furthermore, in several countries stated to have stable consumption (e.g., East Germany and Switzerland), there appear to have been declines after the mid to late 1970s.

The more recent declines in consumption typical of many developed countries have not appeared in many developing countries. Smart (1991) studied alcohol consumption between 1970 and 1980–81 in 155 countries. Developing countries typically showed increases in consumption, but only half the countries in Europe and Latin America showed increases. Eighteen of the twenty-one countries that showed increases of 40 percent or more were in the developing world. However, countries in the developing world still had lower rates of consumption than those in Europe and North America. Data on per capita alcohol consumption have not been analyzed for developing countries from 1980 to the present. Unfortunately, data for these countries on per capita consumption are often sparse for the period before 1970 and are probably less reliable than those for developed countries.

INTERNATIONAL AND NATIONAL DATA ON PATTERNS OF CONSUMPTION

Beverage Preferences

The drinking pattern about which most is known on a worldwide basis has to do with beverage preferences. Allusion has already been made to the tendency to homogenization in developed countries noted by Bruun et al. (1975) and Smart (1989). Holder and Edwards (1995) reviewed trends in preferences in North American and European countries over the period 1971–89. Although the results are complex, a few patterns emerge. Wine-drinking and beer-drinking countries made some movement toward other beverages but remained predominantly in their original category. The greatest homogenization was found in spirit-drinking countries. Unfortunately, there has been no analysis of trends in beverage preferences in developing countries.

Several studies have addressed beverage preferences in European countries. A study by Hupkens, Knibbe, and Drop (1993) of European Community countries showed that between 1961 and 1988 all countries but France and Italy increased their wine consumption, while all countries except Luxembourg increased their beer consumption. There is no reference in the study to changes in spirits consumption. Pyörälä (1990) examined changes in Spain, Portugal, France, and Italy from the 1950s to the 1980s. Total alcoholic beverage consumption declined in all countries except Portugal, and wine consumption declined in all four. In Spain, Portugal, and Italy wine consumption declined as beer consumption increased. However, there was no substitution of wine by other beverages in France, which experienced one of the largest declines.

Some studies of beverage preferences have been made for individual countries. For example, Williams, Chem, and Dufour (1994) showed that in the United States in the period 1977–92 overall alcohol consumption declined by 12.5 percent. Beer and wine consumption fluctuated somewhat over that period, but the 1992 and 1977 levels were about the same. However, spirits consumption showed a declining trend, so that the 1992 level was 32 percent lower than in 1977. There was little variation in those trends among geographic regions.

Simpura, Paakanen, and Mustonen (1995), in their study of Finland between 1984 and 1992, showed how complex changing drinking habits can be. Both mild beer and wine appeared as new beverages in the 1980s and became popular. The proportion of abstainers increased, especially among women, the number of drinking occasions rose for both sexes, and wine drinking at meals increased. Most of the changes involved the ''élites'' at the outset, especially adoption of the wine-drinking culture.

Studies have also been made by Sulkunen (1986, 1989) of changes in France, one of the few countries where alcohol consumption fell between 1965 and 1979. In the first study, Sulkunen (1986) described trends in French drinking, which consists mainly of wine consumption. Abstinence rates, chiefly reflecting a move from wine drinking, increased greatly in France as per capita consumption fell in the 1970s and 1980s. Abstaining was found to be most common among the better-educated classes, but it was expected that abstinence levels would also increase in the lower echelons of French society in time. In a further study, Sulkunen (1989) showed that those at the lowest level of consumption— the middle classes—reduced their consumption most; other groups followed, but later.

Abstinence Levels

All countries have abstainers who do not currently drink alcoholic beverages. In some cases they are lifelong abstainers, many of whom reject alcohol for religious or other reasons. Some abstainers are former social drinkers who have given up alcohol for health reasons like cardiovascular or gastrointestinal problems. Others are former heavy drinkers who have given up drinking because of health, social, or other problems it caused. Of course, the definitions used in various studies on the subject are not standardized.

No internationally comparable data that use the same definition of abstinence are available. However, a rough compilation of available studies was made by Reader's Digest (1991), an unlikely source but the best available. It includes good trend data for eleven countries, including Australia, Canada, United States, Japan, and seven European countries. Among countries with increasing consumption, Iceland and Japan showed a declining abstinence rate, whereas abstinence increased in Finland from the 1970s to the 1980s and into 1990. Among countries with stable consumption, abstinence rates rose in Switzerland, but remained the same in Norway. In Australia and Canada, where overall consumption was declining, abstinence rates increased considerably. In the United States, however, abstinence rates stayed the same for males and declined for females during the period 1979–84, when consumption declined slightly. Clearly, abstinence rates do not accurately reflect changes in overall alcohol consumption. It is likely that unique national factors govern such rates and the changes in them, but so far they have not been well studied. No trend studies have been found of abstinence rates in developing countries.

Sulkunen (1987) made a study of abstinence trends in Finland between 1946 and 1976. He found that there was a large decrease in abstention rates, but almost half of the fall occurred among women. Those aged twenty through twenty-nine, "the wet generation," changed most. This group was better educated, more mobile, and more urban than in previous generations, and women were more often employed outside the home. Similar results were reported by Walsh (1989) for Ireland, where the proportion of abstainers decreased in the 1960s. Rising disposable income allowed more spending on alcohol up to 1972–74, though subsequently both income and drinking declined slightly.

Changes in Drinking Rates over Time

Information on trends in drinking rates comes from repeated surveys in the same geographic areas; few countries have surveys covering a long time period. Consequently, most of the available information comes from studies carried out in the United States, Canada, and some European countries.

In general, research in the United States gives confusing results. Hilton (1988) found no change in heavy drinking between 1967 and 1984, although per capita consumption increased. However, a comparison between 1964 and 1984 did show an increase in heavy drinking among men. There were doubts about the comparability of the questions asked in the two surveys undertaken in 1979 and 1984. A later study showed, with matching questions, an increase in dependence among men but not among women. Mulford and Fitzgerald (1988) failed to confirm Hilton's findings in their study in Iowa. In the period 1961–79 alcohol consumption declined by 12 percent, but there was no decline in heavy drinking or problem indicators. However, there was an increase in reported "trouble due to drinking" and "preoccupied drinking."

Midanik and Clark (1994) reported on data from the U.S. National Household Survey for the period 1984–90. The proportions of current drinkers, drinkers of all beverage types, drinkers whose pattern ranges from one drink a week to five or more drinks on one occasion at least once a week all declined. However, this general downward trend applied only to whites and not to blacks or Hispanics. Surprisingly, Williams, Chem, and Dufour (1994) found a different outcome in the Behavioral Risk Factors Survey done in nineteen American states for the period 1986–92. In fifteen of the nineteen states, average consumption per drinker appeared to be increasing, while in the remaining four there was no clear trend. Differences in survey questions and sampling methods could explain the apparent disparity between the findings of these two studies. Fillmore's analysis (1987) of longitudinal and trend patterns among men also gives complex results. She found that men in their thirties and sixties surveyed in 1979 had higher rates of abstention than those surveyed in 1964. However, rates of heavy drinking were lower only for those in their sixties in 1979.

Several studies in the United States have examined trends among female drinkers. For example, Wilsnack and Wilsnack (1995), in a comparison of national survey data for 1981 and 1991, found that in 1991 fewer women drank heavily, female drinkers drank less frequently, and they had fewer episodes of heavy drinking. However, younger drinkers had more episodes of intoxication in 1991 than 1981. Also, Sedula et al. (1991) found that the prevalence of alcohol consumption among pregnant women decreased between 1985 and 1988. However, the median number of drinks per month did not decline for those who drank. No decline in drinking was found among those under twenty-five years and among the less educated. Declines in female drinking in the United States may be largely among middle-aged and older women.

An interesting study of trends in alcohol consumption in Sweden has been reported by Hauge and Irgens-Jensen (1989). In the period 1976–88 per capita consumption was unchanged. However, reported intoxication on about one occasion a week showed a remarkable decline. Among Swedish military conscripts, 19.4 percent reported such intoxication in 1976, but only 6.2 percent reported it in 1988. Why such a large change took place is not clear, though evidently young drinkers became more cautious about heavy drinking.

Canadian data also show that trends and patterns in alcohol consumption do not always behave in similar ways. Smart and Mann (1995) showed that alcohol consumption in Ontario declined by 19.1 percent between 1975 and 1990. Surveys of adults indicated that the percentage of daily drinkers decreased by 38.1 percent. However, the percentage of persons drinking five or more drinks on any one occasion each month decreased by far less (9.2 percent) than did per capita consumption. Again, the differences cannot be easily explained.

The survey of adults by Adlaf, Ivis, and Smart (1994) in Ontario used by Smart and Mann (1995) showed that during the period 1977–94 the percentage of drinkers remained about the same (80 percent) while alcohol consumption was falling (by about 19 percent). Daily drinking declined by more than 50 percent, but drinking of five or more drinks on an occasion remained about the same, with some fluctuations. Declines in daily drinking from 1984 onward were found for all age groups and both sexes, except for females aged eighteen through twenty-nine. Why that segment should be an exception is not clear.

There have been several trend studies of alcohol consumption patterns among students in the United States. For example, the study of twelfth-grade students by Johnston, O'Malley, and Bachman (1994) found that daily drinking decreased by about 60 percent between 1975 and 1993. Heavy drinking (five or more drinks on one occasion in the previous two weeks) decreased by about one-third. Studies of U.S. college students also showed declines in daily drinking (Meilman et al. 1990) and heavy drinking indicators (Temple 1986) in the early 1980s after earlier increases.

The study by Adlaf et al. (1995) of students in grades seven to thirteen in Ontario showed declines between 1977 and 1995 in most indicators of drinking. The proportion of drinkers decreased by 23 percent, and the reduction was about equal for all grade levels, for both sexes, and for all geographic regions. Heavy drinking (five or more drinks on one or more occasions in the previous month) decreased by 24 percent and daily drinking by 33 percent. However, the frequency of drinking showed much smaller changes (about 10 percent) in the period 1981–95.

The study by Kono and Takano (1992) is an exceptional contribution to knowledge about trends in drinking in Asian countries. They showed that complex changes took place in the 1970s and 1980s. Overall consumption went up, as did heavy drinking. Traditional beverages used for celebrations remained a niche beverage, and beer consumption increased. At the same time, far more women began to drink.

In general, the research literature on trends in the frequency of alcohol consumption shows little consistency. Declines in heavy consumption indicators do not necessarily follow declines in per capita consumption and may occur without such changes. Moreover, trends in the indicators of heavy consumption may vary. However, most countries reporting trends show some downward trend in some patterns of heavy consumption in recent decades. Little is known about how per capita alcohol consumption and patterns vary over time in developing countries.

FACTORS RELATED TO CHANGES IN PATTERNS OF ALCOHOL CONSUMPTION

Economic Factors

Numerous studies have been made of the effects of economic changes, such as those brought on by depression and war, in reducing per capita alcohol consumption (Bruun et al. 1975; Walsh 1989; Holder and Edwards 1995). Also, the real price of alcohol is known to affect overall consumption (Bruun et al. 1975). However, there have been few studies of the effects of economic factors on patterns of consumption or choice of beverage. Because trends in overall consumption and consumption of specific beverage types do not necessarily follow each other, it cannot be assumed that the same factors are involved in both.

Smart (1987) has pointed out that the declines in per capita alcohol consumption in some countries occurred after the OPEC oil crisis in the mid-1970s. In other countries the decline in consumption occurred in the early 1980s. In some countries, such as Canada, unemployment increased and real incomes stopped rising after 1975. In Canada, as mentioned earlier, this led to a drop in alcohol consumption, a large decline in daily drinking, and a smaller decline in heavy drinking. However, many other changes have occurred during the same period; for example, the population has aged, and many other consumption habits have changed. Attributing the decline in daily drinking to economic factors is not feasible at present. Further research is needed to show how different patterns of alcohol consumption respond to changes in economic conditions brought on by such situations as unemployment and war.

Alcohol Controls

Research on the way in which alcohol controls affect patterns of consumption is limited. Giesbrecht and Macdonald (1981) have shown that increasing the prices of fortified wines, often consumed by skid row alcoholics, led to decreases in their consumption. The liberalization of beer sales in Iceland (Olafsdottir 1991) led, as expected, to higher beer consumption. The introduction of sales of wine in privately owned stores has had mixed results, the studies showing no increase in sales (Smart 1986), a small increase (Mulford, Ledolter, and Fitzgerald 1992), or large increases (Macdonald 1986; Wagenaar and Langley 1995).

Major changes in availability may lead to heavier alcohol consumption and intoxication, but these changes may also follow large social changes. In many Eastern European countries the political changes of the 1980s led to much greater availability of alcohol, which was accompanied by heavier drinking and more public intoxication (Wald et al. 1993; Treml 1991). However, many social and economic changes occurred at the same time, and attributing a rise in drunkenness to any one factor is hazardous.

In some cases, greater availability may not lead to greater consumption. Smart and Mann (1995) found that during a period (1975–91) when daily drinking decreased among adults and students in Ontario, physical availability increased. There was no increase in the real price of alcoholic beverages, and the number of on-premise outlets expanded by 134 percent. More research is needed in other countries to see whether such changes have occurred elsewhere and what the reasons might be.

Alcohol Advertising

Research on alcohol advertising generally indicates that increased alcohol advertising has little influence on overall alcohol consumption (Smart 1988; Fisher 1993). Studies of the effects of advertising on the frequency of alcohol consumption or on heavy drinking indicators are not available. On the other hand, research has shown that increased advertising of particular beverages can increase their sales (Smart 1988).

The most recent reviews of alcohol advertising studies have been Fisher (1993) and Calfee (1996). Fisher concluded that such advertising has a weak positive influence on consumption but no impact on experimentation or abuse of alcohol. However, his summary of empirical studies shows that of nine study categories (econometric, experimental, or those dealing with consumption and problem indicators), six showed no effect of advertising, two showed a positive effect, and one showed a negative effect. An equally plausible conclusion would be that, on balance, alcohol advertising has no effect. Calfee's extensive review of the advertising literature also concluded that there is no substantial effect.

Sociocultural Changes: An Antiwetness Trend?

Instead of seeking a simple explanation of particular factors that influence changes in patterns of consumption, it may be better to examine larger cultural changes. For example, Smart (1987) showed that declines in alcohol consumption in Canada were associated with higher unemployment rates and demographic changes but, also, with changes in eating habits. There appeared to be lifestyle changes focusing on consuming less alcohol and tobacco, eating low-cholesterol foods, and taking more exercise. It may be that the reduction in daily drinking that began in the late 1970s was part of a broader trend toward healthier ways of living.

A somewhat similar explanation is suggested in the studies of French drinking habits in the 1970s. Sulkunen (1989) showed that wine drinking decreased at home and that routine use of wine at meals was also falling. Much of that change occurred among the élites, or the better educated classes, in which abstinence is now more valued and daily wine consumption is not.

Smart and Mann (1995) have shown that reduced drinking and daily drinking in Ontario after 1975 was associated with many changes in both prevention and treatment efforts. Alcohol education expanded in schools, as did employee assistance and health promotion programs for employees. More people went into treatment for alcoholism and more joined Alcoholic's Anonymous. Other studies (Smart and Walsh 1996) showed that alcohol control attitudes also became less liberal. Perhaps general changes fostering an antiwet attitude occurred in Canada. This attitude could have supported lower levels of drinking and more participation in treatment and AA programs and set the stage for more government and industry spending on prevention programs.

More studies are needed of how global social and cultural changes lead to changes in drinking patterns, especially heavy consumption.

RELATIONSHIPS BETWEEN CHANGES IN PATTERNS OF CONSUMPTION AND ALCOHOL PROBLEMS

Whether changes in consumption patterns lead to different trends in alcohol-related problems is difficult to assess from the available literature. Most research has related such problems to overall per capita consumption and not to patterns of consumption. Much research has shown a close correlation between per capita consumption and problems such as liver cirrhosis deaths, alcohol-related accidents, and rates of alcoholism (Bruun et al. 1975; Holder and Edwards 1995).

One study (Smart and Mann 1987) showed a close correlation between alcohol consumption and alcohol dependence mortality, alcoholism rates, cirrhosis mortality, and drunk driving for the years 1963–73, when alcohol use was increasing. However, there was no significant correlation for the period 1975–83, a period during which alcohol consumption decreased. Alcohol consumption fell by only 3.4 percent, but liver cirrhosis deaths decreased by 43.2 percent, hospital admissions for alcohol dependence by 69.8 percent, mortality from alcohol dependence by 175 percent, charges of driving while impaired by 15.9 percent, and drunk driving fatalities by 36.4 percent. These data suggest that patterns of alcohol consumption changed remarkably in the direction of less hazardous drinking. However, surveys for 1977 and 1984 in Ontario show little change in daily drinking or heavy drinking. Unfortunately, we do not have survey data for 1975 and 1983. It may be that drinking levels changed mainly for the heaviest drinkers or those with problems, but the surveys do not include sufficient numbers of heavy drinkers. A later study (Smart and Mann 1995) did show that alcohol problem indicators decreased between 1975 and 1990, as did per capita consumption, daily drinking, and heavy drinking.

Studies from the United States also show declines in liver cirrhosis death rates and alcohol-related traffic fatalities between 1977 and 1990. However, it is difficult to establish that these trends are related to falls in heavy drinking or problem drinking, as surveys give conflicting results (Hilton 1988; Mulford and Fitzgerald 1988; Williams, Chem, and Dufour 1994). Health consequences related to drinking patterns are dealt with more fully in chapter 4.

International trend data on drinking problems are difficult to obtain except for liver cirrhosis deaths. These data suggest that patterns of consumption may contribute to such changes, but a thorough analysis is lacking. Table 2.1 provides information for twenty-nine countries that have data on per capita alcohol consumption and liver cirrhosis death rates. Between 1974–76 and 1988–90, twenty countries showed a decrease in alcohol consumption, one had no change, and nine showed an increase. Nineteen showed a decrease in liver cirrhosis rates and ten showed an increase. However, there is no correlation between changes in per capita consumption and cirrhosis deaths. This clearly suggests that changes in drinking patterns (e.g., frequent and heavy drinking) are responsible, but evidence for this is not available at present.

Several countries—Hungary, Romania, Yugoslavia, Czechoslovakia, and the Netherlands—showed a decline in alcohol consumption but an increase in liver cirrhosis deaths. Other countries—Iceland, Ireland, and Switzerland—had increases in consumption but declines in cirrhosis. It is not clear whether lags in the influence of consumption on cirrhosis are important or whether there are shortcomings in the estimates from some countries. However, there is also the possibility that changes in alcohol use patterns or beverages consumed in different countries may account for the differences. More research at the country level is needed to establish which factors are most important.

Time lags may be an important factor in explaining why consumption and cirrhosis rates are not apparently related in some countries. Skog (1987) has shown that when time lags are taken into consideration some anomalies are resolved, as it takes a long time for the effects of changes in consumption to be fully reflected in the liver cirrhosis data, since liver cirrhosis takes many years to develop. Unfortunately, there are no analyses of the time lag needed for changes in alcohol use patterns to have their full effect on overall consumption or problems related to consumption.

CONCLUSIONS

Although in many instances there is a lack of data and a need for more research, especially in developing countries, several tentative conclusions can be advanced about trends in patterns of alcohol consumption.

Table 2.1 *(Continued)*

Table 2.1 Per capita alcohol consumption and deaths from chronic liver disease and cirrhosis for 29 countries: 1974–76 and 1988–90

	Mean per capita consumption (liters absolute alcohol)			Mean liver cirrhosis death rates		
	1974–6	1988–90	Percent change	1974–6	1988–90	Percent change
Wine countries						
France	16.7	12.4	−25.7	33.1	18.7	−43.5
Hungary	12.3	10.7	−13.0	17.9	49.9	+179.0
Portugal	14.3	10.1	−29.4	34.6	25.9	−25.1
Romania	7.4	7.3	−1.4	21.6	33.4	+54.6
Switzerland	10.8	10.9	+0.9	13.5	10.5	−22.2
Yugoslavia	7.6	6.5	−14.5	13.2	18.1	+37.1
Spain	13.8	10.9	−21.0	22.8	20.7	−9.2
Italy	13.4	9.6	−28.3	33.1	28.1	−15.1
Beer countries						
Australia	9.7	8.0	−17.5	8.1	7.0	−13.6
Austria	11.3	8.8	−22.1	32.0	27.3	−14.7
Belgium	9.9	9.8	−1.0	13.4	12.5**	−6.7
Canada	8.7	7.6	−8.0	11.9	8.2	−31.1

Czechoslovakia	9.8	8.7	− 11.2	17.5	22.1	+ 26.3
Denmark	8.8	9.7	+ 12.5	10.6	13.7	+ 29.2
Germany	12.2	10.5	− 13.9	27.6	21.1	− 23.6
Ireland	5.7	7.1	+ 25.6	3.5	2.8	− 20.0
Luxembourg	13.0	12.3	− 5.4	27.4	23.3	− 15.0
Netherlands	8.7	8.2	− 6.1	4.7	5.2	+ 10.1
New Zeland	9.4	7.8	− 17.0	5.5	3.3	− 40.0
Norway	4.2	4.2	0	4.8	6.1	+ 27.1
United Kingdom	8.2	7.6	− 17.1	8.1	6.1	− 25.0
USA	7.3	7.4	+ 1.4	15.1	10.8	− 28.5
Mixed preference countries						
Finland	6.4	7.6	+ 18.8	5.8	10.1	+ 74.1
Iceland	3.0	4.0	+ 33.3	2.1	1.7	− 19.1
Israel	2.9	1.0	− 65.5	6.0	5.9***	− 16.7
Poland	7.0	6.8	− 2.9	10.2	10.1	− 9.8
Sweden	6.1	5.5	− 9.8	11.9	7.3	− 38.7
Cuba	2.0	3.6	+ 80.0	5.5	7.8	+ 41.8
Peru	1.3	1.5	+ 15.4	5.3***	5.5*****	+ 3.8
Mean Rates	8.7	7.8	− 4.9	14.7	14.6	+ 2.3
						(if Hungary is deleted − 4.2)

*1988 only   **1987 only   ***1987–89   ****1977 figure   *****1989 only

- Studies of worldwide trends in per capita alcohol consumption indicate that there were large increases in many developed countries between about 1950 and the mid to late 1970s. However, after that time many developed countries showed decreases in consumption. Those declines did not appear in many developing countries, at least until the 1980s. In many such countries alcohol consumption was still increasing. These conclusions are somewhat tentative because of many problems with per capita consumption data, such as unrecorded consumption, tourism, the conversion factors for absolute alcohol, difficulties in establishing standard drink sizes, and the calculation of the alcohol content of home-produced beverages. These problems are dealt with extensively in chapter 12.

- The best studies of patterns of consumption relate to beverage preferences. A trend to more homogenized consumption appeared in most developed countries between 1950 and 1975 and continued thereafter. It appears that wine- and beer-drinking countries made less change to other beverages than did spirits-drinking countries in the period 1977–89. In some countries, such as France, large declines occurred in wine consumption with no substitution by other beverages. In others (Spain and Portugal), there was substitution by beer. No studies have been made of trends in beverage preferences in developing countries.

- There is limited information on trends in abstinence rates, with good data for only a few developed countries. There is no overall recent trend either upward or downward. Changes in abstinence rates are often not related to changes in per capita alcohol consumption.

- There is no worldwide trend in the frequency of drinking or heavy drinking. Indicators of heavy drinking show different trends from country to country. In some countries, downward trends are more common in some demographic groups (e.g., women and whites in the United States and, in Canada, older males and females but not younger females). Declines in heavy consumption do not always follow declines in per capita consumption; they may occur without them, as in Sweden. Most countries that have reported data on trends have shown declines for some indicators of heavy consumption.

- Factors related to increases and declines in various patterns of alcohol consumption include economic changes, drastic changes in alcohol controls, and sociocultural changes such as newly developing lifestyles. In some countries so many different changes have taken place at about the same time that it is difficult to determine which factors are most important.

- Changes in alcohol problem indicators such as liver cirrhosis rates are difficult to interpret. Although many developed countries have shown recent declines in cirrhosis, these changes are often not correlated with declines in per capita alcohol consumption. Again, complex factors such as patterns of lower drinking and attitude changes as well as better prevention and treatment programs may be involved.

- There is a major lack of data for many countries on trends in patterns of alcohol consumption and the factors responsible for them. This is especially true for developing countries but applies also to many developed countries. There is little information on how long it takes for changes in patterns of alcohol consumption to affect overall consumption or levels of problems.

REFERENCES

Adlaf, E. M., F. J. Ivis, and R. G. Smart. 1994. *Alcohol and Other Drug Use among Ontario Adults in 1994 and Changes since 1977.* Toronto: Addiction Research Foundation.

Adlaf, E. M., F. J. Ivis, R. G. Smart, and G. W. Walsh. 1995. *Ontario Student Drug Use Survey, 1977–1995.* Toronto: Addiction Research Foundation.

Brewer's Association of Canada. 1992. *International Survey: Alcoholic Beverages, Taxation, and Control Policies.* 8th ed. Ottawa: Brewer's Association of Canada.

Bruun, K., et al. 1975. *Alcohol Control Policies in a Public Health Perspective.* Vol. 25. Helsinki: Finnish Foundation for Alcohol Studies.

Calfee, J. E. 1996. *Statement on a Proposal to Restrict Alcohol Beverage Advertising and Promotion in the District of Columbia.* Washington, D.C.: American Enterprise Institute.

Fillmore, K. M. 1987. Prevalence, incidence, and ethnicity of drinking patterns and problems among men as a function of age: a longitudinal and cohort analysis. *British Journal of Addiction* 82:77–83.

Fisher, J. C. 1993. *Advertising, Alcohol Consumption, and Abuse: A Worldwide Survey.* Westport, Conn.: Greenwood.

Giesbrecht, N., and S. Macdonald. 1981. A ban on fortified wine in northwestern Ontario and its impact on the consumption level and drinking patterns. *British Journal of Addiction* 76:281–88.

Grant, M. 1987. Alcohol and drug use: a world perspective. *Australia Drug and Alcohol Review* 6:289–92.

Hauge, R., and O. Irgens-Jensen. 1989. *Alkoholen i Norden* (Alcohol in the Nordic countries). Oslo: Statens Institutt for Alkoholforskning.

Hilton, M. E. 1988. Trends in drinking problems and attitudes in the United States, 1979–1984. *British Journal of Addiction* 83:1421–27.

Holder, H., and G. Edwards. 1995. *Alcohol and Public Policy: Evidence and Issues.* Oxford: Oxford University Press.

Hupkens, C. L. H., R. A. Knibbe, and M. Drop. 1993. Alcohol consumption in the European Community: uniformity and diversity in national drinking patterns. *Addiction* 88:1391–1404.

Johnston, L. D., P. M. O'Malley, and J. G. Bachman. 1994. Drug use continues to climb. Press Release. Ann Arbor: University of Michigan.

Kono, H., and T. Takano. 1992. Patterns and problems of alcohol consumption in Japan. *World Health Forum* 13:326–29.

Macdonald, S. 1986. The impact of increased availability of wine in grocery stores on consumption: four case histories. *British Journal of Addiction* 81:381–87.

Mäkelä, K., et al. 1981. *Alcohol, Society, and the State.* Vol. 1. Toronto: Addiction Research Foundation.

Meilman, P. W., J. E. Stone, M. S. Gaylor, and J. H. Turco. 1990. Alcohol consumption by college undergraduates: current use and 10-year trends. *Journal of Studies on Alcohol* 51:389–95.

Midanik, L. T., and W. B. Clarke. 1994. The demographic distribution of U.S. drinking patterns in 1990: description and trends from 1984. *American Journal of Public Health* 84:1218–22.

Moser, J. 1992. *Alcohol Problems, Policies, and Programmes in Europe.* Copenhagen: WHO Regional Office for Europe.

Mulford, A., J. Ledolter, and J. L. Fitzgerald. 1992. Alcohol availability and consumption: Iowa sales data revisited. *Journal of Studies on Alcohol* 53:487–94.

Mulford, H. W., and J. L. Fitzgerald. 1988. Consequences of increasing off-premise wine outlets in Iowa. *British Journal of Addiction* 83:1271–79.

Olafsdottir, H. 1991. I forandringens tid: Islandsk alkoholpolitik i 1980-arene. (In changing times: Icelandic alcohol policy in the 1980s.) *Nordisk Alkoholtidskrift* 8:342–51.

Österberg, G. 1987. Recorded and unrecorded alcohol consumption. In *Finnish Drinking Habits,* ed. J. Simpura. Helsinki: Finnish Foundation for Alcohol Studies.

Pyörälä, E. 1990. Trends in alcohol consumption in Spain, Portugal, France, and Italy from the 1950s until the 1980s. *British Journal of Addiction* 85:469–77.

Readers Digest. 1991. Eurodata: a consumer survey of 17 European countries. *Reader's Digest.* London: Reader's Digest Association.

Sedula, M., et al. 1991. Trends in alcohol consumption by pregnant women, 1985 through 1988. *Journal of the American Medical Association* 265:876–79.

Simpura, J., P. Paakanen, and H. Mustonen. 1995. New beverages, new drinking contexts? Signs of modernization in Finnish drinking habits from 1984 to 1992, compared with trends in the European Community. *Addiction* 90:673–83.

Single, E., and N. Giesbrecht. 1979. The 16 per cent solution and other mysteries concerning the accuracy of alcohol consumption estimates based on sales data. *British Journal of Addiction* 74:165–73.

Skog, O. J. 1987. *Trends in Alcohol Consumption and Alcohol-Related Damage.* Oslo: National Institute for Alcohol Research.

Smart, R. G. 1986. The impact of consumption of selling wine in grocery stores. *Alcohol and Alcoholism* 2:233–36.

———. 1987. Socio-economic, lifestyle, and availability factors in the stabilization of alcohol consumption in Canada. *Canadian Journal of Public Health* 78:176–80.

———. 1988. Does alcohol advertising affect overall consumption? A review of empirical studies. *Journal of Studies on Alcohol* 49:314–23.

———. 1989. Is the postwar drinking binge ending? Cross-national trends in per capita alcohol consumption. *British Journal of Addiction* 84:743–748.

———. 1991. World trends in alcohol consumption. *World Health Forum* 12:99–103.

Smart, R. G., and R. E. Mann. 1987. Large decreases in alcohol-related problems following a slight reduction in alcohol consumption in Ontario, 1978–1983. *British Journal of Addiction* 82:77–83.

———. 1995. Treatment, health promotion, and alcohol controls and the decrease of alcohol consumption and problems in Ontario, 1975–1991. *Alcohol and Alcoholism* 30:337–43.

Smart, R. G., and A. Ogborne. 1996. *Northern Spirits: Drinking in Canada Then and Now.* 2d ed. Toronto: Addiction Research Foundation.

Smart, R. G., and E. W. Walsh. 1996. Do long-term attitudes toward alcohol controls change during decreasing alcohol consumption? Toronto: Addiction Research Foundation.

Sulkunen, P. 1986. Why is alcohol consumption declining in France? An analysis by socio-professional groups. *Alkoholiipolitika* 3:191–99.

———. 1987. Abstinence. In *Finnish Drinking Habits,* ed. J. Simpura. Helsinki: Finnish Foundation for Alcohol Studies.

————. 1989. Drinking in France, 1965–1979: an analysis of household consumption data. *British Journal of Addiction* 84:61–72.

Temple, M. 1986. Trends in collegiate drinking in California, 1979–1984. *Journal of Studies on Alcohol* 47:274–82.

Treml, V. G. 1991. Drinking and alcohol abuse in the USSR in the 1980s. In *Soviet Social Problems,* ed. A. Jones et al. Boulder, Colo.: Westview.

Wagenaar, A. C., and J. D. Langley. 1995. Alcohol licensing system changes and alcohol consumption: introduction of wine into New Zealand grocery stores. *Addiction* 90:773–83.

Wald, I., et al. 1993. Alcohol policy in the light of social changes. In *Experiences with Community Action Projects: New Research in the Prevention of Alcohol and Other Drug Problems,* ed. T. K. Greenfield and R. Zimmerman. Monograph 14. Rockville, Md.: U.S. Department of Health and Human Services.

Walsh, B. M. 1989. Alcoholic beverages in Ireland: market forces and government policy. *British Journal of Addiction* 84:1163–71.

WHO. 1988. *World Health Statistics Annual, 1987.* Geneva: World Health Organization.

Williams, G. D., D. Chem, and M. C. Dufour. 1994. *Apparent per Capita Alcohol Consumption: National, State, and Regional Trends, 1977–1992.* Washington, D.C.: U.S. Department of Health and Human Services.

Wilsnack, S. C., and R. W. Wilsnack. 1995. Drinking and problem drinking in U.S. women: patterns and recent trends. *Recent Developments in Alcoholism* 12:29–60.

Chapter 3

Individual Characteristics and Drinking Patterns

Wilson Acuda and Barton Alexander

Other chapters have postulated that drinking patterns are more important in determining the outcomes of beverage alcohol consumption than are simple measures of total alcohol consumed. This chapter, then, examines the characteristics of individuals that may predict or at least contribute to different drinking patterns. Responsible drinking is both possible and healthy for the vast majority of people (Ford 1990; Chafetz and Chafetz 1995). An examination of biomedical and psychosocial risk factors suggests that there are specific individuals and groups who are at greater risk of alcohol abuse or dependence than others.

MODELS OF ALCOHOL USE

The pleasure associated with the consumption of alcohol beverages has been heralded in art and literature since the beginning of recorded history. At the same time, the dangers of irresponsible drinking have long been recognized. Cultures have adopted various approaches to managing consumption of alcohol beverages, ranging from prohibition to integration into daily ritual. At the same time, most societies have acknowledged the double-edged nature of drinking: responsible

Wilson Acuda is with the Department of Psychiatry, University of Zimbabwe, Harare. In addition to contributing to the text in its entirety, he is solely responsible for the medical and scientific data. Bart Alexander is with the Coors Brewing Company, Golden, Colorado, U.S.

and irresponsible. The Puritan clergyman Increase Mather, in *Wo To Drunkards,* put it this way in 1673:

> Drink is in itself a good creature of God,
> and to be received with thankfulness,
> but the abuse of drink is from Satan,
> the wine is from God, but the Drunkard is from the Devil.

By the middle of this century, many ideas about the reasons for alcohol abuse had been advanced, to the extent that Jellinek (1960) summarized over 200 definitions, theories, and conceptualizations. Hester and Sheehy (1990) found that these approaches could be summarized in eleven models, presented in table 3.1.

The temperance model is aimed squarely at the product alcohol. This model views alcohol itself as a dangerous drug, to be consumed cautiously, if at all. Its proponents hold that prevention of abuse requires either outright prohibition or restrictive controls over availability and promotion, recently termed *neoprohibition* (Ford 1990).

Several other models focus on the environment in which abuse occurs. For example, the general systems model attempts to focus on the larger system, of which the abuser is only one part, implying that the causal factor is a dysfunctional interpersonal environment. The sociocultural model emphasizes the importance of societal norms, conditions of sales, and nature of the drinking environment. The public health model attempts to integrate these factors, along with recognition of some individual differences. Through its inclusion of the agent (in this case, alcohol), the host (the drinker), and the environment as causal factors, it implies that different approaches may be successful in different communities and for different individuals.

Other models look at those family and community factors that may result in differences among individuals. The educational model views alcohol abuse as the result of a deficit in knowledge about the effects of alcohol. Armed with appropriate knowledge, individuals will make safe and healthy decisions. The conditioning model explains alcoholism as a pattern of learned behaviors that have been reinforced. Treatment involves counterconditioning, aimed at both the individual and the community. The social learning model goes beyond simple conditioning to emphasize the social context in which irresponsible drinking occurs. Causal factors include peer pressure, lack of coping or stress management skills, and modeling of abusive drinking. The moral model emphasizes deficits in personal responsibility or spiritual strength as the cause of excessive drinking. Thus, the legal system and spiritual authorities must motivate appropriate action and punish acts of misconduct.

Other models directly examine the individual. The characterological model focuses on psychopathology or other personality deficits as the cause of alcohol abuse, so that the appropriate treatment must address the underlying psychological problem. The biomedical model emphasizes genetic and physiological factors resulting in alcoholism, suggesting that until a "cure" is developed, diagnosticians should identify those at risk and caution them about their use of alcohol. The American disease model holds that alcoholism is a progressive, irreversible condition characterized by loss of control over drinking. Under this model, those with the disease and those who are at risk of contracting it must abstain from drinking for their entire lives.

This chapter draws on all these models from a particular perspective, that of the individual. It examines the role of individual differences, both biomedical and psychosocial, and how they appear to relate to different drinking patterns.

PATTERNS OF DRINKING AND BIOMEDICAL DIFFERENCES

Genetic and Other Biological Factors

Of all the patterns of drinking, researchers have singled out the pattern of alcohol dependence for study of possible genetic roots. Alcohol dependence is a result of an interaction between biological and environmental factors. Several twin and adoption studies have shown that there is a genetic contribution to the etiology of alcohol dependence, although the exact mechanism of transmission is not known (Cloninger, Bohman, and Figwardson 1981; Goodwin et al. 1973). Monozygotic (MZ) twins have concordance rates for alcohol dependence twice as high as those of dizygotic (DZ) twins. The incidence of alcohol dependence is four times higher among the male biological offspring of alcoholic fathers than among the male offspring of nonalcoholic fathers, regardless of whether they are raised by foster parents or by their biological parents. The genetic contribution to alcohol dependence in women is not as clear. Although the result of the MZ-DZ twin comparisons have been conflicting in some studies (Murray and McGuffin 1993), other studies have found even higher MZ concordance rates for alcohol dependence in male and female twins (Pickens et al. 1991; Kendler et al. 1994). These studies have indicated that there is a 25–50 percent likelihood that the development of alcohol dependence may stem from genetic factors.

Adoption studies in Denmark have shown that alcohol abuse and dependence was nearly four times more likely in adopted-away sons of alcohol-dependent parents than in adopted-away sons of parents who are not alcohol dependent (Goodwin et al. 1973). Other adoption studies have indicated that there may be two kinds of alcohol dependence, one with a major genetic component, in which alcohol dependence is passed on from fathers to sons, and another with a lesser genetic component, in which less severe drinking affects both men and women in the family. This hypothesis was elaborated on by Cloninger, who described two types of alcohol dependence (Cloninger, Bohman, and Figwardson 1981; Cloninger 1987). Type I alcoholism, also called milieu-limited alcoholism, occurs in about 75 percent of alcoholics and affects both males and females. It is

Table 3.1 Models of addictive behaviors and their implications for intervention

Model	Examples	Emphasized causal factors	Implied interventions	Appropriate intervention agent
Moral	Abuse as sin Abuse as crime	Spirituality Personal responsibility	Spiritual direction, moral persuasion, social sanctions	Clergy Law enforcement agents
Temperance	Prohibition Women's Christian Temperance Union	Alcohol	Exhortation Abstinence/prohibition	Abstainers Legislators
American disease	Alcoholics Anonymous.	Irreversible constitution Abnormality of individual	Identification/confrontation Lifelong abstinence	Recovering alcoholics Peer support
Educational	Lectures Affective education	Lack of knowledge Lack of motivation	Education	Educators
Characterological	Psychoanalysis	Personality Traits/dispositions Defense mechanisms	Psychotherapy Risk identification Self-image modification	Psychotherapists
Conditioning	Classical conditioning Operant conditioning	Conditioned response Reinforcement	Counterconditioning Altered contingencies Relearning, "disenabling"	Behavior therapists

Biomedical	Heredity Brain	Genetic Physiological	Risk identification Medical treatment	Diagnosticians Physicians
Social learning	Cognitive therapy Relapse prevention	Modeling Expectancies Skill deficits	Appropriate models/goals Cognitive restructuring, skill training, self-control training	Cognitive-behavior therapists Appropriate models
General systems	Transactional analysis "Adult children of alcoholics"	Family dysfunction	Family therapy Recognition, peer support	Family therapist Support groups
Sociocultural	Control of consumption	Environmental Cultural norms	Supply-side intervention Social policy Server intervention	Lobbyists/legislators Social policy makers Retailers/servers
Public health	World Health Organization National Academy of Sciences	Interactions of host, agent, and environment	Comprehensive, multifaceted	Interdisciplinary

Source: Hester and Sheehy 1990.

referred to as milieu-limited alcoholism because both environmental and genetic factors play a part in the etiology. Type I alcoholism is characterized by adult onset (after twenty-five years of age), a gradually increasing consumption from mild to moderate, and a personality characterized by guilt, worry, dependency, and introversion. There is a lack of positive family history of alcohol abuse and minimal conflict with the law. Type I responds better to treatment than Type II.

Type II alcoholism is found in about 25 percent of alcoholics and is limited to males. It has a strong genetic penetrance from father to son and minimal environmental association. The onset of alcohol dependence is typically before twenty-five years of age, and the drinking pattern is characterized by irresponsible consumption, aggressive behavior, and many involvements with the law. Response to treatment is poor (Cloninger 1987).

A few studies, however, have not demonstrated such a strong genetic contribution to alcoholism. A study based on the Australian twin register found that among males, age of initiation of drinking was uninfluenced by genetic factors but was strongly influenced by the shared environment (Heath and Martin 1988). Among females, a moderate genetic influence and little shared environment effect was found. Current alcohol consumption by adult twins was found to be strongly influenced in both sexes by genetic factors. A fairly recent study by McGue, Pickens, and Svikis (1992) also found only a modest genetic influence on alcohol problems in women and in late-onset alcoholism in men. However, genetic influence was substantial in the etiology of early-onset male alcoholism.

A number of other biological factors have been implicated in alcohol use, abuse, and dependence. The most established biochemical abnormality concerns aldehyde (acetyldehyde) dehydrogenase, an enzyme involved in the metabolism of alcohol. Normally, alcohol is broken down into acetaldehyde and then into carbon dioxide and water by the enzyme aldehyde dehydrogenase. Acetyldehyde normally does not accumulate in the plasma. If it does, it produces very nasty symptoms, such as flushing of the face, nausea, vomiting, palpitations, and hypotension (Wolff 1972, 1973). About 50 percent of certain Asian groups, specifically Japanese, Chinese, and Koreans, have inherited deficiencies of this enzyme. This deters them from using alcohol and reduces the risk of alcohol dependence among them.

Another enzyme that influences the metabolism of alcohol is alcohol dehydrogenase, which metabolizes alcohol into acetaldehyde. About 5–10 percent of the British and German populations and up to 20 percent of the Swiss population are reported to possess the atypical forms of this enzyme (Marshall and Murray 1989). Individuals with these atypical forms can eliminate alcohol more rapidly (about 30 percent faster) than other people. Possession of these forms of the enzyme, which may also be genetically transmitted, may therefore influence alcohol consumption and its complications.

Sons of alcohol-dependent persons have been found to be at increased risk of developing alcohol dependence. A number of physiological differences have been found that could be associated with the increased risk, although it is not clear whether these differences are causal or simply markers. One good example is abnormally low P300 waves in visually evoked potentials. The size of the P300 spike is believed to correlate with the individual's ability to selectively recognize and properly interpret subtle stimuli in the environment. Thus the P300 wave measures the sensory, perceptual, and cognitive responses of the individual (Berman and Noble 1993). In early studies, P300 was found to be reduced in abstinent alcoholics, and this was thought to be the consequence of alcohol abuse (Begleiter, Porjecz, and Tenner 1980). However, subsequent similar studies have found reductions in P300 amplitudes in preadolescent sons of alcohol-dependent fathers compared with preadolescent sons of non-alcohol-dependent parents. The sons had not been exposed to alcohol, but they met the criteria for male-limited, Type II alcoholism described by Cloninger (1987).

There is also some evidence to suggest that sons of alcohol-dependent persons are less sensitive to the acute intoxicating effects of alcohol. This would also put them at increased risk of irresponsible drinking and of developing dependence. Both the P300 abnormality and the decreased sensitivity could be due to genetic predisposition. Other biological abnormalities that have been found in individuals who consume excessive quantities of alcohol include reduced activity of platelet monoamine oxidase and adenylate cyclase.

The discovery of the pleasure-rewarding system in the brain has thrown some light on the physiological basis of craving and drug dependence. Alcohol and other psychoactive substances are believed to activate this rewarding system by stimulating the activity of dopamine. A number of reports have claimed that a particular allele of the dopamine D2 receptor gene is found with increased frequency in alcohol abusers (Blume et al. 1991).

Personality and Psychiatric Disorders

Many individuals in clinical populations do not become alcohol dependent, and many alcohol-dependent persons have no obvious personality vulnerability or psychiatric disorder. However, in clinical practice it is common to find that excessive alcohol consumption is associated with personality vulnerabilities or psychoneurotic disorders. In fact, much of the research on alcohol abuse has been carried out on such clinical populations (i.e., those who are in some form of treatment). These associations do not tell us whether alcohol abuse is a cause or a consequence of the other problems.

Some of the personality traits that have been linked with alcohol abuse and dependence include chronic anxiety, a sense of inferiority, self-indulgent tendencies, antisocial personality disorder, and aggressive and impulsive personality, particularly in adolescents and borderline personalities (Lewis and Bucholz 1991). Other researchers have suggested that there might be a broad-based genetically transmitted personality predisposition, which may be expressed in either alcohol dependence or depression (Winokur et al. 1974).

The unified biosocial model, developed by Cloninger (1986) to address differences in susceptibility to chronic cognitive and somatic anxiety, was later extended to the problem of alcoholism (Cloninger 1987). Howard, Kivlahan, and Walker (1997) evaluated numerous studies that applied Cloninger's tridimensional theory of personality to substance abusers. They concluded that, while factor analyses did not uniformly support the tridimensionality of the measure, novelty-seeking traits distinguished alcoholics from nonalcoholics. In particular, novelty seeking predicted early-onset alcohol abuse and criminality and distinguished alcoholics exhibiting antisocial behavior and persons with antisocial personality disorder from their nonantisocial counterparts. Findings for the harm-avoidance and reward-dependence subscales were less consistent, though harm avoidance had some value in predicting the intensity of substance use.

Recent studies have implicated personality traits that lead to risk-taking behaviors and novelty seeking, including alcohol abuse (Jessor 1987; Berman and Noble 1993; Milkman and Sunderwirth 1994). Mässe and Tremblay (1997) established that high novelty seeking and low harm avoidance predicted early onset of getting drunk, cigarette smoking, and drug use, and the power of prediction was similar at ages six and ten. This approach, when placed in the broader context of lifestyle, has led to large population studies to determine both risk and protective factors (Jessor 1987) and is examined in detail later in this chapter.

The relationship between alcohol abuse and various other psychiatric disorders (such as generalized anxiety disorders, agoraphobia, social phobias, somatization disorders, and depression) has been well recognized, although psychiatric illness is not generally accepted as the major cause of alcohol abuse. Because many psychiatric patients find some of their symptoms distressing, it is postulated that many of them may misuse and abuse alcohol in attempts to relieve the symptoms. In major depression, alcohol may be used in attempts to lift the depressed mood and to self-induce sleep.

A recent longitudinal study of a representative community sample of 1,507 older adolescents (aged fourteen through eighteen years) in the United States found that more than 80 percent of adolescents with alcohol abuse or alcohol dependence had some other form of psychopathology. Importantly, alcohol disorders generally followed rather than preceded the onset of other psychiatric disorders. Increased alcohol use was associated with the increased lifetime occurrence of depressive disorders, disruptive behavior disorders, and drug use disorders (Rohde, Lewinsohn, and Seeley 1996). There was a trend for increased alcohol use among girls to be associated with anxiety disorders.

Manic patients may abuse alcohol to achieve loss of inhibition, feelings of grandiosity, and increased capacity to socialize. Alcohol abuse is common among chronic schizophrenic patients in their attempts to minimize symptoms such as anxiety, depression, insomnia, and hallucinations (Noordsy et al. 1991). Hyperactivity and attention deficit disorder have been associated with abuse of alcohol and other psychoactive substances and may be part of the conduct disorder syndrome (Mannuzza et al. 1989).

Age and Sex

The relationship between age and alcohol abuse has been well documented. On the whole, young people (below thirty years of age) abuse alcohol more than older people (over fifty) and have higher risks of incurring such complications of acute intoxication as accidents, fights, and alcohol poisoning. In adolescents, alcohol abuse is frequently associated with repeated episodes of antisocial behavior. In older people, certain physical changes associated with aging may result in increased susceptibility to the depressant effects of alcohol, decreased rates of metabolism of alcohol in the liver, and decreased percentage of body water. These changes tend to limit excessive alcohol consumption by elderly people but put them at increased risk of developing intoxication and its consequences at lower levels of consumption than younger people.

Irresponsible drinking in elderly people is also likely to coexist with or exacerbate other physical problems. Brennan and Moos (1996) found that, among older individuals who relied heavily on avoidance coping strategies, negative life events were more likely to predict an increase in drinking problems. However, among those with an initial drinking problem, subsequent health-related negative events and stressful incidents involving their friends led to decreased drinking problems.

Alcohol use, abuse, and dependence are much more common in males than in females, the male:female ratios varying from 7:1 to 3:1. The ratio, however, varies widely within age groups and gradually decreases with increasing age. More drinking is generally reported among younger women (Fillmore 1984; Hilton 1988). It is well recognized that females tend to start abusive drinking much later in life than males and probably also develop alcohol problems later. In many societies, the use of alcohol by females is strongly disapproved or is prohibited. This tends to restrict alcohol consumption by females, although it may also promote a different pattern of use, such as drinking at home or in private. However, once alcohol dependence is established in women, the deterioration tends to be faster, so that by the middle-age years females may have the same alcohol problems as males.

Other factors that might influence the use of alcohol by females and increase the risk of alcohol problems involve the metabolism of alcohol in the body. Females tend to develop higher blood alcohol concentrations than males when they consume equal quantities of alcohol. Females also have a lower percentage of body water and a higher percentage of body fat than males, and they tend to metabolize alcohol more slowly. It has recently been found that the "first pass" metabolism of alcohol by gastric tissues is lower in alcoholic women than in alcoholic men. This may explain the increased bioavailability of alcohol and, possibly, the increased rates of hepatic injury in women (Frezza et al. 1990). All these factors increase the risk of development of health complications in female drinkers compared with male drinkers of the same age (see also chapter 4 of this volume on health issues and drinking patterns).

PATTERNS OF DRINKING AND PSYCHOSOCIAL DIFFERENCES

Risk and Protective Factors

As noted above, some researchers have placed personality and other psychological differences in the context of lifestyle. They have then studied representative populations (rather than clinical populations only) in order to establish patterns of relative risk and health. The outcome of these approaches suggests that risky behaviors with respect to alcohol co-occur with other risky behaviors. They also suggest that attention to both risk and protective factors can help prevent alcohol abuse.

For example, when Jessor studied teenagers who engaged in drunk driving, he found that "risky driving behavior emerges from these analyses as an aspect of a larger adolescent lifestyle . . . embedded in the same set of personality, perceived environment, and behavior variables as other adolescent problem behaviors such as delinquency, problem drinking, and illicit drug use." He concluded that "prevention/intervention efforts might well be focused at the level of lifestyle rather than be restricted to the specific behavior—risky driving— alone" (Jessor 1987, 10).

Donovan, a colleague of Jessor, extended the initial research to a sample of young adults. He found that young adults who drove after drinking showed higher levels of personality and social unconventionality, enjoyed taking more risks, and were more hostile and aggressive than those who did not. Variation in drinking and driving was related to a variety of other problem behaviors, including problem drinking, use of illegal drugs, and delinquent behavior. His research provided clear evidence that, in his words, "drinking-driving is part of a larger pattern of involvement in behaviors that violate normative standards, a 'lifestyle' of problem behavior in young adulthood" (Donovan 1993, 609).

The Search Institute in Minneapolis recently investigated a range of risk-taking behaviors among adolescents in the United States (Burns 1994). Its data establish that risk in the areas of alcohol use, tobacco use, illegal drug use, sexuality, depression or suicide, other antisocial behaviors, school problems, and vehicle safety co-occur at significant rates, as shown in table 3.2.

Shedler and Block (1990) explored the psychological and social underpinnings of substance abuse among a diverse population of individuals, whom they tracked from preschool age to early adulthood. The youths who abused substances displayed distinctive traits, including poor impulse control, inability to form close relationships, inability to concentrate, a lack of self-reliance and

Table 3.2 Patterns of co-occurrence among at-risk behaviors, (percent)

At-risk area	Alcohol use	Tobacco use	Illicit drug use	Sexuality	Depression suicide	Antisocial behavior	School	Vehicle safety
				Risk in related area				
Alcohol use		42	27	70	33	49	23	86
Tobacco use	66		35	77	39	53	26	85
Illicit drug use	72	60		84	46	61	32	88
Sexuality	49	34	22		34	41	19	77
Depression/suicide	41	30	21	59		38	18	73
Antisocial behavior	54	37	24	64	34		22	82
School	62	43	31	72	40	53		82
Vehicle safety	41	25	15	52	28	35	15	

Source: Search Institute, as presented in Burns 1994.

confidence, and a tendency to withdraw under stress. The authors concluded that these factors predate initiation of drug or alcohol abuse.

Schulenberg and colleagues (1996) also focused on the transition to young adulthood. Their study examined drinking reported at biennial intervals by a very large sample of young adults (eighteen to twenty-four years) in the United States. They found strong evidence of wide developmental variations in drinking patterns in the population identified. Abusive patterns of drinking were closely tied to difficulties in successfully negotiating the transition to young adulthood, in some cases among those who had few if any problems with adolescence. For some groups, these abusive patterns persisted and developed into adult problem drinking; for others, the patterns moderated as they matured. The authors concluded that a pattern-centered approach, rather than a traditional aggregate-level approach, produces a more complete understanding of developmental patterns in both healthy and risky drinking.

Werner and Smith (1992), who followed all individuals born on the Hawaiian island of Kauai in 1955, reached similar conclusions about risk factors. Their study focused attention on those children who were at highest risk for substance abuse, violence, and mental illness—children who were born in poverty and whose parents abused substances, were physically violent, or suffered from chronic physical or mental illness. In fact, a substantial portion of these children had these problems as adolescents or young adults. In their continued tracking of these individuals, Werner and Smith found that by the age of thirty-two, the majority had become healthy, well-adjusted adults. The researchers were particularly interested in the factors that accounted for this change and concluded that what consistently made the difference for those who developed into healthy, well-adjusted adults was an ongoing relationship with at least one person who provided them with a secure basis for developing trust, autonomy, and initiative.

Researchers working in the United States, the United Kingdom, Lebanon, and Mozambique (Wolin and Wolin 1993; Garbarino et al. 1992; Garmezy 1991; Kurth-Schai 1988; Rutter 1985) have observed two other major protective factors that, in addition to the presence of a caring and nurturing adult, move children toward normal adult development under all but the most persistent adverse circumstances: opportunities for meaningful participation in school or community and high and realistic expectations of the child by significant adults. Burns (1994) has argued that families, schools, and communities can take positive actions that will move youth from risk to resilience. He has outlined individual, family, and community risk and protective factors. By linking specific protective factors with risk factors, he suggests the direction for positive intervention. These relationships are presented in table 3.3.

A prevention analyst in the United States has emphasized the importance of protective factor research: "If we can determine the personal and environmental sources of social competencies, we can better plan preventive interventions focusing on creating and/or building the personal and environmental attributes

Table 3.3   Protective factors recommended for fostering resilience

	Risk factors		Protective factors
Individual and peer	Family		
Early antisocial behavior	Lack of clear behavioral expectations		A relationship with a caring adult role model
Alienation and rebelliousness	Lack of mentoring and supervision		Opportunity to contribute and be seen as a resource
Antisocial behavior in latter childhood and early teens	Lack of caring		Effectiveness in work, play, and relationships
Favorable attitudes toward drug use	Inconsistent or excessively severe discipline		Healthy expectations and positive outlook
Susceptibility to peer influence	Parental positive attitudes toward drug use		Self-esteem and internal locus of control
Friends who use tobacco, alcohol, illicit drugs	Low expectations for children's success		Self-discipline
	History of alcohol and drug abuse		Problem-solving and critical thinking skills
			A sense of humor

Source: Adapted from Burns 1994.

that serve as the key to healthy development'' (Benard 1991, 2). She argued that parents, educational institutions, and community organizations can systematically develop programs that promote the healthy development of youth and young adults. Benard called this process ''fostering resiliency.'' She encouraged specific programs that reduce risk factors and foster protective factors, including mentoring programs, peer programs, and cooperative learning strategies. Glenn and Nelson (1989) have proposed additional programmatic solutions, including community service programs and other opportunities for young people to make valued, significant contributions to their communities. They note that when delinquent young people are recruited into programs to work with and help younger people, ''they tend to shed much of their delinquent behavior as they come to perceive of themselves as needed and significant'' (p. 103).

The importance of attention to protective factors as well as risk factors was underscored by Jessor and his colleagues (1995). They conceptualized protective factors as variables that reflect involvement with and commitment to conventional society, that control against nonnormative activities, and that refer to activities incompatible with normative transgression. In reviewing longitudinal data from a large sample of adolescents, they found the expected interaction between protection and risk in the prediction of problem behavior, yet protection was shown to moderate the relation of risk to problem behavior. Protective factors were also shown to be significant predictors of change in adolescent problem behavior over time. Programs based on the risk and protective factor model have been shown to be effective. Lower rates of alcohol and drug abuse, higher school grades, and reduced drop-out rates are some of the positive results of student assistance programs (Watkins and Chatfield 1995). A longitudinal study showed that early prevention and education resulted in reductions in alcohol and drug use among students through their high school years (Botvin et al. 1995).

Developmental Assets

Recent work in the United States by the Search Institute focused more clearly on individual differences that predict alcohol abuse and other antisocial behaviors (Benson 1996; Search Institute 1996). Its model, based largely on the risk and prevention literature, examines thirty key developmental assets for youth. External assets were

Support
- Family support
- Parents as social resources
- Parent communication
- Other adult resources
- Other adult communication

- Parent involvement in schooling
- Positive school climate

Boundaries

- Parental standards
- Parental discipline
- Parental monitoring
- Time at home
- Positive peer influence

Structured time use

- Involved in music
- Involved in school extracurricular activities
- Involved in community organizations or activities
- Involved in religious activities

Internal assets included

Educational commitment

- Achievement motivation
- Educational aspiration
- School performance
- Homework

Positive values

- Values helping people
- Is concerned about world hunger
- Cares about people's feelings
- Values sexual restraint

Social competencies

- Assertiveness skills
- Decision-making skills
- Friendship-making skills
- Planning skills
- Self-esteem
- Positive view of personal future

Out of 250,000 sixth- to twelfth-graders who were surveyed, the average number of assets was sixteen. Over three-quarters of the young people possessed twenty or fewer assets. The implications for problem alcohol use (defined as six or more uses in the past month or got drunk once or more in the past two weeks) are clear. Only three percent of those with twenty-six through thirty assets reported problem alcohol use, compared with 44 percent of those with zero through ten assets. Similar patterns were found for other problem behaviors, such as sexual activity, violence, other antisocial activity, and school trouble. On the other hand, positive behaviors showed the inverse patterns. Only five percent of those with zero through ten assets were A students, whereas 51 percent of those with twenty-six through thirty assets were. The study concluded that the more internal and external assets students possess, the lower their risk.

The developmental asset model may be more accessible to lay audiences than the research on risks and protective factors and may be more easily translated into action by individuals, families, organizations, and communities. It has been shown to work across diverse populations in the United States, and with appropriate modifications for different cultures it could be useful in other settings.

Societal Norms

While this chapter focuses on individual differences, it must be emphasized that societal norms, reinforced by law and custom, significantly influence behavior by individuals. Heath (1990) found that societal norms that allow for safe and moderate alcohol consumption and responsible abstention, while disapproving of abuse, were most likely to create the environment that fosters healthy decisions about alcohol. He concluded that honest education about the nature and effects of alcohol, combined with instilling norms about the limits of appropriate and inappropriate behavior, "serves as a kind of 'immunization' against alcoholism and drinking problems" (p. 78). Reinforcement of healthy norms, he argued, was likely to be more effective in the long run than increasing emphasis on legal and regulatory controls.

For example, in the United States today, alcohol sales are not permitted on most reservations for Native Americans. Thus, residents may hitchhike miles to reach a bar outside the reservation, and reports of hypothermia and of pedestrian deaths involving vehicles on the return journey are frequent (Gallaher et al. 1992). This pattern of abusive drinking outside the family or local village is not unusual in cultures that prohibit alcohol consumption.

In fact, healthy social norms appear to be strengthened by focusing on the appropriate, rather than the risky, behavior. After trying both approaches on an American college campus, Haines (1993) concluded that by using media to emphasize the healthy norms of the majority of students, he and his colleagues were able substantially to reduce alcohol abuse among the student body. On the other hand, a focus on unhealthy behaviors actually promoted illness. A similar conclusion was reached by Epstein and colleagues (1995) regarding a population of inner-city, minority youths. They found that students had significant misconceptions about the prevalence of drinking among friends and peers. In fact, there is a dearth of data on moderate consumption, particularly across cultures (Ahlström 1994).

CONCLUSION: PATTERNS OF DRINKING AND
INDIVIDUAL DIFFERENCES

It is clear that individual differences—biomedical and psychosocial—are important in understanding different drinking patterns, including alcohol abuse and dependence. Most drinkers do not abuse alcohol, and therefore responsible drinking is possible for the vast majority of people.

Yet the examination of biomedical and psychosocial risk factors in this chapter suggests that there are specific individuals at greater risk for alcohol abuse or dependence. For some of these persons, drinking may interact with genetic or other biological conditions, personality and psychiatric disorders, or age and gender considerations. For others, risk may be predicted by psychosocial risk and protective factors or by the absence of developmental assets. Drinking and other problems may stem from the failure to successfully negotiate a critical developmental transition, such as adolescence or young adulthood. These individuals may "grow out" of their problem behaviors or may encounter difficulties in the next transition. Societal norms, laws, and customs may mediate individual differences and either guide individuals toward responsible behaviors or foster abuse.

Researchers may never agree on the "cause" of abuse, if there is such a single syndrome or model at all. Still, the broad range of individual differences provides significant opportunities for collaboration among governments, the academic community, voluntary organizations, and the alcohol beverage industry. These diverse interests all have a stake in fostering scientific research on the etiology of alcohol abuse, educating young people and consumers, strengthening norms that promote only responsible drinking, and supporting effective prevention strategies for individuals and groups at greatest risk of abuse.

REFERENCES

Ahlström, S. 1994. Variations in drinking norms by subculture and demography. *Contemporary Drug Problems* 21:211–21.

Begleiter H., B. Porjecz, and M. Tenner. 1980. Neuroradiological and nurophysiological evidence of brain deficits in chronic alcoholics. *Acta Psychiatrica Scandinavica* 2:3–13.

Benard, B. 1991. *Fostering Resiliency in Kids: Protective Factors in the Family, School, and Community.* Portland, Ore.: Northwest Regional Educational Laboratory.

Benson, P. L. 1996. *Creating Healthy Communities for Children and Adolescents.* San Francisco: Jossey-Bass.

Berman, S. M., and E. P. Noble. 1993. Childhood antecedents of misuse of substances. *Current Opinions in Psychiatry* 6:382–87.

Blume, K., et al. 1991. Association of the A1 allele of the D2 dopamine receptor gene with severe alcoholism. *Alcohol* 8:409–16.

Botvin, G. J., et al. 1995. Long-term follow-up results of a randomized drug abuse prevention trial in a white middle-class population. *Journal of the American Medical Association* 273:1106–12.

Brennan, P. L., and R. H. Moos. 1996. Late-life problem drinking: personal and environmental risk factors for 4-year functioning outcomes and treatment seeking. *Journal of Substance Abuse* 8:167–80.

Burns, T. 1994. *From Risk to Resilience: A Journey with Heart for Our Children, Our Future.* Dallas: Marco Polo.

Chafetz, M., and M. D. Chafetz. 1995. *Drink Moderately and Live Longer: Understanding the Good of Alcohol.* New York: Madison.

Cloninger, C. R. 1986. A unified biosocial theory of personality and its role in the development of anxiety states. *Psychiatric Development* 4:167–266.

———. 1987. Neurogenetic adaptive mechanisms in alcoholism. *Science* 236:410–16.

Clonigner, C. R., M. Bohman, and S. Figwardson. 1981. Inheritance of alcohol abuse. *Archives of General Psychiatry* 38:861–68.

Donovan, J. E. 1993. Young adult drinking-driving: behavioral and psychosocial correlates. *Journal of Studies on Alcohol* 54:600–613.

Epstein, J. A., et al. 1995. The role of social factors and individual characteristics in promoting alcohol use among inner-city minority youths. *Journal of Studies on Alcohol* 56:39–46.

Fillmore, K. M. 1984. When angels fall: women drinking as a cultural preoccupation and as reality. In *Alcohol Problems in Women,* ed. S. C. Wilsnack and L. J. Beckman. New York: Guilford.

Ford, G. 1990. *Drinking and Health.* San Francisco: Wine Appreciation Guild.

Frezza, M., et al. 1990. High blood alcohol levels in women: the role of decreased gastric alcohol dehydrogenase activity and ''first-pass'' metabolism. *New England Journal of Medicine* 322:95–99.

Gallaher, M., D. Fleming, L. Berger, and C. M. Sewell. 1992. Pedestrian and hypothermia deaths among Native Americans in New Mexico: between bar and home. *Journal of the American Medical Association* 267:1345–84.

Garbarino, J., N. Dubrow, K. Kostelny, and C. Pardo. 1992. *Children in Danger: Coping with the Consequences of Community Violence.* San Francisco: Jossey-Bass.

Garmezy, N. 1991. Resiliency and vulnerability to adverse developmental outcomes associated with poverty. *American Behavioral Scientist* 24:416–30.

Glenn, S., and J. Nelson. 1989. *Raising Self-Reliant Children in a Self-Indulgent World.* Rocklin, Calif.: Prima.

Goodwin, D. W., et al. 1973. Alcohol problems in adoptees raised apart from alcoholic biological parents. *Archives of General Psychiatry* 28:238–43.

Haines, M. 1993. Using media to change student norms and prevent alcohol abuse: a tested model. *Oregon Higher Education Alcohol and Drug Coordinating Committee Newsletter* 1:3–5.

Heath, D. 1990. Flawed policies from flawed premises: pseudo science about alcohol and drugs. In *Controversies in the Addictions Field,* ed. R. Engs. Vol. 1. Dubuque: American Council on Alcoholism.

Heath, A. C., and N. G. Martin. 1988. Teenage alcohol use in the Australian twin register: genetic and social determinants of starting to drink alcohol. *Clinical Experimental Research* 12:735–41.

Hester, R., and N. Sheehy. 1990. The grand unification theory of alcohol abuse: it's time to stop fighting each other and start working together. In *Controversies in the Addictions Field,* ed. R. Engs. Vol. 1. Dubuque: American Council on Alcoholism.

Hilton, M. E. 1988. Trends in U.S. drinking patterns: further evidence from the past 20 years. *British Journal of Addictions* 83:269–78.

Howard, M. O., D. Kivlahan, and R. D. Walker. 1997. Cloninger's tridimensional theory of personality and psychopathology: applications to substance use disorders. *Journal of Studies on Alcohol* 58:48–66.

Jellinek, E. M. 1960. *The Disease Concept of Alcoholism.* New Haven, Conn.: Hillhouse.

Jessor, R. 1987. Risky driving and adolescent problem behavior: an extension of problem-behavior theory. *Alcohol, Drugs, and Driving* 3:1–11.

Jessor, R., et al. 1995. Protective factors in adolescent problem behavior: moderator effects and developmental change. *Developmental Psychology* 31:923–33.

Kendler, K. S., et al. 1994. A twin-family study of alcoholism in women. *American Journal of Psychiatry* 151:707–15.

Kurth-Schai, R. 1988. The roles of youth in society: a reconceptualization. *Educational Forum* 52:113–32.

Lewis, C. E., and K. K. Bucholz. 1991. Alcoholism, antisocial behaviour, and family history. *British Journal of Addiction* 86:177–94.

Mannuzza, S., et al. 1989. Hyperactive boys almost grown up. IV. Criminality and its relationship to psychiatric status. *Archives of General Psychiatry* 46:1073–79.

Marshall, E. J., and R. M. Murray. 1989. The contribution of twin studies to alcoholism research. In *Alcoholism: Biochemical and Genetic Aspects,* ed. H. W. Goedde and D. P. Agarwal. New York: Pergamon.

Mässe, L. C., and R. E. Tremblay. 1997. Behavior of boys in kindergarten and the onset of substance use during adolescence. *Archives of General Psychiatry* 54:62–68.

McGue, M., R. W. Pickens, and D. S. Svikis. 1992. Sex and age effects on the inheritance of alcohol problems: a twin study. *Journal of Abnormal Psychology* 101:3–17.

Milkman, H., and S. Sunderwirth. 1994. *Pathways to Pleasure: The Consciousness and Chemistry of Optimal Living.* New York: Lexington.

Murray, R. M., and P. McGuffin. 1993. Genetic aspects of psychiatric disorders. In *Companion to Psychiatric Studies,* ed. E. Kendell and A. K. Zeallay. Edinburgh: Churchill Livingstone.

Noordsy, D. L., et al. 1991. Subjective experiences related to alcohol use among schizophrenics. *Journal of Nervous and Mental Disorders* 179:410–14.

Pickens, R. W., et al. 1991. Heterogeneity in the inheritance of alcoholism: a study of male and female twins. *Archives of General Psychiatry* 48:19–29.

Rohde, P., P. M. Lewinsohn, and J. R. Seeley. 1996. Psychiatric comorbidity with problematic alcohol use in high school students. *Journal of the American Academy of Child and Adolescent Psychiatry* 35:101–9.

Rutter, M. 1985. Resilience in the face of adversity: protective factors and resistance to psychiatric disorder. *British Journal of Psychiatry* 145:598–611.

Schulenberg, J., et al. 1996. Getting drunk and growing up: trajectories of frequent binge drinking during the transition to young adulthood. *Journal of Studies on Alcohol* 57:200–304.

Search Institute. 1996. *Healthy Communities, Healthy Youth.* Minneapolis: Search Institute.

Shedler, J., and J. Block. 1990. Adolescent drug use and psychological health: a longitudinal inquiry. *American Psychologist* 48:612–27.

Watkins, C., and L. F. Chatfield. 1995. Student assistance programs: we know what's working. *Inter-Connections* 1:2–3.

Werner, E., and R. Smith. 1992. *Overcoming the Odds: High-Risk Children from Birth to Adulthood*. Ithaca: Cornell University Press.

Winokur, G. A., et al. 1974. The division of depressive illness into depression spectrum disease and pure depressive illness. *International Pharmacopsychiatry* 9:5–13.

Wolf, P. H. 1972. Ethnic differences in alcohol sensitivity. *Science* 175: 449–50.

————. 1973. Vasomotor sensitivity to alcohol in diverse Mongoloid populations. *American Journal of Human Genetics* 25:193–99.

Wolin, S., and S. Wolin. 1993. *The Resilient Self: How Survivors of Troubled Families Rise above Adversity*. New York: Villard.

Chapter 4

Health Issues and Drinking Patterns

Amelia M. Arria and Michael Gossop

Researchers, clinicians, and policy makers have long shown great interest in understanding the consequences of alcohol consumption for health. We know that not all people who drink are adversely affected by alcohol and that not all people who experience alcohol-related problems drink the same amount of alcohol or have the same drinking patterns. The growing body of research findings and clinical observations on alcohol and its physical consequences can be divided broadly into three main areas of inquiry:

1.   studies examining the association between per capita consumption and rates of morbidity and mortality both within and across populations,
2.   case control studies estimating the risk of physical illness among alcohol-dependent individuals as compared to controls, and
3.   studies of the association between levels of alcohol consumption and risk of physical outcomes (e.g., prospective studies, dose-response studies).

Several topics in the field of alcohol and health are in need of further exploration, including refinements in the measurement of alcohol consumption; improved comprehension of the mechanisms underlying alcohol's biological action; and a greater appreciation and understanding of alcohol's interaction with

Amelia M. Arria is with Johns Hopkins University, Baltimore, Maryland, U.S. Michael Gossop is with the National Addiction Centre, London, United Kingdom.

sociodemographic characteristics, behavioral factors such as smoking, diet, and exercise, and genetic differences in vulnerability to physical conditions. There are also interesting and important questions about how drinking patterns are associated with health consequences. Compared to the number of studies examining the association between level of drinking and health consequences, far fewer studies have addressed the way in which patterns of alcohol consumption are associated with physical illness.

At various points in this chapter, the reader is referred to comprehensive reviews and other publications that discuss the important association between level of alcohol consumption and specific health consequences, including cardiovascular diseases, liver diseases, neurologic disorders, and accidental injuries. The issue of psychiatric comorbidity, or the co-occurrence of alcohol dependence with psychiatric disorders, is beyond the scope of the chapter and is not covered here; the reader is referred to Mirin and Weiss (1991) as well as to chapter 3 of this volume, for a fuller discussion. This particular chapter attempts a synthesis of the available literature on patterns of drinking and physical health, giving special attention to the various patterns of drinking that may be considered to be in the range of light-to-moderate drinking.

Recently, more attention has been paid to levels of consumption below what might be termed the heavy end of the alcohol drinking continuum, where most individuals concerned would be classified according to psychiatric criteria as alcohol dependent or as problem drinkers. We have learned that the risk of adverse health consequences for alcohol-dependent individuals is much higher than for individuals whose drinking level and pattern lie elsewhere along the spectrum. With the possible exception of coronary heart disease, our understanding of the association between alcohol and health at lower levels of consumption is less clear; and in the studies that recognize an association between light-to-moderate drinking and lowered risk of coronary heart disease there are many unanswered questions about the mechanisms responsible for that association. There are data that support a biological explanation for the association as well as studies suggesting that light-to-moderate drinkers are different in terms of their behavioral risk profile (e.g., frequency of exercise, dietary habits; see Marques-Vidal et al. 1996). Given the absolute number of individuals who can be classified as light or moderate drinkers, it is crucial that more attention be paid to this issue. The recent request by the National Institute on Alcohol and Alcoholism for research proposals having a focus on moderate drinking and health is one example of attempts to fill this gap in our knowledge.

To set the stage for the ensuing discussion, it is important to first reiterate briefly what is meant by *drinking pattern*. To quote from chapter 1,

patterns of drinking may refer . . . to temporal variations in drinking, the number and characteristics of heavy drinking occasions, the settings where drinking takes place, the activities associated with drinking, the personal characteristics of the drinkers and their drinking confederates, the types of beverage consumed, and the clusters of drinking norms and behaviors often referred to as drinking cultures.

The authors draw a clear distinction between drinking level (how much one drinks) and drinking pattern (how one drinks).

Some of these aspects of patterns of drinking will have greater relevance than others for health outcomes. For instance, whether a person drinks a fifth of liquor at home or in a bar probably does not have a bearing on whether his or her liver enzymes become elevated as a result. However, variations in the place where one consumes alcohol might have a bearing on the risk of accidental injury (e.g., drinking at home alone or drinking the same amount while driving a boat). Whether alcohol is consumed during a meal or not is another aspect of pattern that may be relevant to health consequences. We know that alcohol metabolism is slowed when beverages are taken with meals, so that the biological impact may be somewhat attenuated. In addition, the type of alcohol consumed (e.g., home-produced versus industrial-grade alcohol) may have different biological effects. Two recent studies by Alvarez, Del Rio, and colleagues (1993, 1994) on Spanish males and females and another by Madianos, Gefou-Madianou, and Stefanis (1995) in Greece illustrate how questions on drinking during meals and on type of beverage can be incorporated into an epidemiologic survey. However, in these studies no data on health outcomes related to drinking patterns were presented. Some aspects of pattern may be more relevant for chronic disease (beverage type, drinking during meals or not, sustained versus intermittent consumption), while others may be more relevant for accidental injury (drinking during the day at work, drinking while driving), both of which are considered in this chapter.

Probably the drinking pattern aspect most relevant for health outcome is the distinction between binge drinking and sustained drinking. Though there are several definitions (and a number of different terms) for binge drinking and sustained drinking (see Epstein et al. 1995), the most important question from a biological point of view may be whether exposure to alcohol of the organ system or tissue is continuous or intermittent, that is, how frequently intoxicating blood levels are achieved. Changes in this aspect of drinking pattern could have significant health consequences. Furthermore, one can speculate that different organ systems, given their varying adaptive capabilities at the cellular level, react differently to continuous versus intermittent exposures to alcohol. This issue is complicated by the possible interaction of drinking pattern with sex differences in alcohol metabolism and genetic differences in vulnerability to organ damage.

Although advances have been made in the measurement of alcohol consumption, current methods are far from ideal. This is especially true for methods of gathering information about drinking pattern. The methodological problems inherent in alcohol assessment techniques are important to consider when evaluating studies in the area of alcohol and health. Although this topic is covered in more detail in chapter 12, it is important to highlight some issues here to serve as background for the studies discussed in the following pages. Obtaining reliable information about drinking history requires careful development of survey instruments. Often, in a research setting, what to ask about alcohol consumption takes precedence over more subtle issues of how to ask. Knowing how to ask can reduce the likelihood that a respondent will underestimate or overestimate consumption levels.

However, no measure is perfect. Many researchers believe that self-reported alcohol consumption tends to be underestimated. Moreover, alcohol drinking patterns over a life span are difficult to estimate. Because of resource constraints, and also to minimize the burden on respondents, researchers are usually limited to gathering information about alcohol consumption during a short period prior to the time of the survey (e.g., the previous month). Others have been successful in asking questions about alcohol drinking patterns over the life span, using important life events to trigger memories of the specific time period of interest (e.g., the time-line follow-back method). Until recently, epidemiologists in the area of alcohol research did not typically include specific measures of drinking pattern in surveys of the general population. Now, however, because of the recognized need for data on drinking pattern and health outcomes, researchers are beginning to develop and use measures of drinking pattern in their work (see Reynolds, Chambers, and DeVillaer 1992; Russell et al. 1991).

The inclusion of pattern of drinking as well as level of drinking in studies on alcohol and health can open a Pandora's box. Using average level of consumption certainly requires simpler analytic strategies and is probably one of the main reasons that alcohol researchers have limited themselves to analyzing this data. However, within any average level of consumption there are likely to be groups of individuals with different drinking patterns, and analytic results will thus be less informative than if pattern is taken into account. A person who drinks two drinks regularly every day of the week cannot be considered in the same way as someone whose average daily consumption is also two drinks but whose pattern consists of fourteen drinks on a single occasion during the week. To understand, from a public health perspective, how alcohol is related to health in terms of both level and pattern of consumption, we need to start exploring these more complex issues, using sophisticated statistical methodology.

AN OVERVIEW OF HEALTH CONSEQUENCES

According to a substantial research literature, heavy, prolonged alcohol consumption over the life span increases an individual's risk for not only a variety of systemic illnesses but also accidental injury. Similarly, not much controversy exists over the negligible health consequences of light drinking throughout one's life span. (We must take into account, however, the definitions of light-to-moderate drinking, since average-daily-consumption categories group together individuals with different drinking patterns.) Several major epidemiological studies have demonstrated that alcoholism or alcohol dependence is associated with premature death. Further, almost all areas of the body—including the liver, brain, pancreas, cardiovascular system, and immune system—may be affected negatively by long-standing alcohol abuse. Many studies documenting the negative health consequences of alcoholism have employed clinical samples of alcoholics admitted to treatment facilities. (More information on the physical conditions associated with alcohol dependence can be found in several textbooks and publications; see NIAAA 1993.)

The effects of moderate drinking on physical health have received more attention in the recent past and have been studied most extensively with regard to coronary heart disease. One of the most robust ways of discerning the effects of level of alcohol consumption on health is to conduct prospective epidemiological studies, in which alcohol consumption is measured at a baseline date and individuals are followed up at some later date to determine the physical consequences. Reports from several such studies have been published, and the general conclusion has been that light-to-moderate levels of alcohol consumption are associated with mortality rates not significantly greater than rates in nondrinkers. The association between average levels of alcohol consumption and mortality rates has often been described as U-shaped, the highest mortality rates being observed for the nondrinking and heaviest drinking categories of individuals and the light-to-moderate consumers having the lowest rates. (See Shaper 1990 for a comprehensive review of the prospective studies conducted before 1990 on the association between average level of alcohol consumption and mortality.) The U-shaped association appears to be much more pronounced for coronary heart disease (CHD) mortality than non-CHD mortality. Given that CHD is a major cause of death for most of these populations, some argue that CHD is most likely to account for the association. Criqui and Ringel (1994) provide evidence that, while moderate alcohol consumption is associated with a decreased risk for coronary artery disease, it does not appear to be associated with increased longevity, while others suggest that light drinking is associated with lowered overall mortality (DeLabry et al. 1992). This topic is a matter of continued debate. In a thirteen-year prospective study of British male doctors, Doll et al. (1994) reported that lowest overall mortality rates were observed in the group drinking eleven to eighteen units a week, with a unit defined as the equivalent of 8 grams of ethanol (U.K. Department of Health and Social Security 1995). Doctors who reported drinking twenty-nine through forty-two units a week had about 20 percent higher total mortality, and those consuming more than forty-two units a week had about 40 percent higher mortality.

The U-shaped association is not generally disputed. What causes some controversy is its interpretation (Shaper 1990). Does it imply a causal association? Are nondrinkers different from drinkers in ways other than their drinking— ways that cause them to have an elevated risk for mortality? There are also difficulties in deciding where the cutoff line lies between light and moderate drinking. Should it be different for males and females? The issue of whether certain drinking patterns (within the category of individuals classified as light-to-moderate drinkers) are more or less likely to be associated with decreased overall mortality has yet to be examined. There is general agreement that heavy binge drinking is more likely to be associated with premature mortality than other patterns of drinking. This may be partly due to the association of heavy binge drinking with accidental injury and risk-taking behavior. We return to these issues at the end of the chapter and discuss the important implications of pattern of alcohol consumption in relation to overall health.

COFACTORS INVOLVED IN THE ASSOCIATION BETWEEN ALCOHOL CONSUMPTION AND HEALTH

Poor health, in ancient times, was often attributed to the revenge of the angry gods. Later, unsanitary conditions were recognized as major contributors to ill health. More recently, we have identified specific genetic factors that confer either vulnerability or resistance to particular diseases or infections. When discussing alcohol's effect on physical health, we must appreciate that a number of other factors influence our health, both independently of the actions of alcohol and through some interaction with it. Figure 4.1 graphically depicts the complexity of the relationship between alcohol consumption and health. While alcohol certainly has independent effects on organ systems, other agents, such as prescription drugs or illicit drugs and dietary factors, may work synergistically or antagonistically to alter those effects.

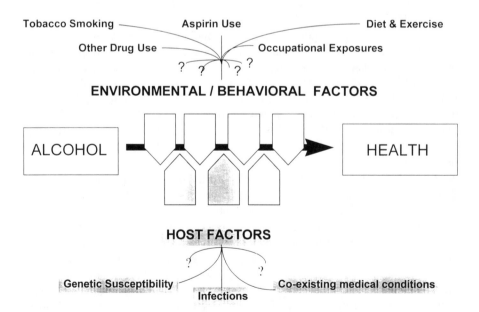

Figure 4.1 The relationship between alcohol consumption and health

Many of the physical conditions discussed below have a host of associated risk factors, including such personal characteristics as age, sex, race, ethnicity, and genetic makeup. For example, preliminary evidence suggests that women appear to have decreased "first-pass" metabolism of alcohol, which leads to increased bioavailability of alcohol (Frezza et al. 1990). This is one possible reason for the observed increased vulnerability among women to alcohol-related liver damage. Macroenvironmental characteristics such as access to health care and environmental quality can also influence health. Smoking, misuse of prescription medications, illicit drug use, and an improper diet all have ramifications for physical health.

The manner in which medications can interact with alcohol is shown by a series of studies conducted by Roine et al. (1990). They investigated the effect of aspirin on blood alcohol concentration, using volunteers, an animal model, and in vitro studies. The results of their experiments supported the hypothesis that ordinary aspirin can increase blood alcohol concentration after ingestion of food. The mechanism appears to involve inhibition of gastric alcohol dehydrogenase (ADH), the enzyme in the stomach responsible for the first-pass metabolism of alcohol. By reducing the activity of gastric ADH, aspirin makes more alcohol available to the systemic circulation. This finding is of clinical significance in that ingesting alcohol in combination with aspirin may potentiate the effects of alcohol. The same research group found similar results with the histamine H_2 receptor antagonist, cimetidine, a drug prescribed commonly by gastroenterologists for ulcers. Like aspirin, cimetidine decreased the activity of gastric ADH and, in turn, increased blood alcohol concentrations (Caballeria et al. 1989).

THE HEALTH BENEFITS OF ALCOHOL CONSUMPTION

Coronary Heart Disease

A substantial body of epidemiological evidence indicates that light-to-moderate drinking (one to two drinks, or 20 to 30 grams of ethanol, a day) is associated with a reduction in risk for coronary artery disease (Klatsky, Freidman, and Siegelaub 1981; Rimm et al. 1991; Maclure 1993; Renaud et al. 1993; Serdula et al. 1995). This effect is seen in men, women, the elderly, and both smokers and nonsmokers. Most of the studies conducted up to the present have considered the impact of either total consumption of alcohol over the life span or average daily consumption during a specified time period. The influence of various drinking patterns, or the variability in drinking across the life span (for example, reducing drinking as one ages), has not been adequately investigated. However, there is evidence that the risk for coronary artery disease increases at high levels of alcohol consumption, especially when it takes the form of binge, or heavy weekend, drinking (Kozarevic et al. 1988).

The well-established risk factors for coronary artery disease include smoking, lack of exercise, high saturated fat intake, low socioeconomic status, and medical conditions such as diabetes and hypertension (Levy and Moskowitz 1982). On the other hand, several behavioral factors have been linked to a decreased risk for cardiovascular disease, including aspirin use, regular exercise, and maintaining low body fat. It is a reasonable hypothesis that individuals who maintain a light-to-moderate level of alcohol consumption also practice good health behaviors, such as regular physical activity, stress reduction, and sound dietary habits. Indeed, the results of several studies support this hypothesis: moderate drinkers tend to smoke less than other groups (Marques-Vidal et al. 1995) and are more likely to have a self-perception of good health (Poiklainen, Vartiainen, and Korhonen 1996). Weaker social networks among abstainers and heavy drinkers, compared to light-to-moderate drinkers, might also account for the J-shaped association between alcohol and mortality (Skog 1995). The differences in lifestyle associated with wine drinking could also explain part of the relation between alcohol consumption and coronary artery disease. Such effects deserve explicit attention in research studies of the effects of alcohol on health. Rather than simply ''adjusting'' for these behavioral factors, thereby essentially removing their effect on the health outcome of interest, it would be useful to include their interactions with alcohol when modeling empirical associations between alcohol and various health outcomes.

Because the finding that light-to-moderate drinking is associated with reduced risk for coronary artery disease has been replicated in several studies, many have tried to answer the more important question of whether or not a causal relationship exists. There are several ''requirements'' to demonstrate causality in a classic epidemiological sense. One requirement is to show convincingly that the association has biological plausibility. In this regard, there are two major hypotheses concerning cellular and molecular mechanisms by which alcohol may exert its ''protective'' effect against coronary artery disease. The first concerns HDL (high-density lipoprotein) cholesterol, the form of cholesterol associated with reduced risk for atherosclerosis. While some studies have shown that chronic alcohol consumption increases some subfractions of HDL, such as HDL3 (Hartung et al. 1990; Langer, Criqui, and Reed 1992), others have observed that this form of HDL cholesterol does not confer protection against atherosclerotic lesions. The work of Criqui and colleagues (1987) suggested that the effect of alcohol is mediated through a pathway alternative to changes in HDL cholesterol. The second possible biological mechanism concerns alcohol's effect on platelet aggregation and subsequent thrombus formation. Acute alcohol consumption reduces platelet aggregation in vitro (Renaud and deLorgeril 1992). In vivo studies have supported these results. Volunteers consuming alcohol in moderate amounts had an increase in their blood concentration of prostacyclin, which is a thromboxane antagonist (Landolfi and Steiner, 1984).

There has been speculation as to the importance of beverage type in conferring cardioprotective effects, and the evidence indicates that all types of alcohol confer the same reduction in risk. In a review of studies on the relationship between beverage alcohol and coronary heart disease, Rimm and colleagues (1991) concluded that the benefit conferred is from the ethanol itself rather than from any other components of each typ: of drink. Earlier work (Renaud et al. 1992) suggested that drinking during meals leads to slower absorption and thus to a prolonged protective effect on, for example, blood platelets at the time they are under the influence of alimentary lipids that are known to increase their reactivity (see Nordoy, Lagarde, and Renaud 1984).

Maclure (1993) discussed the evidence in the literature on alcohol drinking and coronary heart disease in the context of the other requirements for demonstrating a causal association. He concluded that, while the balance of evidence favors a causal association, it is important to convey a responsible public health message concerning alcohol consumption and risk for coronary artery disease. As Maclure aptly noted, "most health professionals still refrain from suggesting that nondrinkers start drinking small quantities of ethanol. Equally effective prevention of heart disease may be achieved by other means, including control of weight and blood pressure, use of aspirin, etc." Given that much of the research in this area has employed measures of average level of consumption and not drinking pattern, more research on which patterns of drinking are associated with the observed decrease in risk for coronary artery disease is warranted so that public health messages can be clearer. It is also necessary for clinicians to understand the balance of evidence concerning alcohol drinking patterns and heart disease so they can help individuals make educated assessments of their own risk levels in the light of competing genetic and behavioral risk factors.

Stroke

Some evidence suggests that a low level of alcohol intake is associated with decreased risk for ischemic stroke (van Gign et al. 1993). A fuller discussion of this topic can be found in the next section of this chapter.

PHYSICAL DISEASE STATES AND PATTERN OF DRINKING

Liver Disease

The association between alcohol abuse and liver cirrhosis is undisputed. A close relationship has also been established linking per capita alcohol consumption and cirrhosis mortality rates, both withi.. and across populations. The association is so strong that cirrhosis mortality is often used as an indicator of aggregate consumption of alcoholic beverages. In the United States, alcohol abuse accounts for approximately 75 percent of cases of advanced end-stage cirrhosis. The spectrum of liver injury produced by alcohol, in order of severity, includes fat accumulation, alcoholic hepatitis (inflammation of the hepatocyte), and finally, cirrhosis. These three conditions may simultaneously exist within the same patient.

Both the amount consumed and the duration of alcohol abuse are correlated with risk for cirrhosis (Lelbach 1975). Although there is a clear relationship between alcohol consumption and alcohol-related hepatitis or cirrhosis, total alcohol consumption does not appear, by itself, to explain why only 17–30 percent of heavy drinkers develop some form of alcoholic liver injury that reaches the attention of a health professional. It has been postulated that other factors may be involved in individual vulnerability to develop cirrhosis, including beverage type and dietary factors in addition to alcohol drinking pattern. The possibility that there may be a genetic susceptibility to cirrhosis or a vulnerability to abnormal immune responses is not discussed here; reviews on this topic can be found elsewhere (see Arria, Tarter, and Van Thiel 1991). With regard to beverage type, there is no clear evidence to suggest that one type of alcoholic beverage is more cirrhogenic than another (Tuyns, Esteve, and Pequignot 1984). It is thought that the amount of alcohol that reaches the liver is the most important determinant of injury, not the concentration of alcohol in any particular beverage.

Given that alcoholic cirrhosis can occur in well-nourished individuals, the hypothesis that malnutrition is a necessary condition for the development of cirrhosis has not been supported. More likely, nutritional factors play a role in modulating the hepatotoxicity of ethanol (Mitchell and Herlong 1986). The prevalence of malnutrition is high in alcoholics with liver disease, and there is some evidence that nutritional therapy is beneficial in improving the rate of recovery from alcoholic liver disease (ibid.). In a recent study by Corrao, Ferrari, and Galatola (1995) of 115 cirrhotic patients and 167 controls, a high lipid intake, combined with low protein and carbohydrate intakes, was found to modify multiplicatively the risk of cirrhosis associated with alcohol intake or chronic hepatitis C infection.

Pattern of alcohol abuse has been postulated to affect risk for alcoholic liver disease and cirrhosis. In one study, patients with elevated liver enzyme levels were more likely to be daily drinkers, were less likely to indulge in binge drinking patterns or have alcoholic blackouts, and showed a tendency toward a less severe pattern of alcoholism (Yates, Petty, and Brown 1987). Although this study examined precirrhotic individuals, the authors suggested that periods of abstinence may be helpful in preventing cirrhosis in patients with a biological risk for alcoholic liver disease. To test this hypothesis in a controlled setting, Gavaler and colleagues (1993) conducted a well-designed experiment in which ovarectomized rats were fed the same total amount of ethanol over a four-month period but in two different patterns. One group was fed intermittently, the other daily. Because there was no difference between the two groups in terms of the liver-body ratio or liver fat infiltration scores upon autopsy, the authors concluded that it was the cumulative amount, not the pattern of ethanol intake, which determined liver injury, at least in this particular animal model.

Although the results of the experiment by Yates, Petty, and Brown (1987) provide support for the hypothesis that liver injury may be more closely associated with daily drinking than heavy intermittent or binge drinking, the issue is still unresolved. From a biological point of view, it is likely that a pattern of heavy, steady exposure could lead to a continuously elevated blood alcohol level that might exceed the liver's capacity for removal. Regular daily consumption is typical of wine-consuming countries such as Italy, France, and Portugal, and the cirrhosis mortality rates of these countries are some of the highest in the world. Intermittent or binge drinking, which is common in Norway and Finland, might confer a lower risk of development of alcoholic liver injury. This hypothesis, however, is purely speculative, since the total per capita amount of alcohol consumed is also higher in the wine-producing countries than in Finland and Norway.

Some have speculated that heavy daily drinking might be less likely to result in negative psychosocial consequences than intermittent bouts of intoxication. In the first case, the psychosocial consequences and overt physical symptoms may not require medical attention. In the latter case, even for frequent binge drinking, the alcohol problem may come to the attention of a health professional before the cumulative dose has reached a high enough level to cause liver disease. This hypothesis may help to explain the observed association between cumulative lifetime alcohol intake and risk for cirrhosis and supports the notion that sustained drinking patterns are more related to cirrhosis than intermittent drinking patterns. More studies examining the issue are needed to test this hypothesis.

Hypertension

Hypertension is an independent risk factor for cerebrovascular hemorrhage (stroke) and coronary artery disease. A number of studies have been directed toward clarifying the influence of alcohol consumption on risk for hypertension. As with other cardiovascular diseases, alcohol-dependent individuals are at higher risk for hypertension than individuals who drink moderately (Keil, Swale, and Grobbee 1993). Evidence from cross-sectional prospective studies and intervention studies supports a causal association between a chronic intake of alcohol in the range of $\geq 30-60$ grams a day and blood pressure elevation in men and women (ibid.). Whether the association between amount of alcohol consumed and hypertension in the general population is linear or J-shaped— teetotalers having a slightly higher rate of hypertension than light-to-moderate drinkers—is still open to question.

Three recent studies have demonstrated the importance of taking drinking pattern into account when explaining the association between alcohol consumption and hypertension. Russell and colleagues (1991) studied 1,635 household residents in Erie County, New York. Using multiple regression analyses, and controlling for thirteen additional risk factors, the authors found a significant positive effect of the frequency of alcohol consumption on both systolic and diastolic blood pressure, whereas drinking quantity did not affect either. Mean systolic and diastolic blood pressure levels were 6.6 and 4.7 millimeters Hg higher, respectively, among daily drinkers than among individuals who drank less than once a week. Significant interaction effects between quantity and frequency were not found in this study. The authors concluded that the previously reported health benefits associated with low average drinks per day are likely to be related to light, weekly drinking and infrequent drinking, rather than to light, daily drinking.

These findings were similar to those of Seppa, Laippala, and Sillanaukee (1994), who found that daily heavy drinkers (mean intake of 151 grams during the weekend) had significantly higher systolic (8 millimeters Hg) and diastolic (6 millimeters Hg) blood pressure levels than teetotalers. The diastolic blood pressure of weekend heavy drinkers did not significantly vary from that of teetotalers, but systolic blood pressure was slightly higher (5 millimeters Hg).

Cardiomyopathy

Cardiomyopathy is characterized by a thickening and dilation of the heart muscle and decreased cardiac efficiency. Although 20–30 percent of cardiomyopathy cases are thought to be attributable to long-standing alcohol abuse, to our knowledge no studies have been conducted on the association between pattern of alcohol consumption and risk for cardiomyopathy.

Atrial Fibrillation

Among the risk factors for atrial fibrillation, or disturbances of the normal electrical conduction system of the heart, is heavy alcohol use (Rich, Siebold, and Campion 1985). Atrial fibrillation following acute alcohol ingestion is sometimes referred to as "holiday heart." Koskinen and Kupari (1991) reported that alcohol consumption was not significantly related to the induction of supraventricular tachyarrythmias other than atrial fibrillation. The pathogenesis of alcohol-induced atrial fibrillation is not well understood. However, there is some evidence that it is a manifestation of alcohol withdrawal.

Stroke

Stroke is a leading cause of death and disability in many industrialized countries, especially in older age groups. Strokes can result either from an occlusion of a blood vessel in the brain secondary to a local or "traveling" embolism (referred to as an ischemic stroke) or from a rupture of an intracerebral artery (referred to as a hemorrhagic stroke). Ischemic stroke is much more common than hemorrhagic strokes. The association between alcohol drinking and stroke differs according to the type of stroke, the evidence suggesting that a moderate level of alcohol consumption is associated with a decreased risk for ischemic stroke and an increased risk for hemorrhagic stroke (van Gign et al. 1993). The occurrence of stroke is difficult to ascertain, and a minor stroke may go undetected during a person's lifetime. Conversely, a stroke may be counted as a cause of death in a person who has suffered from a long-term chronic illness. As in heart disease, several behavioral risk factors are known to contribute to an increased risk for stroke. Because of these methodological issues, studying the true relation between alcohol and stroke is challenging.

In a comprehensive review of earlier epidemiological studies, Camargo (1989) concluded that while some evidence appears to support a J-shaped association for ischemic stroke and a positive linear association for hemorrhagic stroke, there is insufficient evidence to support either an increased or a decreased risk of either type of stroke with recent alcohol use in the low-to-moderate range. It is extremely important to take into account a number of behavioral risk factors for stroke as well as age, race, and sex when examining this association. The association between heavy drinking and all stroke combined is somewhat clearer: a positive dose-response relationship is apparent. Regular heavy and binge drinking have been shown to increase the risk of sudden death secondary to stroke (Hillbom and Juvela 1996). Ethanol in vivo can induce reductions in cerebral blood flow, cerebrovascular spasms, and the depletion of intracellular magnesium (Altura et al. 1993).

With regard to biological mechanisms, alcohol consumption could hypothetically increase the occurrence of hemorrhagic stroke via alcohol-induced hypertension. Alcohol consumption has been shown to reduce fibrinogen concentration in the blood, which in turn would reduce the risk of formation of thrombi in the blood vessels. This is a possible mechanism to explain the association between alcohol consumption and a reduced risk of ischemic stroke with light-to-moderate drinking levels.

Hansagi et al. (1995) conducted an epidemiological study on the association between alcohol consumption and stroke in which 15,077 male and female twins born in Sweden between 1886 and 1925 were investigated. In 1967 and 1968, when this cohort was aged forty-one through eighty-one years, the investigators collected baseline data on alcohol consumption. Unlike many studies, some questions were included to give an idea of how often binge drinking (defined as drinking half a bottle of spirits or two bottles of wine on the same occasion) occurred. Using the Swedish national cause-of-death register, which has been shown to have 97 percent validity in the case of cerebrovascular disease, 769 deaths from stroke were found by the end of the twenty-year follow-up in 1987. Analyses were conducted separately for males and females, controlling for age and smoking status and using lifelong abstainers as a reference category. For men, no statistically significant dose-response associations were observed. Middle-aged and elderly men who were infrequent drinkers, or who reported binge drinking on rare occasions, had an elevated risk of ischemic stroke. For women, different results were seen. A reduced risk of ischemic stroke was found for women in the lowest drinking category, corresponding to two to three glasses of wine a week. Female ex-drinkers were found to have the highest risk of ischemic stroke. No association with hemorrhagic stroke was found in either men or women. The level of overall alcohol intake was relatively low in this cohort: fewer than 1 percent reported a consumption of 40 grams a day or more, and 20 percent of men and 44 percent of women drank no alcohol at the baseline date. The results of this study need to be interpreted cautiously because of the possibility that drinking patterns may have varied considerably over the twenty-year follow-up period. In addition, the study focused solely on mortality rather than morbidity and mortality. Comparatively little is known about the ways in which various patterns of light-to-moderate drinking may be related to stroke, and more research is needed to clarify this matter.

Neurological and Neuropsychological Deficits

Many studies have demonstrated that alcohol abuse or alcoholism is associated with neurological conditions such as Wernicke-Korsakoff syndrome as well as with more subtle neuropsychological deficits such as impairments in memory and attention. When studying the association between alcohol consumption and these impairments, it is important to keep in mind that a number of factors often co-occurring with alcohol abuse can compromise neurological function. These factors include nutritional deficiencies, head injury, and liver disease (Mearns and Lees-Haley 1993; Schafer et al. 1991). In addition, performance on neuro-psychological tests is influenced greatly by educational attainment.

Hunt (1993) discusses the hypothesis that binge drinking may be more closely associated with neurological damage than regular alcohol consumption is. He defines binge drinking as heavy periods of drinking interrupted by periods of abstention that can result in repeated episodes of withdrawal. There is considerable evidence to suggest that there is a positive association between the number of previous withdrawal episodes and the occurrence of seizures during detoxification (Brown et al. 1988). Hunt goes on to describe the possible biological mechanisms for this and other forms of alcohol-induced neurological damage.

Whether these hypotheses hold true at a lower level of alcohol consumption, in which light-to-moderate episodes of drinking may be interspersed with periods of abstinence but not with full-blown withdrawal, remains to be seen. Only recently have studies been conducted to determine whether low-to-moderate levels influence performance on neuropsychological tests. There is evidence both in support of and against the hypothesis that moderate social drinking can result in impairment on neuropsychological tests (Bates and Tracy 1990; Waugh et al. 1989). In one study, episodic drinkers showed fewer deficits than those who drank on a daily basis (Tarbox, Connors, and McLaughlin 1986), but other studies have reported opposite findings. It appears that these studies lack adequate control for maximum quantity of alcohol consumed and that this may be the most important determinant of cognitive impairment (Schafer and Parsons 1986).

Intentional and Nonintentional Injury

Intentional and nonintentional injury are a major cause of morbidity and mortality worldwide. Intentional injuries include acts of violence against another person as well as suicide, whereas nonintentional injuries encompass a broad spectrum of accidents, such as motor vehicle crashes, falls, boating accidents, and fires. The link between alcohol intoxication and increased risk for both types of injury has been well established (Li, Smith, and Baker 1994), though again intoxication is only one predisposing factor among many (Stockwell et al. 1994). It is probable that an individual whose drinking is characterized by frequent bouts of intoxication is more likely to be injured than someone who drinks only one or two drinks a day.

Data from the Michigan Behavioral Risk Factor Survey illustrate how pattern of drinking may be more important than average level of consumption in determining individual risk for motor vehicle crashes. Using these data, Anda and colleagues (1987) found that only 27 percent of drinking drivers reported an average weekly alcohol consumption that would be considered heavy (fourteen or more drinks a week). In contrast, binge drinking (five or more drinks on a given occasion at least once during the month preceding the survey) was reported by more than 90 percent of the drinking drivers in the study. Binge drinking therefore appears to be a better predictor of being a drinking driver than does heavy drinking. These findings have important implications for the prevention of alcohol-related crashes. Prevention efforts should not focus exclusively on the heavy drinker or chronic alcoholic but seek to educate individuals about the risk of accidental injury associated with binge drinking and intoxication.

Li, Smith, and Baker (1994) analyzed the 1986 National Mortality Followback Survey in an effort to understand the association between drinking behavior and cause of death due to injury. Adjusting for several demographic variables, the investigators found that daily drinking, binge drinking, and heavy drinking were each associated with increased relative risk for death by injury. These data were limited by the fact that alcohol consumption information on the decedent was gathered by proxy interview or questionnaire and that the sample included only individuals aged twenty-five through sixty-four years.

Other Physical Disease States

Several other conditions—gastritis, peptic ulcers, immunological disturbances, skeletal muscle disease, bone disease, pancreatitis, renal disease, and hyperuricemia—have been associated with long-standing alcohol abuse, but relatively little is known about the relationship of drinking pattern and the risk for these conditions. There are few data on how alcohol drinking patterns are associated with risk for cancer. Doll et al. (1993) reviewed the evidence on the association between alcohol consumption and various types of cancer. The bulk of studies were inconclusive, with the exception of alcohol and upper airway cancers: a large body of epidemiological evidence suggests that excessive alcohol consumption adds to the risk associated with smoking for cancers of the mouth, pharynx, esophagus, and larynx.

DRINKING PATTERNS AND HEALTH CONSEQUENCES: AN EMPIRICAL DEMONSTRATION

An analysis—taking alcohol drinking pattern into account, and not simply average level of consumption—was conducted in cooperation with the principal investigators of the Baltimore epidemiologic catchment area (ECA) survey program. (More data on the ECA program can be found in Eaton and Kessler 1985.) The first wave of survey data was collected on 3,481 individuals residing in the Greater Baltimore metropolitan area in 1981. Thirteen years later, in 1994, a second wave of data on 1,865 of these same individuals was collected. At the baseline date, a number of individual-level demographic characteristics were assessed, along with drinking history and health status. At follow-up, these same variables were measured, together with more information on health risk behaviors (e.g., smoking and diet) and a number of additional health outcome variables. A major limitation of the data is that morbidity was measured exclusively by self-report. (Details of the causes of mortality among those who had died before follow-up are currently being compiled and will be available for analysis in the near future.)

The results set out here should be considered preliminary since, at the time of this writing, further publication is under way (Arria and Gossop in preparation) and the methods of analysis have not been subjected to the scrutiny of scientific peer review. The primary objective of the analysis was to examine the associations between various drinking patterns and a number of health outcomes at follow-up, including cardiovascular diseases and general psychiatric distress. This analysis builds on previous work by Dryman and colleagues (Dryman, Anthony, and DePaulo 1989; Dryman and Anthony 1989) and Ford and colleagues (1989). This was a secondary data analysis, so the areas of inquiry were limited to information gathered to fulfill the aims of the general ECA program.

Because the Baltimore ECA program did not examine the association between drinking pattern and health outcome as one of its original goals, drinking pattern variables had to be derived from the existing data. Quantity of alcohol consumed in the past month and frequency of alcohol consumed in the past month were cross tabulated at both baseline and follow-up, producing more than 155 groups (of individuals consuming, e.g., one drink every day, one drink every other day, two drinks every day, and so on). These groups were reduced to 11 mutually exclusive groups based on drinking pattern: 9 drinking groups and 2 nondrinking groups (the latter being lifelong abstainers and former drink-ers). This reduction was guided by the frequency distributions of the various drinking categories in this data set as well as by a review of the work of investigators who faced similar data reduction challenges (see Russell et al. 1991). Table 4.1 provides information about the cutoffs used in constructing the nine drinking pattern categories.

About 12 percent of the sample reported in 1981 that they never or rarely consumed alcohol. These individuals were deemed lifetime abstainers and were used as a reference category against which other drinking patterns could be compared. Figure 4.2 illustrates how average level of consumption was distrib-uted among the nine drinking pattern categories. It is evident that some groups had very similar *average level* of consumption but very different *pattern* of consumption (see table 4.1, frequent-moderate versus occasional-heavy). Di-chotomous variables were computed that would denote the presence or absence of each health outcome of interest. This was fairly straightforward for all the health outcomes with the exception of psychiatric distress, which involved scor-ing on a twenty-item scale and then using a standard algorithm to derive a dichotomous variable for the presence or absence of psychiatric distress. With the outcome variables and the eleven drinking patterns defined, a series of descriptive analyses was run to determine the proportion of individuals in each drinking pattern category reporting certain health problems. This series provided a crude comparison of health outcomes between the nondrinking groups and the drinking groups. Finally, using standard multiple logistic regression modeling procedures, a series of analyses was run to investigate the association between drinking pattern and health outcome, adjusting for possible confounding varia-bles such as age, sex, and smoking status.

Table 4.2 presents the results of the analyses for two health outcomes: psychiatric distress and myocardial infarction. It appears that infrequent and occasional light drinkers have a slightly lower risk than abstainers of reporting psychiatric distress when other demographic variables are held constant, a finding that raises new questions about an old hypothesis concerning the possible inter-relationship of light alcohol consumption and tension reduction. The results from the analyses on myocardial infarction show a more than threefold increase in risk for the heaviest consumers compared to abstainers. A slight decrease in the risk for myocardial infarction was observed, but it was not statistically signifi-cant, perhaps owing to the small number of cases in these categories.

Several limitations of this analysis should be noted. First, the analysis is illustrative of a methodology; it may not be possible to generalize the estimates derived to other populations with different sociodemographic characteristics. In addition, more analyses are being conducted to examine the effect of interactions and whether similar results could be obtained if quantity and frequency were used as continuous variables and their interaction modeled. Last, sample size limitations make it difficult to draw strong conclusions from the data. The point in presenting these results here is simply to provide an empirical illustra-

Table 4.1 Nine drinking pattern categories (analysis of 1981 baseline data)

Quantity (number of drinks per drinking day)	Frequency (number of drinking days in past month)		
	1–4	5–20	21–31
1–2	Infrequent-light (N = 720)	Occasional-light (N = 238)	Frequent-light (N = 105)
3–4	Infrequent-moderate (N = 313)	Occasional-moderate (N = 224)	Frequent-moderate (N = 172)
5 or more	Infrequent-heavy (N = 130)	Occasional-heavy (N = 95)	Frequent-heavy (N = 98)

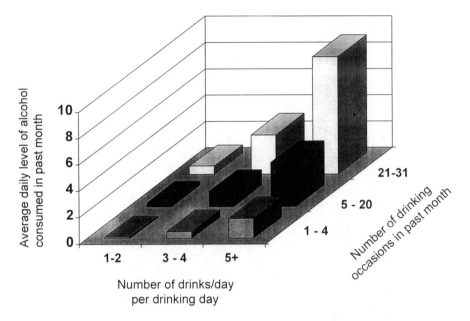

Figure 4.2 Average level of alcohol consumption, nine drinking pattern categories

tion to stimulate further exploration of the importance of patterns of alcohol consumption.

FUTURE DIRECTIONS

The relationship between alcohol and health is, without question, a matter of great importance to scientists, physicians, and policy makers. Unfortunately, there are many obstacles to our understanding of the relationships that may exist between drinking pattern and health. Some of these problems are related to difficulties of conceptualization. Clear and explicit definitions of health, for example, are both surprisingly rare and difficult to specify. (In a slightly different context, Lewis 1958 described the notion of mental health as "invincibly obscure.") But without any agreement as to what constitutes health, there is endless scope for misunderstanding in our discussion of the issues. The World Health Organization has defined health as a state of "complete physical, mental, and social well-being and not merely the absence of disease or infirmity" (WHO 1996). This definition provides a useful reminder that we might regard health in a positive way and not simply in terms of the absence of morbidity, disease, and disability. Indeed, too firm a reliance upon the concept of health as the absence of illness can lead to a restricted and stagnant perspective. Nonetheless, it is in this latter sense that health is most frequently understood by clinicians and health researchers. One of the principal reasons for preferring the negative definition of health is that it is easier to identify and measure ill health.

Table 4.2 The relation of psychiatric distress and myocardial infarctions to alcohol consumption pattern

Consumption pattern	Proportion of sample meeting criteria for psychiatric distress (%)	Estimated odds ratio[a]	Proportion of sample reporting myocardial infarction	Estimated relative risk[b]
Nondrinkers				
Lifetime abstainers	9.8	1.00	5.3	1.00
Former drinkers	13.1	0.99*	9.3	1.04
Current drinkers				
Infrequent-light	11.1	0.63*	3.9	0.87
Occasional-light	14.5	0.76*	3.5	0.61
Frequent-light	18.3	1.00	7.1	0.77
Infrequent-moderate	11.4	1.27	3.9	1.95
Occasional-moderate	11.3	0.90	2.2	0.83
Frequent-moderate	17.2	0.90	4.3	0.63
Infrequent-heavy	10.9	1.42	7.1	1.24
Occasional-heavy	8.6	1.00	17.9	0.48
Frequent-heavy	18.8	0.77	10.8	3.33*

[a]The odds ratio is gauged relative to abstainers and is adjusted for age, sex, and educational attainment. Cross-sectional data from 1981 was used for this analysis.
[b]Relative risk is gauged relative to abstainers and is adjusted for age, sex, educational attainment, smoking status, body mass index, and diabetes. Both baseline and 13-year follow-up data were used in this analysis to obtain an estimate of the relative risk.
*$P < 0.05$.

There are also problems concerning our limited ability to measure the appropriate variables. The problems of conceptualizing positive health, for instance, are immediately translated into practical problems of measurement. One challenge to health researchers involves the creation of measurable concepts of positive health functioning. For many drinkers, drinking is a pleasurable activity that enlivens social activities and enhances relaxation. In these respects, it may serve as a health-promoting activity in its own right, or it may counterbalance other factors that increase the risks of ill health. Indeed, because of the prevalence of coronary heart disease in many countries, the possible health benefits of alcohol in reducing the risks of heart disease is an important area of investigation. Although these effects are extremely difficult to study in empirical research studies, they are of importance and deserve attention.

There are also reasons why we might be less than satisfied with our current ability to conceptualize and measure the complexities of drinking patterns. This is especially relevant to a concern with the health consequences of drinking, where effects may accrue in a gradual, cumulative, and long-term manner. It is clear that drinking behaviors vary in many respects and that, especially over prolonged periods of time, there can be enormous variation in patterns of drinking. Fixed or stereotyped drinking patterns are not typical of most drinkers, and the sheer complexity of patterns of drinking behavior, especially over time, presents a major challenge to researchers. In what ways are we to reduce this complexity to manageable proportions? What are the relevant dimensions by which we should seek to characterize these patterns?

Simple univariate measures have taken us some way toward understanding the relationship between drinking and (ill) health, but more sophisticated measurement approaches would enhance this understanding. The illustration in this chapter, using a two-dimensional system of categorization, provides one example. Current knowledge of the health effects of drinking is largely concerned with certain adverse effects associated with excessive drinking, but our understanding of other health effects, and the effects among ''normal'' drinkers, is still rudimentary. Relatively few studies have looked in detail at these issues, and in many respects our understanding of the precise health consequences of different patterns of drinking remains seriously incomplete.

REFERENCES

Abel, E. L., and R. J. Sokol. 1987. Incidence of fetal alcohol syndrome and economic impact of FAS related anomalies. *Drug and Alcohol Dependence* 19:51–70.

Altura, B. M., A. Zhang, T. P. Cheng, and B. T. Altura. 1993. Ethanol promotes rapid depletion of intracellular free Mg in cerebral vascular smooth muscle cells: possible relation to alcohol-induced behavioral and stroke-like effects. *Alcohol* 10:563–66.

Alvarez, F. J., and M. C. Del Rio. 1994. Gender differences in pattern of alcohol consumption in Spain. *Alcoholism, Clinical and Experimental Research* 18:1342–47.

Alvarez, F. J., D. Queipo, M. C. Del Rio, and M. C. Garcia. 1993. Patterns of alcohol consumption among the general population of Castille and Leon (Spain). *Alcohol and Alcoholism* 2843–54.

Anda, R. F., et al. 1987. Patterns of self-reported drinking and driving in Michigan. *American Journal of Preventive Medicine* 3:271–75.

Arria, A. M., and M. Gossop. In preparation. Alcohol drinking patterns and health consequences in a community sample.

Arria, A. M., R. E. Tarter, and D. H. Van Thiel. 1991. Vulnerability to alcoholic cirrhosis. In *Recent Developments in Alcoholism,* ed. M. Galanter. Vol. 9. *Children of Alcoholics.* New York: Plenum.

Bates, M. E., and J. I. Tracey. 1990. Cognitive functioning in young "social drinkers": is there impairment to detect? *Journal of Abnormal Psychology* 99:242–49.

Brown, M. E., R. F. Anton, R. Malcolm, and J. C. Ballenger. 1988. Alcohol detoxification and withdrawal seizures: clinical support for a kindling hypothesis. *Biological Psychiatry* 23:507–14.

Butterworth, K. 1993. Overview of the biomedical project on alcohol and health. In *Health Issues Related to Alcohol Consumption,* ed. P. M. Verschuren. Washington, D.C.: ILSI.

Caballeria, J., E. Baraona, S. M. Rodamilan, and C. S. Lieber. 1989. Effects of cimetidine on gastric ADH and blood ethanol levels. *Gastroenterology* 96:388–92.

Camargo, C.A. 1989. Moderate alcohol consumption and stroke: the epidemiologic evidence. *Stroke* 20:1611–26.

Corrao, G., P. A. Ferrari, and G. Galatola. 1995. Exploring the role of diet in modifying the effect of known disease determinants: application to risk factors of liver cirrhosis. *American Journal of Epidemiology* 142:1136–46.

Criqui, M. H., et al. 1987. Lipoproteins as mediators for the effects of alcohol consumption and cigarette smoking on cardiovascular mortality: results from the lipid research clinics follow-up study. *American Journal of Epidemiology* 126:629–37.

Criqui, M. H., and B. L. Ringel. 1994. Does diet or alcohol explain the French paradox? *Lancet* 344:1719–23.

DeLabry, L. O., et al. 1992. Alcohol consumption and mortality in an American male population: recovering the U-shaped curve, findings from the Normative Aging Study. *Journal of Studies on Alcohol* 53:25–32.

Doll, R., D. Forman, C. La Vecchia, and R. Wouterson. 1993. Alcoholic beverages and cancers of the digestive tract and larynx. In *Health Issues Related to Alcohol Consumption,* ed. P. M. Verschuren. Washington, D.C.: ILSI.

Doll, R., et al. 1994. Mortality in relation to consumption of alcohol: 13 years' observation on male British doctors. *British Medical Journal* 309:911–18.

Dryman, A., and J. C. Anthony. 1989. An epidemiological study of alcohol use as a predictor of psychiatric distress over time. *Acta Psychiatrica Scandinavica* 80:315–21.

Dryman, A., J. C. Anthony, and J. R. DePaulo. 1989. The relationship between psychiatric distress and alcohol use: findings from the East Baltimore Mental Health Survey. *Acta Psychiatrica Scandinavica* 80:310–14.

Eaton, W. W., and L. G. Kessler, eds. 1985. *Epidemiological Field Methods in Psychiatric Epidemiology: The NIMH Epidemiologic Catchment Area Program.* Orlando: Academic.

Epstein, E. E., et al. 1995. An empirical classification of drinking patterns among alcoholics: binge, episodic, sporadic, and steady. *Addictive Behaviors* 20:23–41.

Ford, D. E., J. C. Anthony, G. R. Nestadt, and A. J. Romanoski. 1989. The GHQ by interview: performance in relation to recent use of health services. *Medical Care* 27:367–75.

Frezza, M., et al. 1990. High blood alcohol levels in women: the role of decreased gastric ADH activity and first-pass metabolism. *New England Journal of Medicine* 322:95–99.

Gavaler, J. S., et al. 1993. "Binge" versus steady drinking: effects on the liver in the ovarectomized rat. *Alcoholism: Clinical and Experimental Research* 17:355–58.

Hansagi, H., et al. 1995. Alcohol consumption and stroke mortality: 20-year follow-up of 15,077 men and women. *Stroke* 26:1768–73.

Hartung, G. H., et al. 1990. Effect of alcohol dose on plasma lipoprotein subfractions and lipolyzyme activity in active and inactive men. *Metabolism* 39:81–86.

Hillbom, M., and S. Juvela. 1996. Alcohol and risk for stroke. In *Alcohol and the Cardiovascular System*. National Institutes on Alcohol Abuse and Alcoholism Research Monograph 31. NIH Publication No. 96-4133.

Hunt, W. A. 1993. Are binge drinkers more at risk of developing brain damage? *Alcohol* 10:559–61.

Keil, U., J. D. Swales, and D. E. Grobbee. 1993. Alcohol intake: its relation to hypertension. In *Health Issues Related to Alcohol Consumption*, ed. P. M. Verschuren. Washington, D.C.: ILSI.

Klatsky, A. L., G. D. Freidman, and A. B. Siegelaub. 1981. Alcohol and mortality: a 10-year Kaiser-Permanente experience. *Annals of Internal Medicine* 95:139–45.

Koskinen, P., and M. Kupari. 1991. Alcohol consumption of patients with supraventricular tachyarrhythmias other than atrial fibrillation. *Alcohol and Alcoholism* 26:199–206.

Kozarevic, D., et al. 1988. Drinking habits and death: the Yugoslavia Cardiovascular Disease Study. *International Journal of Epidemiology* 12:145–50.

Landolfi, R., and M. Steiner. 1984. Ethanol raises prostacyclin in vivo and in vitro. *Blood* 64:679–82.

Langer, R. D., M. H. Criqui, and D. M. Reed. 1992. Lipoproteins and blood pressure as biological pathways for effect of moderate alcohol consumption on coronary heart disease. *Circulation* 85:910–15.

Lelbach, W. K. 1975. Cirrhosis in the alcoholic and its relation to the volume of alcohol abuse. *Annals of the New York Academy of Science* 252:85–105.

Levy, R. I., and J. Moskowitz. 1982. Cardiovascular research: decades of progress, a decade of promise. *Science* 217:121–29.

Lewis, A. 1958. Between guesswork and certainty in psychiatry. *Lancet* 1:170–75.

Li, G., G. S. Smith, and S. P. Baker. 1994. Drinking behavior in relation to cause of death among U.S. adults. *American Journal of Public Health* 84:1402–6.

Maclure, M. 1993. Demonstration of deductive meta-analysis: ethanol intake and risk of myocardial infarction. *Epidemiologic Reviews* 15:328–52.

Madianos, M. G., D. Gefou-Madianou, and C. Stefanis. 1995. Patterns of alcohol consumption and related problems in the general population of Greece. *Addiction* 90:73–85.

Marques-Vidal, P., et al. 1995. Cardiovascular risk factors and alcohol consumption in France and Northern Ireland. *Atherosclerosis* 115:225–32.

———. 1996. Alcohol consumption and myocardial infarction: a case-control study in France and Northern Ireland. Comment. *American Journal of Epidemiology* 143:1089–93.

Mearns, J., and P. R. Lees-Haley. 1993. Discriminating neuropsychological sequelae of head injury from alcohol-abuse-induced deficits: a review and analysis. *Journal of Clinical Psychology* 49:714–20.

Mirin, S., and R. Weiss. 1991. Psychiatric comorbidity in drug and alcohol addiction. In *Comprehensive Handbook of Drug and Alcohol Addiction*, ed. N. Miller. New York: Dekker.

Mitchell, M. C., and F. C. Herlong. 1986. Alcohol and nutrition: caloric value, bioenergetics, and relationship to liver damage. *Annual Review of Nutrition* 6:457–74.

NIAAA. 1993. *Eighth Special Report to the U.S. Congress on Alcohol and Health from the Secretary of Health and Human Services.* Bethesda, Md.: National Institute on Alcohol Abuse and Alcoholism.

Nordoy, A., M. Lagarde, and S. Renaud. 1984. Platelets during hyperlipidemia induced by cream and cod liver oil. *European Journal of Clinical Investigation* 14:339–45.

Plant, M. A., and M. L. Plant. 1992. *Risk Takers: Alcohol, Drugs, Sex, and Youth.* London: Tavistock Routledge.

Poiklainen, K., E. Vartiainen, and H. J. Korhonen. 1996. Alcohol intake and subjective health. *American Journal of Epidemiology* 144:346–50.

RCOG. 1996. *Alcohol Consumption in Pregnancy.* RCOG Guideline 9. London: Royal College of Obstetricians and Gynaecologists.

Renaud, S. C., et al. 1992. Alcohol and platelet aggregation: the Caerphilly Heart Disease Study. *American Journal of Clinical Nutrition* 55:1012–17.

Renaud, S. C., and M. deLorgeril. 1992. Wine, alcohol, platelets, and the French paradox for coronary heart disease. *Lancet* 339:1523–26.

Renaud, S. C., M. H. Criqui, G. Farchi, and J. Veenstra. 1993. Alcohol drinking and coronary heart disease. In *Health Issues Related to Alcohol Consumption*, ed. P. M. Verschuren. Washington, D.C.: ILSI.

Reynolds, D. L., L. W. Chambers, and M. R. DeVillaer. 1992. Measuring alcohol abuse in the community: consumption, binge drinking, and alcohol-related consequences ("alcoholism"). *Canadian Journal of Public Health* 83:441–47.

Rich, E. C., C. Siebold, and B. Campion. 1985. Alcohol-related acute atrial fibrillation: a case-control study and review of 40 patients. *Archives of Internal Medicine* 145:830–33.

Rimm, B., et al. 1991. Prospective study of alcohol consumption and risk of coronary disease in men. *Lancet* 338:464–68.

Roine, R., et al. 1990. Aspirin increases blood alcohol concentration in humans after ingestion of ethanol. *Journal of the American Medical Association* 264:2406–8.

Rossett, H. L., and L. Weiner. 1984. *Alcohol and the Fetus: A Clinical Perspective.* New York: Oxford University Press.

Russell, M., M. L. Cooper, M. R. Frone, and J. W. Welte. 1991. Alcohol drinking patterns and blood pressure. *American Journal of Public Health* 81:452–57.

Schafer, K. W., and O. A. Parsons. 1986. Drinking practices and neuropsychological test performance in sober male alcoholics and social drinkers. *Alcohol* 3:175–79.

Schafer, K., et al. 1991. Cognitive performance of alcoholics: a longitudinal evaluation of the role of drinking history, depression, liver function, nutrition, family history. *Alcoholism: Clinical and Experimental Research* 15:653–60.

Seppa, K., P. Laippala, and P. Sillanaukee. 1994. Drinking pattern and blood pressure. *American Journal of Hypertension* 7:249–54.

Serdula, M. K., et al. 1995. Alcohol intake and mortality findings from the NHANES I follow-up study. *Journal of Studies on Alcohol* 56:233–39.

Shaper, A. G. 1990. Alcohol and mortality: a review of prospective studies. *British Journal of Addiction* 85:837–47.

Skog, O.-J. 1995. The J-curve, causality, and public health. *Addiction* 90:490–92.

Stockwell, T., T. Sitharthan, D. McGrath, and E. Lang. 1994. The measurement of alcohol dependence and impaired control in community. *Addiction* 89:16–74.

Tarbox, A. R., G. J. Connors, and E. J. McLaughlin. 1986. Effects of drinking patterns on neuropsychological performance among alcohol misusers. *Journal of Studies on Alcohol* 47:176–79.

Tuyns, A. J., J. Esteve, and G. Pequignot. 1984. Ethanol is cirrhogenic, whatever the beverage. *British Journal of Addiction* 79:389–93.

U.K. Department of Health and Social Security. 1995. *Sensible Drinking: The Report of an Interdepartmental Working Group.* London: HMSO.

van Gign, J., M. J. Stampfer, C. Wolfe, and A. Algra. 1993. The association between alcohol and stroke. In *Health Issues Related to Alcohol Consumption,* ed. P. M. Verschuren. Washington, D.C.: ILSI.

Waugh, M., et al. 1989. Effect of social drinking on neuropsychological performance. *British Journal of Addiction* 84:659–67.

WHO. 1996. Constitution. In *Basic Documents.* 41st ed. Geneva: World Health Organization.

Yates, W. R., F. Petty, and K. Brown. 1987. Risk factors for alcohol hepatotoxicity among male alcoholics. *Drug and Alcohol Dependence* 20:155–62.

Chapter 5

Social and Behavioral Issues Related to Drinking Patterns

Nii-K Plange

Considerable anthropological data now exist to support the observation that alcoholic beverages exist in almost all societies and that many societies of the past devoted time and resources to the production of alcohol for consumption (Heath 1995a; Lennane 1992; Marshall 1979). In many others, new forms of alcoholic beverages were introduced, accepted, and indeed integrated into an existing context and pattern of use of alcoholic beverages or other mood-altering substances (Plange 1991; Marshall 1979). A few cultures had no alcoholic beverage at all but were soon introduced to them through their contact with other groups.

Differing subcultures, peoples, and groups within nations and cultures have differing forms of alcohol production, distribution, and consumption, and for this reason forms of alcohol use and consumption, or patterns of drinking, are as important an area of study as volume and quantity of consumption. With the emphasis on effects of alcohol use on health and social relations, attention appears to have been duly focused on quantity or dose and on their impact. This emphasis had been enhanced by public health concerns and advances in medical and pharmaceutical sciences. Associated with this are factors such as the level of alcohol content in beverages, dose measurement, and national consumption levels.

Nii-K Plange is a reader in sociology and is head of the Department of Sociology, School of Social and Economic Development, University of the South Pacific, Suva, Fiji.

This approach to alcohol studies reflects the work of Ledermann (1956) and his theory, which quantified consumption within a given population and provided administrations with an observably convenient basis for instituting prevention policies for alcohol use. Dissatisfaction with Ledermann's per capita consumption, or single-distribution, theory produced criticisms and attempts to modify his work (see introduction to this book, as well as chapters 7 and 8). Important as the Ledermann approach has been, it overlooked, indeed ignored, another important aspect of alcohol use, which is illustrated, not in terms of volume or dose, but by the forms, contexts, occasions, and circumstances in which alcohol is consumed (patterns of drinking) and by the outcomes, both social and behavioral, of such patterns. This chapter explores some existing patterns of drinking and their outcomes.

No matter where the emphasis, whether on dosage, quantity, or pattern of drinking, certain characteristics, usually relating to influence of alcohol and outcome, have been recognized. These characteristics appear to have prevailed in earlier human groups or societies as well as in contemporary ones. And indeed, these known aspects of alcohol have been, and remain, reasons why alcohol is consumed or drunk. Alcohol is known to belong to a class of substances that alter mood and behavior. This characteristic has, however, been susceptible to various interpretations. Some cultures perceive in alcohol a "spirit" that possesses those who consume it. In others, alcohol is a devil that overcomes consumers. Still others see it as a substance that makes people lose their heads and become like "sardines" (Marshall 1979) or become elated, jovial, and convivial, participating easily in conversation. These characterizations refer to alcohol's impact on the individual and on consequent social behavior. While social scientists, especially sociologists, anthropologists, and psychologists, have elaborated on alcohol and social (individual) behavior, medical scientists continue to provide a compendium of biological and psychological consequences of alcohol consumption (Lennane 1992).

Medical cautions notwithstanding, alcohol is generally viewed and accepted by many as important to social interaction, social integration, and even bonding of groups in certain circumstances, and it remains an important part of some religious practices. It can thus be said that there is some functional societal role for alcohol distinct from its possible detrimental social and health consequences. That alcohol necessarily has detrimental consequences for health remains unconvincing to observers, especially since there is also evidence that alcohol taken in moderation (though there is little agreement on what this means) is good for health.

ALCOHOL, MOOD, AND BEHAVIOR

The socially desirable aspects of alcohol have always been linked with its capacity to put people "in the mood." It is indeed for this purpose alone that alcohol has gained a pervasive presence in social gatherings of different kinds: weddings, birthday parties, celebrations of promotion, and graduations, to name just a few. Associated with this effect on mood is the property of alcohol to act as a depressant and its capacity to relax people. These properties also account for its common use after work, after dinner, or at a ball game. But what really is "mood"? And to what extent is it induced or sustained by alcohol? Are there particular and culturally specific moods required of or associated with particular occasions? If there are, and if these occasions are not always happy ones, where does alcohol fit in?

Mood is simply defined as a temporary state of emotion or attitude. The mood with which alcohol is usually associated is that of excitement, joviality, and relaxation resulting from the disinhibition produced by its depressant qualities. However, if alcohol use can produce attitudes of gloom and sullenness as well as attitudes of joyousness and conviviality, as conventionally believed and accepted, at what time and in what contexts is each mood possible, appropriate, or indeed relevant? It appears that the behavioral outcome of mood, enhanced by alcohol, is also context dependent, or culturally prescribed. Thus the sociability, enhanced interaction and conversation, joking, and relaxation produced by the drinking of alcohol may occur if the context is suitably structured. Conversely, sullenness and gloom as well as argumentativeness and bad temper are also context specific. Social behavior as a consequence of alcohol drinking can then perhaps be seen more in terms of what Marshall (1979) referred to as altered states of consciousness, meaning "the way persons who carry a shared culture agree to set aside normal rules for acceptable behavior when a particular . . . substance has been consumed." Such behaviors are still within the limits beyond which other behavior in the particular context becomes unacceptable because it is disruptive and disintegrative.

From such a perspective, one can understand the multiple uses and differential outcomes of alcohol in some cultures: at wakes and funerals, childbirth and weddings, installation ceremonies, child-naming ceremonies, and rituals of religious significance. Among the indigenous Accra people of the southern coast of Ghana, for example, alcohol is consumed during wakes and funerals. Relatives arriving at the ceremony are welcomed with a serving of drink (usually a local gin called *akpeteshie*) and a recounting of the events leading to the death. Condolences are expressed, and the pain of death is borne, quietly and gloomily, together. The serving of the drink and the solemn expression of sympathy constitute an integrative symbol and behavior specific to the occasion. Indigenous Fijian culture practices a similar ceremony at deaths, except that the beverage consumed is kava, a local brew made from the roots of a shrub (*Piper methysticum*). In both Ghana and Fiji, the underlying base of the behavior is integration and solidarity with the group. The bonding that drinking together provides is similar to the "mateship" among Australian men drinking in public houses, where the context encourages, indeed requires, the consumption of alcohol with associated behavior that emphasizes group belonging.

Demonstrating the opposite mood and behavior is the occasion of child naming among the Accra people. It is a context for drinking and conviviality, reminiscent of the Sirioni in Bolivia (see Heath 1995b). Sharing in child naming is an "occasion for joyous convivial drinking in which drunkenness seemed to enhance sociability, make jokes funnier, and provide everyone with a welcome time of relaxation and enjoyment." Alcohol consumption beyond certain limits, however, in either of the above contexts, resulting in unacceptable behavior, changes the mood of the gathering. It appears, then, that drinking contexts are also associated with prescribed behaviors, known to the participants.

That such multiple scenarios exist in other cultures lends support to the belief that alcohol contributes to, rather that causes, behavior (Hezel 1984), among them conviviality, which means to feast and to be together in a socially lively way. A convivial person is fond of good company and is lively in groups and interactions. The term thus embodies sociability, one of the enduring positive attributes of alcohol consumption. Alcohol relaxes inhibitions and leads to free-flowing conversation and a joyous mood. In a group situation, it creates a mood conducive to friendly conversation. While certain sociocultural circumstances or conditions might restrain this feeling, in the appropriate situation alcohol provides a general atmosphere of gaiety, enhances interaction, and produces an enjoyable occasion (Heath 1995a). Indeed, this is why alcoholic beverages have become ubiquitous at festive occasions; their depressant qualities disinhibit people and predispose them to conviviality. It is not surprising, therefore, that drinking alcohol is seen in many societies and cultures as a group activity.

The group spirit among team players involved in sports and among fellow professionals and work mates is usually enhanced by the drinking of alcoholic beverages after a game or work. Teams, such as harvesters, might drink some alcohol after their task is completed, athletes may have an after-game drink, university lecturers might proceed to campus clubs to have a drink at the end of the day, and cocktails at professional conferences are often organized to provide the occasion for relaxed interaction and rapport. This particular aspect of alcohol consumption, to enhance group solidarity through relaxed interaction, is almost universal. Among Icelandic seamen (Ásmundsson 1995), Malaysian workers in both bureaucratic and agricultural settings (Arokinsamy 1995), Nigerian students (Oshodin 1995), Fijian youths and adults (Plange 1991), and Guatemalan women (Adams 1995), social gatherings are enhanced by the drinking of alcohol. Alcohol contributes to a friendly and festive atmosphere, in spite of other possible behavioral outcomes, which may be unacceptable, socially disruptive, and problematic. It is indeed an irony that the same disinhibiting characteristic of alcohol that enhances conviviality can also lead to behavioral or social problems, some with important implications for public health.

These problems, some individual and domestic, and others societal, are the damaging aspects of alcohol availability, accessibility, and use, including abuse. They have also been the basis of action for various temperance movements over the past century. It was in response to the observable negative outcomes of disinhibition on both individuals and society, and the quest for policy action toward prevention, that Ledermann's theory became popular. Its popularity lies more in its simplification of a complex problem and in the grounds it provided for action than in its comprehensive coverage of alcohol problems. While the single-distribution theory quantifies distribution and per capita consumption, it is remarkably unable to account for ways in which people drink, who they drink with, and the extent to which patterns of drinking explain some of the related social problems of alcohol. Nor is Ledermann's theory able to explain why countries or groups with high levels of alcohol consumption are not necessarily the ones with alcohol-related problems.

It appears then that many other factors and social contexts influence patterns of alcohol use and, of course, misuse and outcome (Peck 1982). These include family, peer groups, occupation, income, and other life events, many of them unforeseeable. At the same time, however, it is often in these same contexts that the problems associated with alcohol use are experienced (Marshall 1979). Studies on alcohol-related social problems must recognize the importance of the influence of alcohol use and misuse on individuals, the social factors and contexts associated with use, the rules and regulations that define use, and the type of alcohol consumed.

Alcoholic beverages include wine, spirits, beer, and a variety of home brews whose alcohol content is not well known. Consumption of some home brews is erratic and might not be captured with traditional methods of measurement and quantification, which makes the application of Ledermann's theory difficult in developing countries, where large quantities of home brews are produced, sold, and consumed. In other words, recorded per capita consumption of alcohol, especially in developing countries with both traditional and contemporary brews, will be of little significance in determining alcohol policy. In Nigeria, for example, there is the traditional palm wine and the traditional gin, or *gorogoro*; in Ghana there are palm wine, *akpeteshie, pito,* and other fruit-based brews; in the South Pacific Micronesian states there is toddy tapped from the coconut tree and fermented; and in Fiji there are numerous home brews concocted in villages and on sugarcane farms. These are authentic alcoholic beverages, drunk in various ways, and pervasive in these countries. Yet few, if any, are officially or formally quantified and entered in the records. At the same time, tourism contributes significantly to the volume of alcoholic consumption in many of these countries (Casswell 1986), making resident per capita consumption difficult to assess.

Nevertheless, there is a general recognition of alcohol-related problems in all countries in which alcohol is available and accessible (Heath 1995a). These problems fall into two broad categories (Grant and Ritson 1983): (1) problems emerging from or related to alcohol dependence, such as homelessness, indebtedness, family problems, marital problems, sexual problems, absenteeism, employment problems, and stigma; and (2) problems associated with drunkenness, such as social isolation, domestic violence, child abuse, child neglect, passive behavior, aggressive behavior, sexual problems, domestic and industrial accidents, and absenteeism.

For the second category, social expectations, pattern of drinking, and the group with whom alcohol is drunk contribute to the consequences. The availability of alcohol does not per se lead to drunkenness, but rather drinking beyond permissible limits, inexperienced drinking, and drinking with the aim of getting drunk. Other factors also combine with alcohol to lead to dependence: repeated excessive drinking, drinking for relief of the effects of earlier inake, and gradual increases in tolerance levels (Plant 1982).

PATTERNS OF DRINKING AND PROBLEMS

Patterns of drinking (see the introduction and chapter 1, this volume) allow one to see the complex contexts, choices, and forms associated with alcohol consumption as well as temporal variations in drinking and gender differences in levels of drinking and beverage choice. This complexity has led to attempts to relate some aspects of the contexts, forms, and types of drinking to outcomes of drinking, at both the individual and the societal level (Marshall 1979; Adinkrah 1995). Epstein and colleagues (1995) offer an alternative to theses on outcomes of alcohol consumption that emphasize level of drinking, with their attendant methodological problems in identifying level-specific outcomes that can be observed cross-nationally and cross-culturally. Evidently, level of drinking, or per capita consumption, is inadequate in predicting outcomes, since individuals and groups within societies may have different levels and patterns of consumption leading to different outcomes. For example, body weight is a factor in assessing the effect of alcohol on people: the greater the weight the more slowly the effects are felt. Predictably, the same level of alcohol consumed even during a binge will not produce the same level of drunkenness in every individual. Demographic groups distinguishable on the basis of age, sex (Roizen 1983), ethnicity, and even level of education or social status have different levels of consumption and patterns of drinking, and these are influenced by sociocultural norms and values (Bales 1946).

Against this background, drinking patterns and related outcomes become more meaningful. A pattern of drinking that encourages excessive drinking, bingeing, or drinking to get drunk produces adverse consequences, even if these are accepted within local cultural parameters. The following examples from Truk in Micronesia, Fiji in the South Pacific, and Iceland in the North Atlantic, illustrate existing and culturally acceptable but inappropriate patterns of drinking and their negative outcomes for individuals and society at large.

Truk

The pattern of drinking of the young male "weekend warriors" of Truk, in Micronesia, is characteristically binge drinking with the intention of getting drunk (Marshall 1979). Hence, excessive amounts of alcohol (either beer or spirits) are consumed within a short period. These youths are under considerable societal pressure to demonstrate courage, strength, boldness, and capacity for physical combat in a society with no specific roles for youths in transition to adulthood except for publicly established bravery. Thus, risk taking of all kinds remains characteristic of youth in Truk.)Binge drinking and the dangers associated with it, such as getting into fights, are seen as marks of bravery, upon which the youths can build their reputations. Other risks they take include voyaging in a canoe into the open sea and spear fishing beyond the reefs in shark-infested waters. The preferred alcoholic beverage (spirits) and pattern of drinking (together in the bush out of a single bottle) emulate those of North American and Japanese sailors and beachcombers and are linked with boisterous drunken behavior and occasional brawls. The style of drinking—bingeing, consuming excessively, drinking to get drunk—is as much a celebration of bravery and solidarity with the group as it is an eagerness to get drunk quickly.

The outcome of this pattern of drinking is dramatic. Drunken Trukese youth build up an emotionally charged atmosphere in which they unleash their aggression, resulting in brutal fights for the display of the individual's honor, strength, machismo, status, and ability to endure pain (Marshall 1979). Some of these encounters result in homicide and suicide (Hezel 1984). However, the outcomes, violent as they are, are expected and accepted within the Trukese culture as standard behavior and as occasions for youths to let out their aggression. When sobriety returns, they can claim craziness or possession by some spirit and be forgiven. The important analytical issue here is to separate what is culturally acceptable from the nature and outcome of what is acceptable. Trukese culture does not consider suicide, homicide, and brutal and bloody fights instances of good behavior. If these were favorable outcomes and perceived as good behavior, there would be no need to plead craziness or possession by a spirit, nor would the behavior be expected to terminate at adulthood, when moderate drinking is encouraged and practiced (Marshall 1979).

Fiji

(Caught between traditional cultural demands and the requirements of modern urban culture, facing high levels of unemployment and poverty, and sometimes failing in competition with others, young Fijian men may take up alcohol drinking to vent frustrations, deal with the burden of idleness, and also partly to regain confidence lost in other societal endeavors. These factors combine with the chauvinism, machismo, and peer pressure inherent in ethnic Fijian culture to lead to patterns of drinking that emphasize excessive consumption. Thus there are inevitable negative outcomes,)with the result that a disproportionate number of young ethnic Fijians go to prison for offenses committed under the influence of alcohol (Adinkrah 1995).

Like the Trukese, ethnic Fijian youths and young adults usually drink to get drunk. This is done through binge drinking in secluded bushes or in nightclubs and bars. Much less drinking goes on in restaurants, which are generally not patronized by Fijian youth. In the parks or among the bushes, a glass of whatever alcoholic beverage is available is "spinned around" (all drink from one glass, and each must drink his glassful at once to allow the next person his round). Soon, drunkenness sets in, and a convivial situation quickly turns into fights, arguments, assaults on taxi drivers who are "hired" to buy more beer, or even rape of women whose homes are broken into or who are encountered in the vicinity. The drunken youths may commit burglaries as the need for money to continue drinking takes command. The adverse consequences of this pattern of drinking result crimes and, ultimately, encounters with the law. Excessive drinking also takes place in rural villages, and though some of the excesses of drunken behavior are condoned as functional for the village (young men venting their frustrations), there are limits to such acceptance. Excessive drinking also takes place in the home, with friends, and produces domestic quarrels that may end in spousal abuse when drunken husbands try to exert their authority over their wives after the slightest disagreement.

Young Indo-Fijian men also share some of this drinking pattern (although the adverse consequences of social drunken behavior and problems manifest themselves elsewhere.) With access to automobiles, either as employed drivers or in their own vehicles, Indo-Fijians are often involved in motor accidents resulting from excessive drinking. In other cases, intoxication leads to domestic problems. (But Indo-Fijians also face some societal stress, including unemployment, landlessness, and poverty, which may lead to despair and migration into towns in search of survival (Plange 1996). This may also influence alcohol consumption, as an antidote to stress and despair. Some of these factors may contribute to domestic crises, with homicide and suicide as final outcomes.) Indeed, among both ethnic groups, young men tend to indulge in excessive drinking with sometimes violent outcomes (Adinkrah 1995). Small wonder, then, that the Fiji police force reports a high incidence of alcohol-related offenses.

Iceland

Icelanders drink a lot at a time, but infrequently (Ásmundsson 1995), and these occasions are prompted by the intention of having a good time. Among seamen, especially, this pattern may include excessive drinking and drunkenness. Their infrequent bingeing, mostly on spirits, come in the few days' break between spells of many weeks of fishing in the hazardous North Atlantic, where they operate "dangerous, complicated, and expensive equipment, often in bad weather" (p. 124). The outcomes of this pattern of drinking are frequently fatal accidents and arrests by the police. Hence, Icelandic seamen have been documented as "most at risk for alcohol problems" (p. 124). Yet sobriety soon sets in after the risk period and throughout the subsequent work period.

Common Threads

In the cultural examples outlined above, some common denominators emerge: the drinkers are male, the drinkers have minority status in the culture, large quantities of alcohol are consumed in a short time, and the drinkers quickly return to the status quo. These factors need to be considered together with the level of drinking itself. The extent to which drunkenness or excessive drinking, rather than alcoholism or alcohol dependence, characterizes most of the alcohol drinking in the South Pacific is shown by the near unanimous agreement that pathological addictive drinking of the sort commonly labelled alcoholism does not exist (Stein 1982). This position has, however, been contradicted by other findings, which indicate alcoholism and alcoholic psychosis among Melanesians in New Caledonia associated with the frustrations inherent for Melanesians within the structure of New Caledonian society.

Patterns of drinking in many societies include both acceptable forms and drinking to drunkenness. In most of these situations, only a minority of people appear to drink to excess. In some multiethnic societies, such patterns of drinking become associated, sometimes wrongly, with particular ethnic groups so that to be described as "drinking like an X" means drinking to the state of drunkenness. In Australia, Canada, and Guatemala (Adams 1995) it is associated with indigenous populations. In Canada, a minority of drinkers, probably those drinking excessively, also think that it is permissible for a man to drink enough to feel the effects of alcohol (Cheung and Erickson 1995). Drinking to feel the effects could also result in drunkenness, especially since bars and taverns or social gatherings where excessive quantities may be consumed are frequent contexts of Canadian drinking. Among Canadian drinkers, this pattern has often been associated with social problems, including difficulties with friendships and social life, a negative outlook on life, financial difficulties, problems with marriage or home life, and problems with employment and studies (ibid.).

HEALTH AND QUALITY OF LIFE

Perhaps no other era in human history has been as concerned, indeed obsessed, with health, healthy living, and good quality of life as our contemporary period. Scientific research reports continue to emphasize the need for simple prevention health guidelines to enhance the quality of life and add more years to life. Increasingly, therefore, physical and mental exercises of different types are now packaged in instructive programs for the market, and consumers eagerly purchase them. For others, daily exercises of a more modest kind remain the order of the day, as they too have been endorsed as proper and healthy; walking briskly is a case in point. Meanwhile, diet, or more precisely proper nutrition, has also been identified as important to maintaining health, preventing illness and disease, and thus sustaining good quality of life. In response to this, health foods of all varieties abound in the market to cater to customers bent on keeping healthy, even if it means following the fad of the day. And, as one aspect of nutrition, alcohol itself in moderate quantities on a daily basis has also been shown to add quality to life through its cardioprotective effects (Rimm and Ellison 1995).

In general, there appears to be in our contemporary era a rediscovery of the body and its new forms of representation underlined by healthy diet, healthy living, and long life. This rediscovery and representation of life are supported by increased consumerism and by the media. The importance of lifestyle, that is, the choices people consciously make regarding what to do with their time, what to eat, whether or not to smoke, or what pattern of sex they choose, is now emphasized more than ever before. The reason is the near conquest, chiefly in the latter part of this century, of the numerous communicable or infectious diseases, for example smallpox, cholera, tuberculosis, and leprosy, which have in the past afflicted humanity and taken a heavy toll in some populations.

The improvement in quality of life brought about by advances in medical science and in the delivery of health services has been accompanied by new prevention and treatment methods in previously fatal diseases. These achievements have led to an increase in life expectancy in many countries. However, they have not provided enduring good health, longevity, or a disease-free life. Instead, illnesses and diseases that may derive largely from lifestyle—diabetes, cardiovascular diseases, cancer, coronary heart disease, and HIV-AIDS—have increased. They derive from lifestyle insofar as their causes depend on choices the individual makes to smoke, to consume foods rich in saturated fats, to be idle and not exercise, to drink excessively and repeatedly, to indulge in unsafe sex, and to eat foods without appropriate vitamin content. Evidently, then, a particular lifestyle will almost invariably yield certain outcomes.

At the individual level, quality of life means attaining and sustaining good health as a shield against disease. At the collective or societal level, quality of life is a public health issue. Small wonder, then, that there are more and more public health recommendations for selecting particular foods, the use of appropriate dietary supplements, exercising, and the responsible use of alcohol.

These considerations have prompted the notion that some minimum living condition and lifestyle are implied by the concept of quality of life (Mukherjee 1989) and that these can be measured by such indexes as standard of living, style of living, and level of living, which are usually quantified in terms of food consumption, income, living conditions, and health. Scores attributed to each of these are developed from individual responses into a quality-of-life index. Such indexes have been used in national settings, for example in the Swedish Level of Living Survey (Erikson 1993). Cultural differentiation enters into this exercise, as cultures vary and indeed can impose beliefs, attitudes, and values regarding food consumption, substance use, smoking, and lifestyle. In addition, there is the controversial issue of choice of indicator (Brock 1993; Ysander 1993). The influence of culture on quality of life, however, needs to be approached cautiously to avoid a static conceptualization of culture and its influence. Culture and traditions are lived experiences and can generate new knowledge to influence change. It is from this perspective, then, that alcohol and its relationship with quality of life and its measurement can be viewed, especially with regard to food and nutrition.

THE ROLE OF ALCOHOL IN HEALTH AND
QUALITY OF LIFE

Alcohol is consumed in almost all cultures, each with its particular pattern and choice of beverage. The perception of alcohol as being detrimental to health, the individual, and society lies not in the substance itself but in particular patterns of consumption, that is, drinking to the point of drunkenness, addiction, or alcoholism. In these circumstance, alcohol affects health negatively, may contribute to domestic and social problems, becomes an associated cause in motor accidents, and in some cultures predisposes people to violence: assault, rape, and even suicide. It has been shown to contribute to poor quality of life for some individuals (Chubon 1987).

Alcohol's potential negative impacts contrast rather sharply with its positive contributions to health and quality of life. Scientific research and evidence have increasingly underlined this aspect of alcohol. Thus, in all cultures in which alcohol is available it can be used to enhance and sustain quality of life if its consumption follows a responsible pattern. This is exemplified in Mediterranean countries, where the consumption of alcohol in moderation by the majority has contributed to lower rates of cardiovascular diseases (Rimm and Ellison 1995).

In old traditions and cultures, alcohol has tended to be perceived as food (Heath 1995a), since the basic ingredients of alcohol are essentially agricultural food items: wheat, barley, rice, hops, fruits, and even vegetables. The complexities of the breakdown of alcohol within the human body to yield the observed physiological and therapeutic results (see Packer 1996) are beyond the scope of this chapter. Suffice it to say that the ancient sages were not widely off the mark when they insisted that alcohol is food and that, when taken within the limits prescribed by culture, is good for the body. Increasingly, the benefits of moderate use of alcohol by adults have been established by scientists. Turner, Bennett, and Hernandez (1981) reported that, particularly among the elderly, moderate use of alcoholic beverages may improve quality of life by reducing stress and the risk of myocardial infarction. More recent research, such as that carried out on the "French paradox" (Renaud and de Lorgeril 1992, 1993) and in the Copenhagen Heart Study (Gronbaek et al. 1995), has attested to this positive outcome of the responsible use of alcohol.

While wine has been emphasized as beneficial in some studies, such as those on the Mediterranean diet and the Danish study, other evidence underlines the equally positive contribution of beer and distilled spirits in lowering the risk of heart disease if consumed moderately (Rimm and Ellison 1995; Rimm et al. 1996). Most important, however, is the finding that it is the alcohol, as the key consituent of wine, beer and distilled spirits, that provides the protection against heart disease. Rimm and Ellison (1995) concluded that "alcohol reduces the risk of cardiovascular disease in populations throughout the world." In addition, "the benefits stem predominantly from the alcohol itself, not from other constituents of the beverage sources.'' Thus, ethanol has its own benefits for the human body.

Renaud and de Lorgeril (1992, 1993) concluded that there is no other drug that's been so efficient than a moderate intake of alcohol, and the Copenhagen Heart Study has provided added evidence in support of this claim (Gronbaek et al. 1995). Using a sample of 13,000 people between the ages of thirty and seventy-nine, this ten-year study of the relationship between health and alcohol produced results that are surprising, even shocking. What surprised the research scientists most was the finding that even moderate wine intake of up to three to five glasses of wine implied a significantly much lower mortality with regard to all causes. As for spirits, only a small amount, perhaps one drink a month, was beneficial.'' According to Rimm and Ellison (1995), there are three points. The first is that abstinence from alcohol is a major risk factor for coronary heart disease. Secondly, moderate drinking reduces total mortality, thus decreasing moderate drinking in a population would increase mortality rates. And, finally scientific data on alcohol and health should be considered by governments in making policy.

It can therefore be concluded that alcohol does have a positive outcome on quality of life, especially in its capacity to lower the probability of degenerative heart disease and to reduce mortality. But when the use of alcoholic beverages is recommended, it is the pattern of consumption that should always be emphasized and not the beverage per se.

CONCLUSION

The emphasis in this chapter, on patterns of drinking and their outcome, underlines that there are multiple patterns of alcohol use, which lead to multiple health and societal consequences. Excessive drinking has a negative outcome for individuals and for society, and a regulated, moderate, and responsible pattern of drinking has a positive outcome on health and well-being. These demonstrable outcomes are not captured by the single-distribution theory expounded by Ledermann (1956). Nor does the theory lead to an understanding of the French paradox or the Mediterranean diet and their recent confirmation by the Danish study. Individuals who are dependent on alcohol and those who binge to drunkenness exist everywhere, even in regions where beneficial patterns are regarded as the norm. But these people and their patterns of drinking do not negate the positive outcome of alcohol consumption for the large numbers of people who drink moderately. It appears, then, that there is a need for education toward a healthy use of alcohol.

REFERENCES

Adams, W. R. 1995. Guatemala. In *International Handbook on Alcohol and Culture,* ed. D. B. Heath. Westport, Conn.: Greenwood.

Adinkrah, M. 1995. *Crime, Deviance, and Delinquency in Fiji.* Suva, Fiji: Fiji Council of Social Services.

Arokinsamy, C. V. 1995. Malaysia. In *International Handbook on Alcohol and Culture,* ed. D. B. Heath. Westport, Conn.: Greenwood.

Ásmundsson, G. 1995. Iceland. In *International Handbook on Alcohol and Culture,* ed. D. B. Heath. Westport, Conn.: Greenwood.

Bales, R. F. 1946. Cultural differences in rates of alcoholism. *Quarterly Journal of Studies on Alcohol* 6:480–99.

Brock, D. 1993. Quality of life measures in health care and medical ethics. In *The Quality of Life,* ed. M. Nussbaum and A. Sen. Oxford: Oxford University Press.

Casswell, S. 1986. *Alcohol in Oceania.* Research Monograph. Auckland, N.Z.: University of Auckland, School of Medicine, Department of Community Health, Alcohol Research Unit.

Cheung, Y. W., and P. G. Erickson. 1995. Canada. In *International Handbook on Alcohol and Culture,* ed. D. B. Heath. Westport, Conn.: Greenwood.

Chubon, R. A. 1987. Development of a quality-of-life rating scale for use in health care intervention. *Eval. Health Prof.* 10:186–200.

Epstein, E. E., et al. 1995. An empirical classification of drinking patterns among alcoholics: binge, episodic, sporadic, and steady. *Addictive Behaviors* 20:23–41.

Erikson, E. 1993. Descriptions of inequality: the Swedish approach to welfare research. In *The Quality of Life,* ed. M. Nussbaum and A. Sen. Oxford: Oxford University Press.

Grant, M., and B. Ritson. 1983. *Alcohol: The Prevention Debate.* New York: St. Martin's.

Gronbaek, M., et al. 1995. Mortality associated with moderate intakes of wine, beer, or spirits. *British Medical Journal* 310:1165–69.

Heath, D. B., ed. 1995a. *International Handbook on Alcohol and Culture.* Westport, Conn.: Greenwood .

Heath, D. B. 1995b. Changes in drinking patterns in Bolivian cultures: a cautionary tale about historical approaches. *Addiction Research* 2:307–18.

Hezel, F. X. 1984. Cultural patterns in Trukese suicide. *Ethnology* 23:193–206.

Ledermann, S. 1956. *Alcool, Alcoolisme, Alcoolisation.* Institut National d'études Démographiques, Cahier 29. Paris: Presses Universitaires de France.

Lennane, J. 1992. *Alcohol, the National Hangover: The Social and Personal Cost of Drinking in Australia—and What You Can Do about It.* North Sydney: Allen and Unwin.

Marshall, M. 1979. *Weekend Warriors: Alcohol in a Micronesian Culture.* Palo Alto, Calif.: Mayfield.

Marshall, M. 1987. "Young men's work": alcohol use in the contemporary Pacific. In *Contemporary Issues in Mental Health Research in the Pacific Islands,* ed. A. Robillard and A. Maresella. Honolulu: University of Hawaii.

Mukherjee, R. 1989. *The Quality of Life: Valuation in Social Research.* London: Sage.

Oshodin, O. G. 1995. Nigeria. In *International Handbook on Alcohol and Culture,* ed. D. B. Heath. Westport, Conn.: Greenwood.

Packer, L. 1996. Possible factors influencing ageing. *WHO Healthy Ageing Book of Abstracts.* Geneva: WHO, Ageing and Health Programme.

Peck, D. F. 1982. Problem drinking: some determining factors. In *Drinking and Problem Drinking,* ed. M. A. Plant. London: Junction Books.

Plange, N. 1991. Social aspects of drug and alcohol abuse: an overview of the situation in Fiji. *Fiji Medical Journal* 17:4–12.

———. 1996. Evaluation of employment opportunities in Fiji: report prepared for the United Nations Development Programme, Fiji.

Plant, M. A., ed. 1982. *Drinking and problem drinking.* London: Junction Books.

Renaud, S., and M. de Lorgeril. 1993. The French paradox: diet factors and cigarette smoking-related health risks. *Annals of the New York Academy of Sciences* 686:299–309.

———. 1992. Wine, alcohol, platelets, and the French paradox for coronary heart disease. *Lancet!* 339:1523–26.

Rimm, E. B., and R. C. Ellison. 1995. Alcohol in the Mediterranean diet. *American Journal of Clinical Nutrition* 61:1378S–82S.

Rimm, E. B, A. Klatsky, D. Grobbee, and M. J. Stampfer. 1996. Reviews of moderate alcohol consumption and reduced risk of coronary heart disease: is the effect due to beer, wine, or spirits? *British Medical Journal* 312:731–36.

Roizen, R. 1983. The World Health Organization study of community responses to alcohol-related problems: a review of cross-cultural findings. Annex 41. In *Community Response to Alcohol-Related Problems: Phase I,* ed. I. Rootman and J. Moser. Document MNH/83.17. Geneva: World Health Organization.

Stein, H. F. 1982. Ethanol and its discontents: paradoxes in imbrication and sobriety in American culture. *Journal of Psychoanalytic Anthropology* 5:355–77.

Turner, T. B., V. L. Bennett, and H. Hernandez. 1981. The beneficial side of moderate alcohol use. *Johns Hopkins Medical Journal* 48:52–63.

Ysander, B.-C. 1993. Commentary on Erikson. In *The Quality of Life,* M. Nussbaum and A. Sen. Oxford: Oxford University Press.

Chapter 6

Cultural Variations among Drinking Patterns

Dwight B. Heath

Any discussion of the two focal themes of this book—patterns of drinking and patterns of problems—must sooner or later come to grips with the unavoidable fact that there is considerable cultural variation in both. That simple assertion may be disturbing to some, but it has enormous value in terms of the substantive description of the range of human experience. It is also important in terms of theoretical interpretations and practical actions concerning alcohol, its uses, and the outcomes of such usage. From an anthropological perspective, it is remarkable that so simple a chemical substance (C_2H_5OH), often found in nature without human intervention, has undergone such elaborated technological manipulation and been so esteemed by some populations and so condemned by others (with some complex justifications for both attitudes) and that norms on alcohol are so varied, emotionally loaded, and often contradictory.

The exponential growth of the literature about drinking and its outcomes from a cultural perspective, which began in the mid-1900s (Heath 1975, 1987a, 1987b), has slowed markedly during the past decade, and few points need to be added to a summary evaluation of that literature that I wrote at the height of such activity (Heath 1988):

> A global overview of the literature on alcohol allows one to recognize a number of important points to which the sociocultural perspective has made major contributions:

Dwight B. Heath is professor of anthropology, Brown University, Providence, R.I., U.S.

- Drinking is almost always a social act—in many cultures, drinking alone is unthinkable, and in most, drinking together is an act endowed with strong positive meanings.
- Peoples are rarely neutral about drinking—it is often hedged about with a varied lot of norms, to a far greater extent that many other kinds of activity.
- Those norms are often endowed with a strong emotional charge, again more than is the case in many other sets of norms.
- Such affectively loaded norms include expectations about the results of drinking that are regularly patterned among most members of any given population.
- Actual drunken comportment conforms to such patterns, and the fact that it rarely exceeds widely shared limits of propriety indicates that it is strongly affected by social learning.
- In most of the cultures where drinking occurs at all, most drinkers have few, if any, alcohol-related problems in physiological, psychological, social relational, economic, or other terms.
- The phenomenon of dependence or addiction is rare with respect to alcohol, on a worldwide basis.
- Among those individuals who do develop drinking problems, aspects of the cultural context in which they live often play a major role in the etiology of their problem.
- There is no uniform developmental sequence that applies cross-culturally with respect to the way in which various kinds of alcohol-related problems (with the possible exception of certain organic pathologies) manifest themselves.
- For those individuals who seek help in relation to drinking problems, cultural differences can result in potentially harmful misunderstandings; cultural differences can also be helpful in identifying potentially fruitful adaptive strategies for individuals and populations. (pp. 397–398)

As has already been noted above, "level of drinking refers to how much people drink, while pattern of drinking refers to how they drink and the circumstances in which they drink" (see Chapter 1, this volume).

The term *abuse* is commonly used with reference to alcohol, not just by laypersons but as one of only two major diagnoses of psychiatric problems associated with alcohol that are recognized by the American Psychiatric Association (1994). The implication is that there are ways of using beverage alcohol that are not of psychiatric concern but that are "normal" in both sociological and statistical terms, "moderate" in terms favored by the drink industries and used in dietary guidelines for Americans (USDA/USDHHS 1995), or "sensible" as used in the United Kingdom government's recommendations (U.K. Department of Health and Social Security 1995) to its citizens about the role of drinking in a healthful lifestyle.

In this chapter, the emphasis is on cultural variations in drinking patterns and problems, not only to illustrate that no simple and uniform solution promises to lessen the risks or to prevent those harms that are sometimes associated with drinking but also to show that drinking is neither inherently risky nor harmful and that patterns of both thinking and acting can be shaped in ways that further public health and social welfare.

WHY CULTURE MATTERS

Culture has been diversely called "a set of ready-made answers to the recurring questions of life," "an integrated system of patterns of belief and behavior characteristic of a human population," and "a web of meaning." Furthermore, specialists argue about whether it exists "in the minds of the actors," "in the mind of the analyst," or "out there in the real world" (Kroeber and Kluckhohn 1952, 50–72). The reality of any culture is not nearly so abstruse as those comments may suggest.

Perhaps one of the most helpful ways of understanding the concept of culture is by way of analogy: culture is to other behavior as grammar is to speech. A child learns many of the rules of grammar long before being aware of them, or of such a thing as grammar, for that matter. It is a rare five-year old who cannot speak clearly, even imaginatively and inventively, long before being confronted with grammatical details, such as parts of speech, mood, gender, tense, and voice. In much the same way, most individuals incorporate gestures, manner of eating, ideas about themselves in relation to others, a complex worldview, and other customs, mores, norms, or cultural traits long before they have heard anything about culture as such.

In this connection, we must also recognize that a cultural system, like a grammatical system, allows for a broad range of flexibility. For all the rules of grammar, we rarely feel constrained by it; certainly, we do not all talk alike. On the contrary, each of us is constantly improvising, combining the limited set of components that are grammatically available to us in ways that produce new and unique sentences, most of which we have never uttered or heard before and many of which we will never encounter again. It may seem ironic, but historical uniqueness is so commonplace in human speech that we rarely notice it, even though it all occurs within the apparently strict limitations set by a grammatical system. In much the same way, the rules of culture do not constitute a cookie-cutter or punch press from which we emerge as preprogrammed automatons, nor do we usually even chafe under the real limitations they set.

Insofar as culture relates to drinking, it can be said in a fundamental sense that culture determines what is readily available. Before people knew about fermentation, there was no beer or wine; before distillation, no spirits. Pulque, made from maguey sap, is popular in Mexico, and kumiss, or fermented mare's milk, is appreciated by herders in central Asia, but both are virtually unknown elsewhere. Rice is made into beer in the Dominican Republic and into wine throughout eastern Asia. Barley or wheat can be made into vodka or beer just as easily as those drinks can be made from potatoes, maize, or millet, but the techniques, values, and associated meanings are very different. Culture's impact on drink is also seen in ideas about origins. One culture saw beer as a gift of the gods and a valuable good to be sacrificed to them yet, subsequently, came to revile it as an abomination (Ashour 1995). In some cultures, wine is viewed as a comforting and nutritious food integral to the daily diet, while in others it is scorned as poison, damaging to the soul as well as the body.

From an anthropological point of view, one of the most fascinating things about beverage alcohol is the diversity of cultural variations that can be found around the world (Heath 1995a), and the fact that even within a given culture, usages and the meanings and consequences of such use can be very different at different moments in history (Heath 1995b).

ALCOHOL AND ASPECTS OF CULTURE

When we focus on that meaning of the term *culture* that embraces the entire way of life of a people, it is noteworthy that alcohol impinges on virtually every aspect. It is for this reason that I have spoken of alcohol as providing a "window on culture" (Heath 1993, 30). As Duster (1983, 326) said, "Alcohol is to social science what dye is to microscopy . . . [allowing us] to penetrate the structure." Any culture is a complex system of interrelated things, ideas, institutions, and processes, all of which can be classified in myriad ways. Volumes have been written about each, but within the limited scope of this chapter, it seems appropriate simply to refer to some of the universal aspects of culture in alphabetical order under the categories of arts and literature, economics, history, recreation and entertainment, religion and ideology, and social and political relations. Other aspects, such as technology, conflict management, and science, are beyond the scope of so brief a summary.

Arts and literature

Some sorts of esthetic expression, whether graphic, plastic, or verbal, occur in every known society, even those in which there is no writing and in which the people do not speak about art or esthetics as a distinctive notion. Beverage alcohol figures prominently in ancient Egyptian portrayals of life, whether in exquisite bas-reliefs, ceramic miniatures, or paintings. Depictions of the gods who supposedly introduced wine are abundant. Drinking and drinkers play a conspicuous part in opera, drama, novels, folktales, and visual representations, and poetry often waxes eloquent about the pleasures of drink. Beverage alcohol seems almost to be a dominant character in many of the works of such writers as Hemingway, O'Neill, Lowry, Dostoyevsky, and Simenon and is invoked as an integral part of the setting or as the justification for twists in the plot of others. Film and television continue the dramatic tradition (Cook and Lewington 1979). Even without an attempt to sketch in outline the range of variation that can be found in cultures through both time and space, it is apparent that alcohol often plays a significant role in a culture's arts and literature.

Economics

In a broad sense, we can speak of the economic aspect of culture whenever we are dealing with exchanges, whether of goods, services, people, or symbols. Decisions about allocation can be important whenever a foodstuff is converted to alcohol; often, such conversion turns large-volume low-value material into a good that has small volume but high value and that is easily transportable, almost infinitely divisible, does not spoil, but is often readily consumed. Far from being wasteful of foodstuffs, home brewing often enhances their dietary value. A different sort of value lies in the fact that acquisition of beverage alcohol may interfere with the budget of a household or that drunkenness may result in harm to a person or to property. Beverage alcohol itself can be an important item in large-scale trade over long distances, as with the infamous "triangle trade" whereby Antillean molasses was taken to New England to be converted into rum, which was then traded for black people, who were taken from the west coast of Africa and sold as slaves in the West Indies, or who were traded for molasses to make more rum. To a remarkable degree, beverage alcohol was used as a tool in support of colonial expansion in North America, Oceania, and Australia (areas where, curiously, there had been little indigenous production) and in Africa (where home-brewed beers were already commonplace).

In recent years, in much of highland New Guinea, cases of beer have come to be the functional equivalents of pigs in the traditional pattern of feasting, whereby a man's public generosity underscores his social status (Marshall 1982). And drinks are heavily taxed in many jurisdictions, constitute a part of pay for labor in others, and find a ready market in most. Ever since the first body of law was codified in writing (the Code of Hammurabi, in Babylonia around 2000 B.C.), beverage alcohol has been subject to strict regulations, many of which have been designed to protect the consumer.

Sometimes beverage alcohol is paid as part of a wage, and sometimes it constitutes a major item of consumption in budgets that are newly involved in cash as a medium of exchange. Archeological studies of ceramic wine jars attest to long-distance trade in early times and allow us to trace routes of diffusion as well as conquest. In more recent times, the proliferation of allied industries such as can, bottle, and label making and transportation carry the economic impact far beyond the immediate circle of producers and consumers.

History

Contrary to widespread belief, every society has its history, even if it is oral rather than written and even if portions of it are difficult to distinguish from mythology. Without going into the fascinating details of case studies throughout the world, it still seems worthwhile to illustrate the extent to which certain cultures have changed in their approaches to beverage alcohol, if only to correct the assumption that such change is rare or difficult to achieve. The impact of

Islam is one of the most dramatic examples, bringing virtually effective prohibition to a huge population over a vast area, where both drinking and drunkenness
had been highly esteemed in earlier times (Badri 1976). Although the experiment
with national prohibition in the United States is generally viewed as having failed
in most respects (Kyvig 1985), it does dramatically illustrate some of the ex-
tremes in attitudes and behavior that have characterized that country's ambivalence about drink, an ambivalence that is played out politically in an almost
cyclical pattern (Musto 1987).

One of the most striking historical sequences is that of the Seneca Indians
of upstate New York and southern Canada (Wallace 1970). Before contact with
Europeans, they had no beverage alcohol. When first introduced to it in the early
1600s, most rejected it. A few developed a taste for it, and soon it was used as
an adjunct to the traditional religious vision quest. Gradually, it became a major
item in trade. As more Seneca drank and as they were subject to manifold other
pressures, drunkenness became problematic, with associated aggression and vi-
olation of other traditional norms, until a recovering alcoholic named Handsome
Lake articulated his syncretic vision around 1800. He was so successful that the
religion bearing his name remains vital today, with abstinence an important
article of faith among adherents on both sides of the border.

Other examples of major historical changes in drinking beliefs and practices
are numerous around the world. For example, the average citizen of the United
States around 1825 drank more than three times as much as in 1975, half of the
states enacted prohibition around 1850, and the entire nation was officially dry
(by constitutional amendment) from 1920 to 1934 (Rorabaugh 1979). Iceland at
various times prohibited wine, beer, and spirits separately but subsequently
repealed each such ban (Ásmundsson 1995). Two of the most successful examples of nationwide prohibition of all beverage alcohol now are Iran and Saudi
Arabia, although both inherited vast and opulent literature as well as lavish
paintings about the joys of drink and of drunkenness. Finland, parts of Canada,
and the United Kingdom had brief prohibitions, while Sweden experimented
with alcohol rationing for a time.

Much of sub-Saharan Africa is witnessing a massive shift in taste from
home-brewed beers to factory-made beers. Dealers in the United States speak of
a major turn in recent years from "dark goods" (e.g., whiskey and rum) to
"light goods" (e.g., vodka and tequila); the opposite is happening in Eastern
Europe. When U.S. tax rates changed, previously phenomenally successful fruit-
flavored wine coolers were promptly replaced with malt-based counterparts.
Wine sales are increasing in the United States, while those of spirits have continued to decline since around 1980. At the same time, young people in Spain,
France, and Italy are turning from wine to beer. The once-infamous three-martini
lunch has virtually disappeared, as have hosts over eager to keep every guest's
glass full. Nonalcoholic alternatives are popular at parties, and the stereotypical
inebriate is no longer a fit object for humor in North America or Western Europe.
Most of these changes have come about in a single generation, proof that a

culture and its drinking habits can and do change, contrary to the dire predictions of many who view education as a fruitless approach to the prevention of alcohol-related problems.

Recreation and Entertainment

Far from being a ticket to oblivion, drinking usually alters one's mood for the better. In almost all cultures, one of the most common uses of beverage alcohol is precisely that for which it is pharmacologically most apt, as a relaxant that is nontoxic and readily metabolized in moderate quantities. This can reduce fatigue, ease stress, enhance sociability, and otherwise make life a little pleasanter, especially when dealing with other people. This is presumably why beverage alcohol is so often enjoyed on festive occasions (feasts, weddings, parties) and why it is an integral part of many meetings, with toasting an elaborate way of symbolically reaffirming special relationships.

Drinking games are also commonplace, many involving quick, often imaginative, responses. To an almost ritualistic degree, drinking is a frequent accompaniment to such special occasions as picnics, hunting or fishing trips, visits with friends, and the celebration of key events. The relaxation function is probably also an important reason that, in those cultures in which work is done outside the home, a drink is often an important marker of the boundary between labor and leisure, the public and private worlds, the workplace and home. Even if one does not drink enough to feel the effects, there is often a favorable symbolic or psychological response, in which the drink signals an important change of pace or venue (Gusfield 1987).

Religion and Ideology

Beliefs and attitudes about drinking are often intimately linked with religious and ideological systems, whether positively or negatively, and drink itself plays many crucial roles in various religions. For the ancient Greeks, wine was a gift of the god Dionysus, and periodic drunken revels were a form of worship in his name; Romans followed the same pattern, in honor of their wine-giving god, Bacchus. Similarly, ancient Egyptians believed that the god Osiris had brought them the precious gift of beer and taught them how to make it. Halfway around the world, the Aztecs of pre-Columbian Mexico cherished pulque as the gift of the 400-breasted Mayahuel, but their descendants adjusted to calling it "the milk of the Virgin" when they adopted Roman Catholic Christianity. By contrast, most Muslims reject drinking, on the grounds of a Koranic injunction.

Although some ascetic Protestant groups similarly reject drinking, the Bible abounds in favorable references to it, one of the most striking of which was Jesus's designation of wine to symbolize his blood in what has become the Eucharist, or communion, one of the fundamental rites of Christianity. Just as some religions embrace beverage alcohol, others consider it anathema. Among the few prohibitions that have been effective are those that are deeply imbedded in religious values. Even cultures that allow drinking sometimes forbid it in specifically religious contexts, though beer or wine serves as the ideal sacrificial gift to many deities in African and Latin American cultures, and drunkenness is often valued and sought as facilitating direct communication between the drinker and supernatural beings. Although emotions run high on the subject, there is anything but consensus concerning alcohol among the world's religions and ideological systems.

Social and Political Relations

An overwhelmingly striking feature of beverage alcohol in both the historical and the cross-cultural perspective is its predominant association with sociability and hospitality. Whatever else it may be, drinking is quintessentially a social act, and it is unthinkable in many cultures that anyone would use beverage alcohol otherwise. In a recent survey of drinking in twenty-seven nations around the world, every respondent emphasized the use of alcohol as an adjunct to sociability and hospitality as a primary benefit of drinking, even though few of these writers were social scientists (Heath 1995a). There are some societies in which drinking is among the few social activities that exist (Heath 1958) and others in which drinking is an important marker of social status, defining the boundaries among groups or reflecting levels of power and prestige. In many cultures, "Let's have a drink" is the normal greeting to a visitor; in many others, all drinking is social.

Virtually all Jews drink, but they think of drunkenness as a trait of non-Jews. Seemingly endless toasting, with elaborate wordplay as well as large quantities of alcohol, is an essential component of a big meal in Russia and Georgia. The sequence of drinking, from a single glass, strictly conforms to age hierarchy among contemporary Mayas. And a large part of the growing popularity of factory-made beer in many developing countries is said to be conspicuous consumption on the part of wage earners eager to distinguish themselves from peasants. In ancient Rome, women were allowed only limited access to wine, and the widespread use of wine by the general population (rather than just the wealthy) is not more than 150 years old, even in France and Italy.

Most prohibition movements have been imbedded in broader political concerns, and sensitivity to issues surrounding drink are reflected in the ban on drinking by striking workers during the Polish revolution of the 1960s and in the strong reaction to Gorbachev's imposition of strict alcoholic controls during perestroika and just prior to the dissolution of the Soviet Union. Prohibition was written into India's constitution as an aim; virtually all the states subsequently repealed their local restrictions, although some are reinstating them. In the United States, the first federal excise tax (on whiskey) prompted the first local revolt against the new government (the Whiskey Rebellion in western Pennsylvania), which was put down by the first use of national armed forces. No other commodity is dealt with by the U.S. Constitution, which was amended once to impose nationwide prohibition and, again, less than twenty years later, to rescind it (the sole instance of repeal of an amendment in the two centuries during which that document has been the foundation of government in the United States and a model for many other countries).

During the late 1800s, a consortium of nations tried to restrict trade in beverage alcohol in Africa. During the late 1900s, a specialized agency of the United Nations is trying to restrict alcohol consumption throughout Europe (WHO 1981), with the recommendation that the rest of the world should follow suit. Some individual communities become dry under local option, even in countries and states where beverage alcohol is legal and most people drink. It is evident that social and political relations are yet another aspect of culture that impinges on drinking patterns and consequences.

CULTURE AND INDIVIDUAL VARIABLES

A cultural perspective tends to emphasize patterns of drinking whereby self-identified human populations show themselves to be distinctive in some significant respects from others. Even if the members of a given society do not drink at all, their very abstinence (with accompanying attitudes) often allows for meaningful comparison with other populations. One of the themes of this chapter so far has been to show the broad range of variation among such culturally patterned beliefs and practices about drinking, both among different cultures and also in a given culture over time. However, it is simplistic to suggest that styles of thinking and drinking are uniform even within the most homogeneous culture. It is a truism that, however small and unstratified a society may be, each individual is like all others in only some respects; in other respects, each individual is like only some others; and in some respects, each individual is like no others.

Demographic Variables

From the point of view of social science, it is important to focus on that middle range, the so-called demographic variables that allow us to look at subgroups within a population, and we often find that members of such groups are treated much the same and behave in similar ways. Among such groupings that have been used in analyzing subcultural variations within drinking populations, some of the most noteworthy are gender, age, and social categories.

Gender Whether with justification or not, every culture treats people differently on the basis of sex; in fact, the social implications of that biological differentiation are what we call gender. Certain roles are considered right for males and for females; other roles overlap gender or are indeterminate. Males are taught, and sometimes not at all subtly, that they are expected to act differently from females and, often, to think differently; and vice versa. The gradual

process of enculturation or socialization implants ideas about the range of appropriate male or female alternatives and about a range of inappropriate alternatives.
Such general rules are not always strictly prescriptive or proscriptive, but they
do set standards, within which certain patterns become dominant.

Although the stereotypes that people learn in this connection are often
thought to be "natural," or imposed by biology, they are in fact social and
cultural conventions. Nevertheless, it is striking that males everywhere drink
more often, and tend to drink more, than females. In several contexts drinking
is restricted to males, such as certain bars in Spain and Latin America, Greek
cafés during the day, among African herders sipping beer through straws from
the communal pot, Finnish sauna binges, and so forth. But there are also a few
contexts restricted to women: kitchen parties in contemporary New Zealand and
Sweden, drunkenness associated with ritual prostitution in ancient Greece, and
so on. The infamous double standard applies, so that a woman who drinks is
presumed to be sexually promiscuous in many societies, and her drinking may
be morally condemned. To those who have studied changing attitudes about
gender and drink, it is striking that women's drinking tends to become an important issue in public debate at times when their status and power are seen as
challenging to those of men (Heath 1994).

Age   Different patterns of belief and behavior are acceptable (or expected,
or required, or approved, or disallowed) at different ages. The details differ from
one society to the next, but all provide for a period of infantile helplessness,
followed by dependent but increasingly responsible childhood. Some allow for
relative freedom and independence in adolescence, adulthood usually marking
the move by which one establishes a new family. Seniority may be a continuum,
or elders may be afforded special status, depending on what they have achieved
that is valued in their culture.

In relation to drinking, access is often restricted by age. A Jewish boy is
given a ceremonial drop of wine immediately after circumcision, on his eighth
day of life. French and Italian children are often given a few drops of wine
diluted in water to accompany older relatives drinking during a meal; the mixture
is strengthened as the child matures, so that wine drinking is learned as a normal
part of everyday living, an adjunct to food, and part of a pleasant and sustaining
ambience, in which drunkenness and boisterous behavior would be out of place.
By contrast, in the United States, beverage alcohol takes on the mystique of
forbidden fruit because it is legally unavailable in most states until the age of
twenty-one (even though the age of majority for voting is eighteen, and it is
lower for some other legal purposes).

Episodic heavy drinking is often associated with aggressive and other excessive behavior on the part of adolescents, where it is tolerated. By contrast,
moderate drinking, eating, and a wide range of other activities dominate interaction among age-mates in other settings. Epidemiological patterns associated
with age can be important in terms of prevention strategies. For example, the

high rate of accidental deaths among teenagers in the United States appears to be closely linked not only with their predilection for risk taking and their lack of driving experience but also with their pattern of episodic heavy drinking. By their midthirties, most adults in the United States have significantly decreased both their frequency of heavy drinking and their overall quantity of drinking. By contrast, among Hispanics, there tends to be a continuing rise in drinking over much of the life cycle; and among several American Indian tribes and southeast Asian ethnic groups, heavy drinking is a prerogative reserved for the older and more prestigious members.

Social Categories   The social categories most often used to distinguish drinking subcultures in many societies are based on education, occupation, caste or class, religion, and ethnicity.

Formal schooling must be recognized as only a small portion of the lifelong process of education. However, in cultures where it looms large in terms of shaping life chances, it tends to correlate with larger overall consumption, as well as with particular beverages, which may be given more prestige.

Occupational differentiation, while minimal in some societies, plays an important role in self-identification and social stratification in others. Illustrative of such differences are widespread stereotypes (supported by some empirical evidence) that soldiers and sailors are heavier-than-average drinkers, even though both groups may abstain during long periods, like lumberjacks and cowboys. Social workers and librarians are generally abstemious, at least in comparison with artists, writers, miners, and factory workers. There are few efforts at systematic comparison, but detailed studies of selected groups reveal strikingly different patterns of drinking: whether, when, where, how much, and with what outcomes.

In some heterogeneous societies, categorization of individuals by caste (by inheritance, usually regulating marriage opportunities) or by class (usually socioeconomic) is socially important. One example of how caste relates to drinking pattern is in India, where members of the prestigious Brahmin caste seek intoxication with cannabis tea, while members of the warrior Rajput caste drink a local flower-based liquor, each group deploring the other's taste (Carstairs 1954). In the United States, beer consumption is greater among the lower socioeconomic class, and wine consumption is greater among the upper socioeconomic class. Efforts at social climbing can include adoption of beverages that are enjoyed by the group to which one aspires, just as a "a champagne appetite but a beer pocketbook" can signal frustration. Although legal interventions far more often result in problems for lower-class drinkers, largely because of where and how they drink, their overall consumption is often less than that of upper-class drinkers.

Religious groups often show marked differences in rates of both drinking and drinking problems, in part because so many of them proscribe the use of beverage alcohol. While entire families of orthodox Jews drink wine as an important part of weekly rituals, various Protestant groups so favor abstention that they ostracize all drinkers. Muslims are not supposed to drink, while Buddhists and Confucians are free to drink in moderation. In other religions, drunkenness is valued as a shortcut to transcendence. Recent research suggests that nominal affiliation with a religious group is less important as a predictor of drinking than are degree of commitment or involvement.

Ethnicity is used with far too many meanings in alcohol studies, so that it sometimes overlaps or becomes confused with race, religion, nationality, or cultural heritage (Heath 1991). Nevertheless, comparisons between so-called ethnic groups are commonplace. For example, the pattern of low consumption and high rate of problems found among the Irish was contrasted in an early study with universal drinking and a low rate of problems among Jews (Bales 1946). Few black American women drink, but black males who do drink incur high rates of problems. Few American Indian (Native American) women drink, but those who do account for a disproportionate number of cases of fetal alcohol syndrome. Cultural and physiological differences (notably the ''Oriental flush'') were once thought to protect those of East Asian descent from excessive drinking, but both types of protection have recently been questioned. Contrary to popular belief, aboriginal Australians drink in a manner very like their countrymen (Hall and Hunter 1995), and municipal beer gardens were among the least segregated places in South Africa for years before the official end of apartheid. Members of exploited minorities sometimes drink in ways that they think show resistance to—and other times acceptance of—the dominant culture. The rich diversity of ethnicity that can be found in some countries is perhaps the clearest evidence that cultures are not congruent with nation-states (although, for certain comparative purposes, it is sometimes convenient to speak as if that were the case).

Personal Variables

We have been discussing individual variables that relate to social or demographic categories within societies. Individual variables not usually associated with such subcultures are treated as personal variables in the analysis of drinking patterns and outcomes. Among these are attitudes, expectations, and drinking patterns, each of which relate to cultural variations.

Attitudes   Attitude toward drink goes far toward shaping drinking pattern. In France, because wine is considered a food rather than an alcoholic beverage, it is available with school lunches, and airline pilots used to have it with their meals. Children are taught how to drink wine in their family and can buy it easily at grocery stores.

In contrast, in Sweden until recently no one could buy alcohol except by written request, and all alcohol was sold in a state monopoly store. Further, it has been repeatedly demonstrated that members of religious groups that prohibit alcohol are disadvantaged if they experiment with it. To be sure, most of these people do not drink and so have no problems, but among those who do try drinking, the lack of guidelines is such that a high proportion incur problems. If alcohol is forbidden but said to be empowering, sexually arousing, and disinhibiting, is it any wonder that college students, away from home schedules and supervision, often drink heavily and then behave obnoxiously?

Expectations Closely related to attitudes are expectations. There is overwhelming historical and cross-cultural evidence that people learn not only how to drink but also how to be affected by drink through a process of socialization (MacAndrew and Edgerton 1969). Numerous experiments conducted under strictly controlled conditions (double-blind, with placebos) on a wide range of subjects and in different cultures have demonstrated that both mood and actions are affected far more by what people think they have drunk than by what they have actually drunk. It is this expectancy effect that prompts researchers to group individuals according to what they think beverage alcohol will do to or for them (Marlatt and Rohsenow 1980; Holyfield, Ducharme, and Martin 1995). In simple terms, this means that people who expect drinking to result in violence become aggressive; those who expect it to make them feel sexy become amorous; those who view it as disinhibiting are demonstrative. If behavior reflects expectations, then a society gets the kinds of drunks it deserves.

Drinking Patterns An abundance of social survey research has been devoted to identifying drinking patterns with the types of drinkers who exhibit them. Elaborate secondary statistical analyses are often then brought to bear in associating those types of drinkers with certain kinds or rates of problems. For example, in the United States, a person is called an abstainer if he or she has only one drink a year (which allows for a celebratory break from teetotaling in connection with New Year's Eve, a birthday, a wedding, or some such occasion). A striking contrast in terms of cultural norms is the Chilean definition of a moderate drinker as one who is drunk no more than twelve times a year (Medina 1995). In the United States, light or moderate drinking can mean up to two drinks a day, whereas heavy drinking starts at five or six drinks a day, which is far too narrow a range to allow much understanding of those relatively few but important individuals who typically have eight, ten, fifteen, or even more drinks a day. This topic is treated in greater detail elsewhere in this volume (chapter 12), but it is important to mention this shortcoming here for a number of reasons.

An important one is that most of what we know about drinking, in quantitative terms, derives from survey instruments that have been adopted, or only minimally adapted, from U.S. models. For this reason, data at the upper end of the consumption range are extremely poor, and it is impossible to discuss differences among a broad range of drinkers whose patterns have been excessively aggregated. Another difficulty is that such questions often have to do with a certain number of drinks "at a time," or "per occasion," or "per week." The weekly number obscures the significant difference between those who drink a little each day and those who drink none on many days but enough on a few days to make up the difference. For example, the impact of two drinks on each of seven days is very different from that of fourteen drinks on a Saturday night. For just that reason, the United Kingdom's guidelines for sensible drinking were recently rephrased to cover daily consumption. Similarly, five drinks gulped down fast with no food will have an impact markedly different from five drinks spaced throughout a six-hour dinner party. Confusions such as this have prompted the contributors to this volume to emphasize the importance of drinking patterns over that of sheer volume of reported consumption.

In recent years, it has become increasingly evident that sporadic episodes of acute intoxication are associated with both a broader range and a greater frequency of drinking problems than is moderate (nonintoxicating) drinking. Most alcohol-related traffic fatalities involve drivers whose blood alcohol content exceeds the designated level of impairment by at least 50 percent, and a majority of arrests for driving under the influence involve repeaters who admit to driving drunk frequently. The well-known associations between drinking and crime, violence, verbal or sexual aggression, spousal or child abuse, and a host of other objectionable behaviors prove, on close inspection, to be correlations with excessive, rather than with moderate or sensible, drinking, just as most of the physiological damage attributed to alcohol results from long-term heavy drinking. Accidents of all kinds tend also to result from drunkenness rather than from drinking. In sum, most of the risks associated with the use of alcohol should more accurately be associated with its abuse.

The so-called preventive paradox has been proposed. The fact that more moderate drinkers than heavy drinkers admit to having at some time experienced an alcohol-related problem is said to justify requiring all drinkers, rather than only heavy drinkers, to reduce their consumption. The fallacies in such an argument are several. There are about nine times more moderate drinkers than heavy drinkers. Further, many heavy drinkers experience several alcohol-related problems, and these problems are more frequent and far more serious than those experienced by moderate drinkers. National policy should not be based on equating a headache with vehicular homicide or a spouse's scolding with imprisonment for rape. One of the few constants overlooked in my earlier reviews of the cross-cultural literature is the role of acute intoxication as a preamble to those kinds of drinking outcomes that are censured as culturally unacceptable, usually because they interfere with others as well as with the drinker.

CULTURE AND CHOICE OF BEVERAGE

Although many beverage alcohols are used throughout the world, they are usually grouped into three basic types: beer, wine, and spirits. An even simpler dichotomy that is sometimes useful is between fermented beverages (beers and wines, rarely over 18 percent ethanol) and distilled beverages (spirits or liquor, as high as 90 percent ethanol). To a remarkable degree, the outcomes are similar whether the base is a fruit, vegetable, berry, sap, cereal, or tuber, although matters of taste and custom carry immense symbolic and other significance.

For different analytic purposes, it is worth distinguishing home-brewed beers from pasteurized or factory-made beers and legal distillates from illegal distillates (moonshine), although nutritional and other qualities may favor either over the other. Interestingly, although beverage alcohol is usually an important category for tax collectors and for various researchers, it is often ignored in lay usage. Many beer drinkers do not consider beer alcoholic, just as many wine drinkers view wine as food. (Much of French governmental policy is founded on the distinction between wine as food, or hygienic beverage, and beer or spirits as alcohol.) The idea of equating the absolute alcohol in each U.S. "standard drink" or U.K. "unit" is a convenient conceit for those who put considerable stock in statistics that purport to reflect average per capita consumption for various jurisdictions; the weaknesses of such figures are discussed in detail in chapter 12 of this volume.

In keeping with the fallacious but convenient custom of stereotyping, it has become common for those discussing drinking patterns and problems sometimes to refer to a "beer culture," a "wine culture," or a "spirits culture." The real meaning of those terms is that they allow easy categorization, comparisons, and contrasts, even while we recognize how imperfect such categories are. Many readers probably think of Germany as the quintessential beer culture, with images of giant kegs and steins, Oktoberfest, and beer as a major ingredient in cooking. But the fact is, many areas of Germany produce and drink far more wine or spirits than beer. Perhaps ancient Egypt came closer to being a beer culture; beer was a major part of the diet, important in religious ceremonies, and thought to be indispensable to the dead (Ashour 1995). Australia went from being a spirits culture to a beer culture in the late 1800s. Iceland and Denmark both changed from beer to spirits and then back again.

In Zambia many native cultures were based on large-scale use of home-brewed beers, which were important on various counts (Haworth 1995). Home brewing provided a source of income for women, who dominated the trade; beer drinking was important for male sociability; and beer provided a nutritious food for both sexes and all ages. A ceremonial drink of beer was used to seal agreements and contracts, as an adjunct to communal decision making and judicial procedures, and as a gift to the ancestors and certain supernatural beings. As has been dramatically documented by Colson and Scudder (1988), these cultures are now undergoing drastic change as wage earners shift to drinking factory-made beer. Heavy drinking on weekends or paydays is common and is isolated from the traditional pace of life. Women have lost independence and prestige, as well as cash, because there is little demand for their brewing skills. Profits leave the community, and the contexts and meanings of drinking have become very different.

The term *wine culture* refers to areas of France, Italy, Spain, Portugal, Greece, the former Yugoslavia, and other circum-Mediterranean zones where viticulture predominates. Wine is an integral part of daily living and is vaunted in folktales, proverbs, and popular wisdom as a general tonic that strengthens the blood, purifies the body, helps nursing mothers, cures many ills, seals bonds of friendship, rounds out meals, and is otherwise indispensable. Chile and Argentina are examples of nations in the Western Hemisphere that have wine cultures. Georgia and Armenia, once part of the former Soviet Union, are unusual for their wine cultures in an area largely marked by minimal drinking or by spirits drinking.

Spirits cultures may not offer as many reasons to focus on drinking, but they emphasize spirits in whatever drinking does take place. Russia, Finland, Sweden, and Norway exemplify this pattern, while Ireland and Scotland have a similar popular image, although beer may actually be drunk more than spirits.

These three cultures have different drinking patterns and different drinking outcomes. Wine cultures stereotypically have extremely high rates of per capita consumption, coupled with extremely low rates of most kinds of problems, presumably because drinking is so functionally integrated with the culture. The one alcohol-related problem that often occurs in wine cultures is cirrhosis, although it often results from other causes as well. Spirits cultures are often marked by all-male drinking bouts in which drinking is the focus rather than an accompaniment to other activities. Spirits cultures commonly have less concern for moderation; drunkenness is often actively sought and used as an excuse for antisocial or asocial behavior that is thought to result from disinhibition. Beer cultures often have high rates of accidents and gang violence (as among the United Kingdom's infamous "lager louts" following soccer games) but not the lasting psychological and social problems common in spirits cultures.

TYPES OF DRINKING CULTURES

Apart from the very crude identification of cultures with the predominant type of beverage as described above, Eric Single and Victor Leino (chapter 1, this volume) are quite correct in noting that "there is no universally recognized typology of drinking cultures." However, a few typologies have been suggested, each based on different bundles of criteria, and it is appropriate in this context to briefly describe them and the limited heuristic values they offer.

One way of typologizing drinking cultures has been geographic. Even that is not as simple as it might appear, inasmuch as the areas or regions with which cultures are identified are by no means uniform, nor are they easily comparable along dimensions other than patterns of alcohol use. For example, one might speak of a French drinking culture without realizing that there is enormous regional variation in France. There are indeed parts that are famous throughout the world for the quality of their wine, where wine is ubiquitous, esteemed, and widely consumed throughout the day. But other areas produce and use apple cider in similar ways, whereas in still other regions beer or spirits is the predominant beverage.

Of course, nations are not cultures, anyway; some cultures cross the boundaries of nation-states, just as most nation-states contain many cultures (Heath 1995a, 1997). Slightly less inaccurate are references to gross regional differences, as the concept of a Mediterranean drinking culture marked by frequent drinking of wine, usually with meals, a view of drinking as salutary and healthful, and general repudiation of drunkenness. In contrast, Nordic drinking cultures are associated with episodic drunkenness by males, using predominantly spirits without food, and seeking drunkenness as an unhealthful but psychically necessary escape.

Another dichotomous classification of drinking cultures sets ''dry'' against ''wet'' types. A wet culture combines high per capita consumption with generally permissive attitudes toward drinking (by women and youths as well as by men) and acceptance of beverage alcohol as an integral part of everyday living. A dry culture features many abstainers, episodic (and occasionally heavy) drinking, strong sanctions against drinking, and a mystique about alcohol as a powerful substance, unsafe in quotidian contexts. Subtly linked with those relatively overt differences are some less obvious ones: dry cultures are often ambivalent about drinking, and wet cultures seldom think about drinking per se. Drinking tends to be a focus of attention far more in a dry culture than in a wet one, and alcohol-related problems often occur in inverse proportion to consumption. This cross-cultural commonplace is contrary to a misreading of findings by Bruun et al. (1975) that became a pseudoscientific basis for policy recommendations on the part of the World Health Organization, the U.S. National Institute on Alcohol Abuse and Alcoholism, and other agencies. These bodies have stressed restrictions on availability and consumption for all, rather than limitations on excessive drinkers. How such a persistent new temperance movement originated, spread, and came to dominate discussions of alcohol and public health is a fascinating story, nicely chronicled by Room (1990).

Temperance cultures are rare but historically important, each marked by a long sequence of popular movements that have labeled alcohol as an important source of problems (Levine 1992; Room 1992). They occur in the Nordic countries and a few English-speaking areas and are characterized by a lingering ambivalence about beverage alcohol: an appreciation of what moderate amounts can do for enjoyment but a fear of the negative consequences of overindulgence. There is often a moralistic, almost puritanical, substrate to such attitudes, including a distrust of hedonism and more emphasis on the commonweal than on individual independence. The individual is generally viewed as a weak vessel, subject to temptation and corruption by a demonic and powerful substance.

CULTURE AND RISK

Just as culture plays important roles in the shaping of drinking patterns, it also plays important roles in the shaping of risks for different kinds of drinking problems. The fundamental question, What constitutes a problem? is not as clear as most would believe. Beauchamp (1973) could justifiably complain that the main obstacle to public support for alcoholism programs was the virtual invisibility of the problem, because most people saw alcoholics as deviants whose problems had little to do with the rest of the population. Wiener's (1981) early study is still one of the best descriptions of the social process by which competing groups of claim makers negotiate to achieve sufficient consensus so that a given topic—in this instance, alcoholism—becomes identified as a social problem and so comes onto the agenda. Part of the evidence for that study derived from the recognition that there is no single criterion that distinguishes alcoholics (or problem drinkers) from other drinkers, thus bringing the substance alcohol into focus for research from a number of different angles. It is only since then that most people have come to recognize that a biopsychosocial approach is required to understand drinking patterns.

Contrary to popular belief, the prevalence of many alcohol-related problems is not directly related to average annual per capita consumption. Often, in fact, the results are diametrically opposite to those that would be predicted by the distribution-of-consumption model. A brief but striking example is the well-documented contrast between France and Ireland a few years ago. France had almost the highest consumption in the world, whereas Ireland had around the lowest consumption in Europe. Yet the Irish registered high rates of spousal abuse, aggression, psychiatric hospitalization, and many other indexes of alcohol-related problems. France, by contrast, was relatively low in the frequency of those and most other indexes of problem drinking. It is tempting to point to cultural differences as crucial, with frustrated Irish males drinking together at the pub in a context where violence was condoned, acting out in ways that would never be accepted among French familial drinkers, who drink at home in an ambience that did not tolerate abusive drunkenness. Since the 1980s, French and Irish consumption levels have tended to converge, but evidence about the other variables is lacking.

Another anomaly in alcohol-related problems came to light in the southwestern United States, where Hopi Indians live on a small reservation entirely surrounded by that of the Navaho (Kunitz et al. 1971). Investigators were initially surprised to find a high rate of alcohol-related cirrhosis among the Hopi, farmers known for their abstemious ways in virtually all realms of life, compared with a low rate among the Navaho, seminomadic herders with a reputation for sporadic excessive behaviors. Close observation of actual behavior patterns showed that occasional heavy drinking by a Navaho was accepted and kinfolk were supportive. By contrast, a Hopi who drank was ostracized from the village and joined a small band of fellow outcasts in a rural version of skid row, where the lifestyle resulted in sufficient cases of cirrhosis to skew the data among the small Hopi population. Biological and epidemiological indexes can be strongly affected by social and cultural attitudes and relationships.

Few systematic investigations have specifically dealt with religion as a risk factor in relation to drinking problems, but observers who are familiar with the data have long noticed that members of churches that forbid drinking tend very quickly to move from initial experimentation to full-fledged problem drinking. In social and cultural terms, the risk would appear to be that, when proscriptive norms are violated, an actor can be at a loss if there are no prescriptive norms to serve as guidelines as to the limits of acceptability of various actions.

Quantification is weak, partly because there is not yet adequate consensus about what the key variables are and how they might best be measured. Even in those instances where there is apparent agreement about potentially important variables (per capita consumption, quantity and frequency of drinking, death by cirrhosis, blood alcohol level, etc.), data are abundant but not particularly trustworthy. In part, this has to do with difficulties in cross-cultural meanings—not simply translation from one language to another but inconsistency in truly fundamental factors. For example, in most cultures, there is no standard volume for "a drink," and even in the overstudied and overquantified North American and Western European cultures, the range of alcohol content in various drinks is far greater than we admit to in our conventions of mathematical conversion. In some cultures a hangover cannot even be imagined and drinking cannot be conceived as anything but enjoyable. Serious, ambitious, and well-planned recent efforts at achieving cross-cultural comparability of basic diagnostic criteria have foundered, despite enormous investments of time, thought, money, and effort (e.g., Bennett et al. 1993; Helzer and Canino 1992).

It does not in any way detract from the value of new data and findings—especially those that stem from imaginative efforts to combine quantitative and qualitative approaches, as I have long recommended—to admit that the practical implications of a sociocultural perspective have changed little since they were summarized at the height of the popular dialogue about drinking and its outcomes around the world (Heath 1988):

> The increasing attention that has been paid to special populations in recent years is a reflection of the widespread acceptance of the importance of sociocultural perspectives:
>
> - The unquestioned epidemiological fact that different populations have different rates of alcohol-related problems and that they also have different kinds of problems demonstrates the reality of difference in human responses to ethanol. It is often the case that those different kinds and rates of problems can be clearly shown to have a direct relationship to specific patterns of belief and behavior.
> - Such ethnographic data on cultural differences provide insights that may have immediate utility at many levels of practical concern, such as the search for effective measures for prevention. (p. 398)

Without recapitulating illustrative examples that have been described and analyzed by several authors, dealing with cultures at various times and places, it seems appropriate here to mention some of the factors that have been identified at the cultural level of analysis either as putting individuals at risk in connection with drinking or as diminishing such risk.

For example, ambivalence about beverage alcohol appears to be a much more dangerous stance than either open acceptance or rejection of it (Room 1976). Cultures that hedge beverage alcohol around with a special mystique imbue it with symbolic power that can be far more potent than its pharmacological effect, thereby creating risk for those who aspire to participate in those positive symbols.

It has long been known that ethanol has less impact on mood, cognition, coordination, speech, and so on when the organism has a full rather than an empty stomach. Eating before or while drinking is an easy and pleasant way to reduce risk. Also, paying attention to other matters—conversation, activities, and so forth—results in less intoxication (and hence fewer problems) than focusing on drinking as an end in itself or as a means of forgetting, relieving stress, or getting drunk. Avoiding intoxication and adhering to guidelines that distinguish acceptable from unacceptable behaviors also dramatically lessen the risks from drinking.

CONCLUSIONS AND IMPLICATIONS

It goes without saying that the traditional scientific method of experimentation by manipulating variables is out of the question when dealing with human populations and their cultures. Quite apart from ethical concerns, the life span of the human animal and the complexity of any cultural system make that impossible. That does not mean, however, that we must rely on anecdotes and guesswork in our quest for understandings and generalizations in the field of social and cultural studies. Vulcanology, meteorology, and astronomy are no less scientific because their practitioners are similarly unable to manipulate the relevant variables in their studies. Close observation, with minute description, and controlled comparison (often dealing with so-called natural experiments, in which different systems may vary in a few key respects) are valuable, especially when other systems with other differences allow for cautious pattern analysis and even prediction. The same can be done with respect to cultural variations in both patterns of drinking and patterns of problems. As noted previously (Heath 1988):

- Without a good understanding of the norms of a population, it is difficult to make early identification of individuals who are at high risk for many kinds of alcohol-related problems or who are showing early signs that such problems may develop.
- Similarly, a great many of the drinking problems in any population defy diagnosis unless one is familiar with cultural norms and expectations.
- Among the several approaches to treatment that are available, some are appropriate to members of one culture but not another. (pp. 398–399)

A cultural perspective tries to be holistic in describing and evaluating all patterns of drinking and patterns of problems. It is premised on meticulous attention to context and meanings, inasmuch as social norms are subtly imbedded in, reflective of, and responsive to those aspects of culture. Ethnographic comparisons of contemporary cultures and historical comparisons of their pasts both demonstrate that the distribution-of-consumption model is simplistic and inadequate. More complex, but far more promising, is the sociocultural model. Here, the process of social learning is one key, but empathetic concern for meanings and values in all realms of belief and behavior is also a requisite for intelligent analysis and realistic implementation of changes. In dealing with human behavior, a failure to deal with cultural variation is not only self-defeating, but counterproductive.

REFERENCES

American Psychiatric Association. 1994. *Diagnostic and Statistical Manual of Mental Disorders*. 4th rev. ed. Washington, D.C.: American Psychiatric Association Press.

Ashour, A. M. 1995. Egypt. In *International Handbook on Alcohol and Culture*, ed. D. B. Heath. Westport, Conn.: Greenwood.

Ásmundsson, G. 1995. Iceland. In *International Handbook on Alcohol and Culture*, ed. D. B. Heath. Westport, Conn.: Greenwood.

Badri, M. B. 1976. *Islam and Alcoholism*. Takoma Park, Md.: American Trust.

Bales, R. F. 1946. Cultural differences in rates of alcoholism. *Quarterly Journal of Studies on Alcoholism* 6:480–99.

Beauchamp, D. E. 1973. Precarious politics: alcoholism and public policy. Ph.D. diss., Johns Hopkins University.

Bennett, L. A., A. Janca, B. F. Grant, and N. Sartorius. 1993. Boundaries between normal and pathological drinking: a cross-cultural comparison. *Alcohol Health and Research World* 17:190–95.

Bruun, K., et al. 1975. *Alcohol Control Policies in a Public Health Perspective*. Vol. 25. Helsinki: Finnish Foundation for Alcohol Studies.

Carstairs, G. M. 1954. Daru and bhang: cultural factors in the choice of intoxicant. *Quarterly Journal of Studies on Alcohol* 15:220–37.

Colson, E., and T. Scudder. 1988. *For Prayer and Profit: The Ritual, Economic, and Social Importance of Beer in Gwembe District, Zambia, 1950–1982*. Palo Alto: Stanford University Press.

Cook, J., and M. Lewington, eds. 1979. *Images of Alcoholism*. London: British Film Institute.

Duster, T. 1983. Commentary. In *Alcohol and Disinhibition: Nature and Meaning of the Link*, ed. R. Room and G. Collins. Research Monograph 12. Rockville, Md.: National Institute on Alcohol Abuse and Alcoholism.

Gusfield, J. R. 1987. Passage to play: rituals and drinking time in American society. In *Constructive Drinking: Perspectives on Drink from Anthropology*, ed. M. Douglas. Cambridge: Cambridge University Press.

Hall, W., and E. Hunter. 1995. Australia. In *International Handbook on Alcohol and Culture*, ed. D. B. Heath. Westport, Conn.: Greenwood.

Haworth, A. 1995. Zambia. In *International Handbook on Alcohol and Culture,* ed. D. B. Heath. Westport, Conn.: Greenwood.

Heath, D. B. 1958. Drinking patterns of the Bolivian Camba. *Quarterly Journal of Studies on Alcohol* 19:491–508.

———. 1975. A critical review of ethnographic studies of alcohol use. In *Research Advances in Alcohol and Drug Problems,* ed. R. J. Gibbons et al. Vol. 2. New York: Wiley.

———. 1987a. A decade of development in the anthropological study of alcohol use, 1970–1980. In *Constructive Drinking: Perspectives on Drinking from Anthropology,* ed. M. Douglas. Cambridge: Cambridge University Press.

———. 1987b. Anthropology and alcohol studies: current issues. *Annual Review of Anthropology* 16:99–120.

———. 1988. Emerging anthropological theory and models of alcohol use and alcoholism. In *Theories on Alcoholism,* ed. C. D. Chaudron and D. A. Wilkinson. Toronto: Addiction Research Foundation.

———. 1991. Uses and misuses of the concept of ethnicity in alcohol studies: an essay in deconstruction. *International Journal of the Addictions* 25:609–630.

———. 1993. Anthropology. In *Recent Developments in Alcoholism,* ed. M. Galanter. Vol. 11. New York: Plenum.

———. 1994. Cross-cultural perspectives on women and alcohol. In *Women and Substance Abuse,* ed. E. S. Lisansky-Gomberg and T. D. Nirenberg. Norwood, N.J.: Ablex.

———, ed. 1995a. *International Handbook on Alcohol and Culture.* Westport, Conn.: Greenwood.

———. 1995b. Alcohol: history of drinking. In *Encyclopedia of Drugs and Alcohol,* ed. J. Jaffe. Vol. 1. New York: Macmillan.

———. 1997. Culture. In *Sourcebook on Substance Use and Abuse (PP-PP),* ed. R. S. Tarter, R. T. Ammerman, and P. J. Ott. Needham Heights, Mass.: Allyn and Bacon.

Helzer, J. E., and G. J. Canino, eds. 1992. *Alcoholism in North America, Europe, and Asia.* Oxford: Oxford University Press.

Holyfield, L., L. J. Ducharme, and J. K. Martin. 1995. Drinking contexts, alcohol beliefs, and patterns of alcohol consumption: evidence for a comprehensive model of problem drinking. *Journal of Drug Issues* 25:783–98.

Kroeber, A. L., and C. K. M. Kluckhohn. 1952. *Culture: A Critical Review of Concepts and Definitions.* Paper 47. Cambridge: Harvard University, Peabody Museum of American Archaeology and Ethnology.

Kunitz, S. J., J. E. Levy, C. L. Odoroff, and J. Bollinger. 1971. The epidemiology of alcoholic cirrhosis in two southwestern Indian tribes. *Quarterly Journal of Studies on Alcohol* 32:706–20.

Kyvig, D. E., ed. 1985. *Law, Alcohol, and Order: Perspectives on National Prohibition.* Westport, Conn.: Greenwood.

Levine, H. G. 1992. Temperance cultures: alcohol as problem in Nordic- and English-speaking countries. In *The Nature of Alcohol and Drug-Related Problems,* ed. M. Lender and G. Edwards. Oxford: Oxford University Press.

MacAndrew, C., and R. Edgerton. 1969. *Drunken Comportment: A Social Explanation.* Chicago: Aldine.

Marlatt, G. A., and D. Rohsenow. 1980. Cognitive processes in alcohol use: expectancy and the balanced placebo design. In *Advances in Substance Abuse: Behavioral and Biological Research,* ed. N. Mello. Vol. 1. Greenwich, Conn.: JAI.

Marshall, M., ed. 1982. *Through a Glass Darkly: Beer and Modernization in Papua New Guinea.* Monograph 18. Boroko: Institute of Applied Social and Economic Research.

Medina Cárdenas, E. 1995. Chile. In *International Handbook on Alcohol and Culture,* ed. D. B. Heath. Westport, Conn.: Greenwood.

Musto, D. F. 1987. *The American Disease: Origins of Narcotic Control.* Rev. ed. New York: Oxford University Press.

Room, R. 1976. Ambivalence as a sociological explanation: the case of cultural explanations of alcohol problems. *American Sociological Review* 41:1047–65.

———. 1990. Social science research and alcohol policy making. In *Alcohol: The Development of Sociological Perspectives on Use and Abuse,* ed. P. M. Roman. New Brunswick: Rutgers University, Center of Alcohol Studies.

———. 1992. The impossible dream? Routes to reducing alcohol problems in a temperate culture. *Journal of Substance Abuse* 4:91–106.

Rorabaugh, W. J. 1979. *The Alcoholic Republic: An American Tradition.* New York: Oxford University Press.

U.K. Department of Health and Social Security. 1995. *Sensible Drinking: The Report of an Interdepartmental Working Group.* London: HMSO.

USDA/USDHHS. 1995. *Nutrition and Your Health: Dietary Guidelines for Americans.* 4th ed. Washington, D.C.: USGPO.

Wallace, A. F. C. 1970. *The Death and Rebirth of the Seneca.* New York: Knopf.

WHO. 1981. *Global Strategy for Health for All by the Year 2000.* Health for All Series 3. Geneva: World Health Organization.

Wiener, C. 1981. *The Politics of Alcoholism: Building an Arena around a Social Problem.* New Brunswick, N.J.: Transaction.

Part Two

Policies and Programs

As the first section of this book demonstrated, patterns of drinking are more useful and more flexible predictors of both positive and negative outcomes of alcohol consumption than is the traditional approach originally proposed by Ledermann which emphasizes levels of consumption. Strong empirical evidence supports an approach to alcohol policy development in which it is more relevant to focus on individual problematic drinking behaviors.

In light of such evidence, a fresh approach to alcohol policies is needed that is able to take into account individual variations in drinking behavior, cultural context, and individual outcomes. Such a model requires that policy measures move away from a general population approach and address harmful patterns of drinking within their social and cultural context.

The following section of *Drinking Patterns and Their Consequences* reviews the model of the "single distribution theory," reassessing available empirical data on current strategies for harm reduction. Addressed is the effectiveness of various control measures on reducing adverse outcomes of alcohol consumption, both from a historical perspective and with a focus on measures currently implemented in a number of countries around the world.

As control measures are largely based on social cost, the authors evaluate both the theory and practice of social cost estimation within the context of alcohol consumption. It is proposed that the current measures of social cost may result in incorrect policy prescriptions and may thereby detract from areas truly meriting public intervention. This section also examines how greater emphasis on patterns of drinking rather than levels of consumption would affect the assessment of social cost and thereby also any approaches to prevention.

Finally, the implications of a paradigm shift toward a model focusing on patterns rather than levels of drinking as more reliable predictors of outcomes require that different perspectives be taken into account when developing policy models. The contributions to this section examine methodologies that have been used in previous approaches to intervention. A more informal approach to alcohol policy development is proposed, which emphasizes patterns of drinking and educational measures within their appropriate cultural context. It is suggested that this more integrative approach would provide a viable alternative to the more rigid control policies of the past.

Chapter 7

The Distribution of Alcohol Consumption

John B. Saunders and Simon de Burgh

Alcohol consumption is often considered purely as an individual behavior, but it is strongly influenced by a person's social network and the culture in which he or she is living. Factors that influence drinking behavior include the alcohol consumption of friends and family, the extent to which drinking is sanctioned or encouraged by that culture, and the cost of, and access to, alcoholic drinks. A recurring challenge for scholars and researchers has been to develop a conceptual model to relate individual consumption to population consumption. If such a model could be devised, it could lead to approaches that, when applied to whole populations, would reduce alcohol problems at a fraction of the cost of interventions directed at individuals.

The purpose of this chapter is to review work on population consumption distributions. To introduce this work, we first describe some of the ways in which alcohol use and misuse have been conceptualized by alcohol researchers. We then examine the work of Ledermann, who described the single-distribution theory of alcohol consumption (Ledermann 1956). This was an early attempt to fit drinking behavior into a mathematical model. We discuss the extent to which the empirical evidence supports Ledermann's model as well as prevention the-

John B. Saunders is with the Centre for Drug and Alcohol Studies, Department of Psychiatry, University of Queensland, Australia. Simon de Burgh is with the Drug and Alcohol Unit, Prince of Wales Hospital and National Drug and Alcohol Research Centre, University of New South Wales, Australia. Part of this work was supported by the Thyne Reid Educational Trust.

ories inspired by it. We then review developments in distribution theory, examine the implications of alcohol's beneficial effects, and discuss the relevance of distribution theories for the development of alcohol policies.

INDIVIDUAL VERSUS POPULATION PERSPECTIVES OF ALCOHOL USE AND MISUSE

The Disease Concept

In the 200 years that alcohol problems have been the subject of scientific enquiry, the concept that there is a discrete disease, alcoholism, has received much support. Alcoholism is held by proponents of this view to be of largely biological causation and to have a predictable natural history. In this formulation, an underlying abnormality drives the behavior, which is little influenced by the cost and availability of alcohol or by sociocultural issues. When the disease is established in an individual, the pattern of alcohol consumption is essentially unvarying. The prevalence of alcoholism in the population inevitably influences the overall level of consumption in that society. Put simply, the more alcoholics in a community, the higher the level of consumption, whether or not the drinking behavior of other individuals is influenced by them.

The disease concept reached its apotheosis with the work of Jellinek (1952) in the years following the Second World War. In 1952 he published his formulation of alcoholism as a unitary disease and developed this by describing five subtypes, at least two of which were considered to be disease entities (Jellinek 1960). Gamma alcoholism, typical in Anglo-Saxon countries, was characterized by increased tolerance to alcohol, withdrawal symptoms, craving, and loss of control over drinking. Delta alcoholism, seen in wine-producing countries, was similar but "instead of loss of control there is inability to abstain" (ibid.). The main implication of the disease model was that for most cases the recommended goal was total abstinence.

The Quantitative Tradition

A contrary tradition took root in France in the 1950s. Instead of alcoholism as a condition, the focus of study was the relationship between the occurrence of various diseases and levels of consumption by individuals (and populations). In a series of case-control studies, Péquignot (1960) investigated the risk of morbidity from various diseases (such as cirrhosis, various cancers, pancreatic disease, and psychosis) at various levels of alcohol intake. For example, the risk of cirrhosis was found to increase above a threshold of 80 grams alcohol per day. This threshold was subsequently revised downward (Péquignot et al. 1974) to 40 grams a day for men and 20 grams a day for women. The relationship between alcohol intake and the risk of certain other conditions (e.g., chronic pancreatitis) was a linear one, with no evidence of a threshold level.

The Epidemiological School

At the same time in France, Ledermann (1956) introduced the concept that the level of alcohol consumption in the population as a whole was the primary determinant of the rate of occurrence of alcohol-related problems. In population studies there was no evidence of a bimodal distribution of alcohol intake, no separate "hump" in the curve indicating a population of "alcoholics" distinct from "normal drinkers." Subsequently, alcohol-related problems were shown to have a unimodal distribution, implying a continuum of risk, not a separation of "safe" and "harmful" drinking (Cartwright, Shaw, and Spratley 1978). In fact, among adherents of the epidemiological outlook it became accepted that moderate drinkers produce more alcohol problems, because there are many more of them than of heavy drinkers. This is the preventive paradox, a prominent concept since the mid 1980s (Kreitman 1986).

Psychological and Sociological Models

Two other prominent schools of thought have contributed to our understanding of alcohol use and misuse. In social learning theory, substance misuse is seen as the result of the way the individual has learned to use that substance, mediated by interactions between the individual's personality and the social and cultural environment (Bandura 1977). Alcohol-related problems are seen as diverse events, each with its particular set of causes and not showing any special tendency to cluster, as would be expected if there were an underlying syndrome. A sociological perspective sees health as primarily a product of the social and economic environment. Psychological and sociological models have tended to avoid labeling or dose-response considerations, which smack too much of a biomedical influence.

The Dependence Model

In 1976 Edwards and Gross introduced the concept of a dependence syndrome. It encapsulated a set of behaviors and physiological features that were considered to provide the driving force for persistently harmful drinking. They included impaired control over drinking, orientation of life around alcohol, continued drinking despite harm, and in many cases, tolerance and withdrawal symptoms on cessation of drinking. The dependence syndrome did not imply any causative mechanisms or any direct relationship to the quantity of alcohol consumed (Edwards, Arif, and Hodgson 1981). This concept has been widely accepted as an appropriate middle ground between the disease concept and those traditions that see quantity of alcohol consumed as the primary issue.

Conclusions

Thus, alcohol problems can be examined from several perspectives, which may be complementary or compete. Among clinicians, the categorical disease model continues to hold sway in many countries, especially in North America. In Western Europe a quantitative, dose-response model linking individual and population consumption to problems has been paramount, and it has strongly influenced policy recommendations of the World Health Organization. Distribution theory has been most closely aligned with this tradition. Meanwhile, general health professionals have adopted an intuitive position with little conceptual content: for instance, "Excessive drinking causes problems, so limit your drinks," or "Drinking in certain situations is risky, so if (for example) you drive, don't drink." This is the patterns and limits policy, which is now receiving serious attention from policy theorists and is the subject of this book.

DISTRIBUTION THEORIES

Ledermann's Single-Distribution Model

In the years following the Second World War, in a setting of high, indeed prodigious, intake of alcohol, Ledermann observed that the mortality of the French was high compared with other European countries. In a series of epidemiological studies he linked high alcohol intake to high mortality rates (Ledermann 1956). The French public took a liberal view of alcohol and regarded the casualties of alcohol as an unfortunate few, separate from ordinary drinkers. Ledermann argued that ordinary drinking was the problem and that the French drank too much. He took a population view of an individual behavior.

Like many behaviors and natural phenomena, drinking in a population can be represented graphically by plotting average intake against the number or percentage of drinkers. Ledermann made this process familiar to the alcohol field. As with many other phenomena, Ledermann's (smoothed) curve had two notable features: the bulk of drinkers gathered in one peak near the zero end of the curve, and there was a long tail or skew to the right containing the minority of heavy drinkers. Importantly, there was no separate peak of heavy drinkers. The immediate conclusion was that heavy drinkers did not form a separate population but were part of the continuum of the distribution.

Ledermann's pivotal hypothesis was that the proportion of drinkers with an intake over a specified amount, say 100 grams of alcohol per day, had a fixed relationship to the population average intake. He argued that heavy drinking cannot be reduced by interventions aimed at heavy drinkers alone but only by reducing overall population drinking. The Ledermann approach to preventing alcohol problems therefore consists of general discouragements to drinking: reduced availability, increased taxes on alcohol, and mass propaganda.

This supposed fixed relationship (between population mean and percentage of heavy drinkers) was expressed in the Ledermann formula, a statistical device that joined all distributions into one mathematical family. Thus it was suggested that the same formula would predict the proportion of heavy drinkers in both a population with low mean intake (e.g., Norway) and one with a high mean intake (e.g., France). Hence the alternative name, single-distribution theory. This feat was to be achieved by two key assumptions. The first was that all distributions could be described satisfactorily by a lognormal curve (a curve with a long tail to the right). When the logarithm of each value is plotted (instead of the untransformed value), the distribution reverts to the familiar bell-shaped Gaussian, or normal, distribution curve. The second assumption was that for any population of drinkers there would be the same tiny proportion (0.03 percent) with an intake above an extreme value, which was taken to be 1 liter of (pure) alcohol per day. Of course, there is no reason to believe that any such constant proportion exists in reality, and Ledermann gave no justification for the assumption (Skog 1985). It was simply a device to provide a formula that linked all distributions in one mathematical family.

There was also a third assumption in the Ledermann theory: that it applied to homogeneous populations. Apart from the question of how much variety might be permitted in a homogeneous population, it is immediately clear that populations containing both men and women are not homogeneous with respect to alcohol intake. Ledermann mentioned a further term in the formula to accommodate heterogeneity, but such a term would disconnect the mathematical relation between distributions; they would no longer form a single-distribution family. Indeed, the heterogeneity term received no further attention from him.

There was, all the same, a more valid idea in Ledermann's proposal, even though obscurely and incompletely expressed (de Burgh 1990). Drinking is a social ("contagious") activity, so that changes in drinking habits are brought about by social pressures. Drinkers, light or heavy, tend to influence others' drinking, so that changes spread through the drinking population. This picture is intuitively attractive, and it was later developed explicitly by Skog (1985). Ledermann, however, used it in an attempted justification of the lognormal form: the law of proportionate effect states that a variable (e.g., the size of a plant) tends to be distributed lognormally if the effects of stimuli are proportionate to the original value of the variable (Aitchison and Brown 1957). Or put another way, the effects are multiplicative rather than additive.

The mathematical basis for Ledermann's curve was weak. Moreover, the rationale for the prevention theory inspired by it was poorly developed and, in fact, contrived (de Burgh 1990). While the control-of-consumption approach is supposed to follow from Ledermann's curve, it actually predates it by at least five years. Ledermann and Tabah (1951) noted falls in excess mortality among men following alcohol control measures in Sweden (in 1885 and 1917) and Denmark (in 1917) and during the Second World War alcohol restrictions in France. Later papers referred to the quantity of alcoholic beverages available to the population (Ledermann 1952) and to the consequent advantages of taxation of alcohol and control of outlets (Ledermann 1953). In 1953 Ledermann proposed that alcohol consumption was distributed lognormally. The curve proposed in 1953 differed from the well-known 1956 curve, having a greater dispersion, with more light and heavy drinkers. No family of curves was proposed. In other words, the 1956 Ledermann formula was concocted to support an existing view. This view made perfect sense in the France of the 1950s, but it was a common-sense idea, not a technical one.

In 1964 Ledermann published another monograph with more empirical data, with which to demonstrate his model. However, although this work showed a connection between mean consumption and prevalence of heavy drinkers, it did not test the theory. There was no test of the statistical significance of the idea, the hypotheses of lognormality, or the existence or value of the constant, θ, which gives the figure of 0.03 percent as the prevalence of heaviest drinkers (Skog 1982). Even so, when unsuitable or inadequate data sets are removed from Ledermann's collection, a fairly consistent relationship between heavy drinking and average consumption is evident (ibid.). We consider later whether that relationship implies a statistical law and what it means for prevention policy.

The Career of the Curve

In the 1960s Ledermann's ideas aroused interest overseas. At the Addiction Research Foundation in Toronto, Seeley (1960) showed that liver cirrhosis mortality in Canada correlated remarkably well with changes in per capita alcohol consumption and that the correlation between consumption and the relative price of alcohol was also strong. When the price went down, consumption went up. The Canadian group was in tune with Ledermann's thinking, for it recognized the need for distribution data to interpret these relationships.

Other reactions were skeptical, with doubts about whether North American population consumption would obey any statistical law. Also, the Ledermann formula underestimated the number of alcoholics, as judged by the Jellinek formula (using cirrhosis mortality rates) and survey results (de Lint and Bronetto 1964). However, doubt turned to enthusiasm when a number of distributions were examined to test the Ledermann model. Purchase order forms (de Lint and Schmidt 1968) and blood alcohol concentrations of drivers (Smart and Schmidt 1970) were found to fit the Ledermann curve. Also, Schmidt and de Lint (1970) reapplied the Ledermann formula to estimate the number of alcoholics. They used an empirically derived intake for an "alcoholic" of 150 milliliters per day, instead of Ledermann's 200 milliliters, and found that the discrepancy with the Jellinek formula disappeared. The effect of the numbers falling into place in this way must have been most persuasive.

On the other hand, these tests represented only a limited range of times and cultures. Blood alcohol readings taken from drivers are not equivalent to population consumption. The purchase orders only included information on a third of drinkers (de Lint and Schmidt 1968) and therefore should not have conformed to the Ledermann curve (de Burgh 1990). Even the finding of lognormality was considered invalid by other authors (Skog 1983; O'Neill and Wells 1971).

Nevertheless, the findings convinced the Canadian group. It held that the Ledermann curve had been validated for a variety of populations and began using the Ledermann formula to estimate the number of alcoholics in various countries from per capita consumption figures (de Lint and Schmidt 1971). It continued in this vein over many years, describing the epidemiology of alcoholism as if the Ledermann formula gave highly accurate estimates for any population. It did not subject the formula to further critical analysis or development but relied on the evidence already mentioned and on correlations between consumption figures and cirrhosis mortality. The Canadian group also accepted Ledermann's view of what the model meant for prevention policy: "Since the rates of alcoholism rise and fall with the overall level of alcohol use in a population, a reduction in the per capita alcohol consumption must lead to lower rates of alcoholism. For this reason the taxation of beverage alcohol and, in general, all control measures that reduce accessibility appear to be effective, particularly if there is also a wide acceptance of the public health value of such controls" (de Lindt and Schmidt 1971).

The Canadians later conceded that Ledermann's model could only be a rough approximation (Schmidt and Popham 1978), but they, along with many allies, maintained that the model could be regarded as a quasi-mathematical law. That is, "the general character of the distribution is unalterable" (Popham, Schmidt, and de Lint 1978). The degree of commitment to this view is surprising given the limited amount of evidence. A partial explanation is provided by Schmidt and Popham (1978), who referred to the view prevalent in the 1960s that favored increasing the availability of alcohol in order to "demystify" and "civilize" drinking habits (Chafetz 1967). This view ignored the medical consequences of chronic heavy consumption. Schmidt and Popham (1978) admitted to some overstatement and oversimplification in their earlier work in order to secure a hearing for heterodox ideas.

Room (1978) has pointed out an irony in the shift of thinking in the Canadian group. The first policy comments of de Lint and Schmidt (1968) connected with their distribution work were quite tentative. It was the policy-making arm of the Addiction Research Foundation that seized upon their research analysis "as an organizing tool for a coherent alcohol policy position" (Room 1978). The researchers then rose to the task and began presenting the observed distribution regularities as a law. In the manner of Ledermann, the form of the distribution was now held, for all practical purposes, to be unalterable. As in Ledermann's case, empirical findings seem to have been put to the service of existing policy thinking.

The Nordic Contribution

The single-distribution theory received more critical attention in Finland and the Scandinavian countries. Mäkelä (1969) tested Ledermann's hypothesis with representative population data. Consumption was indeed very skewed, but less so than the lognormal distribution, and several of Ledermann's data sets fitted the lognormal distribution poorly. Mäkelä pointed out that, like other distribution models, the lognormal curve does not accommodate nondrinkers. Skog (1971) also criticized Ledermann's work for its statistical shortcomings and tested it against data from a number of Scandinavian surveys. Distribution of consumption often deviated significantly from the lognormal, tending to have fewer heavy drinkers than predicted, sometimes in data sets with very good coverage of overall consumption. However, in support of Ledermann's general idea, distribution curves tend to lie parallel when plotted on log probability paper, though not in the fan shape he proposed. In other words, all levels of consumption tend to move in concert as the mean changes, a phenomenon that can be called the Ledermann effect. It is probably a manifestation of social interaction and the social nature of drinking. Changes in drinking habits spread through society.

Skog (1980) developed the contagion idea and went on to construct a simple mathematical model (Skog 1985). In this model, determinants of individual drinking behavior combined multiplicatively, and changes spread through a social network. Social interaction accounted for the Ledermann effect, and multiplicativity accounted for the skewed distribution. Skog (1983) also plotted the proportion of heavy drinkers against mean consumption in some Scandinavian and French populations. He showed that in general, within that range of consumption, the proportion of heavy drinkers in a population rises in proportion to the square of mean consumption, as Ledermann had predicted. However, several data points fell outside the predicted curve. In further testing of his model, Skog showed, using population consumption data from several European countries, that when average population consumption increases, the average intake of each quintile of the drinking population increases, but not in exact parallel on a lognormal plot.

Some years before, Bruun and colleagues (1975) presented a well-argued case for the Ledermann approach. It retained its standing in the debate for many years. In fact it has only recently been superseded by an equivalent volume (Edwards et al. 1994). Bruun and colleagues did not accept Ledermann's formula as a natural law but argued that his prevention approach was supported empirically. They concluded that the dispersion of distributions with the same mean alcohol intake was similar. From that they argued a close relationship between mean and heavy consumption. They further presented evidence that alcohol problems are related to the prevalence of heavy drinking and went on to argue that control of alcohol problems depends on control of heavy drinking, which in turn depends on controlling the general level of drinking. They adduced that this may be achieved through limiting the availability and maintaining the price of alcohol.

CONTRARY VIEWS

Smith (1976) and especially Duffy (1977a, 1977b, 1978, 1980, 1986) strongly criticized both Ledermann's statistical procedures and the arguments of Bruun

Table 7.1 Expected proportion of drinkers consuming over 150 ml pure alcohol per day, for different values of mean consumption and dispersion parameters

Mean consumption (liters/year)	Dispersion (S.D. of natural logarithms)	Excessive users per 100,000 drinkers
4	1.4	510
4	1.2	280
10	1.2	2170
10	1.0	1290

From Duffy and Cohen (1978).

and colleagues (1975). Duffy tested consumption distributions from Canada and Great Britain and found substantial divergence from the distribution predicted by the Ledermann theory, especially in the percentages of very heavy drinkers. He questioned whether the approximations offered by the Ledermann model were satisfactory and challenged proponents of the model to state the limits of the approximation. He did not agree that the differences in the dispersion of different populations were "quite small," as Bruun and colleagues (1975) had

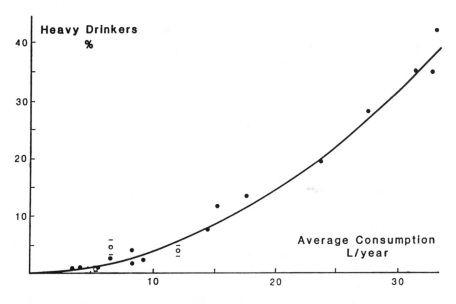

Figure 7.1 Relation between per capita consumption (litres pure alcohol per year) and the proportions of drinkers consuming over 100 ml pure alcohol per day, from various survey populations. Solid points and fitted curve are redrawn from Skog (1983). Open circles are added data: South Australian women, 5.4 L/year, and men, 12.1 L/year (Australian Bureau of Statistics 1984); Panjabi men, 6.6 L/year (Mohan et al. 1980). Bars represent 95% confidence intervals. Reproduced from de Burgh (1990) with kind permission.

stated. They were statistically significant and in some cases quite large. In any case, small variations in the dispersion could have a large effect on the expected number of heavy drinkers (Duffy and Cohen 1978; Table 7.1).

Figure 7.1 displays the empirical relationship of the prevalence of heavy drinkers to mean consumption. Skog's (1983) data points have been plotted. They show a steeply rising curve, as predicted. However, when per capita consumption of alcohol was less than 10 liters per year, the proportion of heavy drinkers was found to vary by a factor of two or more for populations with similar consumption means (Table 7.1). In fact, the more recent survey data added to Skog's suggest that variability can be a factor of four (de Burgh 1990).

To many bystanders the controversy between opposing experts was unsettling and potentially damaging to public health efforts. At a conference on the Ledermann curve, the participants were warned (Davies 1977): "If it goes out from a group like this that the Ledermann type of curve is wrong, or a myth, or something of that sort, that would be used by people who do not understand the refinements of our discussions."

THE PREVENTIVE PARADOX

In 1986 Kreitman put forward the argument, already accepted for risk factors such as raised blood pressure (Rose 1981), that there is more to be gained from reducing moderate drinking than from concentrating solely on extreme cases (heavy drinkers). This is the preventive paradox. Though individual risk is small for moderate drinkers, their contribution to population risk is greater than that of heavy drinkers because there are so many of them. Kreitman quoted studies in which drinking problems among moderate drinkers outnumbered heavy drinkers' problems for this reason. The same phenomenon had been noted earlier (Moore and Gerstein 1981).

The Kreitman argument has important consequences for public health policy. Orthodox health promotion follows the reasoning that risk rises with consumption and advises safe upper limits. Kreitman (1986) applied limits suggested by the Royal College of Psychiatrists (1979), namely fifty standard drinks per week for men and thirty-five for women, to several prevalence studies. He showed that even complete adherence to these limits would reduce problem drinking by, typically, 20 percent. For comparison, he calculated the reduction in problem drinking when the alternative approach of inducing all drinkers to reduce their drinking (by 10 percent, 20 percent, and so on) was applied. The same gain as a fully successful safe-limits approach was achieved by a 20 percent drop in general consumption.

Thus, the control-of-consumption approach gained a new rationale. Ledermann relied on the causal chain, according to which availability influenced mean consumption, which influenced the proportion of heavy drinkers, which in turn influenced the prevalence of alcohol-related problems. Kreitman's case was easier to argue and could be thought of as neo-Ledermann prevention thinking (de

Burgh 1990). Availability influenced all or any drinking, which in turn influenced the prevalence of problems. By price maintenance, restricted availability, and education measures, all drinkers would be persuaded to cut down. Heavy drinkers might be resistant, even remembering the Ledermann effect, but moderate or even light drinkers would yield public health gains because of their greater numbers. There was no need to argue the link between per capita alcohol intake and alcohol problems on the basis of distribution theory, because the prevalence of problems among the moderate range had been established empirically.

However, Kreitman's work had certain flaws (de Burgh 1990, 1992; Sinclair and Sillanaukee 1993). Random errors in classifying drinkers and problem drinkers reduce the relative risk of heavy versus moderate or light drinking, so that the proportion of drinkers with problems would be understated in heavy drinkers and inflated in moderate drinkers. Kreitman's examples used seven-day recall for consumption but longer periods, such as a year, for problems (naturally enough, given the frequency of most alcohol problems). Heavy drinkers who had a low level of consumption in the previous week would have had their past problems attributed to moderate drinking, and moderate drinkers who drank more in the previous week would, therefore, have had their low rate of problems attributed to heavy drinking. Acknowledging the problem, Kreitman repeated the exercise using measures of habitual consumption and found similar results. However, confident interpretation of consumption-problems studies requires either a short recall period for drinking and problems, concurrently, or prospective measurement, with repeat measurements of consumption. Prospective or concurrent measurement would also deal with a lag bias, which is probably present in the data that Kreitman used. Heavy drinkers who either did or intended to cut down consumption because of problems in the past would have tended to report problems as a heavy drinker but current consumption as a moderate drinker, while moderate drinkers moving to the heavy category would have tended to report the lower rate of problems from their moderate pasts.

A further problem was that prevalence of problem drinking is not the same as extent of alcohol problems, and this effect is important if comparing different classes of drinker. A 10-drinks-per-week drinker who drinks excessively one day at lunch may report trouble at work and become a "case" in Kreitman's data. A 120-drinks-per-week drinker may be useless every afternoon at work but will only count as one "case." Both frequency and severity of problems in individuals can be expected to be worse among heavy drinkers, but this difference will not be expressed in a count of cases. When these criticisms were published by Sinclair and Sillanaukee (1993), their strength was not acknowledged by some (e.g., Crawford 1993; Kreitman 1993). The biases proposed are likely, not merely speculative, and they exaggerate the preventive paradox.

Though the preventive paradox was supposed to be only a proposition, it rapidly became the enlightened view. It avoided the interminable arguments about whether lowering per capita intake would reduce the proportion of heavy drinkers, because it concluded that all drinkers were at risk and should reduce their consumption. The consequences of Kreitman's argument are that measures to reduce alcohol consumption are best applied to the population as a whole. This proposition sees hazardous, or risky, drinking as a legitimate target for prevention efforts but not exclusively or even predominantly so.

Kreitman (1986) stated that "there is little point in reporting on further tests of data," in the belief that the preventive paradox had been adequately established. On the contrary, a U.S. Air Force study quoted by Kreitman in support of the paradox also contained data that contradicted it: among the personnel surveyed, nearly all (93 percent) reporting alcohol-related harm exceeded the rather generous limits (about ten standard drinks as a maximum and seven for the daily average).

A recent study (Stockwell et al. 1996) specifically examined the question, with illuminating results. In population-based data the authors found that, of all those reporting at least one alcohol-related problem, nearly 60 percent were in the low-average intake category, in conformity with the preventive paradox. Only 25 percent were in the high-intake category. However, when the risk level was defined by the level of consumption on the heaviest recent drinking day, 84 percent of those with at least one problem fell into the high-risk category and only 4.5 percent in the low-risk group. The amount of alcohol consumed on the day harm was experienced was the best predictor of harm. Of all problems experienced, 87 percent occurred after high consumption on a particular occasion. Thus, the preventive paradox does not apply "when measures and problems of intoxication are matched" (Stockwell et al. 1996).

FURTHER WORK ON DISTRIBUTION THEORY

Skog (1993) devised the concept of the consumption containment rate (CCR) and applied it to consumption data from several countries. The CCR for a given intake is the conditional probability that a hypothetical drinker will drink no more than that amount after reaching that level. A CCR curve is equivalent to a plot of age-specific mortality rates for those who have survived to a certain age (instead of the population average age at death). The concept of survival is converted to the notion of a drinker progressing from the lowest to some higher level of intake. In short, it is a statistical concept. The CCR has interesting properties, especially for examining the tail of a distribution, but its visual display does not offer straightforward interpretation. Skog's analysis concluded that CCR curves are different for populations with low consumption but similar for populations with heavy consumption, regardless of culture. This is a plausible result, given that drinkers of any culture have physiological limits toward which they will converge with increasing intake.

Lemmens, Tan, and Kibbe (1990) acknowledged that formal mathematical (parametric) distributions have not been fruitful and showed a method of displaying the relationship between two empirical (i.e., surveyed) distributions. The percentiles of alcohol intake are plotted against each other, and confidence intervals are drawn around the resulting line. If a straight line can be drawn between the confidence intervals, the null hypothesis of a nonlinear relationship cannot be rejected; that is, the two distributions may be related in a linear way. Lemmens and his colleagues compared Dutch surveys in 1970, 1981, and 1985 and found that they bore a linear relationship to each other, a formal demonstration of the Ledermann effect in a population undergoing a change in total consumption. In a companion article, Tan, Lemmens, and Koning (1990) attempted to broaden the significance of their findings, but the hope of identifying a universal mathematical model for alcohol distributions has not been realized.

SAFE LIMITS

The concept of safe, or low-risk, levels of alcohol consumption does not have its origins in distribution theory but is primarily empirically derived. As mentioned earlier, a series of epidemiological studies was conducted in France from the 1950s onward (Péquignot 1960; Péquignot et al. 1974; Péquignot, Tuyns, and Berta 1978). These studies had the aim of defining the risk of various chronic disorders associated with given levels of alcohol consumption. Over the subsequent twenty-five years, this work, together with case control and cohort studies from many other countries, identified dose-response relationships for a range of conditions (English et al. 1995). These data are reviewed elsewhere in this volume. Suffice it to say that from these studies there developed the concept of gradations of risk from various levels of alcohol intake. More recently, this has been supplemented by analyses of the risk of harm associated with various patterns of drinking.

Recommendations about safe, low-risk, or nonhazardous drinking have been drawn up by health organizations in several countries. In some cases (e.g., the United Kingdom until 1995, Australia, and the Scandinavian countries), the advice has been phrased in terms of a weekly limit of standard drinks, or units. In others (e.g., the United Kingdom since 1995), advice on limits for daily drinking has been given, in recognition of the adverse effects of binge drinking and because of the wish not to sanction consuming the weekly "ration" on one occasion. The safe limits approach targets risky behavior. As a primary prevention strategy directed to the whole population, it involves education programs, media campaigns, and the like. As a secondary prevention strategy, it involves screening for hazardous drinking at the population level and the provision of brief, structured advice for those who engage in hazardous alcohol use (Babor et al. 1987; Saunders 1987; Babor and Grant 1992; Bien, Miller, and Tonigen 1993; Saunders et al. 1993).

The safe limits approach does not specify any form of distribution. It recognizes that there is a spectrum of alcohol use and misuse and a wide variety of patterns of drinking in different cultures. It also allows that different forms of harm arise from different styles of drinking. It is empirically, rather than theory, driven.

CONSUMPTION AND HARM

Harm increases with increasing alcohol consumption, other things being equal. However, the argument is not straightforward, for there is a variety of possible relationships between amount and pattern of drinking, on the one hand, and harm, on the other. For example, harm may have a monotonic relationship to average (daily or weekly) consumption. The relationship may be linear, exponential, quadratic, or other. There is no safe zone for drinking, and with increasing intake the risk of disease increases, as well. Certain cancers, for instance, fall into this category. Alternatively, there may be a threshold above which harm increases with increasing drinking. Several of the chronic medical effects of alcohol, including chronic liver disease, appear to be in this category.

Acute intoxication from alcohol, accidents and violence, and various domestic, legal, and occupational problems, which must surely match medical harm in most societies, have no clear relationship with average intake. The primary determinant seems to be the severity of the drinking episode and the setting for drinking, although it must be recognized that knowledge in this area is very incomplete.

THE BENEFICIAL EFFECTS OF ALCOHOL

The rationale for basing alcohol policies on distribution theory has been called into question by the increasing evidence for the health-protecting effects of alcohol. There is a consistent finding that moderate drinkers have lower mortality rates than nondrinkers or heavy drinkers (Marmot et al. 1981), principally from the protective effect of alcohol against coronary heart disease (Ashley et al. 1994; Doll et al. 1994; English et al. 1995; Marmot 1984; Saunders 1995). By using the data sets established in the United States and Great Britain to identify coronary heart disease risk factors, epidemiologists have shown there is a lessened risk of mortality at low levels of consumption (approximately 5 to 30 grams of alcohol daily) and an elevated risk above this amount. The relationship between alcohol intake and risk has been portrayed as a U-shaped or J-shaped curve.

Social consequences may be analogous. Social benefits extend beyond the obvious ones of good cheer, conviviality, and relaxation and could influence the expression of psychopathology in beneficial as well as harmful ways. The idea was implicit in Bales' (1946) formulation of drinking cultures, in which he saw alcohol as having a function in the release of societal tension. It is easier to understand such release in traditional societies, in which energy can be channeled safely through socially sanctioned settings and occasions. In societies in which these controls have been weakened, it is equally easy to see the release of tension tip over into violence. Some measures of social benefit and harm have been plotted against consumption (Mäkelä and Simpura 1985; Mäkelä and Mustonen 1988). Adverse consequences such as quarrels, property damage, and trouble with the police rose more sharply than benefits as consumption increased. But benefits, including being funnier and wittier, expressing feelings, and getting to know someone better, were reported by more respondents. Neither medical nor social consequences, therefore, can be argued as having a monotonic relation to alcohol consumption.

THE EFFECTS OF RESTRICTIONS ON ALCOHOL AVAILABILITY AND ASSOCIATED HARM

If the theory of a single distribution of alcohol consumption were supported by the evidence, and if the relationship between consumption and harm were shown to be monotonic, a powerful argument could be mounted for developing policies aimed at reducing per capita intake. Such policies would include fiscal controls (for example, increasing the level of taxation on alcoholic beverages), stricter licensing laws (governing the hours when alcoholic drinks can be sold and the number of points of sale), controls on advertising and promotion, and restrictions on the alcohol content of drinks.

There are several pieces of evidence that restrictive legislation can indeed reduce alcohol-related harm. The classical example is the enactment of prohibition in thirteen states of the United States between 1919 and 1932. Mortality from cirrhosis fell by 40 percent, and there was a reduction in other alcohol-related illnesses. However, the deleterious effects of prohibition have become part of folk wisdom. The production of alcohol became linked increasingly to crime syndicates, and the experience was judged generally to have been counterproductive. A second experiment occurred in France during the Second World War. In 1941 rationing of wine to a limit of 1 liter per adult per week was introduced. Cirrhosis mortality declined from fifty per 100,000 in 1940 to seven per 100,000 in 1945 (Ledermann 1964). Rationing was abandoned in 1947, and within five years cirrhosis mortality had returned to its prewar level.

The essential question is whether decline in consumption leads to fewer drinkers in the high-consumption zones, as predicted by distribution theories. A few paired surveys, done when general consumption was increasing, are available. In the United States (Room and Beck 1974), the proportion of men who drank enough to be intoxicated (five drinks) at least once a week increased over time, but the proportion of women did not. Adults in Iowa were surveyed in 1958, 1961, and 1979 (Fitzgerald and Mulford 1981). In 1979 rates of light and moderate drinking had increased over previous years, but heavy drinking had not. Former nondrinkers had probably joined the drinking population at the low end of the distribution. However, Hilton and Clark (1987), reporting on changes in U.S. national survey results over the period 1967–84, found a small increase in male abstainers. Per capita consumption rose 11.8 percent in that time; changes in drinking habits were small but were consistent with the Ledermann effect.

Kuusi (1957) tested the effect of introducing beer and wine stores into rural Finnish communities. Interviews were conducted before and after introduction of the stores, and changes were compared with changes in two control communities. The effects of increased availability were a decline in the consumption of spirits and illicit liquor and an overall increase in consumption due to beer and wine drinking. Drinks per occasion hardly changed, and the increased consumption was due to increased frequency of drinking. Later, after licensing laws were liberalized throughout Finland, the proportion of heavy drinkers increased as predicted among women, but there was only a small increase among men (Simpura 1980). In the Netherlands between 1958 and 1989 there was a threefold increase in alcohol consumption in the general population. The proportion of heavy drinkers increased, but there were exceptions in various age and gender groups (Neve et al. 1993).

A pair of surveys in London (Cartwright, Shaw, and Spratley 1978) showed that there was a significant increase in the proportion of drinkers consuming more than 70 milliliters per day, and the fourfold increase was somewhat greater than predicted by the Ledermann formula. Two publications (Dight 1976; Knight and Wilson 1980) reported surveys taken at times (1972–78) when consumption in Scotland was rising. There was no increase in heavy drinking, but the data are not fully comparable. Subsequently, there was a decline in consumption in Scotland. In repeat surveys of drinkers conducted in 1978–79, and again three years later, Kendell and colleagues found that heavy drinkers had reduced their consumption, while light drinkers had increased theirs (Kendell, de Roumanie, and Ritson 1983; Kendell 1984). The opposing trends represented a failure of the Ledermann effect to operate; at the same time, the results suggested that heavy drinkers responded to the adverse economic conditions being experienced at the time.

Norström (1987) examined changes in consumption and cirrhosis mortality in Sweden since 1950. Cirrhosis had quadrupled, while per capita alcohol consumption had risen by only 50 percent. His analysis suggested that most or all of the excess mortality was attributable to a change in the shape of the consumption distribution after the Bratt rationing system was abolished in 1955. Heavier drinkers during rationing increased their consumption relatively more after its abolition. This analysis does not argue against populationwide control measures, but it provides an example of the tail of the distribution being manipulated disproportionately by a targeted approach.

TARGETED APPROACHES

By targeted approaches we mean that specific patterns of drinking, particular high-risk groups or specific types of alcohol-related harms, are identified for action. Educational, legislative, and other approaches are then developed with the intent of reducing these harms. One of the most effective examples is the introduction of random breath testing in Australia. In December 1982, the state of New South Wales introduced random testing combined with an upper legal limit of 50 milligrams of alcohol per 100 milliliters of blood for fully registered drivers and 20 milligrams per 100 milliliters for provisionally registered drivers. Within a week there was a decline in the number of motor vehicle fatalities, and after three years the reduction was 30 percent. Fatalities have continued to decline since then. The legislation was enacted vigorously in New South Wales, and most adults have had a random breath test several times. In states where the legislation was enacted less vigorously there was no reduction, or a much smaller reduction, in road accident deaths (Homel 1993; Smith 1988).

Targeted approaches can also be applied to specific high-risk groups such as young drivers and, as mentioned earlier, to persons with existing hazardous use. Since the 1970s the legal age for drinking has been raised from eighteen to twenty-one years in some North American jurisdictions. As these changes often happen abruptly in response to public concern about motor vehicle deaths in young people, the consequences can be inferred with some confidence. Raising the legal age usually leads to decreased rates of traffic casualties among those of the affected ages and a little younger, while lowering the age has the opposite effect (Smith 1988).

There is now compelling evidence for the effectiveness of brief interventions for hazardous alcohol use, when these are offered to hazardous drinkers identified during routine screening, usually in primary-care settings. In a recent World Health Organization collaborative study, there was a statistically significant reduction in alcohol intake of around 30 percent among hazardous drinkers who, on the basis of random assignment, received five minutes of advice (Babor and Grant 1992). There was also a significant effect on frequency of intoxication.

Targeted approaches can also be applied in the drinking environment. Measures such as the use of shatterproof drinking glasses have been introduced. Monitoring of licensed premises by community police with the specific intent of reducing unruly behavior has been shown to reduce road accidents and assaults in the proximity (Jeffs and Saunders 1983; see also chapter 15, this volume).

COMPARATIVE APPROACHES TO REDUCING HARM

The effects of different approaches to reducing harm have been modeled by de Burgh (1990), using data from six published cohort studies. The first model examined the effect of the control-of-consumption ("less is best") approach. In this example, 10 percent of persons in each drinking category (as defined in the particular study) moved to the category below, with 10 percent of the lightest drinkers, therefore, becoming nondrinkers. This would be equivalent to a consumption control measure based on the Ledermann effect, though the percentage reduction in each category would not be exactly that of a single-distribution model. In two cohorts, mortality decreased by 0.2 percent and 0.4 percent, respectively. In three, mortality increased by 0.4 percent to 1.7 percent. In one analysis of the Kaiser-Permanente cohort, the number of drinkers in the top category was hypothetically doubled, to account for undersampling of heavy drinkers in an employed population (and indeed, in any survey). In this example, mortality still increased by 1 percent (de Burgh 1990). A safe limits approach, having the effect that 10 percent of hazardous drinkers reduced their intake to the next lowest category, resulted in a consistent decrease in mortality of 0.3 percent to 1 percent in all six cohorts.

The greatest reduction in mortality was seen in a model where abstainers were encouraged to become light drinkers. It was assumed that 50% of nondrinkers would move to the lowest drinking category. It was also assumed that 10% of the higher moderate and heavy drinkers would use such a message as an excuse to move up one category. In this example, mortality decreased by 1.3–3.6% (de Burgh 1990).

The mortality changes seen here depend mostly on the proportions of abstainers and heavy drinkers in each population. The hypothetical movements represent, of course, no more than an illustrative exercise. Nonetheless, the results are suggestive. They are also supported by Pearson and Terry (1994), who calculated that if consumption of alcohol in the United States ceased, there would be a saving of approximately 81,000 deaths per annum, but a simultaneous increase of approximately 100,000 deaths (principally and predictably from coronary heart disease) per annum. Thus, there would be a net increase in the number of deaths of 19,000 each year. Similar figures can be calculated for Australia using etiological fractions determined by English and colleagues (1995). Alcohol-related mortality amounted to 6,354 cases in 1986. It is estimated that there were 8,255 fewer deaths than would have occurred if consumption were zero, thus giving a net saving of 1,901 lives (Holman and English 1995).

CONCLUSIONS

The single-distribution model provided a mathematical link between individual and societal use of alcohol. It performed the important function of "pricking overinflated theories" (Room 1973), namely, the fiction that alcohol problems occur only in a distinct group of "alcoholics" and are unrelated to alcohol consumption itself. Supporters of the Ledermann approach have contributed to public health thinking through their emphasis on populationwide prevention measures. Indeed, given the huge quantities of alcohol consumed by large segments of the population in some post–Second World War European countries, the single-distribution theory can be seen as a useful child of its time. However, in view of the effectiveness of targeted approaches to reduce alcohol-related harm, and the evidence for the physical and social benefits of moderate alcohol consumption, the relevance of any distribution theory for alcohol policy is doubtful.

The emphasis on distribution theory over the last forty years has been at a price. The evident importance of the patterns, settings, and sociocultural contexts of drinking on particular occasions has been neglected. The Ledermann approach is therefore a limited one. This would not necessarily be a criticism were it not for the stifling effect it has had on policy development. Indeed, one can argue that the focus on distribution theory has concealed more than it has revealed. Many policy theorists have confined their attention to measures that manipulate price and availability or price alone (Popham, Schmidt, and de Lint 1978). Although price maintenance relative to incomes may suppress consumption (Seeley 1960), the potency of price as a tool of control must be limited if incomes keep on rising. Admittedly, it makes sense to maintain prices so that alcohol is more expensive than, say, soft drinks. But beyond that a tax on alcohol high enough to be effective is likely to be regarded as unfair, to be unpopular with the public, and to be used as a justification for illegal production (Taussig 1978). Ledermann's publications did lead to work that indicates a tendency for drinking behavior to change in concert within a population. Hence, scientific support is given to a prudent policy approach that would not permit artificial stimulation of demand for alcohol, even if it is good for the economy.

The main value of the Ledermann approach and the distribution theories it inspired has been as scientific window dressing for alcohol policies that have their origins in a desire for central control of consumption. The practical impact of this approach has been limited: control policies that derive from the Ledermann model have been too unpalatable to enforce in the political realm in normal circumstances. While policy experts advised restricted availability and increased taxation on alcohol, governments in most countries continued to liberalize rather than restrict trading conditions. The only (partial) exception are the Nordic countries, where alcohol problems have been seen as a consequence of a lack of regulation on individual behavior.

Meanwhile, those involved in application rather than theory—primary-care and health promotion professionals, for instance—have adhered to an intuitive, or commonsense, position with little ideological content. This has advised limiting drinks per occasion or per week. Governments have felt more comfortable with this type of advice to the public, and there is now a considerable body of scientific evidence to support this position (Holman et al. 1995).

In summary, there is no foundation for the belief that reducing total consumption in a society should be the primary way of reducing alcohol problems. The worth of any control measure has to be tested empirically and judged by its effects, not by whether it conforms to a theory. Theories do not necessarily translate into effective action, and there are many ethical, practical, and political considerations that need to be acknowledged. Expert opinion is properly only one of many inputs into the decision-making process in democratic societies. Societies have the right to make decisions most relevant to their own cultures, structures, and aspirations. Thus, distribution theory has been a useful intellectual exercise in drawing attention away from the concept of alcoholism as an individual problem uninfluenced by the wider society. The general principle of adopting population-based measures to reduce alcohol misuse and specific harms is unarguable. But having a theory of distribution of consumption driving a health policy smacks of H. L. Mencken's dictum: "For every problem, no matter how difficult, there is an answer that is simple, direct—and wrong."

REFERENCES

A.B.S. 1984. *Alcohol Consumption Patterns, South Australia, October.* Catalogue No. 4304.4. Adelaide: Australian Bureau of Statistics. (Also, unpublished data from Information Services, A.B.S., G.P.O. Box 2772, Adelaide, S.A. 5001, Australia.)

Aitchison, J., and J. A. C. Brown. 1957. *The Lognormal Distribution, with Special Reference to Its Uses in Economics.* London: Cambridge University Press.

Ashley, M. J., et al. 1994. Moderate drinking and health: report of an international symposium. *Canadian Medical Association Journal* 151(suppl. 1):1–12.

Babor, T. F., and M. Grant. 1992. *Project on Identification and Management of Alcohol-Related Problems: Report on Phase II, a Randomised Clincal Trial of Brief Interventions in Primary Health Care.* Geneva: World Health Organization.

Babor, T. F., P. Korner, C. Wilber, and S. P. Good. 1987. Screening and early intervention strategies for harmful drinkers: initial lessons from the Amethyst Project. *Australian Drug and Alcohol Review* 6:325–39.

Bales, R. F. 1946. Cultural differences in rates of alcoholism. *Quarterly Journal of Studies on Alcohol* 6:480–99.

Bandura, A. 1977. Self-efficacy: toward a unifying theory of behavioral change. *Psychological Review* 84:191–215.

Bien, T. H., W. R. Miller, and J. S. Tonigen. 1993. Brief interventions for alcohol problems: a review. *Addiction* 88:315–36.

Bruun, K., et al. 1975. *Alcohol Control Policies in Public Health Perspective.* Vol. 25. Helsinki: Finnish Foundation for Alcohol Studies.

Cartwright, A. K. J., S. J. Shaw, and T. A. Spratley. 1978. The relationships between per capita consumption, drinking patterns, and alcohol-related problems in a population sample, 1965–1974. Part III. Implications for alcohol control policy. *British Journal of Addiction* 73:247–58.

Chafetz, M. 1967. Alcoholism prevention and reality. *Quarterly Journal of Studies on Alcohol* 28:345–50.

Crawford, A. 1993. Much ado about nothing. *Addiction* 88:595–598.

Davies, D. L. 1977. The epidemiology of alcoholism. In *The Ledermann Curve.* London: Maudsley Hospital, Alcohol Education Centre.

de Burgh, S. P. H. 1990. Epidemiology and alcohol policy. Ph.D. diss., University of Sydney.

———. 1992. Alcohol policy and the preventive paradox. In *Drug Problems in Our Society: Dimensions and Perspectives,* ed. J. White. Proceedings of the Window of Opportunity Conference, December 1991. Drug and Alcohol Services Council, Adelaide, Australia, 137–140.

de Lint, J., and J. Bronetto. 1964. Alcohol prevalence estimation and alcohol consumption. Addiction Research Foundation, Toronto.

de Lint, J., and W. Schmidt. 1968. The distribution of alcohol consumption in Ontario. *Quarterly Journal of Studies on Alcohol* 29:968–73.

————. 1971. Consumption averages and alcoholism prevalence: a brief review of epidemiological investigations. *British Journal of Addiction* 66:97–107.

Dight, S. E. 1976. *Scottish Drinking Habits*. London: HMSO.

Doll, R., et al. 1994. Mortality in relation to consumption of alcohol: 13 years' observation on male British doctors. *British Medical Journal* 309:911–18.

Duffy, J. C. 1977a. Estimating the proportion of heavy drinkers. In *The Ledermann Curve: Report of a Symposium*, pp. 11–24. London: Alcohol Education Centre.

————. 1977b. Alcohol consumption, alcoholism, and excessive drinking: errors in estimates from consumption figures. *International Journal of Epidemiology* 6:375–79.

————. 1978. Comment on "The Single Distribution Theory of Alcohol Consumption." *Journal of Studies on Alcohol* 39:1648–50.

————. 1980. The association between per capita consumption of alcohol and the proportion of excessive consumers: reply to Skog. *British Journal of Addiction* 75:147–51.

————. 1986. The distribution of alcohol consumption patterns: 30 years on. *British Journal of Addiction* 81:735–42.

Duffy, J., and G. Cohen. 1978. Total consumption and excessive drinking. *British Journal of Addiction* 73:259–64.

Edwards, G., A. Arif, and H. Hodgson. 1981. Nomenclature and classification of drug- and alcohol-related problems: a WHO memorandum. *Bulletin of the World Health Organization* 59:225–42.

Edwards, G., and M. M. Gross. 1976. Alcohol dependence: provisional description of a clinical syndrome. *British Medical Journal* 1:1058–61.

Edwards, G., et al. 1994. *Alcohol Policy and the Public Good*. Oxford: Oxford University Press.

English, D. R., et al. 1995. *The Quantification of Drug-Caused Morbidity and Mortality in Australia, 1995*. Canberra: Australian Government Publishing Service.

Fitzgerald, J. L., and H. A. Mulford. 1981. The prevalence and extent of drinking in Iowa, 1979. *Journal of Studies on Alcohol* 42:38–47.

Hilton, M. E., and W. B. Clark. 1987. Changes in American drinking patterns and problems, 1967–1984. *Journal of Studies on Alcohol* 48:515–22.

Holman, C. D. J., and D. R. English. 1995. An improved aetiological fraction of alcohol caused mortality. *Australian Journal of Public Health* 19:138–141.

Holman, C. D. J., D. R. English, E. Milne, and M. G. Winter. 1995. Meta-analysis of alcohol and all-cause mortality: validation of NH&MRC recommendations. *Medical Journal of Australia* 163:141–45.

Homel, R. 1993. Random breath testing in Australia: getting it to work according to specifications. *Addiction* 88 (suppl.): 275–345.

Jeffs, B. W., and W. Saunders. 1983. Minimising alcohol-related offences by enforcement of existing licensing legislation. *British Journal of Addiction* 78:67–78.

Jellinek, E. M. 1952. Phases of alcohol addiction. *Quarterly Journal of Studies on Alcohol* 13:673–84.

————. 1960. *The Disease Concept Of Alcoholism*. Schenectady: New College and University Press.

Kendell, R. E. 1984. The beneficial consequences of the United Kingdom's declining per capita consumption of alcohol in 1979–1982. *Alcohol and Alcoholism* 19:271–76.

Kendell, R. E., M. de Roumanie, and E. G. Ritson. 1983. Effect of economic changes on Scottish drinking habits, 1978–1982. *British Journal of Addiction* 78:365–79.

Knight, I., and P. Wilson. 1980. *Scottish Licensing Laws.* London: HMSO.

Kreitman, N. 1986. Alcohol consumption and the preventive paradox. *British Journal of Addiction* 81:353–63.

———. 1993. Sinclair and Sillanaukee's storm in a teacup. *Addiction* 88:598–599.

Kuusi, P. 1957. *Alcohol Sales Experiment in Rural Finland.* Helsinki: Finnish Foundation for Alcohol Studies.

Ledermann, S. 1952. Une mortalité d'origine économique en France: la mortalité d'origine ou d'appoint alcoolique. *Semaine Médicale* 28:418–21.

———. 1953. L'alcoolisation excessive et la mortalité des Français. *Concours Médicaux* 75:1485–96, 1583–98, 1675–82, 1767–74.

———. 1956. *Alcool, Alcoolism, Alcoolisation. Données scientifiques de caractère physiologique, économique et social.* Cahier 29. Paris: Presses Universitaires de France, Institut National d'Etudes Demographiques.

———. 1964. *Alcool, Alcoolism, Alcoolisation.* Vol. 2. Paris: Presses Universitaires de France.

Ledermann, S., and F. Tabah. 1951. Novelles données sur la mortalité d'origine alcoolique. *Population* G:41–56.

Lemmens, P., E. Tan, and R. Kibbe. 1990. Comparing distributions of alcohol consumption: empirical probability plots. *British Journal of Addiction* 85:751–58.

Mäkelä, K. 1969. Alkoholinkulutuksen Jakautuma. Social Research Institute of Alcohol Studies, Helsinki.

Mäkelä, K., and M. Mustonen. 1988. Positive and negative experiences related to drinking as a function of annual alcohol intake. *British Journal of Addiction* 83:403–8.

Mäkelä, K., and J. Simpura. 1985. Experiences related to drinking as a function of annual alcohol intake and by sex and age. *Drug and Alcohol Dependence* 15:389–404.

Marmot, M. G. 1984. Alcohol and coronary heart disease. *International Journal of Epidemiology* 13:160–67.

Marmot, M. G., G. Rose, M. J. Shipley, and B. J. Thomas. 1981. Alcohol and mortality: a U-shaped curve. *Lancet* 1:580–83.

Moore, M. H., and D. R. Gerstein, eds. 1981. *Alcohol and Public Policy: Beyond the Shadow of Prohibition.* Washington, D.C.: National Academy Press.

Neve, R., J. P. M. Diedericks, R. A. Knibbe, and M. J. Drop. 1993. Developments in drinking behaviour in the Netherlands from 1958 to 1989: a cohort analysis. *Addiction* 88:611–21.

Norström, T. 1987. The abolition of the Swedish alcohol rationing system: effects on consumption distribution and cirrhosis mortality. *British Journal of Addiction* 82:633–41.

O'Neill, B., and W. T. Wells. 1971. Blood alcohol levels in drivers not involved in accidents and the lognormal distribution. *Quarterly Journal of Studies on Alcohol* 32:798–803.

Pearson, T. A., and P. Terry. 1994. What to advise patients about drinking alcohol: The clinician's conundrum. *Journal of the American Medical Association* 272:967–968.

Péquignot, G. 1960. Enqute par interrogatoire sur les circonstances diététiques de las cirrhose alcoolique en France. *Annales Medic-chirurgicales du Center* 17:1–21.

Péquignot, G., C. Chabert, H. Eydoux, and M. A. Courcoul. 1974. Augmentation du risque de cirrhose en fonction de la ration d'alcool. *Revue de l'Alcoolisme* 20:191–202.

Péquignot, G., A. J. Tuyns, and J. L. Berta. 1978. Ascitic cirrhosis in relation to alcohol consumption. *International Journal of Epidemiology* 7:113–20.

Popham, R. E., W. Schmidt, and J. de Lint. 1978. Government control measures to prevent hazardous drinking. In *Drinking*, ed. J. A. Ewing and B. A. Rouse. Chicago: Nelson-Hall.

Room, R. 1973. Notes on the implications of the lognormal curve. *The Drinking and Drug Practices Surveyor* 7:18–20.

———. 1978. Social science research and alcohol policy making. Paper presented at conference, Utilization of Social Research in Drug Policy Making, Washington D.C., May 1978.

Room, R., and T. Beck. 1974. Survey data on trends in U.S. consumption. *The Drinking and Drug Practices Surveyor* 9:3–7.

Rose, G. 1981. Strategy of prevention: lessons from cardiovascular diseases. *British Medical Journal* 282:1847–51.

Royal College of Psychiatrists. 1979. *Alcohol and Alcoholism*. London: Tavistock.

Saunders, J. B. 1987. The WHO project on early detection and treatment of harmful alcohol consumption. *Australian Drug and Alcohol Review* 6:303–8.

———. 1995. Alcohol as a health benefit. *Drug and Alcohol Review* 14:3–6.

Saunders, J. B., et al. 1993. Development of the alcohol use disorders identification test (AUDIT): WHO collaborative project on early detection of persons with harmful alcohol consumption. II. *Addiction* 88:791–803.

Schmidt, W., and J. de Lint. 1970. Estimating the prevalence of alcoholism from alcohol consumption and mortality data. *Quarterly Journal of Studies on Alcohol* 31:957–64.

Schmidt, W., and R. I. Popham. 1978. The single-distribution theory of alcohol consumption. *Journal of Studies on Alcohol* 39:400–19.

Seeley, J. 1960. Death by liver cirrhosis and the price of beverage alcohol. *Canadian Medical Association Journal* 83:1361–66.

Simpura, J. 1980. Decomposition of changes in aggregate consumption of alcohol in Finland, 1968, 1969, and 1976. *Journal of Studies on Alcohol* 41:572–76

Sinclair, J. D., and P. Sillanaukee. 1993. The preventive paradox: a critical examination. *Addiction* 88:591–95.

Skog, O.-J. 1971. Alkoholkonsumets Fordeling I Befolkningen. Statens Institutt for Alkoholforskning, Oslo.

———. 1980. Social interaction and the distribution of alcohol consumption. *Journal of Drug Issues* 10:71–92.

———. 1982. *The Distribution of Alcohol Consumption. Part I. A Critical Discussion of the Ledermann Model*. SIFA Monograph 64. Oslo: National Institute for Alcohol Research.

———. 1983. *The Distribution of Alcohol Consumption. Part II. A Review of the First Wave of Empirical Studies*. SIFA Monograph 67. Oslo: National Institute for Alcohol Research.

———. 1985. The collectivity of drinking cultures: a theory of the distribution of alcohol consumption. *British Journal of Addiction* 80:83–99.

————. 1993. The tail end of the alcohol consumption distribution. *Addiction* 88:601–610.

Smart, R. G., and W. Schmidt. 1970. Blood alcohol levels in drivers not involved in accidents. *Quarterly Journal of Studies on Alcohol* 31:968–71.

Smith, D. I. 1988. Effectiveness of restrictions on availability as a means of preventing alcohol-related problems. *Contemporary Drug Problems* 15:627–84.

Smith, N. M. H. 1976. Research note on the Ledermann formula and its recent applications. *Drinking and Drug Practices Surveyor* 12:15–22.

Stockwell T., D. Hawks, E. Lang, and P. Rydon. 1996. Unravelling the preventive paradox for acute alcohol problems. *Drug and Alcohol Review* 15:7–15.

Tan, E., P. Lemmens, and A. Koning. 1990. Regularity in alcohol distributions: implications for the collective nature of drinking behavior. *British Journal of Addiction* 85:745–50.

Taussig, M. K. 1978. Comment on "The Single Distribution Theory of Alcohol Consumption." *Journal of Studies on Alcohol* 39:1643–46.

Chapter 8

The Impact of Alcohol Control Measures on Drinking Patterns

Stephen Whitehead

The alcohol control theory has been an important part of the alcohol policy debate since the mid-1950s. It reached the height of its popularity and acceptance among campaigning organizations and advocacy groups after the publication in 1975 of *Alcohol Control Policies in a Public Health Perspective* (Bruun et al. 1975), usually referred to as the Purple Book.

Since then, the theory has been increasingly challenged, for a number of reasons. First, the original theory upon which the control-of-consumption approach was based has been shown to contain a number of weaknesses and inconsistencies. This topic is addressed in greater detail in chapter 7 of this volume. In addition, the harm-reduction approach (i.e., the reduction of alcohol misuse, not use) has been shown to be more effective (Plant, Single, and Stockwell 1997). Finally, there is evidence that for some individuals, moderate drinking carries with it protective health benefits, especially with regard to coronary heart disease.

THE LEDERMANN HYPOTHESIS

As applied to alcohol consumption, the control-of-consumption theory, also known as the single-distribution theory, was first proposed by Sully Ledermann,

Stephen Whitehead is with International Distillers and Vintners, London, United Kingdom.

a French demographer, in a 1956 publication (Ledermann 1956). On the basis of nine limited surveys, Ledermann described the relationship between average per capita consumption and the number of heavy drinkers in any population as fixed and predictable. According to the hypothesis, if average consumption doubled, the number of problem drinkers would increase fourfold, and if it tripled the increase would be ninefold.

These claims had immediate appeal to members of advocacy groups campaigning against drinking because they appeared to provide a "scientific" method of calculating the proportion of heavy drinkers in a population. More important, they also seemed to demonstrate that alcohol-related problems could be reduced simply by lowering average per capita consumption. Simplified interpretations of Ledermann's theory were therefore readily accepted by a number of influential academics and others involved in the alcohol debate. It is possible that they accepted and promoted the Ledermann conclusions as a basis for policy because these supported many of their own preconceptions about drinking.

POST-LEDERMANN

When the control-of-consumption theory came under closer scrutiny, serious doubts about its applicability to solving alcohol-related problems were raised. The main criticism was that, far from proving a steady relationship between average per capita consumption and the prevalence of heavy drinking in a population, Ledermann had based his model on the assumption that it exists. His mathematics were found to be weak and speculative (Duffy 1977; Smith 1976) and based on the presumption of a homogeneous population. It was pointed out that Ledermann's conclusions had been refuted by empirical data from Britain, America, Scandinavia, and elsewhere (Plant 1979). The extensive criticism put into serious question the premise that it is possible to reproduce the distribution of alcohol consumption within a population on the basis of the average per capita consumption alone.

Despite this trenchant and expert criticism of the original model, the debate about how to prevent alcohol misuse is still influenced by a belief among numerous advocacy groups and campaigning organizations that any increase in average per capita consumption must increase the number of heavy drinkers and, therefore, the number of alcohol problems in a population. This belief was the inspiration for the target set by the World Health Organization Regional Office for Europe that in all countries in the region consumption by the year 2000 must be 25 percent less than what it was in 1980. The same belief presumably inspired Edwards and colleagues (1994), who attempted to bring the Purple Book up-to-date and whose message to the individual and to society is that "less is better." This and a related publication, *The WHO European Alcohol Action Plan* (WHO 1993), are important contributions to the alcohol policy debate. Both are addressed principally to policy makers, and while the authors acknowledge the role of harm-reduction measures in reaching high-risk populations, their principal concern is to achieve across-the-board reductions in alcohol consumption because the control theory remains central to their purpose.

Probably the main reason for the acceptance of the reduction in per capita consumption approach is that it appears to be common sense. In fact, this term was used in a recent publication by EUROCARE (Eurocare 1995), in which reference was made to it as a "commonsensical" assumption. Based on this line of reasoning, the more people who drink, the more are at risk of developing alcohol problems. In practice, the implications for policy of this approach are that any increase in per capita consumption must be prevented because it will result in more heavy drinking and, therefore, in more alcohol-related problems.

One researcher (Tuck 1980) has pointed out that there are at least fifty-one logical possibilities of how the distribution of drinkers (light, moderate, heavy) could change in a situation of increasing national consumption. She has demonstrated that the number of light and moderate drinkers can increase without an accompanying rise in the number of heavy drinkers and that an increase in occasional or light drinking need not inevitably result in a growth in moderate and heavy drinking.

THE PREVENTIVE PARADOX

Another theory, related to the control-of-consumption theory, is frequently referred to as the preventive paradox (see chapter 7 for a detailed discussion). The preventive paradox was so named by Kreitman (1986), who argued that the majority of alcohol problems are caused by low-to-moderate consumers who, although they are a low-risk group, collectively produce more problems because they outnumber by far the heavy drinkers. He therefore concluded that a significant reduction in alcohol-related problems would be brought about only by an across-the-board decrease in drinking and not just by a reduction in consumption by heavy drinkers.

This hypothesis can be questioned on several grounds. Kreitman did not take into account the severity of the problems suffered or the frequency of occurrence. In addition, drinkers who had cut down on their drinking because of a persistant problem would be classified as light or moderate, but the problem would be a legacy of heavy drinking. Many of the problems must be caused by people who are normally light or moderate drinkers and episodically drink too much. However, the fundamental objection to the hypothesis, as pointed out by Duffy (1986) when it was first proposed, is that, like its parent theory, the preventive paradox relies on the assumption that whatever an individual's present level of consumption, its reduction will always be beneficial. This assertion is not compatible with the recent body of medical evidence, which suggests that light-to-moderate drinking is actually beneficial to health. It therefore follows that measures designed to reduce average consumption levels within a population are not bound to have public health benefits and may have adverse consequences for certain individuals.

THE HEALTH BENEFITS OF SENSIBLE DRINKING

There is now an abundance of robust scientific evidence contradicting the alcohol control approach that less is always better. It has been demonstrated that the curve relating alcohol consumption to total mortality is U-shaped. That is to say, increases in consumption starting from nil initially decrease the risk of premature death, but at higher levels this effect is reversed so that the risk first becomes equal to that of nondrinkers and then continues to increase as consumption increases. The claim that the higher mortality among abstainers results from including former heavy drinkers who had stopped drinking because of ill health (the sick quitters) has been shown to be invalid.

It was this sort of evidence that resulted in the conclusion in a World Health Organization technical report (WHO 1994) that consumption of 30 grams of alcohol a day is associated with lower cardiovascular risk and that the existence of a U-shaped curve of mortality associated with drinking could no longer be doubted. The U.K. Interdepartmental Working Group on Sensible Drinking (U.K. Department of Health and Social Security 1995), after its comprehensive consideration of the evidence, reached a similar conclusion.

Claims that there are no substantial reductions in risk for men under thirty-five years and for premenopausal women are understandable given that coronary heart disease is not an important cause of death in those groups. However, as hardening of the arteries begins at a young age and because alcohol has been shown to increase high-density cholesterol in males aged twenty to thirty years, it is reasonable to assume that the benefits are not restricted to the older age group (Kendell 1995; Poikalainen 1995). With regard to women, a study of nurses in the United States (Stampfer et al. 1980) strongly suggests a protective effect in premenopausal women. Another claim is that the reduction in risk by drinking lightly can be obtained by other means, for example, by not smoking, by engaging in physical activity, and by eating a low-fat diet. This claim has been questioned (Kendell 1995), because it assumes there is no additive effect, which seems unlikely.

CONTROL POLICY OPTIONS

Despite the evidence on the health benefits of alcohol, control theorists still insist that governments must adopt policies to reduce consumption across the board. They argue in favor of rigorous policies to control (i.e., to reduce) the consumption of alcohol by a number of means. These include, inter alia, price increases, restrictions on advertising, limiting hours of sale and number of outlets, rationing, prohibition, increasing the legal drinking age, policies to deter drinking before driving, and the creation of monopolies. The relative effectiveness of these options is discussed below.

Price

The taxation of alcoholic beverages is essentially for the purpose of raising revenue. It is not generally regarded as primarily a tool for controlling consumption, although it is used as such in some countries (e.g., Norway and Sweden). However, in most societies, alcoholic drinks are perceived to be luxury items and, as such, candidates for taxation.

The main reason for the argument that taxation should be employed to reduce consumption is that, like most commodities, alcoholic drinks are price elastic, that is, demand is sensitive to price changes. Price elasticity reflects the extent to which a unit change in demand is caused by a unit change in price, up or down. A commodity is said to have a high price elasticity if the demand reacts strongly to price changes, so that purchases go up steeply if prices come down, and vice versa. A product is said to be inelastic with respect to prices if purchases stay much the same regardless of price changes.

In the interpretation of elasticity values, the points of departure should be the social, cultural, and economic circumstances characteristic of each country and period studied. It has been observed that elasticity values relating to different regions, different periods, and different types of alcoholic beverage vary considerably. For example, in English-speaking countries, it has been found that demand for beer has been less price elastic than the demand for wines and spirits (Godfrey 1989, 1990; Hogarty and Elzinga 1972). In contrast, demand for wines has been found to be relatively unresponsive to price in France and Spain (Labys 1976). One study has found the effect of price on consumption to be short term (Johnson et al. 1992), while another has found that elasticity varies with type of beverage (Lau 1975). Market conditions are different from country to country and should, therefore, be considered individually. In addition, demand estimations are difficult to calculate exactly (Ornstein 1980) and price elasticities even more so. Elasticity measurements are a mathematical explanation of what has happened in the past, entering relevant factors into the equation. Elasticity measurements cannot predict changes in consumption and may not be valid when large price changes are involved.

Of much more importance for patterns of drinking is the effect of price increases on different types of consumer. It is frequently claimed that heavy drinkers are at least as responsive to price increases, and sometimes more so, than light-to-moderate consumers. The study most frequently cited is by Kendell, de Roumanie, and Ritson (1983) and concerns the effect of rises in price on consumption as revealed in before and after surveys. It was claimed that heavy drinkers reduced their consumption much more than other drinkers after excise duties were increased. A more recent study (Manning, Blumberg, and Moulton 1995) has shown that moderate consumers of alcoholic beverages show more price elasticity than light or heavy drinkers. Therefore, the contention that price increases will have a marked effect on heavy drinkers and should be used to improve public health is questionable. The probability is that the most marked effect would be on light-to-moderate drinkers and could push their consumption below the level at which most health advantage is obtained, thereby increasing the incidence of cardiovascular disease and premature death among a large section of the population. This would not benefit public health.

Advertising

In some countries, the interests of the alcohol beverage industry are perceived to be at odds with those of public health. A commonly held assumption among advocacy groups and organizations campaigning against drinking is that alcohol advertising is effective; otherwise, manufacturers would not spend so much money on it. Yet industry proponents argue that the main purpose of advertising is not to increase the overall level of consumption but to induce a shift in market share by affecting brand choice and brand loyalty. Simply stated, the main objective of advertising is to persuade customers to continue to enjoy, or to switch their preference to, the brand being advertised.

There is considerable empirical evidence to support this notion (Österberg 1992; Partanen and Montonen 1988) as well as for the conclusion that advertising does not have a strong impact on alcohol consumption (Smart 1988). In a review of the literature on the impact of advertising on drinking, Fisher (1993) concluded that there is little reason to believe that advertising increases consumption to the point at which meaningful adverse social consequences result.

A recent review (Ambler 1996) has suggested that the main impact of advertising is to persuade consumers to change the brand of products they consume. Published research has not demonstrated unequivocally that there is a causal relationship between advertising spending and the aggregate demand for alcohol products (Calfee and Scheraga 1994; Duffy 1989; Lee and Tremblay 1992; Saffler 1992; Smart 1988; Sturgess 1992; WHO 1988). Restrictions on advertising do not automatically result in declines in total alcohol consumption. International studies have shown that no health benefits can be expected from alcohol bans (Harrison and Godfrey 1989; Saffler 1991). When a ban on advertising of almost sixty decades was lifted in the Canadian province of Saskatchewan, there was no perceptible impact on total alcohol sales (Makowsky and Whitehead 1991). A study in British Columbia reached similar conclusions (Smart and Cutler 1976). Conversely, there have been instances in which increases in advertising spending are juxtaposed against declines—some very marked—in consumption (e.g., Italy, France, Germany, the Netherlands, Spain, and the United Kingdom).

Finally, there is little support for the notion that alcohol advertising influences social conditioning to alcohol, thereby leading to misuse (Adlaf and Kohn 1989; Connolly et al. 1994; Strickland 1982, 1983). Similarly, there is little evidence to support the idea that alcohol abusers are influenced by advertising to increase consumption (Sobell et al. 1993). At the same time, evidence from some former Eastern bloc countries showed that significant increases in consumption often occurred despite the prohibition of advertising.

Licensing Hours

It is frequently claimed that increased drinking is associated with increased hours of sale, and vice versa, and that decreased drinking follows the elimination of some days of sale. However, there is published evidence (Duffy 1992) that extensions of the hours of sale in Scottish public houses in 1976 did not lead to increases in alcohol-related problems, which many who were opposed to the changes had predicted. Bruce (1980) also researched the effects of these changes and found no difference in average consumption, a small decline in rates of consumption, and a reduction in accelerated drinking at the end of permitted hours. A Norwegian study (Nordlund 1985) showed that a Saturday closing of outlets did not decrease level of alcohol consumption. Research by Knight and Wilson (1980) and by Duffy and Plant (1986) confirmed these findings.

In England and Wales, the 1988 Licensing Act extended the hours during which licensed premises were permitted to sell alcohol. The result of these changes was monitored by the Office of Population Censuses and Surveys (Goddard 1991), and it was concluded that although the results of the surveys were difficult to interpret, the extensions to the permitted hours (afternoon opening and, in many parts of the country, later evening closing) did not lead to a marked increase in overall alcohol consumption. It is probable that the Association of Chief Police Officers in England and Wales has been guided by this experience in proposing to the government that twenty-four-hour opening of licensed premises would not have adverse social consequences.

In Norway in the early 1980s there was an experimental one-year Saturday closing of state-controlled liquor stores (Norway is a monopoly country). This had little effect on consumption, as consumers simply adjusted their purchasing patterns. Alcohol-related disturbances certainly declined on Saturdays, but according to Nordlund (1985, 1989) they increased on Fridays. Presumably, the net effects of this experiment were not considered beneficial because the legislation was repealed.

Density of Outlets

It has been suggested that there is an association between outlet density and the consumption of alcohol. Yet classic economic theory would suggest that outlet density would change in response to demand. Statistics for the United Kingdom as they relate to per capita consumption and the number of licensed premises showed an interesting relationship between outlet density and consumption. Between 1980 and 1992 per capita consumption was virtually unchanged, but the number of licensed outlets increased by about 12 percent, from 177,343 to 199,567. There are probably many reasons for this lack of correlation. Some licensed premise owners might have been satisfied with lower returns from their business. Others might have diversified into food, for instance, and relied less on the profits from alcoholic drinks.

Rationing

In some societies rationing systems have been imposed but have been found to be an ineffective way to reduce problem drinking. The Bratt rationing system (named after the doctor who invented it) was adopted in Sweden in 1914 as an alternative to prohibition. It coexisted with an illicit trade in alcoholic drinks, abuse of nonbeverage alcohol, the prescription of alcohol by sympathetic medical practitioners, and a widespread disregard of the law. Rationing was introduced in Greenland in 1979 and was abolished in 1982. After it was abolished, there was a 60 percent increase in consumption, as measured by official statistics, and emergency room cases increased. But during rationing a large black market flourished; many casualties were probably concealed.

While rationing might have some success in reducing some alcohol-related problems, it is not generally considered a viable policy option in societies in which a free market economy and individual rights and freedoms are valued.

Prohibition

Over the course of history, prohibition for other than religious reasons has been less than successful. In pre-Christian China, prohibition was tried and abandoned forty times over a period of 2000 years. More recently, in the twentieth century, prohibition has also been shown to be an ineffective and even counterproductive measure.

Yet prohibition does have some benefits. In the United States and Canada there was undoubtedly a marked reduction in alcoholic cirrhosis mortality and other alcohol problem indicators during the period of its enforcement. But it could be argued that there are many aspects of social policy that are as important as alcohol problems. The rise in organized crime in the United States, which was associated with prohibition, was undoubtedly a serious and costly social outcome. In addition, alcohol consumption, the very issue at which the measure was aimed, increased significantly between 1923 and 1933, as the trade in illicit alcohol became established (Bruun et al. 1975).

The case of Truk in Micronesia is sometimes quoted as an example of successful prohibition (Edwards et al. 1994; Marshall and Marshall 1990). Yet, as Partanen (1993) makes clear, this is an example of moral considerations being accorded more importance than measurable criteria of success. But prohibition in Truk did not produce positive results in public health terms. Many other countries have tried prohibition for nonreligious reasons: Norway, Finland, the United States, Canada, Iceland, and the Soviet Union. All of these experiments were abandoned after brief periods because the measure caused more problems than it solved.

Legal Drinking Age

Most developed countries have a minimum age under which it is illegal to purchase alcoholic beverages; in most, the relevant law has been in place for many years and there are few serious attempts to either raise or decrease this age. In North America, however, there have been numerous changes in the law to raise the age, usually in the interests of road safety, and most studies on the effectiveness of this measure have taken place there. The U.S. General Accounting Office (1987) reviewed thirty-two relevant studies and concluded that in states where the minimum age for purchase had been raised from eighteen to twenty-one years, reductions in drink-related road accidents declined by 5–20 percent. The same study did not, however, reveal a drop in the general level of alcohol consumption, and this was confirmed by other studies (Hingson et al. 1983; Williams et al. 1983).

Although a longer term effect of raising the drinking age has been argued by some (O'Malley and Wagenaar 1991), not all studies have provided unequivocal support for this measure. Cross-sectional studies of Toronto high school students showed that a lowering in minimum drinking age did not coincide with an increase in alcohol consumption, but rather that increased consumption has preceded the new legislation (Smart and White 1972). Other evidence from Canada found that, although increases in the drinking age temporarily reduced consumption in the short term, there was no effect on long-term consumption (Johnson et al. 1992).

If road accidents among young drivers are a principal cause for concern, it might make for greater road safety if the minimum driving age were also raised. The dramatic improvements in road safety in the United Kingdom, particularly among young riders and drivers, have occurred by means of measures that target education and public awareness and not through changing the legal alcohol purchase age.

Drinking and Driving

The Legal Limit   Scientific assessment of an appropriate legal blood alcohol concentration (BAC) for drivers is usually based on Borkenstein's Grand Rapids study of the early 1960s. The United Kingdom level of 80 milligrams per 100 milliliters is based on this study. The results of this study have been reanalyzed recently (Hurst, Harte, and Frith 1995), and the significant increase in risk is now thought to occur between 50 and 70 milligrams per 100 milliliters. There is therefore some justification for setting the legal limit either at the lower level or somewhere between the two, and several countries have done so (e.g.,

Belgium, France, Australia, Portugal, Norway). However, after considering all the evidence, the 1992 Report to Congress by the U.S. Department of Transportation recommended the 80 milligrams per 100 milliliters and not the lower level, which the reanalysis of the Grand Rapids study suggested.

What the level should be for a particular country is a matter for local judgment. Obviously, it should not be set at a level at which impairment for the majority of drivers is unlikely, because this would expose citizens to serious penalties when they had put no one at significant risk. To set the limit too low would generate too great a workload for the police and would generate public hostility, which would only hinder enforcement. This appears to have happened in Sweden (Aberg 1993), where the limit was lowered in 1990 from 50 to 20 milligrams per 100 milliliters. If satisfactory progress is being made on the drunk driving front, then no radical changes should be made.

Young drivers form a special category. They are at increased risk because they are both inexperienced drinkers and inexperienced drivers. The obvious implication is that a lower BAC level is justified for such drivers. In Australia such limits have been introduced, with beneficial results. However, in the United Kingdom marked improvements have occurred in young driver safety without further restrictions being imposed on them.

Random Breath Testing   Random breath testing involves frequent, widespread, and publicly visible checks along roadways, during which police stop drivers at random and require them to provide breath samples. Since its introduction in Australia, there has been a 22 percent drop in fatal crash levels and a 36 percent drop in alcohol-involved traffic accidents. However, several factors need to be considered before adopting such a policy in countries where it is not police practice.

Although it was originally supposed that random breath testing alone caused the reduction in drunk driving accidents in Australia, it is now believed that the publicity campaigns that preceded and accompanied it were essential for creating and maintaining an awareness of the drunk driving problem (Moore et al. 1993). Further, because the system is random, very low success rates are achieved: usually fewer than 2 percent of drivers stopped are over the legal limit. This means that random breath testing might not be an efficient use of police time. In the United Kingdom, when targeted testing was carried out, positive detection rates of 30 percent were achieved.

In the United Kingdom in the last decade, alcohol-related road deaths have declined from 33 percent of all road deaths to 17 percent; other alcohol-related accidents have declined by a similar amount. In the same period, vehicle numbers have increased by 25 percent, and mileage traveled has increased by 35 percent. These remarkable successes have been achieved without lowering the legal drinking limit and without random breath testing. The conclusion must be that different approaches may work in different countries.

There have been some promising attempts to change attitudes toward drinking and hazardous drinking patterns. For example, modification of the drinking environment in bars and restaurants has been shown to have a marked effect on alcohol misuse and on drinking and driving. Server training aimed at reducing the risk of intoxication of customers, in particular, was found to reduce the chances of intoxication by one half, while absolute consumption and the rate of consumption remained unaffected (Saltz 1987). Furthermore, in Oregon, for instance, reductions in single-vehicle nighttime traffic crashes were observed following server training (Holder and Wagenaar 1990).

Monopolies

It is sometimes suggested that competitive market forces drive the sale of alcoholic beverages upward as it responds to demand. To avoid this, monopolies have been established in some countries (e.g., Finland, Norway, Sweden). The intention is to decrease consumption or to prevent it from rising by eliminating competition and curtailing availability.

The effectiveness of monopolies in controlling consumption can be questioned. In the European region, out of twenty-three countries for which reliable data are available, over the period 1980–92, declines occurred in fifteen countries with no monopolies. In some (Italy, Poland, France, and Spain), these declines were significant. In Finland, a monopoly country, there was a significant increase in consumption. In Sweden, another monopoly country, there was virtually no change in the official statistics, but unrecorded consumption was thought to have increased to about 40 percent of recorded consumption.

CONCLUSION

The continuing emphasis on alcohol control policies by some reflects a predisposition to regard alcohol use rather than misuse as the source of harm. The effectiveness of control measures depends heavily on the particular drinking culture of the country in question. It has been observed that countries that impose stricter regimes may have a higher prevalence of alcohol problems (Peele and Brodsky 1996). In addition, so-called temperance countries appear to have both a higher death rate from heart disease and a greater number of Alcoholics Anonymous groups per unit population (ibid.).

The control-of-consumption approach, sometimes also referred to as the whole population approach, was considered by the U.K. Interdepartmental Working Group on Sensible Drinking (Moore et al. 1993), which concluded that there were difficulties in applying this approach, especially in the United Kingdom. The group did not presume to include other countries in their conclusions, but nevertheless what they had to say applies to such countries. The Working Group on Sensible Drinking concluded that the causal link between average per capita consumption and alcohol misuse and problems is still poorly understood.

Consequently, there does not appear to be any reason why the approach should apply universally. Seeking to modify individual behavior that is not harmful in order to influence those indulging in harmful behavior poses an ethical problem. In its recommendations, the group was probably strongly influenced by the evidence for the health benefits of sensible drinking.

The following, from a recent paper (Charlton 1995) on the population strategy for preventive medicine, probably best sums up the issue.

> Given the inevitable resource costs of any preventive intervention, the probability of inconvenience and intrusion, and the possibility of harmful outcomes when interfering with human physiology, "conclusive evidence" of causation and effectiveness might be regarded as a *minimum ethical criterion* which must be satisfied before considering a public health intervention. . . . Good intentions are not enough when it comes to imposing interventions upon an unconsenting population. Although effectiveness is a necessary precondition of a preventive implementation, it is not sufficient because it cannot be assumed that the public health should be the overriding goal of policy. Health must be balanced against other principles, such as justice, freedom, and happiness. (p. 609)

REFERENCES

Aberg, L. 1993. Behaviours and opinions of Swedish drivers before and after the 0.02% BAC limit of 1990. *Proceedings of the 12th International Conference on Alcohol Drugs and Traffic Safety.* (Cologne) 1992:1266–70.

Adlaf, E. M., and P. M. Kohn. 1989. Alcohol advertising consumption and abuse: a covariance-structural modelling look at Strickland's data. *British Journal of Addiction* 84:749–57.

Ambler, T. 1996. Can alcohol misuse be reduced by banning advertising? *International Journal of Advertising* 15:167–74.

Bruce, D. 1980. Changes in Scottish drinking habits and behavior following the extension of permitted hours. *Health Bulletin* 38:133–37.

Bruun, K., et al. 1975. *Alcohol Control Policies in Public Health Perspective.* Vol. 25. Helsinki: Finnish Foundation for Alcohol Studies.

Calfee, J., and C. Scheraga. 1994. The influence of advertising on alcohol consumption: a literature review and an econometric analysis of four European nations. *International Journal of Advertising* 13:287–318.

Charlton, B. G. 1995. A critique of Geoffrey Rose's "population strategy" for preventive medicine. *Journal of the Royal Society of Medicine* 88:607–10.

Connolly, G. M., S. Caswell, J. Zhang, and P. A. Silva. 1994. Alcohol in the mass media and drinking by adolescents: a longitudinal study. *Addiction* 89:1255–263.

Duffy, J. C. 1977. Estimating the proportion of heavy drinkers. In *The Ledermann Curve: Report of a Symposium.* London: Alcohol Education Centre.

———. 1986. The distribution of alcohol consumption, 30 years on. *British Journal of Addiction* 81:613–19.

————. 1992. Scottish licensing reforms. In *Alcohol and Drugs: The Scottish Experience*, ed. M. A. Plant, E. B. Ritson, and R. J. Robertson. Edinburgh: Edinburgh University Press

Duffy, J. C., and M. A. Plant. 1986. Scottish liquor licensing changes: an assessment. *British Medical Journal* 292:36–39.

Duffy, M. H. 1989. Measuring the contribution of advertising to growth in demand: an econometric framework. *International Journal of Advertising* 8:95–110.

Edwards, G., et al. 1994. *Alcohol Policy and the Public Good*. Oxford: Oxford University Press.

EUROCARE. 1995. *A Summary of Alcohol Policy and the Public Good: A Guide for Action*.

Fisher, J. C. 1993. *Advertising Alcohol Consumption and Abuse: A Worldwide Survey*. Westport, Conn.: Greenwood.

Goddard, E. 1991. *Drinking in England and Wales in the Late 1980s*. London: OPCS.

Godfrey, C. 1989. Factors influencing the demand for alcohol and tobacco: the use and abuse of economic models. *British Journal of Addiction* 84:1123–38.

————. 1990. Modelling demand. In *Preventing Alcohol and Tobacco Problem*, ed. A. Maynard and P. Tether. Aldershot: Avebury.

Harrison, L., and C. Godfrey. Alcohol advertising controls in the 1990s. *International Journal of Advertising* 3:167–80.

Hingson, R., et al. 1983. Impact of legislation raising the legal drinking age in Massachusetts from 18 to 21. *American Journal of Public Health* 73:163–70.

Hogarty, T. F., and K. G. Elzinga. 1972. The demand for beer. *Review of Economics and Statistics* 54:195–98.

Holder, H. D., and A. C. Wagenaar. 1990. Mandated server training and reduced alcohol-involved traffic crashes: a time-series analysis of the Oregon experience. *Accident Analysis and Prevention* 26:89–97.

Hurst, P. M., D. Harte, and W. J. Frith. 1995. The Grand Rapids dip revisited. *Accident Analysis and Prevention* 26:647–54.

Johnson, J. A., E. H. Oksanen, M. R. Veall, and D. Fretz. 1992. Short-run elasticities for Canadian consumption of alcoholic beverages: an error correction mechanism/cointegration approach. *Review of Economics and Statistics* 74:64–74.

Kendell, R. E. 1995. Alcohol policy and the public good. *Addiction* 90:187–89.

Kendell, R. E., M. de Roumanie, and E. G. Ritson. 1983. Effect of economic changes on Scottish drinking habits, 1978–1982. *British Journal of Addiction* 78:365–79.

Knight, J., and P. Wilson. 1980. *Scottish Licensing Reforms*. London: HMSO.

Kreitman, N. 1986. Alcohol consumption and the preventive paradox. *British Journal of Addiction* 81:353–63.

Labys, W. C. 1976. An international comparison of price and income elasticities for wine consumption. *Australian Journal of Agricultural Economics* 20:33–36.

Lau, H.-H. 1975. Cost of alcoholic beverages as a determinant of consumption. *Research Advances in Alcohol and Drug Problems* 22:211–45.

Ledermann, S. 1956. *Alcool, Alcoolism, Alcoolisation*. Cahier 29, Institut National d'Etudes Demographiques. Paris: Presses Universitaires de France.

Lee, B., and V. J. Tremblay. 1992. Advertising and the U.S. market demand for beer. *Applied Economics* 24:69–76.

Makowsky, C. R., and P. C. Whitehead. 1991. Advertising and alcohol sales: a legal impact study. *Journal of Studies on Alcohol* 52:555–67.

Manning, W. G., L. Blumberg, and L. H. Moulton. 1995. The demand for alcohol: the differential response to price. *Journal of Health Economics* 14:123–48.

Marshall, M., and L. B. Marshall. 1990. *Silent Voices Speak: Women and Prohibition in Truk.* Belmont, Calif.: Wadsworth.

Moore, V. M., et al. 1993. Drink driving: drivers' perceptions about detection and their effect on behavior. *Proceedings of the 12th International Conference on Alcohol Drugs and Traffic Safety.* (Cologne) 1992:1210–15.

Nordlund, S. 1985. *Effects of Saturday Closing of Wine and Spirits Shops in Norway.* Oslo: National Institute of Alcohol Research.

———. 1989. *State Monopolies and Alcohol Prevention.* Helsinki: Social Research Institute of Alcohol Studies.

O'Malley, O. M., and A. C. Wagenaar. 1991. Effects of minimum drinking age laws on alcohol use, related behaviors, and traffic crash involvement among American youth, 1976–1987. *Journal of Studies on Alcohol* 52:478–91.

Ornstein, S. L. 1980. Control of alcohol consumption through price increases. *Journal of Studies on Alcohol* 41:807–18.

Österberg, E. 1992. Effects of alcohol control measures on alcohol consumption. *International Journal of the Addictions* 27:209–25.

Partanen, J. 1993. Failures in alcohol policy: lessons from Russia, Kenya, Truk, and history. *Addiction* 88 (suppl.):1295–345.

Partanen, J., and M. Montonen. 1988. *Alcohol and the Mass Media.* EURO Reports and Studies 108. Copenhagen: World Health Organization.

Peele, S., and A. Brodsky. 1996. The antidote to alcohol abuse: sensible drinking messages. In *Wine in Context: Nutrition, Physiology, Policy.* Proceedings of the Symposium on Wine and Health, Reno, Nevada.

Plant, M. A. 1979. *The Ledermann Curve: A Review of the Recent Debate.* London: Brewers' Society.

Plant, M., E. Single, and T. Stockwell, eds. 1997. *Alcohol: Minimising the Harm.* London: Free Association.

Poikalainen, K. 1995. A Public Enemy or a Public Friend. *Addiction* 90:187–89.

Saffer, H. 1991. Alcohol advertising bans and alcohol abuse: an international perspective. *Journal of Health Economics* 10:65–79.

———. 1992. Alcohol advertising and alcohol abuse: econometric evidence. Paper presented at NIAAA Working Group on the Effects of Mass Media on the Use and Abuse of Alcohol, Washington, D.C.

Saltz, R. F. 1987. Roles of bars and restaurants in preventing alcohol-impaired driving: An evaluation of server intervention. *Evaluation and Health Professions* 10:5–27.

Smart, R. G. 1988. Does alcohol advertising affect overall consumption? a review of empirical studies. *Journal of Studies on Alcohol* 49:314–23.

Smart, R. G., and R. E. Cutler. 1976. The alcohol advertising ban in British Columbia: problems and effects on beverage consumption. *British Journal of Addiction* 71: 13–21.

Smart, R. G., and W. J. White. 1972. *Effects of Lowering the Legal Drinking Age on Postsecondary Students in Metropolitan Toronto.* Toronto: Addiction Research Foundation.

Smith, N. M. H. 1976. Research note on the Ledermann formula and its recent applications. *Drinking and Drug Practices Surveyor* 12:15–22.

Sobell, L., M. Sobell, T. Tonetto, and G. Leo. 1993. Severely dependent alcohol abusers may be vulnerable to alcohol cues on television programmes. *Journal of Studies on Alcohol* 49:85–91.

Stampfer, M. D., G. A. Colditz, W. C. Willett, and F. E. Speizer. 1980. A prospective study of moderate alcohol consumption and the risk of coronary heart disease and stroke in women. *New England Journal of Medicine* 319:267–73.

Strickland, D. E. 1982. Alcohol advertising organizations and influence. *Journal of Advertising* 1:307–19.

Sturgess, B. T. 1992. Dispelling the myth: the effects of total advertising expenditure on aggregate consumption. *Journal of Advertising* 1:210–12.

Sturgess, D. E. 1983. Advertising exposure, alcohol consumption, and misuse of alcohol. In *Economics and Alcohol: Consumption and Control,* ed. M. Grant, M. Plant, and A. Williams. New York: Gardner.

Tuck, M. 1980. *Alcoholism and Social Policy: Are We on the Right Lines?* Home Office Research Study 65. London: HMSO.

U.K. Department of Health and Social Security. 1995. *Sensible Drinking: The Report of an Interdepartmental Working Group.* London: HMSO.

U.S. General Accounting Office. 1987. *Drinking Age Laws: An Evaluation Synthesis and Their Impact on Highway Safety.* Washington, D.C.: Government Printing Office.

WHO. 1988. *Alcohol Policies: Perspectives from the USSR and Some Other Countries.* Copenhagen: World Health Organization.

———. 1993. *European Alcohol Action Plan.* EUR/RC42/8. Copenhagen: World Health Organization.

———. 1994. *Cardiovascular Disease Risk Factors: New Areas for Research.* Technical Report 841. Geneva: World Health Organization.

Williams, A. F., P. L. Zador, S. S. Harris, and R. S. Karpf. 1983. The effect of raising the legal minimum drinking age on involvement in fatal crashes. *Journal of Legal Studies* 12:169–79.

Chapter 9

The Social Costs of Alcohol Consumption: Definitions, Measurement, and Policy Implications

Richard Dubourg and David Pearce

Any reasonable evaluation of the arguments being used to determine the right, or optimal, level of alcohol consumption must rest on a comparison of the costs and benefits accruing to the individual consumer and to society as a whole. Alcohol gives legitimate pleasure (a benefit), but its misuse also imposes losses on society (a social cost). The cost-benefit framework helps to establish what is and what is not a legitimate social cost of alcohol consumption, to indicate what can and cannot be added together, and to illuminate the issue of choice of policy instrument for controlling excessive alcohol consumption.

Essentially, the consumption of alcohol and alcoholic products can be viewed from two perspectives. The first is the perspective of the individual consumer. An individual decides at what level, how frequently, and in what manner he or she wants to consume alcohol by considering the personal costs and the benefits incurred from each. The individual will continue to buy and consume alcohol as long as the enjoyment gained compensates for the expenditure incurred. The individual will also wish to consider any impacts increased consumption might have upon his or her health, performance at work, and so on. At lower levels of consumption, these adverse impacts are likely to be minor,

Richard Dubourg is a European Commission Research fellow at the Centre for Social and Economic Research on the Global Environment (CSERGE), University College London and University of East Anglia. David Pearce is associate director of CSERGE and professor of economics, University College London.

but they might increase significantly at higher levels, so that most individuals will generally refrain from drinking patterns that involve the frequent consumption of large amounts of alcohol.

But what happens if the individual does not take every cost and every benefit into account when choosing how much alcohol to consume or how often to consume it? This might occur for three reasons. First, although this is unlikely, the individual may be unaware of all of the negative consequences of consuming alcohol or of all of the beneficial effects of consuming moderate amounts of alcohol. Second, the individual may be aware of the possible negative consequences but may be unable or unwilling to modify his or her consumption because this consumption has become habitual. Last, the individual may ignore consequences that accrue to other people, for example, the risks borne by others from accidents that may be induced by immoderate consumption. Some of the costs and benefits of drinking thus become external to the decision to drink, and as a result individuals are likely to make the incorrect decision when judged from a social point of view. What matters from society's point of view, then, are the social costs and benefits of individual patterns of alcohol consumption.

The justification for any specific corrective government intervention or policy will depend on a comparison of the costs and benefits resulting from that intervention, but incorrect decisions made by individuals about how to consume alcohol suggest at least the scope for some such intervention. In turn, incorrect consumption decisions are likely to be signaled by the presence of unrecognized external costs and benefits. Indeed, the nature of those externalities is likely to influence directly the type of policy that would be best suited to address the problem; in turn, the nature of the externalities will depend on the pattern of alcohol consumption, because consumption tends to affect type of cost. However, in exercises to estimate the social costs of alcohol consumption, not only is the pattern of consumption rarely mentioned, but even the very costs themselves are misclassified and incorrectly defined. This is likely to lead to ineffective and inefficient policy making and to distract attention away from those areas that truly merit public intervention.

THE EXTERNAL COSTS OF ALCOHOL CONSUMPTION

What matters for social policy toward alcohol are the external costs of alcohol consumption. As suggested earlier, alcohol consumers might be unaware of, or judge inaccurately, the full costs and benefits that accrue to them through alcohol consumption and related activities. However, it is commonly known that certain drinking patterns involving heavy consumption may carry with them increased health risks. In fact, it is more likely that people are unaware of the health benefits thought to accompany moderate consumption. Similarly, people are aware that being drunk increases the risk of having accidents while driving, at work, or in the home. Even if their judgment of those risks is impaired at the time of any accident, individuals can be expected to have accounted for this in the decision to drink (and get drunk) in the first place.

That alcohol consumers might be aware of the associated costs but are unable to curtail their consumption is a technical question best left to those qualified to answer it (see chapter 3, this volume). However, a body of economic research suggests that even severe drug addicts are able to, and do, respond to relevant mechanisms such as price changes (see Pearce, Dubourg, and Calthrop 1996 for details). Moreover, we might ask whether alcohol policy is the appropriate route for addressing alcoholism, for alcoholism is a far more complex phenomenon than a mere compulsion to drink. It involves a whole range of factors relating to the alcoholic's own character and personal circumstances. In the same way that suicide is increasingly being seen as a symptom of mental illness (see section on suicide and depression, below), perhaps alcoholism needs to be seen as more than just excessive drinking, and policy and treatment should be formulated accordingly.

Some of the costs generated by alcohol-related behavior may fall on people other than the drinker, so that he or she has no incentive to take these into account when deciding how much to drink. Costs and benefits such as these are rife in the environmental sphere. For instance, someone might decide to drive to work despite the fact that the (net) benefits derived are less than the extra costs imposed on others in the form of air pollution, noise pollution, and traffic congestion. Similarly, an industrial company might continue to emit waste into rivers or the atmosphere, even when the costs of installing abatement technology are much less than the benefits that surrounding residents would gain in terms of a cleaner environment. Such externalities also arise in alcohol use. When an individual decides to drink and drive, he or she may not consider the extra accident risk imposed on other road users. Or when an individual decides to drink at work, he or she may not consider the possible reduced productivity. And if drinking causes the drinker to draw on health or accident insurance more often, the premiums might not reflect this.

Hence, the costs imposed by drinkers on third parties, and for which no compensation is paid, are the only costs relevant for policy. Other costs are not. The costs of purchasing alcohol, for example, are not relevant to decisions about how much or how frequently alcohol should be consumed, since consumers willingly pay these costs in return for the benefit of alcohol consumption, whether that benefit is simply pleasure or a mix of pleasure and personal health. Such costs are said to be internalized. In the same way, the displeasure associated with, say, a hangover is an internalized cost, since any rational person would expect that such an event will follow heavier than moderate drinking. The general rule, then, is that as long as costs are internalized, they are already accounted for in the private cost-benefit calculation; they are not relevant to social cost-benefit calculations and are not, therefore, relevant to social policy. It matters a great deal, then, what external costs are and how they are measured. Here we consider the definition of external cost and compare this definition with the determinants of external costs most often found in the literature.

In what follows, we examine the way social costs have been defined and measured in the literature on alcohol consumption. We pay particular attention to the question of whether costs are internalized. We also address explicitly the relationship between pattern of alcohol consumption and generation of costs. This permits us to assess to what extent existing social cost studies are legitimate and accurate and what the effect might be of taking a full, economic approach.

THE DIFFERENT COSTS OF ALCOHOL CONSUMPTION

Premature Mortality among Drinkers

There is a large literature on the impact of alcohol consumption on mortality rates. A growing consensus now exists that light and moderate alcohol consumption may have some protective effects in terms of reduced all-cause mortality and of mortality from cardiovascular disease and ischemic stroke in particular (Ashley et al. 1994; Doll et al. 1994; English et al. 1995). These benefits tend to be especially relevant to particular sections of the population according to their sex, age, diet, and of course, drinking pattern. Moreover, the risks of other illness is thought to be related to abusive patterns of consumption. Finally, heavy and immoderate drinking is thought to be associated with increases in the risks of all relevant diseases, although there is some disagreement as to the definition of heavy drinking.

A large number of studies have estimated the costs of premature mortality thought to be the result of alcohol consumption (see also chapters 1, 2, and 7 in this volume). In the United Kingdom, McDonnell and Maynard (1985) have used figures estimated by Holtermann and Burchell (1981), based on the value of output lost as a result of premature death, that is, the discounted present value of the earnings stream over the life cycle. They calculated costs of £567.7 million in 1983, which translates to about £950 million in 1993 prices. However, they admitted to some inadequacies in the data they employed. Other studies have, of course, generated different numbers. An estimate of the costs of substance abuse in Canada by Single and colleagues (1996) suggested that the estimated cost of alcohol abuse in Canada for 1992 was $7.5 billion. The lower values obtained in the study than in a previous analysis (Adrian 1988), which placed the cost at $11.8 billion, were due to its more conservative operating principle.

This human capital approach, which focuses on loss in output, was also used for the case of Japan by Nakamura, Tanaka, and Takano (1993). They estimated the premature mortality costs of alcohol abuse to have been ¥923 billion in 1987, or over US$6 billion. This figure includes estimates of the value of nonmarket services, such as housekeeping. However, the study has a serious weakness in that it used a 1980 United States ratio, originally estimated by Harwood et al. (1984), for the ratio of alcohol-attributable deaths to total deaths. Clearly, the assumption of an identical ratio, in spite of potentially wide differences in the public health and drinking patterns of the two countries, introduces significant uncertainty into the results.

Finally, Rice et al. (1990) estimated the mortality costs of alcohol use in the United States to have been $27 billion in 1985, indexed to just under $37 billion in 1990 (Rice 1993). This figure incorporated estimates not only for those life-threatening conditions thought to be the direct result of alcohol consumption, such as cirrhosis of the liver, but also for deaths due to road accidents, suicides, and so on. One-fifth of these costs were accounted for by the former category, giving figures of $5 billion in 1985 and $7 billion in 1990, which are more comparable with those of McDonnell and Maynard (1985). Some commentators have questioned the role of alcohol as a causative agent, at least in all of such cases rather than an associated factor (Josephson and Haberman 1980).

These figures, if correct, suggest that the premature mortality costs of alcohol use might be a significant burden on these and other countries. However, the relevance of such calculations to social cost estimates and policy formulation is doubtful. In particular, premature mortality costs borne by drinkers cannot be described as external costs. As long as individual drinkers are aware of the potential health risks that might accompany their drinking—and there is no reason, given the wide publicity and the ongoing public debate in this area, to suppose that they are not—then a positive decision to drink indicates that drinkers have decided that these health risks are outweighed by the positive aspects of drinking, namely, taste, enjoyment, and socializing. From a social point of view, if no one else is affected by the individual's decision, then that decision is the correct one, and there is no reason for society, represented by the government, to intervene.

This is an important issue and one to which we will return. The explanation for repeated errors in the literature regarding social costs is the result of a failure to recognize that social well-being is a function of the well-being of individuals in society. This failure accounts for the reliance placed upon the human capital model to value health losses. The implications are graphically illustrated in the study by McDonnell and Maynard (1985), in which alcohol-related premature mortality was counted as a cost to industry rather than to drinkers. Such a position suggests, for example, that a decision by a person to join, say, the civil service rather than a private firm should also be classed as a cost to industry. Even further, it argues for alcohol-related mortalities to be treated as a benefit to some companies, undertakers, for instance, who will presumably gain from the increased demand for their services.

There is little difference when we recognize that, individually, the greatest health risks are borne by those people whose patterns of drinking are immoderate or abusive. For even though heavy drinking can be associated with serious health implications, it is the value of the risk of those impacts that is relevant to the individual's consumption decision. This explains why some people are prepared to submit themselves to what others might regard as unacceptably high risks of death in pursuit of, say, the enjoyment of partaking in dangerous sports. It is the risk of death, not death itself, that the mountaineer or racing driver trades off against enjoyment. Emphasizing the apparent importance of health risks associated with alcohol consumption, while denying the existence of any associated enjoyment, pleasure, or other benefits (as, for instance, Eurocare 1995 does), not only contradicts common observation but also removes any ability to explain the existence of drinking in the first place. Such a narrow approach does little to advance the debate or to formulate reasonable, democratic, government policies.

Morbidity among Drinkers

Many of the points raised above in connection with premature mortality can be reiterated here. The estimation of morbidity costs in terms of human capital lost, for example, fails to recognize that it is the individual's own valuation of his or her health that is relevant to the drinking decision and that any morbidity health costs resulting from drinking are costs to the drinker and are, therefore, internal, so that the decision whether to drink or not can be regarded as the correct one. However, some of the impacts of alcohol-induced morbidity might well be borne not by the drinkers themselves but by their employers. That is, the employers of alcohol abusers bear the costs of absence through sickness, absenteeism, time spent on visits to doctors and medical centers, and reduced productivity.

McDonnell and Maynard (1985) used data from the United Kingdom Office for Population Censuses and Surveys to estimate the number of extra days of sick leave in a year taken by drinkers, as opposed to nondrinkers, and then multiplied this by an estimated value of a day's work. This approach was, as they acknowledged, subject to the criticism that it did not account for the reason for sick leave (for instance, drinkers were also more likely to be smokers). Nor did they account for the fact that moderate drinkers might take fewer days of sick leave than either heavy drinkers or nondrinkers. If an assumption of 40 percent extra days attributable to alcohol was used, a figure of £176 million would be obtained for 1983, or £404 million if all extra days of sick leave were alcohol related (£292 million and £671 million, respectively, in 1993 prices). This latter figure is an overestimate. However, McDonnell and Maynard ultimately rejected these estimates in favor of an updating of the figures obtained by Holtermann and Burchell (1981), which were based on a study of seventy-three male alcoholics. This gave a figure of £641 million (1983; £1.06 billion in 1993), but the validity of this procedure must be in doubt.

However, the crucial question is whether such costs are borne by the employer and, if so, whether they are external to the individual drinking decision or internal to it, given that drinkers tend to receive lower wages in recognition of their lower productivity and performance. In fact, the way Harwood et al. (1984), Rice et al. (1990), and Nakamura, Tanaka, and Takano (1993) treated this issue was by calculating that heavy drinking results in an impairment factor (the extent to which earnings are reduced by alcohol abuse) of 21 percent. That is, the wages of alcohol abusers are 21 percent lower than those of nonabusers. These assumptions led Rice et al. (1990) to estimate the reduction in wages to be $24 billion for the United States in 1985 ($30 billion, or £20 billion, in 1993) and Nakamura, Tanaka, and Takano (1993) to estimate a ¥4,400 billion reduction in wages for Japan in 1987 (¥4,868 billion, or £26 billion, in 1993).

Hence, Harwood et al. (1984) accounted for the fact that abusive and immoderate drinking patterns were most likely to be associated with extra sickness and absenteeism, while McDonnell and Maynard (1985), by allocating all extra sick leave to drinking alone, did not. On the other hand, Heien and Pittman (1989) have provided a comprehensive demonstration of the weaknesses of the analysis by Harwood and colleagues. In addition, Nakamura, Tanaka, and Takano (1993) continued to transfer the Harwood results directly to the Japanese context, further compounding the analytical errors. However, the greater error arose in the assignment of these costs as external costs. To the extent that wages were lower as a result of alcohol-related productivity losses, this simply meant that costs were internalized. As a result, whether the Harwood-derived cost estimates were right or wrong, they should still be excluded from assessments of the economic costs of alcohol abuse.

A number of studies have attempted to estimate the effects of alcohol consumption on earnings. The results of Harwood et al. (1984) are typical in that many studies have found some depressing effect. However, more recent studies have challenged this conclusion. Berger and Leigh (1988) found that drinkers in the United States earned more than nondrinkers, but their analysis was limited in that it distinguished only between nondrinkers and drinkers and related only to workers, thereby missing individuals for whom drinking was associated with unemployment. This analysis also did not differentiate between the earnings of individuals with different drinking patterns.

Mullahy and Sindelar (1993), however, have found that alcoholism had a more significant impact on the likelihood of working than on wage rates and that much of the impact on wages disappeared once account was taken of correlated variables, such as schooling. Most recently, French and Zarkin (1995) accounted for variations in workers' consumption levels and found that moderate consumption was associated with the highest wages; heavy drinkers, abstainers, and light drinkers were paid less, on average. This could reflect the higher social and other relevant variables linked with moderation, but it could also reflect the smaller number of days lost from sick leave and absenteeism and the higher productivity that might accompany the improved health associated with beneficial patterns of alcohol consumption.

What is evident is that, whatever the exact relationship, wages respond to changes in productivity and efficiency related to alcohol consumption and are likely to vary with individual drinking patterns. As a result, it is not certain that these losses should be counted either as social costs (in the sense implied by social cost studies) or externalities. It has been suggested that "as precise data are scarce, there do not appear to be available reliable estimates of the economic burden imposed by alcohol problems on workplaces. However, common sense suggests that the burden must be substantial" (Eurocare 1995, p. 56). Yet the literature demonstrates that, at least for the majority of drinkers, this is not true. To quote Cook (1991), summarizing his review of the alcohol-work literature, "these results obviously cast doubt on the importance of drinking in reducing 'industrial efficiency'" (p. 62).

Medical Treatment Costs

Medical treatment costs are also often included in social cost studies and can represent a significant proportion of the estimated total costs. Their estimation usually involves multiplying expenditure on the treatment of a given illness by the proportion of illness cases thought to be caused by alcohol consumption. Heien and Pittman (1989) have strongly criticized the way this procedure has been performed for the U.S. National Institute of Alcohol Abuse and Alcoholism, a method that Rice et al. (1990) employed. Similarly, the accuracy with which attribution of treatment costs has been made to alcohol is open to debate. As mentioned, Josephson and Haberman (1980) questioned to what extent alcohol was a causal agent in illnesses. As shown by recent medical evidence, some patterns of drinking may have beneficial medical consequences while others may be detrimental to health. Moreover, attribution is complicated by the fact that many heavy drinkers are also smokers or have high-fat diets. On the other hand, data on, for instance, visits to doctors often have not specified the reason for the treatment, so some underreporting is likely to occur (McDonnell and Maynard 1985).

It is true, however, that at least in Europe most health care is paid for not by the drinker but by some agency, such as a national health service. Heavy drinkers place a greater burden on medical services than moderate drinkers and abstainers. However, all drinkers pay taxes that nondrinkers do not pay because of the excise duty on alcohol in most economies. Whether treatment costs are internalized or not, therefore, hinges on whether (heavy) drinkers' additional contribution to government tax receipts is sufficient to cover the costs of their health services. In this regard, the importance of taking a full life-cycle view of individuals' respective demands on collectively provided health services should be recognized. For instance, heavy drinkers' greater demands on health services while they are alive needs to be balanced by the fact that they tend to have shorter life expectancies and, hence, do not draw on pension and health service funds for as many years. On the other hand, heavy drinkers also tend to retire earlier than others, offsetting this effect. Only Manning and colleagues (1989, 1991) have accounted for these effects. However, drinking patterns are dynamic, and many individuals change theirs over the course of a lifetime. This change is generally not taken into account, as discussed in full below.

Accidents on the Roads

Several recent studies claim that alcohol-related motor vehicle accidents are one of the most serious external costs of alcohol. The social costs of car accidents (i.e., the internal and external costs) include the loss of well-being to driver and passengers and to their friends and relations, medical and police costs, and damage to property. Some of these costs are internal to the driver and passengers and hence are not included in calculating the external costs of accidents. The driver is assumed to know the risk of having an accident, at least approximately, before deciding to drive, and so this cost is classified as internal. Similar logic is applied to passengers. Even in the case of drunk drivers, it can be assumed that, by deciding to drink, drivers and passengers voluntarily expose themselves to increases in accident risk.

However, if drivers do not take into account increased risks posed to other drivers from their decisions to drive, this is an external cost. The empirical evidence on this relationship is not clear. Intuitively, one might expect the relationship to be positive and linear, but while the number of vehicle kilometers driven in the last decade has grown dramatically, the number of fatal accidents has fallen sharply, due to a host of other factors. Maddison et al. (1996) reviewed the relevant literature and suggested that the nature of the relationship of drivers and protected road users (e.g., other drivers or motorcyclists) was different from that of drivers and unprotected road users (e.g., pedestrians and cyclists). Hence, while the great majority of accidents involving unprotected road users can be treated as external, only a proportion of protected users' costs can be so treated. The exact relationship is further complicated by the insurance and criminal justice system, whereby drivers inflicting damage on others may face some cost of their action in terms of compensation paid to the victim or of legal sanctions, such as driving bans, fines, or imprisonment (see table 9.1).

The economic cost of accidents is quantified in terms of the change in risk to road users. Empirical evidence exists on the amount of money people are willing to pay to change the risks they face, which can be thought of as the premium people will pay for certain safety features on a car, for example.

Table 9.1   Estimated external costs of traffic accidents in the United Kingdom, 1993

Victims	Number of injuries			External cost (£ billion)
	Killed	Serious injury	Slight injury	
Protected road users	2,392	30,201	202,968	0.4–4.9
Unprotected road users	1,422	14,808	54,229	2.5–4.4
Total	3,814	45,009	257,197	2.9–9.4

Source: Maddison et al. 1996, boxes 7.10 and 7.13.

Medical costs and police administration costs are added to produce estimates of the marginal costs of road traffic accidents (table 9.1). They are based on statistical values, that is, on the value people place on the risks of suffering a casualty (Jones-Lee 1989): for life, £700,000 to £2 million; for injuries, £6,000 to £72,000. Because the great majority of costs of accidents to unprotected road users are external, they account for a large proportion of total costs. The large range in the estimates for protected road users reflects the different assumptions that can be made about the relationship between additional vehicle flow and the risk to other drivers. The estimates in table 9.1 do not account for the economic costs imposed on people trying to avoid accidents from motor vehicles, nor do they adequately deal with the complex interrelationships between traffic flow, traffic speed, and the nature of the accident. Nonetheless, we consider these estimates reasonable.

Evidence suggests that at least partial responsibility for some of these accidents in the United Kingdom can be ascribed to alcohol. These costs are then the legitimate external costs of alcohol misuse. McDonnell and Maynard (1985) have cited evidence suggesting that one-tenth of traffic accidents in England and Wales are alcohol related. Jones-Lee (1993), however, noted that during the period 1978–90, between 20 and 30 percent of road fatalities were found to have blood alcohol levels exceeding 80 milligrams per 100 milliliters. Eurocare (1995) quoted a figure of 14 percent for road deaths that are alcohol related, although it cited no reference, while ETSC (1995) claimed that across the European Union alcohol was the main factor in more than one in five fatal road crashes. Heien and Pitman (1993) referred to a 1990 National Highway Traffic Safety Administration report and a study by Rice et al. (1990), which together suggested that 13.5 percent of fatalities in 1985 were external costs of alcohol use.

Clearly, there is some disagreement here. In particular, it is unclear how different studies account for causality in road traffic accidents, that is, for the fact that some accidents in which alcohol was involved would have happened anyway and were not necessarily the fault of the drinking driver. As a result, it is difficult to assess the extent to which reduced alcohol consumption would lead to reduced road traffic accidents. Let us assume, however, that in the absence of alcohol, traffic accidents of all types would fall by 10–20 percent. Combining this assumption with the estimates made of the external costs of accidents in the United Kingdom suggests that in 1993:

Traffic-accident-related external costs of alcohol

   $= 0.10–0.20 \times$ £2.9 billion $-$ £9.4 billion

   $=$ £0.29 billion (ECU 0.36 billion)

      $-$ £1.88 billion (ECU 2.35 billion) per year

These figures might provide some estimate of the accident cost that could be ascribed to drunk driving in the United Kingdom. However, they should not necessarily be apportioned equally among drunk drivers, because the risk of having an accident is related directly to blood alcohol concentration (BAC) (Glucksman 1994). For instance, a case-control study from the United States suggested that a BAC of 80 milligrams per 100 milliliters doubled the risk of causing an accident when compared with a BAC of 0 milligrams per 100 milliliters; 100 milligrams per 100 milliliters increased the risk seven times; 150 milligrams per 100 milliliters increased risk ten times; and 200 milligrams per 100 milliliters increased risk twenty times (Allsop 1988). Thus, drivers who have been drinking heavily would appear to impose a greater external cost on other road users than do other drinking drivers.

However, the picture is complicated even further when we recognize that some internalization of accident costs already occurs as a result of existing regulatory systems of prosecution and fines for drunk driving. Kenkel (1993a) pointed out that although drivers with higher BAC imposed greater risks on others, they were also more likely to be apprehended by the police. In fact, he found that expected penalties in the United States from drunk driving already increased with the driver's BAC by about the right relative amount, at least for the BAC levels he examined. However, he also found that the expected absolute penalty levels were too low by around 50 percent, under conservative assumptions, and possibly by an order of magnitude.

This discussion suggests that the figures we present are likely to be toward the top of the range of estimates of the appropriate external cost because of this existing internalization. However, it also indicates that a simple definition of external costs of alcohol consumption is extremely difficult to arrive at because of the multitude of pathways by which costs and benefits are borne and paid for. A simple framework for presenting social costs runs the risk of failing to recognize the full extent to which costs and benefits are distributed, hence providing inaccurate estimates of the true social costs of alcohol consumption.

Accidents in the Home, at Work, and Elsewhere

It is not surprising that individuals under the influence of alcohol are more likely to be involved in domestic accidents than other people (Glucksman 1994). Moreover, the increased risk of accident is unlikely to be restricted entirely to heavy drinkers, although the absolute increase in risk will generally increase with certain patterns of consumption. As was the case with road accidents, even if people who are drunk might not be aware of the full accident risks they face (which would signal an externality in terms of the classification set out at the beginning of this chapter), it is reasonable to assume that they are fully aware before they decide to drink and recognize the link between their drinking decision and potential associated risk increases. As a result, the costs that accompany these higher accident rates accrue almost entirely to drinkers themselves and are, therefore, internal. The exception is likely to be accident insurance payments, which come from insurance policies that cannot or do not discriminate according to drinking status. This is a legitimate market failure and results in quasi-external costs because it implies that drinkers are receiving insurance coverage at less than the expected value of their claims. This tends to result in an increase in premiums for all policyholders imposed by those who are heavy drinkers.

It is possible that, in certain situations, drinkers might not just increase their own risks of being involved in an accident but also the risks faced by others. An important class of such risks might relate to the workplace. Eurocare (1995) reported International Labour Office claims that 20–25 percent of accidents at work involved intoxicated people injuring themselves and innocent victims. This implies that less than 25 percent of workplace injuries were related to innocent victims and could, therefore, be classified as external. Unfortunately, little other evidence on this question is available.

However, just as the evidence reviewed above supports the possibility that employers are compensated for reductions in productivity due to heavy drinking by paying lower wages, so a similar story might hold here for workplace accidents. If this were the case, then it would imply that alcohol-related workplace accident costs are internalized. This possibility should not be dismissed, although supportive evidence is lacking. It is also unclear to what extent the colleagues of heavy-drinking workers might be compensated for any increased accident risk they might face. This would seem to reduce the scope for internalization in wage rates. More work needs to be done in this area.

Alcohol and Crime

According to Pernanen (1991), alcohol is strongly associated with crimes against property and the person. Glucksman (1994) referred to a number of studies that purport to link alcohol use with rapes, burglaries, and murders. Others, however, have stressed that what has been demonstrated is only an association, rather than a causation, between crime and drinking. (Indeed, Pittman and Heien 1991 used this argument for the total exclusion of crime costs in their study of the external costs of alcohol consumption.) Moreover, that association tended to be between crime and heavy drinking (Glucksman 1994) and to be stronger for victims of crime than for perpetrators. This is potentially important, because it implies that a portion of what would otherwise have been classified as external crime costs of alcohol use—the costs of being the victim of a drinker's action—might more accurately be described as internal.

However, what is hardly in doubt is that the true relationship between alcohol and crime is highly complex. Ensor and Godfrey (1993) have attempted to reflect this complexity in a model of crime and alcohol use. Like most economic models of crime, deterrent and encouraging factors predominate as explanatory variables. Deterrents were sentence severity and the probability of detection; encouraging factors were low wages and crime opportunities. Alcohol was an encouraging factor, perhaps acting by reducing the perceived risk of capture. Alcohol was also postulated to impact upon particular crimes, especially impulsive ones, which required little planning and organization.

Ensor and Godfrey encountered difficulties in obtaining ideal data to test their model effectively. Reliance had to be placed on data on recorded crime, whereas the model was specified in terms of level of criminal activity. Moreover, the authors were forced to consider total annual consumption as their alcohol variable, thereby making demand specification difficult. These weaknesses seem to have had some effect on the results. Consideration of burglaries and fraud had to be abandoned because of poor estimation diagnostics. Mixed support was received for the other four types of crime considered: theft, robbery, criminal damage, and violence. For instance, although alcohol consumption was a generally positive and statistically significant factor in crime levels, the probability of detection (a priori, a major determinant of crime) was not. Other variables were also poorly determined. Similar difficulties were encountered with attempts to model the probability of detection. Alcohol was not found to be a determinant in regional analyses.

These results would seem to support the idea that alcohol consumption and crime are not closely related. As a result, the procedure of Nakamura, Tanaka, and Takano (1993) of attributing only 0.07 percent of total legal and adjustment costs of crime to alcohol may not have been so wide of the mark. On the other hand, much of the problem might have come from Ensor and Godfrey's (1993) concentration on total annual alcohol consumption as the relevant factor explaining crime, since this was obviously an extremely crude specification and probably only weakly representative of the true relationship between drinking and the decision to commit any particular crime.

Suicide and Depression

Social harms such as suicide and depression are often argued to be closely associated with alcohol consumption and to represent one of the main classes of the social cost of drinking. For instance, Gunnell and Frankel (1994) have suggested that in the United Kingdom, the United States, and Sweden alcohol-dependent people have twenty times the average risk of suicide and account for 15–25 percent of the suicides. There is some doubt whether these events should be treated as external costs of drinking, however. There is no need to adopt the cynical line that suicide affects the individual himself, so that, beyond some consideration of the pain and grief of friends and relatives, all costs are internalized. We can simply appeal to the fact that suicide and other such tragedies are increasingly seen as the symptoms of mental illness rather than of alcohol use. This change in professional opinion is reflected in the treatment of suicide costs in Noble (1978) and Harwood et al. (1984), whose work represents somewhat the official U.S. view. In Noble, 25–37 percent of suicides were attributed to alcohol use, whereas Harwood and colleagues attributed all of them to mental illness.

The case for treating these as external costs of drinking would rest on arguments relating to drinkers' lack of awareness of the costs of consumption or to their inability to alter their drinking in response to those costs. Even accepting these arguments, it is unlikely that, for instance, a blanket tax on all drinking would be justified by policy analysis. This is reinforced by the claim that suicide is related to heavy drinking. Rather, a much more efficient and effective policy is likely to be one of targeting for treatment mentally ill people at risk of suicide. This is, in fact, the type of policy outlined by the United Kingdom white paper, *The Health of the Nation* (1992).

THE SOCIAL COSTS OF ALCOHOL CONSUMPTION

The previous discussion suggests that much of the literature purporting to estimate the social costs of alcohol consumption is misguided and largely incorrect. Dubourg, Pearce, and Calthrop (1997) have provided a comprehensive assessment of the effect of adopting more economically defensible cost definitions on some existing estimates. For instance, McDonnell and Maynard (1985) estimated a figure of £1.6 billion in 1983 for England and Wales. However, this was inflated by £568 million through the human capital treatment of alcohol-related mortality. On the other hand, McDonnell and Maynard failed to account adequately for the costs of road accidents, which Dubourg, Pearce, and Calthrop estimated at between £0.27 billion and £1.7 billion in 1993, deflated to £0.17–£1.13 billion in 1983, for comparison. The result was a revised estimate of the external costs of alcohol consumption in England and Wales of £0.65–£2.24 billion in 1993, compared with an indexed £2.68 billion in the original study. Dubourg and colleagues concluded that, although McDonnell and Maynard's original estimate was only slightly greater than the upper bound of their modified figure, its composition was fundamentally different, with a shift away from output-based components to ones based on concepts of individual welfare.

Dubourg, Pearce, and Calthrop (1997) also considered the body of research carried out by Manning and colleagues (1989, 1991) for the United States. The latter study differed from others in a number of respects. First, it concentrated on patterns of heavy drinking, namely, on those who reported drinking more than two standard (United States) drinks per day, largely in recognition of the fact that many of the costs of alcohol consumption do not accompany moderate drinking. Moreover, the emphasis on two reported drinks per day was intended to account for the fact that drinking levels may have been underreported and that actual drinking levels were closer to five standard drinks per day. The comparison was then made between heavy drinkers and so-called controlled heavy drinkers, because heavy drinkers tended to differ from other drinkers in more respects than just their drinking. The pattern of heavy drinking was correlated with various other lifestyle patterns. For instance, heavy drinkers tend to have a higher propensity to smoke and to have different education histories. Failing to control for

these other potentially relevant factors would bias the estimates of external
attributable to alcohol use.

Second, Manning and colleagues' analysis differed from others in taking a
life-cycle approach to the question. For example, heavy drinkers tended overall
not to live as long as other members of the population, which implied that they
have a shorter time in which to draw on pension funds. However, heavy drinking
also tended to be associated with a propensity to retire earlier, largely because
of ill health. This increased the drain on pension fund resources; on balance, the
authors estimated that it is this latter effect that predominates. This implies a
social-level externality of heavy drinking. Moderate drinkers, on the other hand,
tended to have higher life expectancies, but because of their generally better
health might have been expected to retire later than other people, all things being
equal. This might suggest that the social-level externality would be positive in
this case.

The context of Manning and colleagues' study was the United States, and
hence the pension externality operated by increasing the private health insurance
contributions of those other members of the population who participated in group
insurance funds and whose contributions were not therefore linked to lifestyle
status. Insurance also covered medical care, sick leave, life insurance, and
nursing costs, which were estimated to result in an externality cost equivalent of
$0.20 per ounce of alcohol drink in excess of two reported drinks per day (at a
discount rate of 5 percent per annum).

A number of points can be raised at this stage. First, the fact that private
insurance funds were under consideration begged the question of why the extra
costs of heavy drinking were not recognized in higher insurance contributions.
If private companies provide group insurance as, for example, an employee
prerequisite, then we might take this as evidence that they have decided that it
is in company interests not to discriminate between their employees according
to health (and drinking) status. Second, it is unclear what the results of a similar
analysis would be under different health care systems, for instance, the United
Kingdom's National Health Service, as this would depend on the particular
features of the country's taxation and health service allocation mechanisms.
Third, Manning et al. advocated a public fiscal policy to correct the failure of
group insurance schemes to adjust for relevant lifestyle and health indicators. It
is an empirical question whether it is more efficient and cost effective to address
the root cause of an economic distortion directly or via some other pathway.
However, there is a general presumption in favor of the former, and certainly
Manning and colleagues have adopted a drinks-based tax approach quite arbi-
trarily. Indeed, they seemed more concerned about covering costs than about
reallocating resources to pension and health provision. By levying a tax on all
drinking to cover the social costs resulting from heavy drinking, one economic
distortion is being corrected by introducing another. A full policy cost-benefit
analysis would not recommend the same policy mechanisms to address these
failures.

ıl costs considered by Manning et al. required some in- to the lives of nondrinkers lost in motor vehicle accidents volved. The study cited a U.S. Department of Transpor- imated that of the 22,400 people who died in alcohol- ın the United States in 1985, 7,400 were nondrinkers. ᴜuggested by Heien and Pittman (1993). However, not all ..ᴄiated accidents are caused by alcohol, and not all nondrinking passengers ride with drinking drivers involuntarily. On the other hand, no account has been taken of nonfatal casualties of road accidents, which might entail a significant cost.

The 7,400 number was then valued according to the willingness-to-pay principle at $1.66 million per statistical life lost, to give an external cost of $0.58 per excess ounce of ethanol. This external cost estimate was heavily dependent on the chosen value for statistical life. If these numbers were updated to 1993, a figure more in the region of $2.2 million would be expected, which would increase the external cost element to $0.77 per excess ounce. No account, however, was taken of the cost already paid through existing laws governing drunk driving. Note also that Manning et al. attributed a cost imposed by a restricted section of the population (i.e., those who drink and drive) to the behavior of individuals who reported alcohol consumption equivalent to two drinks or more per day, when there is no necessary link between the two (and without offering evidence in favor of any such link). Moreover, they distributed this cost across all drinkers, on the grounds that it is not possible to levy a tax on alcohol consumption above some level or limit (see below).

The final class of external costs relates primarily to material damage caused in road accidents and crime. Respectively, these account for $4.2 billion and $3.1 billion, resulting in a per excess ounce cost of $0.35. The source for these estimates was Harwood et al. (1984), and they were used directly by Manning et al. despite the fact that the considerations of externality given to them are not clear. Pittman and Heien (1991) argued that, even accepting the causal role of alcohol in these cases, they could not all be classed as external and, accordingly, weighted these figures by 0.2 in their reassessment of the NIAAA studies. Ostensibly, Manning et al. were concerned with the deficit in insurance payments accruing to heavy drinkers to cover these events. But there is no evidence to indicate that Harwood et al. (1984) accounted for this. As a result, the suspicion is that these figures were used without sufficient scrutiny. The $0.35 external cost estimate is therefore in doubt, and Dubourg, Pearce, and Calthrop (1997) leaned toward Pittman and Heien's (1991) line in thinking that it is too high.

Manning et al. (1989, 1991) reported a central estimate of the external cost of excess alcohol consumption of $1.19 per ounce, under the assumption of a 5 percent discount rate. They then multiplied this figure by 0.4, on the grounds that it was not possible to tax only those drinks consumed in excess of the reported two per day limit, to arrive at their alcohol tax estimate. Hence, Manning et al. levied the external costs of heavy drinking on all drinkers. The result, using the authors' figures for alcohol consumption, was an estimate of the total external costs of heavy drinking in the United States of \$24.8 billion in 1986 (\$32.7 billion in 1993). Dubourg et al.'s (1997) adjustments of Manning's 1986 data imply a revised figure of \$19 billion (\$25.1 billion in 1993).

The study by Manning and colleagues is clearly an improvement on other studies examined here. Its classification of externality, if not beyond contention, is certainly more robust, and the features of controlled drinkers and a life-cycle approach are clearly advanced. The study is weak in the costs of regulation, however, and improvements could be gained from more detailed consideration of accidents and crime and from the relationship with individual patterns of drinking.

DISCUSSION AND CONCLUSIONS

The previous discussion suggests that taking an economic view of social cost measurement as it relates to alcohol consumption would result in the following differences when compared with approaches now generally employed in the literature.

First, the economic approach implies a radically different pattern of the burden of costs, away from those that contribute to or reduce economic activity and output and toward those that generate or harm individual and social welfare. It recognizes that costs that are relevant to economic and public policy are incurred without compensation or associated price for those who generate them, for it is these costs that imply the real misallocation of resources. Existing approaches appear to classify costs solely in terms of size, whether they are internalized or not. In this regard also, the economic approach is more sophisticated, accounting for the full set of pathways via which cost internalization can occur, be it directly through tax contributions or indirectly through the legal system, for example, or through market wages. By taking a simplistic view of cost-benefit pathways, existing approaches risk providing a distorted and inaccurate picture of true social costs and benefits.

Second, the economic approach acknowledges a more complex pattern of cost-generating behavior than the literature currently does. It recognizes that the size and nature of external costs is generally a direct function of discrete patterns of alcohol consumption and does not attribute these costs solely to drinking. Chronic heavy drinking tends to be associated with social costs relating to pension and health service provision, and moderate drinking might imply some overall social benefit in these terms. On the other hand, bouts of acute heavy drinking (or binge drinking, which can imply any level of average consumption over the longer term) are more likely to be linked to acute costs such as accidents; hence the importance of cost generation through the combination of drinking with other activities—for example, driving—as well as the need to separate out harmful drinking behaviors. This increased complexity helps to explain the principles of policy formulation inherent in the economic approach.

Third, by highlighting those areas in which real distortions and failures occur, the economic approach has a predisposition in favor of policies targeted on the true causes of these failures. For it is targeted policies that in theory should be most efficient. Existing studies, however, are generally used to justify controls and regulations that affect all drinkers by attempting to cut average consumption. The difficulties with these recommendations are twofold. First, they play down the link between type of drinking behavior and generation of external costs. This might produce policies that imply no necessary impact upon the cost-generating behavior of interest. For instance, policies to reduce average consumption might have only marginal impact upon the incidence of binge drinking (which can still be consistent with very low annual consumption) and hence on the level of drinking-related accidents. Second, they tend to overlook the legitimate benefit that many derive from drinking and that is reflected in the amounts people are prepared to spend on alcohol consumption. As a result, blanket restrictions can imply a significant cost in terms of the reduced enjoyment of those drinkers who are affected by, but not the subject of, such policies. Indeed, given the current analysis of the pattern of cost-generating behavior associated with alcohol consumption, population policies will tend to suffer at the hands of cost-benefit appraisal, as they are likely to imply high costs (through their impact upon innocent consumers) and uncertain benefits (through their tenuous link to their target).

Indeed, whatever the balance of costs and benefits, an assessment of the appropriate policy response needs to be based on a weighing of the impacts of individual policies. For example, Kenkel (1993a, 1993b) found that policies that targeted drunk drivers were more efficient than blanket controls on alcohol availability. What remains the case is that the great majority of social cost studies use erroneous and simplistic definitions of social cost. This does not mean that correctly specified studies will necessarily result in lower overall estimates. However, they will imply a radically different distribution of costs and significantly different implications for policy design. Except in those cases where transaction costs associated with targeting are high, policies directed at those activities that do generate externalities are likely to be more efficient and equitable. There can be no justification for making all drinkers suffer for the costs imposed by those who combine excessive drinking with some other form of activity.

REFERENCES

Adrian, M. 1988. Social costs of alcohol. *Canadian Journal of Public Health* 79: 316–22.

Allsop, R. E. 1988. *Alcohol and Road Accidents: A Discussion of the Grand Rapids Study*. Crowthorne: Transport and Road Research Laboratory.

Ashley, M. J., et al. 1994. Moderate drinking and health: report of an international symposium. *Canadian Medical Journal* 151:1–20.

Berger, M. C., and J. P. Leigh. 1988. The effect of alcohol use on wages. *Applied Economics* 20:1343–51.

Cook, P. 1991. The social costs of drinking. In *The Negative Social Consequences of Alcohol Use,* ed. O. G. Aasland. Oslo: Norwegian Ministry of Health and Social Affairs.

Doll, R., et al. 1994. Mortality in relation to consumption of alcohol: 13 years' observations on male British doctors. *British Medical Journal* 309:911–18.

Dubourg, W. R., D. W. Pearce, and E. Calthrop. 1997. *The Social Costs of Alcohol Consumption: Definitions and Measurement.* Working Paper GEC96.20. London: Centre for Social and Economic Research on the Global Environment.

English, D. R., et al. 1995. *The Quantification of Drug-Caused Morbidity and Mortality in Australia, 1995.* Canberra: Commonwealth Department of Human Services and Health.

Ensor, T., and C. Godfrey. 1993. Modelling the interactions between alcohol, crime, and the criminal justice system. *Addiction* 88:477–87.

ETSC. 1995. Reducing Traffic Injuries Resulting from Alcohol Impairment, 1995. In *Counterbalancing the Drinks Industry: A Eurocare Report to the European Union on Alcohol Policy.* St. Ives: Eurocare.

Eurocare. 1995. *Counterbalancing the Drinks Industry: A Eurocare Report to the European Union on Alcohol Policy.* St. Ives: Eurocare.

French, M. T., and G. A. Zarkin. 1995. Is moderate alcohol use related to wages? Evidence from four worksites. *Journal of Health Economics* 14:319–44.

Glucksman, E. 1994. Alcohol and accidents. *British Medical Bulletin* 50:76–84.

Gunnell, D., and S. Frankel. 1994. Prevention of suicide: aspirations and evidence. *British Medical Journal* 308:1227–33.

Harwood, H. J., D. M. Napolitano, P. L. Kristansen, and J. J. Collins. 1984. *Economic Costs to Society of Alcohol and Drug Abuse and Mental Illness: 1980.* RTI/2734/ 00-01FR. Research Triangle Park, N.C.: Research Triangle Institute.

The Health of the Nation. 1992. London: HMSO.

Heien, D. M., and D. J. Pittman. 1989. The economic costs of alcohol abuse: an assessment of current methods and estimates. *Journal of Studies on Alcohol* 50:567–79.

———. 1993. The external costs of alcohol abuse. *Journal of Studies on Alcohol* 54: 302–7.

Holtermann, S., and A. Burchell. 1981. *The Costs of Alcohol Misuse.* GES Working Paper 37. London: HMSO.

Jones-Lee, M. W. 1989. *The Economics of Safety and Physical Risk.* Oxford: Blackwell.

———. 1993. Personal willingness to pay for prevention: evaluating the consequences of accidents as a basis for preventive measures. *Addiction* 88:913–21.

Josephson, E., and P. Haberman. 1980. Trends in problem drinking. In *An Assessment of Statistics on Alcohol-Related Problems,* ed. E. Josephson. Washington, D.C.: Distilled Spirits Council of the United States.

Kenkel, D. S. 1993a. Do drunk drivers pay their way? a note on optimal penalties for drunk driving. *Journal of Health Economics* 12:137–49.

———. 1993b. Drinking, driving, and deterrence. *Journal of Law and Economics* 36:877–913.

Maddison, D., et al. 1996. *Blueprint 5: The True Costs of Road Transport.* London: Earthscan.

Manning, W. G., et al. 1989. The taxes of sin: do smokers and drinkers pay their way? *Journal of the American Medical Association* 261:1604–9.

———. 1991. *The Costs of Poor Health Habits*. Cambridge: Harvard University Press.

McDonnell, R., and A. Maynard. 1985. The costs of alcohol misuse. *British Journal of Addiction* 80:27–35.

Mullahy, J., and J. L. Sindelar. 1993. Alcoholism, work, and income. *Journal of Labour Economics* 11:494–520.

Nakamura, K., A. Tanaka, and T. Takano. 1993. The social cost of alcohol abuse in Japan. *Journal of Studies on Alcohol* 54:618–25.

Noble, E. P., ed. 1978. *Third Special Report to the U.S. Congress on Alcohol and Health*. Washington, D.C.: GPO.

Pearce, D. W., W. R. Dubourg, and E. Calthrop. 1996. *The Social Costs of Alcohol Consumption*. London: Amsterdam Group.

Pernanen, K. 1991. *Alcohol in Human Violence*. New York: Guildford.

Pittman, D. J., and D. H. Heien. 1991. Economics and alcohol. *Current Opinion in Psychiatry* 4:415–18.

Rice, D. P. 1993. The economic cost of alcohol abuse and alcohol dependence. *Alcohol Health and Research World* 17:10–11.

Rice, D. P., S. Kelman, L. S. Miller, and S. Dunmeyer. 1990. *The Economic Costs of Alcohol and Drug Abuse and Mental Illness: 1985*. Publication ADM90-1649. Washington, D.C.: U.S. Department of Health and Human Services, Alcohol, Drug Abuse, and Mental Health Administration.

Single, E., L. Robson, X. Xiaodi, and J. Rehm. 1996. *The Costs of Substance Abuse in Canada*. Ottawa: Canadian Centre for Substance Abuse.

Chapter 10

Alcohol Abuse:
Cost Effectiveness and
the Economic Impact of
Policies and Programs

Rhonda Galbally, Chris Borthwick, and Roy Batterham

If the analysis of cost and of the effectiveness of interventions in the area of alcohol abuse were simple, interventions would also be simple. The fact that interventions are demonstrably difficult, and that it is no simple matter even to demonstrate any intervention effect at all, should warn us that work on cost-effectiveness cannot profitably be conducted on the basis of the somewhat simplistic assumptions on which many previous attempts were founded.

One such assumption has been the primacy of the message. Knowledge of health risk is comparatively easy to assess, and if it could be assumed that knowledge of the risks of a particular behavior translated seamlessly into an avoidance of that behavior, then population surveys would translate with comparative ease into numerical data on the effect of any particular intervention. Regrettably, this is not so. Information, even information systematized into education and resulting in communication, does not necessarily alter behavior. Behavior is influenced by such a multiplicity of personal, social, and environmental factors that it becomes increasingly difficult to determine the influence of any intervention on any outcome.

Another such assumption has been the universal undesirability of alcohol. Cost analyses of alcohol abuse have hitherto been largely conducted as if alcohol were a substance like tobacco, with no threshold toxicity level and no health

The authors are with the Victorian Health Promotion Foundation, Carlton, Victoria, Australia.

benefits. This approach merged alcohol abuse, which was by definition undesirable, with total alcohol use, and simply modified the latter to extract the former. Alcohol abuse estimates have thus been made on the basis of total consumption statistics.[1] Collins and Lapsley (1991), for example, estimated that if all drinkers consumed no more than the recommended limit, consumption would fall by 30 percent and, therefore, assumed that 30 percent of consumption represented abuse. Success under such an approach could be measured only by an overall reduction in consumption and would involve an assumption that any decrease represented a general shift of the distribution and, therefore, a reduction in the number and severity of abuse incidents in high-risk groups. The effects of a general shift in the curve are not as straightforward as this approach assumes, and the possibility of differential changes in various subgroups, or changes in patterns of drinking rather than quantities of drinking, cannot be so easily disregarded.

The methodologies of previous estimates and previous interventions provide some indicators of the factors that ought to be taken into consideration in future estimates and evaluations.

THE COST OF ALCOHOL ABUSE:
AVAILABLE MODELS

While recent Australian health promotion interventions have been founded on harm-reduction concepts and have thus been targeted at particular settings and behaviors—drunk driving, adolescent binge drinking, domestic violence—rather than general discouragement of consumption, Australian cost assessments have tended to produce global estimates of the effects of the total elimination of alcohol abuse. They are thus better adapted to casting light on global or national policy moves—on the relation of changes in alcohol taxation levels to national economic cost, for example (Richardson 1991)—than on the relative merits of particular intervention strategies.

When it comes to devising models of the cost of alcohol abuse there is an embarrassment of choices. Collins and Lapsley (1991), for example, list several (including Adrian 1988; Ashton and Caswell 1984; Chetwynd and Rayner 1985; Crawford and Ford 1984; Gorsky, Schwartz, and Dennis 1988; McDonell and Maynard 1985; Parker et al. 1987; Schramm 1977; Siegel et al. 1984). No two studies used the same methodology or even factored into the equation the same set of variables. None considered pattern effects. Richardson noted also "an unacceptably wide range of variation in the estimates of cost," with the lowest estimate being (as a fraction of gross national product) only 9 percent of the highest (Richardson 1991, 843).[2]

---

1. Or in some studies, on production statistics; the relation between national production statistics and national consumption statistics, the latter mainly derived from self-report data of variable accuracy, is also problematic.
2. Differences between surveys undertaken with the same methodology at different times are

While the work done by these authors in separating out the components of economic loss in this area is unquestionably valuable, the sheer number of models in itself conveys a message: no existing system has been generally accepted as entirely satisfactory; any new model will have to compete with a range of existing models; there is no formal or informal adjudication process whereby a model can be given definitive status; and any person who disagrees with any estimate may with no loss of credibility shop around for a model with a more acceptable outcome. These factors may in themselves caution us against expecting that any new evaluation protocol can conclusively settle professional disputes that have divided the field for some years.

No previous evaluation, furthermore, has taken into account the increasingly accepted protective effect of moderate alcohol consumption. For example, Doll (1996, 33) writes, "[t]he benefits in terms of prevention are not small. A probable reduction of 30–40 percent in mortality from such a common condition as ischaemic heart disease in middle and old age constitutes a large benefit." In the design of health care programs there are certainly difficulties in taking account of the U-shaped curve (Marmot and Brunner 1991), in which moderate use produces health benefits while excessive use causes health risk. Encouraging even moderate drinking may move the general consumption curve upward and thus increase the number of abusers. Nonetheless, these difficulties in the design of interventions cannot absolve us from factoring any protective effect of alcohol consumption into our global economic calculations. If public policy is directed toward discouraging consumption, and if this policy is effective, the number of moderate drinkers as well as the number of abusers may fall.

Several studies (see Lazarus et al. 1991) have recorded a higher all-causes mortality rate among nondrinkers than moderate drinkers and among people who have given up drinking than those who continue to drink. A major review by Holman and Armstrong (1990) recorded an all-cause mortality risk for drinkers of 0.88—a significant reduction—and thus points to some lives saved to offset the years of life lost elsewhere. That study still, however, worked on an etiological fractions approach that factors the protective effect of alcohol consumption into only the statistics for ischemic heart disease and not the statistics for all causes, thus diminishing the effect of the offset considerably.[3]

A more fundamental objection to the alcohol cost estimates listed lies in their comparison of the cost to society of present consumption without any feasible expectation of the outcomes of intervention programs but with a hypothetical society that consumed no alcohol. Here, in fact, we encounter the same basic problem that we find in so many studies that have tried to calculate the

---

also large enough to raise questions; see the discussion below of Armstrong and Holman (1990) and English et al. (1995).

3. It is perhaps evidence of the caution with which researchers regard any positive public statement on alcohol consumption that the subsequent review in the same series (English et al. 1995) calculated its 1995 mortality risk ratios not between drinkers and nondrinkers, as in the 1988 review, but between moderate drinkers and heavy drinkers, thus eliminating any statistics that might be seen as recommending moderate drinking over abstaining.

social cost of alcohol abuse or alcohol consumption. It is meaningless to assume an imaginary society with no alcohol problems, to compare it to the actual society with its alcohol problems, and to say that this difference is the actual societal cost of alcohol is meaningless, because the alternative society is not deduced from the actual society. Even if these studies show that the imaginary society would be much better than our actual society, they cannot show the way to a better, problem-free society (Österberg 1989).

This lack of contact between the models and the world is illustrated by the total lack of any reference in any study to the presumed gain of 7 percent that would under these presumptions have been achieved by the actual fall in per capita alcohol consumption in the last decade.[4] Because the cost losses were derived a priori rather than observed, it is not possible to measure in the real world any of the predicted effects of changes in their variables.

(PROGRAM EVALUATION)

Evaluation of treatment programs should in many ways be more straightforward than evaluation of health promotion initiatives, dealing as it does with short-term changes in identified individuals. Even so, no consensus has been hitherto attainable in this field on any assessment-dependent issue, and debates on such particular issues as the relative effectiveness of brief and long-term treatment programs (Galaif and Sussman 1995) and of abstinence and controlled drinking models (Agosti 1994) continue unabated.

In the wider field of health promotion, some progress has been made in reaching agreement on the effectiveness of particular methodologies. Message-based campaigns on the old model are increasingly falling out of favor. School programs, for example, are known to be ineffective if based solely on knowledge transfer (Hansen 1992). One obvious problem is that children who rebel against social constraints on alcohol, smoking, and sex tend to be the same students who rebel against the authority and teaching function of the school and are thus the group most resistant to its health messages (Nutbeam et al. 1993). The wider problem of the overlapping and interdependence of such health risk factors as smoking, alcohol abuse, unsafe sex, and depression has been well covered by Hibbert and colleagues (1996). The interdependence of problems can best be covered by interdependent interventions. This necessity adds to the complications of evaluation by further attenuating the linkages between a multidisciplinary intervention and single risk factor indexes or any single morbidity outcome.

4. Between the 1988 and 1995 reviews mentioned above (Armstrong and Holman 1990; English et al. 1995), the estimated number of lives recorded as lost each year from alcohol-related causes in Australia certainly fell (from 6,354 to 3,660), but this change is far too large to be consistent with any causal hypothesis connected with changes in alcohol consumption, and English and colleagues have not claimed this, attributing the fall to a reanalysis of the benefits of alcohol in ischemic heart disease.

The success of mass media campaigns is also increasingly subject to quali-fication. Reduction in road deaths, and in particular reduction in road deaths due to alcohol, represents one of the undoubted successes of Australian practices. Interventions in this area have included legislative change (compulsory seat belt legislation, random breath-testing laws), changes in enforcement practice (speed cameras, increased police presence), and massive and expensive mass media advertising campaigns (conducted in Victoria by the Transport Accident Com-mission). The contribution of mass media to this success is less straightforward. An independent evaluation of the campaign (Cameron et al. 1993) found that when the advertising was supporting programs in which there was a clear police enforcement effort (where police were vigorously stopping, arresting, and pros-ecuting people for drinking and speeding), the advertisements had an effect; when the advertising was not backed by a police enforcement campaign, there was no evidence to show that the advertising had any effect.

A combination of measures has reduced smoking rates drastically in Cali-fornia. A significant factor was an increase in excise taxes, which rose from $0.10 per pack in 1988, to $0.35 in 1989. A major study of the effect of the advertising component of this campaign has been done, though there were some difficulties with the figures in that half the initial survey population dropped out (Fortmann et al. 1993). Of those who stayed in, there was a reduction in smoking rates of 7.5 percent in the treatment cities and a reduction of 4 percent in the control cities. Again, however, the main drop was at the beginning of the survey, and smoking rates in the control cities are now falling as fast as or faster than in the treatment cities. The highest and lowest overall reductions occurred in the control cities, where there was no treatment campaign. These findings support the view of O'Connor (1988, 195) that "rather than being a hypodermic needle, we now begin to look at mass communication as a sort of aerosol spray. As you spray it on the subject, some of it hits the target; most of it drifts away; and very little has an effect." One might also add here that the drifting spray diffuses widely beyond the target area, complicating comparisons.

A more general survey of mass media campaigns (Redman, Spencer, and Sanson-Fisher 1990) concentrating on seat belt use and cardiovascular risk be-haviors discarded most published evidence on the grounds of insufficiently sim-ilar control groups, insufficient baseline data, and inadequate sampling methods.[5] The authors concluded that the few remaining adequately controlled studies offer little evidence that the mass media can directly alter health-related behavior if used alone. This conclusion may be based in part on methodological grounds, in that the rigor in evaluation standards the authors regarded as essential must of necessity eliminate most large campaigns. The authors approved only studies in which subjects agreed to chemical sampling (to avoid self-report bias) and that have consent and follow-up rates of over 75 percent. Any large population that

---

5. Redman and colleagues regarded city-to-city comparisons as insufficiently controlled.

meets these requirements is likely almost by definition to be untypical. The difficulty would seem insuperable.

Most Australian campaigns in any case now supplement mass-media advertising with community programs. As Redman, Spencer, and Sanson-Fisher (1990) noted, "Such combined programmes have resulted in much greater changes in behavior than the media-alone interventions." However, they go on to comment that "the media role may be less important than has been argued. . . . Those [studies] which emphasized the community viewpoint rather than the media appear to have maximized behavior change. . . . There is currently no evidence that the media component makes a major contribution to the effectiveness of such combined programs" (p. 99).

This view may underestimate the effect of advertising in inducing slow changes in the general culture, or the climate of opinion as opposed to immediately supporting community action; in other words, strategic rather than tactical effects. As pointed out by Caswell, Ransom, and Gilmore (1990, 11), "a primary role for health promotion mass-media campaign is seen as problem amplification or, in other words, keeping the issue high on the public agenda and stimulating debate. . . . A feasible role of the mass media in health promotion is often described as a reinforcer of already existing behaviors and attitudes and of current trends."

Sustainability of change depends on alteration of the culture. Alcohol use has been for millennia a central element of human culture. Fischer's (1994, 160) jest that "Civilisation is a careful construction for the production and distribution of alcohol" is a caricature but a recognizable one. Moreover, "behaviours and their supporting attitudes are deeply embedded in social relationships and the cultural environment and as such are not easily changed by interventions such as mass-media campaigns. . . . A more appropriate set of objectives for mass-media campaigns aimed at alcohol-related problem prevention would be a shift in societal attitude to alcohol use . . . [and] changing the climate of opinion about public policies which may contribute to the prevention of problems" (Caswell, Ransom, and Gilmore 1990, 15). As cultural change is not entirely under the control of even the most enlightened public policy, harm-minimization approaches thus present themselves. These accept that risk behavior will continue and, while attempting to reduce its incidence and intensity, also place considerable emphasis on ensuring that the consequences of that behavior are minimized.

Compulsory seat belt use legislation, referred to above, represents one such intervention. HIV-AIDS poses particular threats to people practicing unsafe sex, in particular to people practicing anal sex, and to intravenous drug users. Australia has to varying degrees adopted harm-minimization approaches in both populations with considerable success. Harm-minimization arguments have been used to support the decriminalization of illicit drug use, and it has been suggested that many protective interventions are feasible only if legal sanctions are not an impediment to participation. These arguments have nowhere been effective against the competing desire to protect the ethical self-image of society. Many interventions, however, have gone some way to bridging this conceptual divide by providing legal support services to reduce the impact of illegal drugs on their users. The most notable of these are the needle exchange schemes now supported by governments in all Australian states, which by issuing the tools of illegal drug use at concessional rates have contributed markedly to inhibiting the spread of HIV-AIDS among the injecting population (Feacham 1996).

A particularly pointed example of harm minimization in the area of alcohol abuse is the requirement under Australian food regulations for the fortification of flour with thiamine to reduce Wernicke-Korsakoff syndrome. This intervention seeks to reduce neither alcohol consumption nor alcohol abuse; it addresses only the physiological impact of that abuse. Some success has been reported (Jiong Ma and Truswell 1995).

A general observation on these various movements in health promotion would be that present-day health promotion is moving away from appeals to populations in the mass toward embedding interventions in actual settings and real communities, in an attempt to establish a virtuous circle between environment and culture.

THE DEVELOPING WORLD

A corollary of this move toward matching particular problems with particular solutions is that the experience of the developed West is not necessarily directly transferable to other areas, with different cultures and different circumstances, even when mortality and morbidity statistics in the West and the developing world seem to be converging in many respects. Neither traditional nor advanced health promotion practices can be taken as universally applicable. While there is certainly a place for old-fashioned public information campaigns in nations with low levels of general education, these cannot substitute for attempts to raise those levels. More progressive health promotion campaigns founded on, for example, a close reading of cultural meanings in the disadvantaged youth of Sydney are still less easily packaged.

In practice, health promotion in developing nations is largely conceived and administered under medical hierarchies and largely directed toward immediate and global risk factor reduction rather than locally mediated development, the latter indeed often being regarded as inherently undesirable. The rhetoric of empowerment endorsed by developing nations through their participation in the Ottawa Charter for Health Promotion and subsequent World Health Organization health promotion pronouncements is not always given great weight in public health policy.

THE ECONOMIC EVALUATION OF
HEALTH PROMOTION INTERVENTIONS:
GENERAL CONSIDERATIONS

Whatever approach is taken, determining whether any significant health promotion activity has been successful is not straightforward or easy. Determining which of two similar but not identical activities has been more successful adds to that initial difficulty. Comparing different approaches to health promotion on the basis of data collected in different circumstances using different protocols in different forms raises the task to the status of a metaproblem. These difficulties are not accidental but are for the following reasons inherent in the nature of the discipline.

Contamination of the Data by Social Change

Health data cannot be quarantined from other social indexes. Risk factor data in all their aspects are inevitably crossed by gradients of socioeconomic status that have a large independent effect on health and mortality (McClelland, Pirkis, and Willcox 1993). While these confounding variables can be to some extent compensated for statistically at the data collection stage, it nonetheless remains the case that global health interventions have a differential impact on different classes and income levels, and policies dealing with other economic and social issues apparently unrelated to health will influence health outcomes more forcibly than will direct health interventions.

Contamination of the Data by Culture

The construction of a culture supportive of health involves working with social and cultural meanings. This has the complicating effect that the more successful the intervention in creating a self-replicating change dynamic in the population, the less the direct effect of the intervention can be measured and the less difference there will be between the target population and control groups, a confounding effect that can be detected in most major population studies (Jousilahti et al. 1994).

Long Time Lines and the Discount Rate

Estimating the economic impact of health promotion interventions is always difficult, involving as it does extended lead times of up to several decades between intervention and health gain. Modifying organizations and structures cannot be done overnight, providing supportive environments for health is an extended process, and building changes into a culture cannot be instantaneous. If all these positions are secured, there are nevertheless many health benefits that will take some years or decades to accrue. This exceptionally long lead time not only allows maximum scope for the operation of confounding variables but also requires that cost analysis incorporate some discount for delays in enjoyment. Cost and cost-benefit calculations are highly susceptible to changes in the discount rate.

PREVENTION AND PARADOX

Difficulties in evaluation need not necessarily lead to pessimism over outcomes. Over the last three decades there have clearly been major health gains in many areas, for example, heart disease, accident prevention, screening in women's health, and limiting the potential toll of HIV-AIDS. What remains unclear, however, is the exact contribution of health promotion activities, and particularly individual discrete programs, to this process. With heart disease, for example, most of the large, community-based demonstration projects have shown some decrease in risk factor prevalence (in the short term, at least) but have had markedly less success in reducing the incidence of coronary heart disease and negligible success in decreasing mortality in target populations any faster than the substantial downward trends occurring generally across the Western world.

A recent editorial in the *American Journal of Public Health* addressed the contrast between the relatively disappointing effects of individual projects and the substantial changes in risk factors, morbidity, and mortality over a period of decades (Susser 1995). The journal editors sought a resolution of this seeming prevention paradox[6] by suggesting that improvements in public health rely on the emergence of a social movement toward health and that the role of individual programs in furthering the development of such movements remains unclear. The editors suggested that new methods need to be developed for teasing out the effects of particular programs in terms of (1) their direct local effects, (2) their influence in continuing, extending, and disseminating a growing social movement, and (3) their contribution to community empowerment.

These changes in the direction of evaluation interlock with emerging paradigms in health promotion theory. Recent conceptualizations of health promotion have broadened the focus of health causation from a concentration on immediate risk factors to include the contextual and social antecedents of disease and have also favored a cognitively based psychology, which views individuals—and communities (Hawe, Degeling, and Hall 1990)—as active, problem-solving, prioritizing agents (Statchenko and Jenicek 1990). This broadened perspective led in the first instance to a greater emphasis on the environmental factors necessary if people were to be able to adopt a healthy lifestyle: availability of healthy food at an appropriate price, the positive influence of peer groups and families, smoke-free environments, and so forth. More recently, emphasis has shifted toward the notion of enablement of both individuals and communities. At the level of individuals, this has led to a focus on such concepts as locus of control, self-efficacy, and more generally, mastery (Bennet and Hodgson 1992) and, at the community level, to a focus on concepts of community control and empowerment that include strengthening the capacity of the community to deal

6. Not to be confused with the preventive paradox (Wodak 1991), in which it is argued that the majority of alcohol casualties in a community come from the large proportion of the population drinking moderately rather than the small proportion drinking heavily.

not only with the targeted health risk but also with its other structural social problems.

At the same time as this increasing tendency to seek comprehensive psychosocial explanations for the occurrence of disease, there has also been a shift from conceiving of health simply as the absence of disease to a view of health based on wellness. As Stevenson and Burke (1992) have suggested, the ironic situation may then arise in which the attempt to consider health globally, without conceptual specificity, can drive bureaucrats back to a dependence upon crude performance indicators for their decisions. However, it is not necessarily the case that specificity, at least in the format with which policy makers are familiar, is attainable. Global economic estimates rest to a considerable degree on reductionist paradigms that have proved incapable of driving effective interventions; concepts that have proved inadequate at one level of agency are not necessarily rescued from futility by being aggregated globally. We may have to learn to be content with other, less precise, measures.

These differences in evaluative expectations derive in part from fundamental ideological discontinuities. Perceptions of health promotion may differ markedly in their views on the mechanisms by which, and the extent to which, the choices of the individual are limited by social structures. At one extreme, the individual is viewed as an almost completely autonomous being who has both the capacity and the responsibility to act in a sensible and productive manner. At the next level, practical constraints (including ignorance) on the individual are acknowledged, but it is presumed that once these are dealt with the individual will then do the sensible thing. A deeper level still recognizes the effect of social and conditioning influences, such as peer pressure and lack of hope regarding the future, but nonetheless views risk behavior as essentially irrational. At the deepest level, society is seen as having a profound impact on the individual's fundamental sense of identity and upon the very basis of his or her rationality, and behaviors that are seemingly irrational to others may be strategic and rational in terms of the individual's response to a particular set of external circumstances in order to meet a particular set of internal needs. From here it is a short step to the phenomenological position that what matters in research is the ability to interpret what meaning events have for groups and individuals.

Phenomenological studies seek to illuminate the needs that groups and individuals consider important, the strategies they use to meet those needs, the manner in which both are influenced by society, and the implications of all of this for "healthy" behavior. They then seek to use those insights to help individuals and groups to achieve more effective and life-enhancing strategies for meeting their needs, using a combination of individual assistance and social activist approaches. Phenomenological evaluation is directed toward understanding rather than simply measuring. Its use therefore inherently involves the exercise of judgment and the construction, rather than the discovery, of answers.

MACROSTRATEGIES

If health promotion evaluation is to guide policy makers in deciding between feasible alternative strategies it must deal with these paradoxes by reconceptualizing its evaluations. Following the lead of Susser (1995), we may attempt to compare differing policy approaches in terms of (1) their direct local effects, (2) their influence toward continuing, extending, and disseminating a growing social movement, and (3) their contribution to community empowerment. Some of these considerations are plainly more straightforward than others, and their simplicity is inversely proportional to their power. To the extent that direct local effects can be extracted from the matrix of health, they tend toward the trivial: the number of people who have seen the advertisement or the number of people who express changed opinions to pollsters. By the time measurements reach more significant indexes, such as the number still indulging in the undesired activity, other effects must be considered that are neither direct nor local.

Changes in accident rates, alcohol-related crime rates, and domestic violence rates can in some cases be reliably linked to legislative and enforcement changes. The fall in road deaths in Victoria attributable to seat belt legislation (Cass et al. 1990) and random breath testing (Homel 1994) showed up in statistics within a year. Legislation's more indirect effects, mediated through cultural change (where, for example, the inconvenience of nominating a designated driver for a party increases the number of low-alcohol celebrations and, eventually, alters views of what constitutes celebratory behavior), are slower to emerge and harder to measure but are probably of more significance in the long term.

Changes in national alcohol policy, on the other hand, do not generally show up clearly in mortality statistics except in the extreme cases of tragic disasters such as the former Soviet Union's antialcohol drive (Korolenko, Minevich, and Segal 1994). Changes across a population in such areas as cardiovascular health status and cirrhosis tend to be gradual and slow. The larger the arena, the greater the number of confounding factors; macrostrategic comparisons are inherently more liable to doubt than are studies of particular interventions.

Educational approaches have been expanded from the previous information transfer goals to encompass working with and collaboratively modifying social and cultural meanings of behavior patterns. Current models of health promotion, emphasizing as they do the interrelated nature of the societal and individual problems that manifest themselves as risk behavior and the necessity for interrelated intervention, provide further complexities in separating out the particular impact of any element. Qualitative measures dealing with the development of autonomous coping skills in individuals and communities will also be necessary, and because these involve working collaboratively on the definition of goals this will also provide challenges in matching initial agency goals to community-determined strategies and outcomes.

Similarly, the third item—capacity-building to empower communities to identify and deal with their perceived needs—can also be recorded and evaluated

(Milio 1996), although such evaluations are not necessarily directly comparable across programs and settings. Capacity and empowerment will, after all, take different forms according to circumstance and setting. Health promotion programs in the workplace now increasingly recognize that "the most effective organisations have a decentralised and flexible structure and a culture that fosters empowerment, skill development, and accountability" (Chu, Driscoll, and Dwyer, in press); the health of the workplace is now seen not simply as the sum of the health status of the individual workers but primarily as the health of the organization as a whole. School programs attempt to support the self-esteem of the students through providing them with a voice in their own education. The notion of community empowerment seeks to give the disempowered the tools to solve not simply their day-to-day difficulties but also to build the capacity to act on the wider issues of social relations that affect their health. These different empowerments require different indexes, and these indexes are neither scalar nor universal. A demonstration of the success of one project does not necessarily establish a general rule.

A greater program emphasis on patterns of drinking behavior—taking an interest in particular drinks, places, rhythms, occasions, activities, confederates—reaches into the realm of personal and social meanings, matches the movement in health promotion to rich description rather than reductionist dichotomies, and corresponds with one general trend in policy evaluation. The task of the health promoter under this paradigm is not to impose one meaning on subjects in the mass but to determine the input points where personal meanings are transformed into social meanings, and vice versa, and then to cultivate a redirection of those meanings toward health.

This will require a reconceptualization of what constitutes evaluation. New disciplines will become relevant. The semiotics of alcohol use have not been studied as exhaustively as the comparable semiotics of cigarette use, tending to be lumped into the broad undifferentiated characterization of peer group pressure, and the process of evaluating changes in social meaning is in its infancy. Nonetheless, the greatest gains in smoking control have come from the pronounced shift in the social meaning of smoking from an approved ritual to a solecism ranking close to deliberate insult; the greatest risk to smoking control among the young is its status as a signifier for revolt and "cool." The fall in alcohol consumption, along with the fall in tobacco consumption and in the context of the entire personal health movement, similarly represents just one facet of an increasingly risk-averse culture.

The nature of the political process, the multifactorial nature of the experience of alcohol in any country, and the intersectoral interests that converge in its administration and control, make it unlikely that any uncontestable conclusion can be drawn from any macroeconomic evaluation system, and judgments based on values and goals will still be necessary. In this endeavor, guidance must be sought from general principles of modern health promotion: the uncontested success of harm-minimization approaches, a preference for work in mesoenvironments such as settings and communities, and a willingness to engage with the particular.

REFERENCES

Adrian, M. 1988. Social costs of alcohol. *Canadian Journal of Public Health* 79:316–22.

Agosti, V. 1994. The efficacy of controlled trials of alcohol misuse treatments in maintaining abstinence: a meta-analysis. *International Journal of the Addictions* 29:759–69.

Armstrong, B., and C. Holman. 1990. *The Quantification of Drug-Caused Morbidity and Mortality in Australia, 1988.* Canberra: Commonwealth Department of Human Services and Health.

Ashton, T., and S. Caswell. 1984. Estimated cost of alcohol to the New Zealand public hospital system. *New Zealand Medical Journal* 97:683–86.

Bennet, P., and G. Hodgson. 1992. Psychology and health promotion. In *Health Promotion: Disciplines and Diversity,* ed. R. Bunton and G. Macdonald. London: Routledge.

Cameron, M., et al. 1993. *Evaluation of Transport Accident Commission Road Safety Advertising.* Melbourne: Monash University Accident Research Centre.

Cass, D., T. Ross, R. McNeil, and P. Hill. 1990. Seat belts save lives. *Medical Journal of Australia* 153:571.

Caswell, S., R. Ransom, and L. Gilmore. 1990. Evaluation of a mass-media campaign for the primary prevention of alcohol-related problems. *Health Promotion International* 5:9–17.

Chetwynd, J., and T. Rayner. 1985. The economic cost to New Zealand of lost production due to alcohol abuse. *New Zealand Journal of Medicine* 97:694–97.

Chu, C., T. Driscoll, and S. Dwyer. In press. Health promoting workplace: an integrative perspective. *Australian Journal of Public Health.*

Collins, D., and H. Lapsley. 1991. *Estimating the Economic Costs of Drug Abuse in Australia. Canberra: National Campaign against Drug Abuse.*

Crawford, R. J., and K. Ford. 1984. Humanitarian and financial costs in alcoholics: a preliminary study of 15 cases. *New Zealand Medical Journal* 97:481–84.

Doll, B. 1996. Beneficial effects of alcohol on vascular disease. *Addiction* 91:32–33.

English, D. R., et al. 1995. *The Quantification of Drug-Caused Morbidity and Mortality in Australia, 1995.* Canberra: Commonwealth Department of Human Services and Health.

Feachem, R. G. A. 1996. *Valuing the Past—Investing in the Future: Evaluation of the National HIV/AIDS Strategy.* Canberra: Commonwealth Department of Human Services and Health.

Fischer, T. 1994. *The Thought Gang.* London: Minerva.

Fortmann, S., C. Taylor, J. Flora, and D. Jatulis. 1993. Changes in cigarette smoking prevalence after five years of community health education: the Stanford Five-City Project. *American Journal of Epidemiology* 137:82.

Galaif, E., and S. Sussman. 1995. For whom does Alcoholics Anonymous work? *International Journal of the Addictions* 30:161–84.

Gorsky , R., E. Schwartz, and D. Dennis. 1988. The mortality, morbidity, and economic costs of alcohol abuse in New Hampshire. *Preventative Medicine* 17:736–45.

Hansen, W. 1992. School-based substance abuse prevention: a review of the state of the art in curriculum. *Health Education Research* 7:403–30.

Hawe, P., D. Degeling, and J. Hall. 1990. *Evaluating Health Promotion.* Sydney: McLennan and Petty.

Hibbert, M., et al. 1996. *The Health of Young People in Victoria: Adolescent Health Survey.* Melbourne: Centre for Adolescent Health.

Holman, C., and B. Armstrong. 1990. *The Quantification of Drug-Caused Morbidity and Mortality in Australia, 1988.* Canberra: Commonwealth Department of Human Services and Health.

Homel, R. 1994. Drink-driving law enforcement and the legal blood alcohol limit in New South Wales. *Accident Analysis and Prevention* 26:147–55.

Jiong Ma, J., and A. Truswell. 1995. Wernicke-Korsakoff syndrome in Sydney hospitals: before and after thiamine enrichment of flour. *Medical Journal of Australia* 163:531–34.

Jousilahti, P., et al. 1994. Trends in cardiovascular disease risk factor clustering in eastern Finland: results of 15-year follow up of North Karelia Project. *Preventative Medicine* 23:6–14.

Korolenko, C., V. Minevich, and B. Segal. 1994. The politicization of alcohol in the USSR and its impact on the study and treatment of alcoholism. *International Journal of the Addictions* 29:1269–85.

Lazarus, N., G. Kaplan, R. Cohen, and D. Leu. 1991. Change in alcohol consumption and risk of death from all causes and from ischaemic heart disease. *British Medical Journal* 303:553–56.

Marmot, M., and E. Brunner. 1991. Alcohol and cardiovascular disease: the status of the U-shaped curve. *British Medical Journal* 303:565–68.

McClelland, A., J. Pirkis, and S. Willcox. 1993. *Enough to Make You Sick: How Income and Environment Affect Health.* Canberra: National Health Strategy Unit.

McDonell, R., and A. Maynard. 1985. The costs of alcohol misuse. *British Journal of Addiction* 80:27–35.

Milio, N. 1996. *Engines of Empowerment.* Chicago: Health Administration Press.

Nutbeam, D., C. Smith, L. Moore, and A. Bauman. 1993. Warning! school can damage your health: alienation from school and its impact on health behavior. *Journal of Pediatric and Child Health* 29:525–30.

O'Connor, J. 1988. The revered role of mass media in drug education: can the expectations be fulfilled? Paper delivered at the Third National Drug Educators Workshop, Fremantle, Australia.

Österberg, E. 1989. A world that does not exist. *Addiction* 5:525–26.

Parker, D., et al. 1987. The social and economic costs of alcohol abuse in Minnesota, 1983. *American Journal of Public Health* 77:982–86.

Redman, S., E. Spencer, and R. Sanson-Fisher. 1990. The role of mass media in changing health-related behavior: a critical appraisal of two models. *Health Promotion International* 5:85–99.

Richardson, J. 1991. A wider view of alcohol in Australia: the economic cost and policy implications. *Medical Journal of Australia* 154:842–44.

Schramm, C. 1977. Measuring the return on program costs: evaluation of a multi-employer alcoholism treatment program. *American Journal of Public Health* 67:50–51.

Siegel, C., C. Haugland, A. Goodman, and J. Wanderling. 1984. Severe alcoholism in the mental health sector: I. a cost analysis of treatment. *Journal of Studies on Alcohol* 45:504–9.

Statchenko, S., and M. Jenicek. 1990. Conceptual differences between prevention and health promotion: research implications for community health programs. *Canadian Journal of Public Health* 81:53–59.

Stevenson, H. M., and M. Burke. 1992. Bureaucratic logic in new social movement clothing: the limits of health promotion research. *Canadian Journal of Public Health* 83:S47–53.

Susser, M. 1995. The tribulations of trials. *American Journal of Public Health* 85:156–58.

Wodak, A. 1991. A wider view of alcohol in Australia: 1. the social cost. *Medical Journal of Australia* 154:838–39.

Chapter 11

Community Reactions to Alcohol Policies

Dwight B. Heath and Haydée Rosovsky

Alcohol policies are developed within a socioeconomic context largely as a result of historical and cultural traditions and also under a variety of international or global influences. Alcohol policies, their development, and their impact are also related to the ways in which other policies are made, perceived, and applied within a given society. The purpose of this chapter is to discuss some of the elements that influence alcohol policies and their impact not only among the members of a society, especially decision makers, but also in the interactions between those constituencies.

The overwhelming majority of people around the world who drink do so precisely because they find it pleasant and enjoyable. Although some have also seen that drinking is risky, dangerous, or harmful to a few and in limited contexts, most people tend to associate it more often with hospitality, sociability, camaraderie, relaxation, celebration, eating, or some combination of those positive things (Hanson 1995; Heath 1995). For those who think of beverage alcohol in such a positive light, restrictions on availability tend to be viewed as puritanical deprivation of simple pleasures or as inappropriate governmental intrusion into their private lives. There is another considerable constituency of people who, even if they have no interest in drinking, care so deeply about the freedom

Dwight B. Heath is professor of anthropology, Brown University, Providence, Rhode Island, U.S. Haydée Rosovsky is with Consejo Nacional contra las Adicciones (CONADIC), Mexico, D.F., Mexico.

of choice of the individual that they consider such controls, like most other governmental restrictions on behavior, to be unjustified. Others may be sympathetic to the aim of curtailing drinking, for whatever reasons, yet still believe that formal controls are neither the ideal nor most effective way of doing so. And there are others, such as the members of a religion or a movement (such as Muslims or ascetic Protestants), who believe that prohibition of alcoholic beverages, or at least strict controls on them, are necessary.

In some countries there is a positive correlation between the majority of people's feelings about issues and the resulting policies. Alcohol policies may emerge in different societies in different ways. In some societies, alcohol is an important political issue, and alcohol policies are usually decided through the consultation of the will of the people. But in other societies, in which alcohol is not part of the political agenda, policies are developed without taking into consideration, or even exploring, the feelings of the society at large. In some societies, important segments of the population may feel that official alcohol policies are too weak, that governments should be more strict in alcohol control and pay more attention to alcohol's relationship to public health and well-being.

No matter how well conceived any policy may be, its effectiveness is likely to be dependent upon popular reactions on the part of members of the community, whether independently or collectively. These reactions may impede the implementation of even the most well-intentioned policy. It is appropriate in this context to examine some of the reasons for the gap between the aims of elected or otherwise responsible decision makers and their limited ability to effect changes in the workaday lives of common people, whose resistance (whether active or passive) can be a major obstacle. Let us briefly touch on some of the reasons that resistance to official alcohol policies is so widespread.

In the first place, it should never be assumed that attitudes toward alcohol and alcohol-related problems are uniform. Some of the more dramatic cultural variations that set off one society, nation, or population from another with respect to alcohol use and its outcomes are discussed elsewhere (see chapter 6, this volume; Heath 1982). However, there are also variations both among component communities and even within most individual communities (Heath and Cooper 1981). It would be far too ambitious a task (and of only tangential relevance to our present concerns) to review the many and varied meanings that social scientists have attached to the word *community* (Miner 1968; Redfield 1960), but for our present purposes, let it stand for any meaningful reference group among which individual members share a sense of "we-ness" (as contrasted with "they-ness," for those outside the group). Sometimes, such a community may have clear geographic or political boundaries; on other occasions, it may refer to an age cohort, members of one gender, a socioeconomic class, or another socially distinguishable category not necessarily concentrated in a given location. Even in such general terms, we can unequivocally assert that a number of elements of community reaction affect the efficacy of alcohol policies, even if (and perhaps especially if) they were not taken into consideration when a particular policy was being formulated.

THE VARIETY OF ALCOHOL POLICIES

In most contemporary discussions of alcohol policy, it is presumed that the focus will be on limitations on availability and restrictions with respect to use (Edwards et al. 1994; Moore and Gerstein 1981). Prohibition is an extreme form, but there is a wide range of other factors that can be manipulated by formal controls, such as taxation, licensing, and advertising restrictions (Grant 1985). Logically, we should not lose sight of the fact that an alcohol policy can also be permissive. This is not merely a semantic or philosophical game. It is a reality that a free and open market is no accident in any modern nation. Similarly, allowing all people equal access to any commodity is a political decision that is not taken lightly. For that matter, there are examples of alcohol policies that, far from being intended to curtail consumption, enhance or promote it. It was once commonplace that beverage alcohol served as a tool in commercial and colonial expansion, and laborers were obliged to accept drink in lieu of other payment for at least part of their wage (Jankowiak and Bradburd 1996). A widespread recent trend in the world economy is the adoption of free-market strategies within a global framework. Many countries, especially those struggling to develop, tend to give priority to stimulating industrial production, trade, and tax revenues, sometimes at the cost of public health concerns. But historically, calls to curtail drinking have tended to be more common and strident, and they continue to be so at present, in some societies, especially those with a temperance tradition or other abstentionist background, which usually has some roots in religion.

There have been controls on drinking, and especially on excessive drinking, for a long time in many areas of the world (Heath 1997; Moser 1979). Sometimes authorities have invested earnest efforts in imposing and enforcing various types of formal controls, with differing degrees of success or failure (Mäkelä et al. 1981; Single, Morgan, and de Lint 1981). Without attempting to provide an encyclopedic coverage, a few examples should be mentioned here in order to demonstrate that the idea is not as rare as one might suppose, and that it is not restricted to a specific geographical region or a given religion.

For example, although drinking was banned in the early part of the Zhou dynasty in China (over 3,000 years ago), it subsequently became elaborated as an important part of artistic appreciation (Xiao 1995). Various tsars declared prohibition in Russia at different times in the 1800s, but more often they monopolized the lively commerce in drink (Sidorov 1995). Throughout much of the Arabic world, both drinking and drunkenness were eloquently praised in song and verse, until the Koranic injunction against them was construed by most Muslims as making abstinence an article of faith, as it remains today, in the few prohibitions that appear to be successful (e.g., in Saudi Arabia and the Islamic

Republic of Iran; Badri 1976). Half of the component United States of America voted themselves dry for at least a few years in the mid-1800s in response to a widespread and explicitly Protestant religious reform movement (Rorabaugh 1979). In Great Britain at the same time, prohibition legislation was proposed but defeated; in Ireland, people flocked to sign abstinence pledges at the prompting of a charismatic Catholic priest (Stivers 1976).

Sweden tried prohibition briefly, and then rationing, before settling on an austere state monopoly (Nyberg and Allebeck 1995). Iceland banned spirits for some years, and subsequently beer, but neither experiment interrupted the periodic excessive drinking pattern that is popular in that country (Ásmundsson 1995). Various provinces in Canada (Smart and Ogborne 1986), like some states, counties, and towns in the United States, enacted local prohibitions, of which some are still in effect (Musto 1987). European colonial powers often tried to keep native populations from getting alcohol, whether in North, Central, or South America (Mancall 1995), on Pacific islands throughout Oceania (Marshall 1976), and in Australia (Hall and Hunter 1995). They even banded together, under the aegis of the League of Nations, to try to keep most of sub-Saharan Africa dry in the early 1900s (Pan 1975).

National prohibition in the United States (1920–34) was, ironically, credited with having fostered the development of large-scale organized crime, the popularity of drinking among women, and widespread disregard for the law (Sinclair 1964). Given the opportunity in recent years, some Native American tribes in the contiguous United States have chosen to keep their reservations dry (May 1992), as have some communities of Native Alaskans, bands of First Nations in Canada, and communities of Aborigines in Australia (Hall and Hunter 1995). Prohibition is even mentioned in the national constitution of India as an ideal to be aimed for, but few states enacted it, and some that did subsequently repealed it (Mohan and Sharma 1995). Clearly, there are occasional communities in which local people choose prohibition as an appealing alternative to socially disruptive excesses, although most prohibitions that are imposed from the remote, larger, and dominant culture tend to be violated by smuggling, home brewing, illicit distillation, and corruption, all of which subvert both the ban on drink and the broader public order.

But prohibition is by no means the only form of control that has been attempted or that is still recommended. As early as the first written code of laws (in Babylonia around 2000 B.C.), regulations spelled out who should and who should not be served in wine shops as well as strict rules as to measures and other provisions for consumer protection (Harper 1904). Taxation of drink has long been an important source of revenue for governments (and ostensibly a means of decreasing consumption). The licensing of those who produce, distribute, and sell beverage alcohol is another control measure that has long been widespread and generally accepted.

A bewildering variety of other formal controls are in effect in various jurisdictions, and some are subject to frequent revision. One common restriction is that only certain kinds of outlets may sell drinks (whether restaurants, private clubs, pubs or bars, stores that handle nothing else, or others). Another type of restriction is for the retail trade (and sometimes also the wholesale trade, including production) to be monopolized by the state. Within the United States there is a patchwork of regulations whereby selling drinks is allowed in some states only if food is also served and in other states only if food is not served. Some states require that the interior of a drinking establishment be visible from the street, whereas others require the opposite. Some states set maximum prices and others minimum prices; until recently, one state disallowed the advertising of prices altogether. Some places set a maximum number of sales outlets per 10,000 population; others set a minimum distance from schools or churches. The hours of sale are regulated and so are the days of sale. Some places specify a minimum age for purchase of beverage alcohol and others for possession or consumption. Mexico was the first nation to mandate that every beverage alcohol container should carry a label warning: "Abuse of this product is harmful to health" (Cooper 1992, 30). Some other nations have subsequently developed their own warnings, some of which are mandatory on containers, some on advertisements, and others on signs to be prominently displayed in any establishment where drinks are sold (Davies and Walsh 1985; Holder and Edwards 1995).

During recent years, there have been increasing controls on advertising in various jurisdictions. Although beer and wine have long been advertised on television in the United States, and no law forbids the advertising of spirits, the manufacturers have agreed among themselves for decades not to do so. Recently, one company broke with that agreement, and soon others rejected it, although there are some who call for a ban on the advertising not only of spirits but of all beverage alcohol. The utter absence of advertising in the former Soviet Union and several of its satellite countries did not lessen consumer demand for drink, but some Western European and Latin American nations are experimenting with limiting advertisements to print or doing away with them altogether. Inasmuch as there is no clear and compelling scientific evidence that advertising adds to drinking or to costs in terms of health and social welfare, there are critics who care little about alcohol but who feel strongly about any abridgment of the right to free speech. Some of the restrictions on advertising relate to content, others to whether colors may be used, some to placement, some to the products, and some to the anticipated audience.

Furthermore, although alcohol policies often purport to be shaped in the interests of public health, other purposes may be more important. This is especially the case with respect to taxing and licensing, where fiscal interests may predominate (Grant, Plant, and Williams 1983). Similarly, social control may be important when dealing with who may drink, how much, when, where, and so forth. Drinking establishments are often suspected of being places where seditious or revolutionary plots are devised, where workmen air their grievances and organize for collective action, or where other activities are played out that an incumbent regime may want to suppress. Certainly, withholding drink from young people says something about power relationships within a population; differential access among males and females carries similar meanings.

Nor should we expect all of a country's policies toward alcohol to be congruent. The benefits that an administration reaps from high taxes on drink may outweigh the costs of drinking; this is especially the case when the state is also involved as a seller, or sometimes even as the sole producer, of alcoholic beverages. The fostering of economic development, maintenance of agriculture, employment opportunities, and the prestige of having one's own drink can all be attractive incentives for encouraging production and consumption, especially in developing countries (Maula, Lindblad, and Tigerstedt 1990).

Policies about alcohol do not occur in a vacuum but are intimately linked with other public policies. The integration of culture must not be overlooked in weighing the implications of any new policy. Unforeseen problems have marred the implementation of well-intentioned alcohol policies. For example, it is commonplace that prohibition results in the proliferation of illicit production of alcohol, and when the product is not well made it can result in large-scale poisoning, including deaths. Too great a price increase can have the same effect, or it can drive some individuals to drink nonbeverage alcohols (such as paint thinner, industrial solvents, cleaners, or cologne), with the same result. Sharp price increases also often encourage alcohol smuggling. Shortening the hours of sale in retail outlets can stimulate the proliferation of unsanitary and illegal unlicensed outlets or of consumption on the street.

Elsewhere in this volume (see chapters 7 and 8), the rapid diffusion of the control model as a prescription for lessening the full range of so-called alcohol-related problems has already been described. In addition, the package of controls recommended by the World Health Organization has been remarkably consistent, despite its repeated insistence on cultural uniqueness and the need to tailor policies to the distinctive social and cultural context of each situation (WHO 1981). Among the controls it recommends are (in no particular sequence) increased taxation, the indexing of prices so that they rise with inflation, restrictions (or bans) on advertising, increased minimum age for purchase or consumption, fewer outlets, shorter hours of sale, and warning labels, all of which are designed to restrict availability and consumption, with the expectation that doing so will diminish risk and harm.

ALCOHOL-RELATED PROBLEMS

In one sense, it is ironic that the term *alcohol-related problems* has gained such widespread currency. It is a concept with little historical depth and is often misused to imply causality when that remains unproven. It was well within living memory (less than twenty-five years ago) that a graduate student complained that the United States could never mount an effective campaign against drinking because it was not perceived and defined as a social or public problem (Beauchamp 1973). At that time, alcoholism was already a target, but most people thought of it as simply a personal problem for the alcoholic and for those individuals close enough to him or her to be harmed by the aberrant behaviors that characterized that exotic disease.

At about the same time, several European scholars were expressing concern over the approach, even in research, that dealt with alcoholics as if they were distinguishable from other drinkers (WHO 1980). Such terminology was declared fallacious, since there is no dichotomous criterion that sets alcoholics off from all other drinkers. The term *alcohol-dependence syndrome* was chosen to signal that persons at one extreme of the continuum not only have difficulty stopping once they start to drink but also that they continue to drink even when they know they will regret the outcomes—that they let drinking and its sequelae interfere with normal role expectations (as parent, spouse, employee; WHO 1977). The deleterious outcomes, dubbed alcohol-related disabilities (Edwards et al. 1977), ranged from cirrhosis to absenteeism, suicide, homicide, spouse and child abuse, rape, fighting, impaired driving, difficulty at work or at school, strained social relationships, and feelings of guilt.

A flurry of epidemiological studies established correlations, sometimes statistically significant, between quantity and frequency of drinking, on the one hand, and many of those problems, on the other (Mäkelä et al. 1981; Single, Morgan, and de Lint 1981). For most readers, the very term alcohol-related problems connotes or implies causality, despite the fact that serious researchers are careful to point out that they are dealing with correlations and explicitly reject causal interpretations. The nature and rate of alcohol-related problems is almost as varied among different cultures as are the kinds and ways of drinking. For these reasons, policies must differ, and it is also important that they take into consideration likely reactions on the part of the community or communities.

COMMUNITY REACTIONS

Among community factors that must be taken into account is religion. A high proportion of Muslims or ascetic Protestants in the population could result in strong pressures favoring prohibition, whereas Catholics and agnostics might well oppose strong controls (albeit for different reasons). Age and marital status may also be relevant; a population of predominantly young unmarried men would often support cheap and easy availability, whereas older married couples might not. Political stance also matters: libertarians may reject restrictions even if they themselves do not drink. People whose livelihood is linked with beverage alcohol are likely to be permissive regarding drinking.

Demonizing alcohol, believing it to be the source of many kinds of trouble, is counterintuitive for large segments of most populations, who associate alcoholic beverages with camaraderie, enjoyment, celebration, rest after work, and as an accompaniment to food (Heath 1995; Pernanen 1991). Many people see drinking as a harmless and enjoyable adjunct to their workaday lives or a reasonable way of celebrating special occasions (Hanson 1995; Partanen 1991).

Scare tactics in public education are not only ineffective but also counter-productive, because any misrepresentation that is recognized by an audience makes the source less credible on all subjects.

No population welcomes increased formal controls that obtrude upon its daily life, and some will actively oppose them. Almost all of the many countries that have tried prohibition as a policy have found the costs high because of violations. Illicit production and smuggling not only erodes respect for law and order but can form the basis of organized crime and large-scale corruption. Increased taxes, restrictions on sales, licensing, minimum purchase age, bans on advertising, and similar controls that are regularly invoked as effective means of restricting availability are, like other governmental controls on individual auton-omy, viewed as intrusive, especially by the majority to whom they also seem inappropriate (Popham, Schmidt, and de Lint 1976). Many who would accept such measures if they were targeted at the small portion of the population re-sponsible for most of the social costs of alcohol abuse consider it unjust that they should also be penalized. This is particularly true when governmental intrusion results in abuse of the populace, whether it is petty bribery of policemen or more serious official corruption.

Virtually any governmental initiative is suspect in those developing countries whose population has become accustomed to official corruption, especially when the initiative interferes with and increases the cost of those few pleasures afforded to hard-working low-paid members of society with little voice in government. These members of society tend to be accustomed to exploitation, and although they may not be wholly resigned to it, they rarely have access to channels for expressing their grievances (although this is gradually changing in some coun-tries). Many communities resent increasing government intrusion into the mar-ket. In addition, many persons are, justifiably or not, concerned by regulatory, police, and judicial restrictions on their private lives. Such restrictions can result in outright opposition, especially when they are administered discriminately and undemocratically and when corruption, personalism, favoritism, and other abuses are commonplace.

If formal controls do more harm than good, what hope is there of diminishing the damage that sometimes stems from excessive drinking? The majority of social scientists point to informal controls: attitudes, values, norms, and other expec-tations that are generally agreed upon and shared by the members of a commu-nity. Although informal controls may lack the apparent power of formal controls, they make up for that by being accepted and enforced by peers, friends, relatives, and others who are close and emotionally important to the actor. That is why a French or Italian man who drinks many times as much as his counterpart in Finland or the United States may never be drunk. To become so would be viewed as inappropriate, and his honor, social standing, and reputation and that of his family would be jeopardized.

Both historical and cross-cultural experience have demonstrated that infor-mal controls can be just as effective as, and usually far more effective than, formal controls in curtailing the negative sequelae of drinking. One of the principal reasons that informal controls have been so little discussed is because, despite the fact that they predominate in human experience, they are rarely named. Socialization and enculturation, the fundamental processes by which the neonate is gradually shaped into what elders consider a human being, operate almost exclusively on the basis of informal controls. Gossip, shaming, and shunning are extreme forms of sanction for breeches of informal controls, but conformity to them can result in esteem, a position of leadership, friendship, and a variety of other forms of social acceptance. For that matter, there is no reason that formal and informal controls should be construed as mutually exclusive. Drinking, like other human behavior, may best be managed by a combination of formal and informal controls.

THE SOCIOCULTURAL AND EDUCATIONAL MODEL

No matter what specific controls may eventually be brought to bear, education about beverage alcohol and the outcomes of its use should be a cornerstone. But at the same time as there has been an increasing demand for controls on alcohol, there has been a growing reaction against an educational approach to public health. Those who are eager to lessen not only the availability of beverage alcohol but also the knowledge and decision-making capability of any with whom they disagree have made systematic efforts to discredit education as a means of lessening or preventing alcohol-related problems in future generations (Hanson 1997; Heath 1989). Unfortunately, the specific programs to which some of their criticisms are directed have in fact been disappointing because they hoped to accomplish too much, too fast, and with inappropriate methods and inadequate resources. Although many school jurisdictions (in all states in the United States) have instructional programs in place, such programs are often poorly planned and ineffectively carried out. Too often they are a brief add-on to a course in biology or health, taught by people who have little knowledge of the subject, little interest in it, or even an aversion to it.

To a remarkable degree, the presumption (at least in the United States) is that any discussion of alcohol must be about alcoholism. Scare tactics and sloganeering are all too frequent; examples are such messages as "Just say no," "Impairment begins with the first drink," and "Alcohol is a stepping-stone to illicit drugs," most of which are false. Often, the teacher is uncomfortable with the subject and so, even if knowledgeable, tends to be hesitant in response to questions or discussion. Reticence, like misinformation, is often recognized by students, whose personal experience and acquaintances may demonstrate the inappropriateness of such instruction. But it is a myopic view of education that does not look beyond the classroom when the aim is to change attitudes and behaviors at all ages and levels of society.

Regardless of whether the approach is called social marketing or health promotion, the aim is to prompt people to change their behavior in the absence of immediate reward (Heath 1997). It can be done, and has been done, with considerable success, perhaps most notably in the Framingham Heart Study (Castelli 1990; Levy 1993). For over some thirty years, there has been a sustained and pervasive effort to educate members of that community about appropriate ways to minimize the risk factors associated with coronary heart disease, long the major cause of death among adults in the United States (and in other highly urban, industrial societies). The model is that of long-term education (in the broadest sense of that word), in recognition that cultural attitudes and behaviors cannot be changed quickly. Beyond that, it must be accepted that people need reinforcement and that newcomers and young people need to get the same or related message at later times. Another fundamental cornerstone of success in such a venture is recognition that it is not enough to change a few individuals; rather, there has to be a change in the social environment. The desired innovation must become normal as a way of thinking about or doing something.

To accomplish this requires more than just a few hours of pedagogical instruction in the schools (Hanson 1997). In Framingham, short courses were made available to adults at convenient times and places as well as training sessions and collaboration with food service personnel to ensure that heart-healthy alternatives were available in restaurants, grocery stores, catering businesses, and so forth. Appropriate and graded exercise programs were introduced by civic groups such as scouts, youth clubs, the elder center, and city employees, and involving the maximum cross section of the population. Physicians and pharmacists were given pointers on how to help clients and were encouraged to bring up the subject, no matter what else might have been the patient's or customer's primary concern. There is no reason to doubt that a similarly coordinated approach would be effective with respect to drinking.

In the early stages, it may be felt that increased popular awareness of the issue and of desired alternatives is a measure of success, but that must be only a starting point. Public opinion is indeed a potentially powerful force, but the exciting finding in Framingham is that systematic longitudinal studies show actual changes in behavior on the part of many individuals, and those changes are reflected in dramatic epidemiological changes for the population, namely, lowered rates of stroke and heart attack, significantly reduced average levels of damaging cholesterols, fewer and less severe cases of hypertension, and even increased overall life expectancy (Kannel 1989; Castelli 1990; Levy 1993). Obviously, none of these changes can with confidence be said to have been "caused by" the heart health program alone, but the bundle of them together is highly suggestive. Concerns about diverse diet, with more fruits, vegetables, and complex carbohydrates combined with less meat and saturated fats, regular exercise, conscious efforts at stress reduction, and a host of other changes have become routine. There has been a major change in many aspects of the culture of that city and region. Some other cities are adopting similar programs.

If we were to apply that model to the reduction of risk from beverage alcohol, one of the first focuses might be demystification of the substance, with a campaign that would let everyone know enough biology, chemistry, and physiology to appreciate what ethanol is and how it interacts with the human body. The myth of disinhibition should be exposed through historical and ethnographic examples, and there should be open discussion of real risks (as contrasted with the sensationalized versions of risk that have become imbedded in folk belief). If done with appropriate safeguards, there can be enormous impact from a double-blind experiment. Private and commercial hosts should be coached about the importance of having food available when alcohol is served and also the appropriateness of offering attractive nonalcoholic drinks. Journalists, teachers, and law enforcement officers should be sensitized to the fact that inappropriate behavior should be censured, whether a person is drunk or not. That may be one of the major lessons for everyone to learn eventually, but a few pacesetters can do much to foster the idea. Drunkenness as such should be deglamorized, and asocial or antisocial behavior should be negatively sanctioned, preferably by the peer group.

No occasion should have drinking as its focus (unless it is arranged for moderate tasting of wines, for example), although drinking may well serve as an accompaniment to many kinds of occasion. To make drinking a normal adjunct to daily living has served the Mediterranean cultures well in terms of lessened risk of drinking problems, especially in comparison with other cultures, in which drinking is relegated to back rooms, garages, or outdoor trips, and kept from women, children, and youths. In many societies, alcohol use starts at an early age, along with food and in a familiar environment, with no examples of heavy drinking except in occasional and well-controlled social settings. Even in drinking cultures that have a more stigmatized view of drinking, people start to drink in their early teens. But the legal drinking age in some countries is eighteen or twenty-one. These high limits result in many young people's drinking before the legal age. This can damage their view of the law and of the dominant system, promoting both risk taking and a generally countercultural attitude. Would it not be better to teach youngsters to see drinking alcohol as one of the good things of life that should be handled with care in order to be enjoyed? But making a change in that direction would mean a dramatic shift in alcohol policies among large sectors of society, many of whom are already convinced, more by indoctrination than by fact or observation, that teenage drinking is tantamount to car accidents, disinhibited sexual behavior, and loss of control, no matter how much is drunk and under what circumstances.

Changes in attitudes and behaviors likely to reduce both harm and risk often draw on the natural experiments represented by cultures whose patterns of drinking have proven to be less associated with problems. A recent review of the few community interventions that have been attempted in this connection (Gorman and Speer 1996) shows that skills-based training adds little to the above mix unless broad community participation is included. But the specific details of such a program would have to be shaped to conform to the local situation and to prevailing attitudes and tolerance of change. Obviously, the demographics of a community are important in terms of the proportion of the population in the various age groups. Religion could be a factor, where significant "dry" sentiment prevails. Economic factors could play out in different ways.

But the major point is that culture must be recognized as more a product of human behavior than a determinant of it. All cultures change, and parts of a culture can be changed deliberately. But such changes are usually not abrupt, nor are they easy. Those who have expressed concern about drinking problems with regard to public health and social welfare should embrace efforts at shaping patterns of drinking that would lessen harm (to individuals, to those who are close to them, and to the society at large) and that would prevent the recurrence of patterns that result in such harm.

A worldwide perspective suggests that no single alcohol policy or combination of policies is adequate. Formal controls on availability have proven to be relatively ineffective, although they still tend to be favored by governments everywhere. Complex issues do not lend themselves to simple solutions. A long-term perspective featuring education, resocialization with an emphasis on informal controls, and respect for each unique cultural context would appear most likely to achieve positive community reaction, including active engagement and commitment, without which any policy is doomed to be ineffective.

REFERENCES

Ásmundsson, G. 1995. Iceland. In *International Handbook on Alcohol and Culture,* ed. D. B. Heath. Westport, Conn.: Greenwood.

Badri, M. B. 1976. *Islam and Alcoholism.* Takoma Park, Md.: American Trust Publications.

Beauchamp, D. E. 1973. Precarious politics: alcoholism and public policy. Ph.D. diss., Johns Hopkins University.

Castelli, W. P. 1990. Diet, smoking, and alcohol: influence on coronary heart disease. *American Journal of Kidney Disease* 16:41–46.

Cooper, A. M. 1992. Mexican experience with warning labels on alcoholic beverage containers: a cautionary tale. *Moderation Reader* (May–June): 29–32.

Davies, P., and D. Walsh. 1985. *Alcohol Problems and Alcohol Control in Europe.* London: Croom Helm.

Edwards, G., et al., eds. 1977. *Alcohol-Related Disabilities.* Offset Publication 32. Geneva: World Health Organization.

———. 1994. *Alcohol Policy and the Public Good.* Oxford: Oxford University Press.

Gorman, D. M., and P. W. Speer. 1996. Preventing alcohol abuse and alcohol-related problems through community interventions: a review of evaluation studies. *Psychology and Health* 11:95–131.

Grant, M., ed. 1985. *Alcohol Policies.* Regional Publications, European Series, 18. Copenhagen: WHO.

Grant, M., M. Plant, and A. Williams, eds. 1983. *Economics and Alcohol: Consumption and Controls.* London: Croom Helm.

Hall, W., and E. Hunter. 1995. Australia. In *International Handbook on Alcohol and Culture,* ed. D. B. Heath. Westport, Conn.: Greenwood.

Hanson, D. J. 1995. *Preventing Alcohol Abuse: Alcohol, Culture, and Control.* Westport, Conn.: Praeger.

———. 1997. *Alcohol Education: What We Must Do.* Westport, Conn.: Praeger.

Harper, F. F. 1904. *The Code of Hammurabi, King of Babylon.* London: Luzak.

Heath, D. B. 1982. In other cultures, they also drink. In *Alcohol, Science, and Society Revisited,* ed. E. L. Gomberg, H. R. White, and J. A. Carpenter. Ann Arbor: University of Michigan Press.

———. 1989. The new temperance movement: through the looking-glass. *Drugs and Society* 3:143–68.

———, ed. 1995. *International Handbook on Alcohol and Culture.* Westport, Conn.: Greenwood.

———. 1997. Between zero tolerance and a free market: the anthropological case for liberalization of drugs. In *Formal and Informal Control of Drugs: Using Scientific Evidence to Reduce Social Consequences,* ed. O. F. Pomerleau. Ann Arbor: University of Michigan, Substance Abuse Research Center.

Heath, D. B., and A. M. Cooper. 1981. *Alcohol Use and World Cultures.* Toronto: Addiction Research Foundation.

Holder, H. D., and G. Edwards, eds. 1995. *Alcohol and Public Policy: Evidence and Issues.* Oxford: Oxford University Press.

Jankowiak, W., and D. Bradburd. 1996. Using drug foods to capture and enhance labor performance: a cross-cultural perspective. *Current Anthropology* 37:717–20.

Kannel, W. B. 1989. Epidemiological aspects of heart failure. *Cardiology Clinics* 7:1–9.

Levy, D. 1993. A multifactorial approach to coronary heart disease risk assessment. *Clinical and Experimental Hypertension* 15:1077–86.

Mäkelä, K., et al., eds. 1981. *Alcohol, Society, and the State.* Vol. 1. *A Comparative Study of Alcohol Control.* Toronto: Addiction Research Foundation.

Mancall, P. C. 1995. *Deadly Medicine: Indians and Alcohol in Early America.* Ithaca: Cornell University Press.

Marshall, M. 1976. A review and appraisal of alcohol and kava studies in Oceania. In *Cross-Cultural Approaches to the Study of Alcohol: An Interdisciplinary Perspective,* ed. M. W. Everett, J. O. Waddell, and D. B. Heath. The Hague: Mouton.

Maula, J., M. Lindblad, and C. Tigerstedt, eds. 1990. *Alcohol in Developing Countries.* Publication 18. Helsinki: Nordic Council for Alcohol and Drug Research.

May, P.A. 1992. Alcohol policy considerations for Indian reservations and bordertown communities. *American Indian and Alaska Native Mental Health Research* 4:5–59.

Miner, H. 1968. Community-society continua. In *International Encyclopedia of the Social Sciences.* Vol. 3. New York: Crowell Collier and Macmillan.

Mohan, D., and H. K. Sharma. 1995. India. In *International Handbook on Alcohol and Culture,* ed. D. B. Heath. Westport, Conn.: Greenwood.

Moore, M. H., and D. R. Gerstein, eds. 1981. *Alcohol and Public Policy: Beyond the Shadow of Prohibition.* Washington, D.C.: National Academy Press.

Moser, J. 1979. *Prevention of Alcohol-Related Problems: An International Review of Preventive Measures, Policies, and Programmes.* WHO/MNH/79.16. Geneva: World Health Organization.

Musto, D. F. 1987. *The American Disease: Origins of Narcotic Control.* Rev. ed. New York: Oxford University Press.

Nyberg, K., and P. Allebeck. 1995. Sweden. In *International Handbook on Alcohol and Culture*, ed. D. B. Heath. Westport, Conn.: Greenwood.

Pan, L. 1975. *Alcohol in Colonial Africa*. Helsinki: Finnish Foundation for Alcohol Studies.

Partanen, J. 1991. *Sociability and Intoxication: Alcohol and Drinking in Kenya, Africa, and the Modern World*. Helsinki: Finnish Foundation for Alcohol Studies.

Pernanen, K. 1991. *Alcohol in Human Violence*. New York: Guilford.

Popham, R. E., W. Schmidt, and J. de Lint. 1976. The effects of legal restraint on drinking. In *The Biology of Alcoholism,*, ed. B. Kissin and H. Begleiter. Vol. 4. *Social Aspects of Alcoholism*. New York: Plenum.

Redfield, R. 1960. *The Little Community*. Chicago: University of Chicago Press.

Rorabaugh, W. J. 1979. *The Alcoholic Republic: An American Tradition*. New York: Oxford University Press.

Sidorov, P. 1995. Russia. In *International Handbook on Alcohol and Culture*, ed. D. B. Heath. Westport, Conn.: Greenwood.

Sinclair, A. 1964. *Era of Excess: A Social History of the Prohibition Movement*. New York: Harper.

Single, E., P. Morgan, and J. de Lint, eds. 1981. *Alcohol, Science, and the State*. Vol. 2. *The Social History of Control Policy in Seven Countries*. Toronto: Addiction Research Foundation.

Smart, R. G., and A. C. Ogborne. 1986. *Northern Spirits: Drinking in Canada, Then and Now*. Toronto: Addiction Research Foundation.

Stivers, R. A. 1976. *A Hair of the Dog: Irish Drinking and American Stereotype*. University Park: Pennsylvania State University Press.

WHO. 1977. *Manual of the International Statistical Classification of Diseases, Injuries, and Causes of Death*. Vol. 1. 9th ed. Geneva: World Health Organization.

———. 1980. *Problems Related to Alcohol Consumption*. Technical Report 650. Geneva: World Health Organization.

———. 1981. *Global Strategy for Health for All by the Year 2000*. Health for All, 3. Geneva: World Health Organization.

Xiao, J. C. 1995. China. In *International Handbook on Alcohol and Culture*, ed. D. B. Heath. Westport, Conn.: Greenwood.

Part Three

A New Approach

In order to move toward a more integrative approach to alcohol policies that takes individual variables into account, new approaches must be developed. These new methodologies would allow a more accurate description of patterns of alcohol consumption and consequently also of their outcomes. In addition, such an approach would allow for intervention strategies to be tailored to the needs of specific populations particularly at risk while taking into account differences in drinking patterns and particular cultural requirements.

This final section of the book examines some of the implications of the proposed paradigm shift for the development of alcohol policy. First and foremost, a stronger emphasis on patterns of drinking requires a change in the current approach to research and measurement in the alcohol field. Although levels of alcohol consumption are a useful research tool, they must be complemented with other parameters which reveal more detail about specific drinking behaviors and their relationship with particular problems. In addition, in order to meet the requirements of a diverse population, any approach to research and policy development must be tempered with a sensitivity toward diverse cultures and drinking behaviors.

Similarly, given the diversity in drinking patterns and outcomes, any approach to prevention, education, and screening must also cover the full spectrum of use from abstainers and very light drinkers to excessive and dependent drinkers, again with an emphasis on different cultural settings and perspectives.

Such a novel perspective on policy models also creates the opportunity for new partnerships to be forged in a combined effort toward the prevention of alcohol abuse and health promotion. An effective approach to this end would involve the cooperation of governments, health advocacy organizations, the academic community, as well as commercial interests. These collaborative efforts are examined from four different perspectives, and public–private partnership is offered as an idea whose time has come.

The concluding chapter of *Drinking Patterns and Their Consequences* re-emphasizes the theme of harm reduction as it applies to alcohol. The authors propose implications of a shift in focus toward patterns for the future development of policies and strategies. The way ahead lies in greater attention to measures that focus on preventing problems associated with particular harmful patterns of drinking and less attention to general population measures that restrict access to alcohol.

Chapter 12

The Implications for Measurement and Research

Marjana Martinic

Current approaches to research on alcohol-related problems are broad and inter-disciplinary. They combine biomedical approaches with epidemiology and with fields as seemingly far removed as sociology, ethnography, and economics. The main area of alcohol research, however, draws upon epidemiological data with a focus on the measurement of consumption and on indicators of alcohol-related problems. These problems range from somatic manifestations to social pathology and economic costs. Clinical studies have also yielded much information, and research on genetics and in the field of neuroscience appears to hold considerable promise. However, levels of alcohol consumption are often used as the primary measurement tool. Much attention has been paid to how changes in level of consumption affect the incidence and prevalence of alcohol-related problems.

Levels of consumption are an important measurement in alcohol research. However, they rely on aggregate measures, revealing little information about the role of specific drinking behaviors. The importance of individual drinking patterns within different contexts has long been recognized. In their analysis of drinking behaviors in colleges and universities in the United States, Straus and Bacon (1953) set about to answer a number of questions directed at individual patterns of drinking. In addition to measuring levels of consumption, the survey

Marjana Martinic is with the International Center for Alcohol Policies, Washington, D.C., U.S.

addressed a number of additional factors, such as drinking context and cohorts, beverage type, prevailing customs, and attitudes about drinking. Work by Jellinek (1960) also examined patterns of drinking, in particular their potential relationship with the development and onset of alcoholism. This relationship to variation in drinking patterns was addressed within the context of different cultures.

As Room (1996) points out, there has long been awareness of the importance of drinking patterns, that the amount consumed on a single occasion might carry with it different consequences than the average level of consumption. However, historically, little importance has been given to the full complexity of different patterns or to their role within the context of general medical epidemiology. Recently, there has been a shift in the emphasis placed by researchers on the role of drinking patterns. It is becoming more widely recognized that different patterns of alcohol consumption are associated with different problems and, conversely, that problems can be predicted if consumption patterns are known (Bondy 1996; Dawson 1996; Grunewald, Mitchell, and Treno 1996; Rehm et al. 1996; Rossow 1996). This relationship is discussed in some detail in chapter 1 of this volume. The main objective of the present chapter is to examine how a continued greater emphasis on patterns of consumption could contribute to alcohol research and to the prevention of alcohol-related problems.

THE IMPORTANCE OF DRINKING PATTERNS

In order to study alcohol-related problems effectively, it is necessary to examine the behaviors that give rise to them. It has been shown that behaviors such as heavy drinking on frequent occasions are better predictors of certain alcohol-related problems than is per capita consumption (Single and Wortley 1993; Rehm et al. 1996). These behaviors and the problems associated with them vary across cultures. It is therefore not sufficient simply to address the levels at which alcohol is consumed. Instead, it is necessary to derive information on the specific patterns that are associated with the consumption of beverage alcohol by different groups and in different societies. These specific patterns should be drinking behaviors that are repeated with regularity and consistency. They should be robust behaviors that can be described and preferably measured in a reproducible way.

The necessity for the description of specific patterns is illustrated by studies such as that by Poldrugo et al. (1989) in which alcohol-related morbidity in northern Italy was compared to that in the United States. The most prominent alcohol-related diagnosis in northern Italy was liver cirrhosis, while alcoholism and an association with drug dependence and personality disorders were more frequent in the United States. The implications of this difference become clear when one discovers that the drinking patterns in the two countries differ considerably. It is therefore possible to use different drinking patterns as predictors of specific problems. In fact, Poldrugo and colleagues suggested that a pattern of consumption that encourages binge drinking (United States) rather than steady daily consumption (Italy) increases the likelihood of alcohol dependence and is a useful predictor of maladaptive behaviors.

Even when the incidence of alcohol-related problems within a single country is considered, it is important to keep in mind differences in drinking patterns. In the case of the United States, for instance, the culture surrounding alcohol varies widely from one region to another. Surveys have shown that the South has higher rates of abstention than the rest of the country, more frequent instances of heavy consumption, and a generally higher rate of alcohol-related problems (Cherpitel 1996). Therefore, particularly in large and multicultural societies, drinking patterns play a key role in the prediction and understanding of alcohol-related problems.

Drinking patterns and problems can be broken down further still by gender, age, ethnicity, and socioeconomic status (Rehm et al. 1996). Patterns of drinking among men are different from patterns of drinking among women (Fillmore et al. 1991; Dawson 1993). Within multicultural societies, moreover, patterns of drinking also vary with heritage and with degree of cultural integration (Marin and Posner 1995). Even identified groups, such as individuals with alcohol-related problems, show variation in patterns and consequences of drinking. This is illustrated by Epstein et al. (1995), whose attempt to describe drinking patterns among alcoholics showed that these could be broken down into several discrete subtypes. Each of these drinking patterns differs with respect to the onset of alcohol-related problems and carries with it different implications for measurement, research, and treatment.

A further variable that must be taken into consideration when measuring drinking behaviors and alcohol-related problems is beverage type. Most drinkers do not consume one type of product exclusively, making it difficult to assess the effects of a single beverage type. However, there is evidence that different beverages are associated with different drinking patterns and problems (Smart 1996). This distinction appears to be true across cultures. According to the 1993 Spanish National Household Health Survey, for instance, younger Spaniards consume more beer and distilled spirits, while older individuals are generally wine drinkers (Del Rio, Prada, and Alvarez 1995). Gender differences also play a role, with men consuming higher levels of alcohol than women. In addition to demographic differences, the consumption of beer and spirits follows a weekly pattern, while wine is consumed daily.

The preference for one beverage over another has been shown to correlate with significant differences in lifestyle, personality, and consumption pattern (Burke, Puddey, and Beilin 1995). Other correlates of beverage preference such as smoking, education, socioeconomic status, general health (Klatsky, Armstrong, and Kipp 1990), and ethnicity (Herd and Grube 1996) have been described and should be taken into consideration when correlating patterns with problems.

Often related to choice of beverage is the context of drinking. This factor is significant in determining drinking patterns, as different contexts have been shown to be related to different sets of problems. The temporal component of drinking has been described as having an effect on adverse consequences. In particular, late-night drinking appears to be more strongly associated with job- and school-related problems (Dawson 1996). Two other important variables are drinking location and drinking cohorts. This is illustrated by research on drinking behaviors of immigrant groups in the United States. The studies show that Italians (Simboli 1985) and Cubans (Page et al. 1985) traditionally show a low incidence of drinking problems. This appears to be due largely to drinking patterns in which alcohol is consumed in conjunction with meals or rituals and in the context of family. In both cultures, inebriation and heavy drinking are not generally accepted.

Another pattern of drinking—bingeing—also correlates significantly with drinking context. In the United States, for instance, binge drinking is often associated with college and university students. Men are more likely than women to engage in binge drinking and do so predominantly within the social context of fraternities (Wechsler et al. 1994, 1995a, 1995b). The consequences and problems associated with this pattern of drinking range from hangovers and inability to attend classes to injury or even fatalities and affect not only the drinkers themselves but others around them (Wechsler et al. 1995c).

Nor are these patterns of drinking and the problems associated with them confined to the United States. Research from Japan indicates that the social context of university clubs changes the patterns of drinking of both men and women and increases the frequency of observed alcohol-related problems (Umezono et al. 1995). Other research has also demonstrated the importance of drinking locale. A study conducted by the Addiction Research Foundation in Canada suggested that young people, often under the legal drinking age, who drink in controlled settings such as bars experience the fewest alcohol-related problems (Smart, Adlaf, and Walsh 1996).

It is clear from the evidence that patterns such as binge drinking in college fraternities depend on both drinking locale and drinking cohorts. Such patterns differ significantly from patterns such as daily moderate consumption of alcohol with family meals, and the types of problems associated with each behavior and experienced by each group are significantly different. Accordingly, it seems reasonable to suggest that it should be possible to separate out discrete drinking patterns and that the problems associated with each should be addressed in context.

APPROACHES TO MEASUREMENT

Current approaches to the measurement of alcohol consumption and alcohol-related problems have yielded a wealth of information. Most important, they have demonstrated that the association between alcohol use and resulting problems is not unidimensional and that, in addition to levels of consumption, a number of variables must be taken into account (Bondy 1996). However, three main areas would benefit from added attention in order for the emphasis on patterns of drinking to be increased. First, information on patterns should be easily obtainable from measurement of drinking. Currently used variables do not always yield adequate information on drinking behaviors. Second, the relationships between consumption and problems are complex and are not always fully explored when a correlation is made between the two. Finally, much can be learned from studying populations not at risk and populations whose drinking behavior is not associated with problems. Current research places a strong emphasis on clinical samples or on populations already at risk for alcohol-related problems. The following sections examine each of these topics in turn.

The Measurement of Alcohol Consumption

Measurement of alcohol consumption must be designed in such a way that specific patterns can be separated from broad measures of consumption. In general, studies have relied on two principal variables, measurement of quantity and measurement of frequency (Cahalan, Roizen, and Room 1969; Greenfield 1986; Room 1990a; Straus and Bacon 1953). While this approach has yielded valuable information, it has been criticized for being inaccurate and for not providing enough information about patterns of drinking.

Unidimensional measurements of quantity, for instance, are inappropriate for many purposes, such as differentiating between drinkers who are "moderate in amount, steady in frequency" and drinkers who are "heavy in amount, occasional in frequency" (Pearl 1926). While both groups may consume the same amounts over a given period of time, the pattern of the former may be one of daily consumption, while the latter may confine all drinking to a single day or to the weekend. Since most adverse consequences of drinking are closely related to heavy drinking (Room 1990a), it is important to be able to make these distinctions. Hence, information provided by volume alone is not sufficient.

In addition to being inadequate for describing patterns of drinking, measurement of volume is inherently problematic. There is little consensus on a standardized definition of the basic research tool, namely the units by which consumption is measured (Rehm et al. 1996). Measurement of volume relies heavily on the concept of a "drink," which takes on different meanings depending on the source and context. This problem is very well illustrated by Turner (1990) in a review of definitions of a standard drink used in 125 epidemiological studies. The author found that a standard drink, as defined by different researchers, can range from the equivalent of 20 grams of ethanol to 48 grams of ethanol.

The problem of defining a standard drink is compounded by a number of factors. It is necessary to take into account cultural preferences for grams versus ounces of ethanol, American versus British fluid ounces, and measures of alcohol content as a percentage by weight or by volume. While a number of governments around the world have attempted to define the concept of a standard drink, these definitions cover a broad range, from the equivalent of 8 grams of ethanol in the

United Kingdom (U.K. Department of Health and Social Security 1995), the equivalent of 10 grams of ethanol in Australia (National Health and Medical Research Council 1992), to the equivalent of 19.75 grams of ethanol in a Japanese *go*, or standard drink (Turner 1990). Research from different countries must therefore be standardized for valid comparisons to be possible (Miller, Heather, and Hall 1991).

In instances in which levels of consumption are related to harm, the issue of ''drinks'' becomes particularly complicated. It is difficult to draw comparisons between epidemiological studies, especially at the international level, when a drink in one country can be the equivalent of more than twice a drink in another country. This difference in culture-specific definitions of drink sizes is illustrated in reports from the cross-cultural applicability research (CAR) study, jointly sponsored by the World Health Organization, the National Institute on Alcohol Abuse and Addiction, and the National Institute on Drug Abuse in the United States (Bennett et al. 1993). Even more complicated is any attempt at standardization when dealing with measures such as the jar of beer to which a newly wed man or one who has paid his taxes is entitled in Nigeria (Oshodin 1995) or the practice of sharing beer from a large receptacle with a changing group of drinking companions, common in some parts of Africa. Such vague definitions and discrepancies in measure introduce further variation into the definition of related terms such as moderate drinking and binge drinking. A standardized unit that could be used internationally would make valid comparisons possible. A little-heeded plea has been made for universal reporting in grams of ethanol or in metric fluid volume units (Miller, Heather, and Hall 1991).

The standardization of measurement is particularly problematic in research that relies on self-reporting by individuals. The respondent to a questionnaire must estimate the size of the drink consumed, taking into account both alcohol content and container size, two variables that are difficult to gauge. In a study published in 1989, Stockwell and Stirling have shown that most people are unable to estimate the size of a drink accurately. In addition, there is particular difficulty in estimating the strength of low-alcohol or extra-strong drinks. The deviation is highest for distilled spirits and lowest for wine (Lemmens 1994). The problem of correctly estimating the strength of a drink is especially difficult in an off-premise setting in which container size may vary considerably and partially filled glasses replenished. Questionnaires therefore need to be designed in a way that would take this variation into account. It may be easier for an individual to estimate the number of bottles or partial bottles consumed than to estimate the number of standard drinks consumed. It has been reported that subjects typically underestimate the amount of alcohol they consume (Fuller, Lee, and Gordis 1988).

In addition to the problem of correctly estimating the amount of alcohol consumed, self-report data are limited by the ability or the willingness of respondents to recall their alcohol consumption accurately (Midanik and Harford 1994). There is a general tendency toward underreporting alcohol consumption, which is particularly pronounced among alcoholics (Butterworth 1993). According to a report by the International Life Sciences Institute, one result of such underreporting is that consumption levels associated with certain health risks may be higher than indicated by available data (ibid.). Similarly, health problems experienced by some abstainers may be associated with a past history of heavy consumption that they have failed to report. In some societies, the social unacceptability of drinking and alcohol production may also lead to underreporting for fear of exposure or consequences. Conversely, self-report data may also result in overreporting, particularly among young people, who may consider heavy drinking a means of achieving social status (Forman and Linney 1991). The problems inherent in self-report data are further underscored by the finding that such data generally generate lower estimates of total alcohol consumption than data derived from sales (Single and Wortley 1994).

To ensure higher reliability of self-report data, the design of criteria and questions should be such that the answer yields the desired information. Questions about quantity and frequency must be worded in a clear and unambiguous way. In some cases, response validity can be improved by asking multiple questions in a given survey regarding the same behaviors. Alternatively, several methods of measurement can be used simultaneously to test the reliability of the response, or where possible, the size of the sample used in the survey can be increased. While these modifications will not guarantee the reliability of self-report data, they can nonetheless improve upon it.

Another problem, with self-report questionnaires in particular, is the measurement of drinking frequency. One way to obtain information about frequency is the summary method: questions are asked about the number of occasions on which more than a given number of drinks was consumed. The time interval being considered is generally the previous twelve months. While this approach may yield information about general consumption, it reveals nothing about pattern of drinking. In addition, the method is highly inaccurate, as it relies heavily on memory. Another approach is the so-called recent-period summary. This method includes a summary of drinking over a shorter period of time, such as the past thirty days, and can also reveal information about the number of occasions on which more than a given number of drinks was consumed. Since the time interval is shorter than that used in the summary method, the degree of inaccuracy is lower. It is possible also to include questions about other variables, such as type of occasion or context. The disadvantage of this is the possibility that the interval studied may not be representative of an individual's consumption pattern over longer periods (Room 1990a).

One strategy that overcomes these problems has been suggested by Room (1990a). This approach focuses on the most recent drinking occasions or days on which alcohol was consumed (drinking days). This approach has the advantages of providing information about both pattern and context and of revealing information on the drinking patterns of consumers who drink infrequently. Questions are included about quantity consumed, beverage type, length of the drinking occasion, setting, and drinking companions. In addition, this approach could be used to evaluate the drinking experience itself by addressing the subjective assessments of the degree of pleasure derived.

Valuable information about problems can be obtained by questions relating to drinking style (Yu 1995). Starting the day with a drink or a preference for drinking alone, for instance, are both indicators of heavy or problem drinkers (Fine, Scoles, and Mulligan 1975; Miller and Windle 1990). One example of such a comprehensive approach is that employed by Yu and Williford (1992). This study used three measurement concepts: problem drinking, consumption, and style. Problem drinking assesses the intensity of the problem, taking into account the self-perception of the drinker and the family drinking history. Consumption measures quantity, frequency, and type of beverage consumed. Style assesses when, where, and with whom the respondents drink. The combination of these variables allows for a picture to be formed that takes patterns into consideration.

The Measurement of Problems

The second area that would benefit from further attention is that of the relationship between consumption and problems. It is easy to draw correlations between two events, but the validity of such associations may be questionable. Other variables must be taken into consideration to ensure that the association made is not spurious and actually the result of other factors.

Drinking patterns change over time and often reflect a broader societal change. The increase in per capita consumption of alcohol in Japan over the past several years, for instance, is largely attributable to the increase in consumption by women. This reflects the changing role of women in a postindustrial urbanized society and a concurrent change in traditional values (Takano, Nakamura, and Watanabe 1996). Similar changes have also been observed in the United States. Examination of drivers convicted of driving under the influence or driving while intoxicated in the state of New York between 1978 and 1988, for example, showed that the trend was toward a decrease in the proportion of male offenders aged twenty and younger and an increase in the proportion of female offenders (Yu, Essex, and Williford 1992). To understand fully the implications of this changing pattern, it needs to be viewed as a reflection of changes in the role and lifestyle of women as well as of changes in attitudes of the public and the police with respect to female drinking and driving.

Valid conclusions about relationships can be drawn only if the study group is carefully selected and adequate controls are available. A comparative study conducted among Vietnam veterans (Wish et al. 1979) illustrated the complexity of this problem as well as the need to assess other underlying factors. The study showed that upon their return to the United States, Vietnam veterans as a group experienced an increase in alcohol-related problems. These problems stabilized but remained at a higher level than in a control group made up of men who had not entered the armed forces. Several factors confound this study. Legal access to alcohol was limited in Vietnam because many of the enlisted men were under the legal drinking age applied within the U.S. armed forces and also because lower-ranking men were limited to beer. Therefore, many of the servicemen turned to narcotics, which were cheap and easily available. On their return to the United States, alcohol was cheaper than narcotics and the survivors of the war were over the age of twenty-one; as a consequence, the levels of consumption of alcohol and narcotics were reversed.

An understanding of the relationship between alcohol consumption patterns and patterns of problems can also be put to use in other contexts. Problems can be used as indicators of consumption and can be employed as a first approach to measurement and, ultimately, to prevention. Certain types of injury may be particularly associated with elevated levels of drinking and could be used to screen emergency room patients. Similarly, excessive dental abrasion, for instance, may indicate chronic and heavy alcohol consumption and alcohol-related problems (Robb and Smith 1990). Observations such as this further underscore the need for a deeper understanding of the relationship between drinking patterns and alcohol-related problems. Without adequately understanding one, it is not possible to interpret the other.

Yet the interpretation of the relationship between patterns and problems has its pitfalls. These problems are particularly salient in the assessment of risk. One issue to be addressed in risk assessment is that of attribution of causality. For a causal relationship to be established, a statistical correlation between two events must be shown: the occurrence of one event must be necessary for the occurrence of the second. The traditional approach to establishing such a relationship between alcohol consumption and adverse consequences is by calculating the mean number of problems and correlating them with another measure, such as volume of alcohol consumed (Harford, Grant, and Hasin 1991; Midanik et al. 1996). From this, the contribution of alcohol to the problem is assessed by means of multivariate analysis and risk curves. However, risk curves generally rely on the idea of a classic dose-response relationship, which in the case of alcohol research can be easily confounded by a number of factors that defy neat mathematical description and that require a more rigorous approach in the attribution of causality. Such factors include diet, lifestyle, ethnicity, general health, obesity, smoking, and other behavioral factors, which are discussed in some detail in chapters 3 and 4 of this volume.

A second issue that merits further attention are the potential sources of measurement error in risk assessment. One source of error is self-report data, a topic discussed elsewhere in this chapter. An equally important source of error is reliance on the mean number of problems associated with different levels of consumption. As discussed earlier in this chapter, an approach that relies on aggregate data may obscure significant variation in individual drinking patterns, each of which contributes, to a different degree, to the particular problem at hand. Recent attempts have been made to use data from large-scale surveys and to reanalyze them in a way that will reveal additional insights into particular problem areas. This approach is presented in chapter 4 of this volume as well as in recent work by Midanik and colleagues (1996). Although first steps have been made in this direction, much further work is necessary if true insight is to be gained into the relationship between alcohol consumption and problems.

In addition to obscuring variation in drinking patterns, aggregate data may also hide errors that can make interpretation and risk assessment difficult (Edwards et al. 1994). Average measures generally underestimate alcohol intake (Midanik 1994), and the resulting statistical errors in mean and variance can significantly distort subsequent calculations of risk function (Fillmore and Johnstone 1996). Such errors may be especially important when examining the potential risks associated with low-to-moderate levels of consumption. In this instance, the importance of examining individual patterns rather than aggregate data becomes critical.

Finally, risk curves take into account the special characteristics of the populations upon which they are based (Edwards et al. 1994). This issue is particularly relevant in the case of cross-cultural research. The cultural component is an important one in the interpretation of when an outcome can be ascribed to alcohol. The subjective assessment of risk associated with alcohol varies significantly depending on the age, gender, cultural context, tolerance to alcohol, exposure, and environment of the group to be considered. Pernanen (1993) suggested that, whereas the explanatory models favored in North America include factors relating to the individual, European models stress social and structural causes. However, neither of these two approaches may be entirely relevant within the context of developing countries.

Applicability of Findings

The selection of appropriate study and control groups is closely associated with the third point raised in this section, namely that most of the epidemiological evidence on alcohol and alcohol-related problems is derived from information on individuals who either are at risk for or have already developed alcohol-related problems (Popham, Schmidt, and Israelstam 1984). The validity of using at-risk populations such as those included in clinical studies must be questioned. In particular, there is the concern of extrapolating the findings of such studies to the general population. Recent medical evidence has further complicated this issue. It has been reported by a number of researchers that moderate alcohol consumption may in fact have beneficial health effects and that complete abstention from alcohol may even be a risk factor, particularly in the case of coronary heart disease (Rimm et al. 1996). This finding suggests that much can be learned from studying drinking patterns that do not result in problems and that such information may be more applicable to the general population than information gathered from clinical samples. Furthermore, moderate consumers may be better than abstainers as controls for measuring alcohol problems. There has been a recent effort by the U.S. National Institute on Alcohol and Alcoholism (NIAAA) to encourage this line of research in order to provide a better understanding of the mechanisms involved in the effects of alcohol.

To understand fully the relationship between consumption and alcohol-related problems, an interdisciplinary approach must be adopted. This approach should take into consideration a number of variables, such as risk factors. Biological predisposition plays a significant role in the development of alcohol-related problems. This includes factors such as genetic predisposition, family history of alcohol-related problems, and ethnicity. Ethnic differences in response and sensitivity to alcohol have long been understood (Wolff 1972). It has been demonstrated that a mutation in the gene for the enzyme alcohol dehydrogenase can serve as a predictor for excessive alcohol use (Couzigou et al. 1994; Tu and Israel 1995). This mutation is commonly found in individuals of Asian descent. It has been shown that, as a consequence, Asian males are more susceptible to alcohol-related liver damage than are Caucasian males (Wickramasinghe et al. 1995). In addition to predisposing genetic factors, other biomedical factors must also be taken into consideration when assessing alcohol-related problems and correlating them with levels of consumption. Among the most important risk factors are general physiological state, health, age, diagnosis of affective disorder, and use of psychotropic or psychoactive substances.

Along with biological factors, environmental and social influences also play a role in the development of alcohol-related problems and must be taken into consideration in examining patterns and consequences of drinking. For instance, corporal punishment has been identified as a risk factor for alcohol abuse (Straus and Kantor 1994). There is evidence that frequent binge drinking during late adolescence and early young adulthood may be a predictor of harmful behavior as well as of long-term problems with alcohol later in life (Schulenberg et al. 1996). A recent study focusing on the relationship between alcohol consumption and macroeconomic conditions suggests that the intake of beverage alcohol is sensitive to fluctuations in economic conditions (Ruhm 1995). Hence, these interdisciplinary factors merit further examination and should also be included in any comprehensive analysis of the relationship between consumption patterns and their consequences.

One additional component must be taken into consideration when addressing the validity of studies. This is the dimension of time. The most promising method of approaching this issue is the use of longitudinal studies that allow the determination of antecedents of a particular behavior and that also take into account any significant risk and predisposing factors (Fillmore 1990). So, for instance, youthful behavior may be a predictor for certain drinking patterns as well as for alcohol-related problems. Research suggests that antisocial behavior in boys may indicate a tendency toward the development of alcohol-related problems (Robins 1984). In addition to antisocial behavior, abuse during childhood, lower social status, living in an urban area, low intelligence or poor education, and change in parents' marital status during primary school are also predictors of adult alcohol problems (Amundsen 1982). The longitudinal approach also allows the incorporation of incidence and prevalence information, such as the age at which drinking was initiated, into the assessment of problems over time. The recent (1996) study by Schulenberg and colleagues mentioned above, which examined the patterns of drinking of adolescents during the transitional years into young adulthood, serves as an example of the range of information that can be derived from a longitudinal approach.

Thus, longitudinal research combines temporal and contextual approaches and can be designed to take into account a number of variables. At the individual level, longitudinal studies can be used to follow variations in patterns of drinking and in the development of problems over a defined interval or across the course of a lifetime. At the aggregate level, this approach can be used to examine trends in consumption, consumption patterns, and problems. In both cases, other variables can also be incorporated. Social and economic changes that might have taken place during the interval studied can be related to the data. So, for instance, changing levels of alcohol consumption can be correlated not only with changes in alcohol sales but also with variables such as changes in disposable income, industrialization or demographic changes within the region studied, and changing gender roles in a given society. More than any other approach, longitudinal studies offer a means of addressing issues that often require the integration of variables from other disciplines.

RESEARCH PRIORITIES AT THE NATIONAL AND INTERNATIONAL LEVEL

Trends in alcohol consumption and alcohol-related problems have shown a worldwide increase in both (Grant 1990). The focus of alcohol research therefore needs to be shifted toward parts of the world in which alcohol consumption and problems are a recent development. The preponderance of the evidence collected on alcohol consumption and alcohol-related problems has been derived from studies conducted in the developed world, particularly in Europe and North America. While the conclusions of these studies may generally hold true for the developed countries, they are not necessarily relevant or applicable within the context of developing countries, where the problems associated with alcohol may be quite different.

Different concepts exist across cultures with respect to drinking and the definitions of alcoholism and alcohol abuse. While the physical components of alcohol-related problems are easily assessed across cultures, the psychological components—such as shame, anxiety, or guilt associated with drinking and especially with alcohol abuse—may be very different (Batel 1996). Studies have shown that there is wide variation in the culture surrounding alcohol and that experiences with consumption and with alcohol-related problems and disabilities are also widely divergent (Babor et al. 1986; Heath 1995). In addition, the developing world is experiencing a rapid change in cultural orientation. With the influx of Western values from Europe and North America, the traditional role of alcohol is giving way to new and often harmful drinking patterns (Eide and Acuda 1996). It is therefore essential to encourage research by local researchers in developing countries. Particular attention should be paid to the prevailing conditions and culture, and local researchers intimately familiar with both seem best equipped to do so. The ramifications of such an emphasis with respect to prevention are also important, as priorities in individual developing countries may be quite different.

International collaborative research is one means by which research can be conducted in countries that have limited resources to carry out such work on their own. Such collaborative projects have been undertaken by a number of international and national agencies worldwide. The World Health Organization and the NIAAA have sponsored a number of cross-cultural projects, such as the cross-cultural applicability research study (Bennett et al. 1993; Room et al. 1996; Temple et al. 1988). Within individual countries, national agencies have also implemented efforts to foster research in collaboration with other countries. Collaborative projects are extremely valuable, as they put alcohol research into its appropriate cultural context. At the same time, they also extend across cultures, identifying commonalities in behaviors as well as similarities in patterns of both drinking and problems. In addition, they can contribute to the development of cross-culturally valid instruments for screening, intervention, and prevention.

For a cross-cultural approach to be valid, it is necessary to demonstrate that similar results can be achieved using different instruments within a given culture. For this purpose, the use of instruments must be carefully controlled. Diagnostic criteria such as those based on the ICD-10 (WHO 1992, 1993) have been a valuable research tool applicable across cultures. However, many approaches currently in use apply paradigms and measurement tools designed in the European or North American context to the developing world. The instruments used in measurement are often written in English and may not be completely applicable within a different culture. Translation and back translation are used frequently as a means to ensure cross-cultural validity, but they may not be adequate.

Several international diagnostic instruments have proven to be valid and applicable across cultures: the CIDI (composite international diagnostic interview; Robins et al. 1989; WHO 1993), the SCAN (schedules for clinical assessment in neuropsychiatry; Wing et al. 1990; WHO 1992), and the AUDIT (alcohol use disorders identification test), developed as a result of a WHO collaborative project on early detection of hazardous and harmful alcohol consumption (Babor et al. 1992; Saunders et al. 1993). The AUDIT is a simple tool that is sensitive to hazardous consumption and to alcohol-related problems (Farrell 1989).

While the existing research tools have proven useful for cross-cultural analysis, there is a need to design new tools that would take a broader interdisciplinary approach to measuring the relationship between drinking patterns and alcohol-related problems. Such instruments must be designed in such a way as to take into account the idiosyncracies of different cultures and the meanings and interpretations of alcohol use among different peoples. Questions should be phrased in a way that is sensitive to and reflects the way of life and traditional values of a given society. This has been demonstrated by Segal (1996) in research conducted on native Alaskan communities in which the answer elicited depended entirely on the wording of the question. Cross-cultural research therefore requires the inclusion of social and anthropological perspectives, epidemiology, and the participation of researchers familiar with the particular culture. Finally, it requires the use of culturally sensitive instruments. Cross-cultural research provides a powerful tool by which to understand commonalities as well as differences in the etiology and incidence of alcohol-related problems.

Methodology that combines ethnography with epidemiology has been designed and used in other fields. One such example is work conducted in several Latin American societies on cultural variation in beliefs about the etiology of illness syndromes and the effectiveness of folk remedies, in which ethnographic approaches have been combined with epidemiology. In these studies, the interview schedules used were designed to take into account both intra-and inter-cultural variations in beliefs (Trotter 1981; Weller et al. 1993). Such culturally sensitive approaches could also be designed or simply modified to examine both patterns of drinking and the manifestations of alcohol-related problems.

EFFECTIVENESS RESEARCH

Considerable attention has been devoted to research on the effectiveness of control measures and programs directed at prevention and education. While basic research is essential for an understanding of alcohol consumption and its relationship to problems, research on effectiveness is a means of determining whether policies created as a result of this understanding are working. This section provides a broad overview of the estimated effectiveness of specific types of intervention and the manner in which research on drinking patterns could contribute to more effective prevention measures.

Almost all countries have legislation dealing with the production and sale of alcohol beverages in order to control product quality and to satisfy the public health needs raised by the abuse or misuse of alcohol. These measures vary, but most rely on the basic principles of supply and demand. The underlying premise is that by curtailing supply it is possible to lower consumption and, consequently, problems. For the most part, control measures are directed at the availability of alcohol beverages by means of production and retail control, regulation of hours of availability, age restrictions, taxation, zoning, or regulation of advertising (Österberg 1992, 1993). However, other measures that are directed at the community level and that advocate education and prevention measures are also commonly used.

On the whole, studies have shown that changes in price and availability have an effect on total per capita alcohol consumption. What has not been considered in great detail is how changes in alcohol policy affect patterns of consumption. It has been shown, for instance, that moderate drinkers show a higher degree of price elasticity than do heavy or infrequent drinkers, such that an increase in the price of beverage alcohol is likely to affect the very consumption patterns that should be encouraged (Manning, Blumberg, and Moulton 1995). Similarly, while the restriction of alcohol sales may lower per capita consumption, it may simultaneously increase the production or consumption of home-produced or smuggled beverages (Hauge and Amundsen 1994), which bring with them an entirely different set of complications, such as unrecorded consumption and low-quality products with potential health risks.

There has been a recent increase in the body of available evidence on the effectiveness of measures to control alcohol. New statistical tools have been designed to permit a more detailed analysis of the effectiveness of measures. Particular developments have occurred in two areas. First, there has been an increase in the scope of available prevention programs and in approaches to evaluation studies (Room 1990b). Second, there has been a shift from a focus on the effectiveness of control policies for alcoholics to the effectiveness of measures for the general population. This shift represents a first step away from a focus on measures of total consumption and toward a focus on the ramifications of control policies for individual patterns of consumption.

As in basic research on patterns and problems of alcohol consumption, longitudinal research is becoming increasingly important in evaluating the effectiveness of policies. To study control measures, it is important to study their impact over time under changing social, political, and economic conditions. New statistical methods have been designed (Room 1990b) that can be applied in longitudinal research. These methods have been applied to experimental designs in policy making, most of which were designed and implemented in Scandinavian countries (Österberg 1981; Room 1986, 1990b). With the exception of natural experiments, single control measures are rarely implemented by themselves, making it difficult to assess the individual effects of changes in policy. New approaches to longitudinal studies on the impact of policy measures on different consumption patterns are therefore necessary, as many variables need to be taken into account simultaneously.

In addition, longitudinal studies on control measures are important because regulations are closely tied to the cultural context of alcohol within countries. While most of the available evidence on the effectiveness of control measures stems from countries with a long tradition of alcohol research (Österberg 1993), the effectiveness of such measures in developing countries in which conditions are in constant flux can only be gauged across time. As is the case with basic research, effectiveness research should therefore be examined within countries and from the appropriate cultural and historical perspective.

A changing focus toward the effectiveness of measures for particular patterns of consumption also means that educational measures can be designed to target patterns that have proven to be particularly harmful. Educational measures are a powerful tool in prevention, as they can produce changes in social norms and in the acceptability of certain behaviors. A number of educational programs, sponsored by governments, public interest groups, and the beverage alcohol industry, already exist worldwide. Many of these programs are targeted at young children and adolescents in order to address harmful behaviors before they develop. Other programs are directed at the service industry to train servers in how to recognize and prevent problems. Finally, a number of public service efforts are aimed at modifying behaviors associated with the consumption of alcohol at the grassroots level. Such educational measures are perhaps among the most effective tools for eliminating harmful drinking behaviors and for promoting those patterns that emphasize moderation and a healthy drinking style.

SUMMARY

The body of evidence already available in the field of alcohol research is rich and varied. More than most other areas of research, the study of alcohol consumption and alcohol-related problems allows for a broad and interdisciplinary approach. Herein also lies the strength of this field as a tool for successful intervention and prevention, based on a thorough understanding of problems by taking into account multiple contributing factors.

It is because of this multidisciplinary approach that the field of alcohol research lends itself especially well to a shift in focus toward patterns of consumption. Rather than using only one dimension, such as levels of consumption, in research and the implementation of policy, it should be possible to include several measurement tools simultaneously. Such a multifaceted approach also would place greater emphasis on the diversity of alcohol-related problems in different cultures. Only by bearing in mind that alcohol-related problems cannot be measured by the same yardstick across cultures will it be possible to continue to expand our knowledge in an increasingly complex and changing world.

REFERENCES

Amundsen, A. 1982. Who became patients in institutions for alcoholics? Paper presented at the International Council on Alcohol and Addictions Epidemiology Section Meeting, Helsinki, Finland.

Babor, T. F., et al. 1986. Concepts of alcoholism among America, French-Canadian, and French alcoholics. In *Alcohol and Culture*, ed. T. F. Babor. New York: New York Academy of Sciences.

Babor, T. F., J. R. de la Fuente, J. Saunders, and M. Grant. 1992. *AUDIT: The Alcohol Use Disorders Identification Test, Guidelines for Use in Primary Health Care*. Geneva: World Health Organization.

Batel, P. 1996. Comments on Room et al.'s WHO cross-cultural applicability research on diagnosis and assessment of substance use disorders: an overview of methods and selected results. *Addiction* 91:221–22.

Bennett, L. A., A. Janca, B. F. Grant, and N. Sartorius. 1993. Boundaries between normal and pathological drinking. *Alcohol Health and Research World* 17:190–95.

Bondy, S. J. 1996. Overview of studies on drinking patterns and consequences. *Addiction* 91:1663–74.

Burke, V., I. B. Puddey, and L. J. Beilin. 1995. Mortality associated with wines, beers, and spirits. Letter. *British Medical Journal* 311:1166.

Butterworth, K. 1993. Overview of the biomedical project on alcohol and health. In *Health Issues Related to Alcohol Consumption*, ed. P. M. Verschure. Washington, D.C.: ILSI.

Cahalan, D., R. Roizen, and R. Room. 1969. *American Drinking Practices: A National Study of Drinking Behavior and Attitudes*. Monograph 6. New Brunswick: Rutgers Center for Alcohol Studies.

Cherpitel, C. 1996. Regional differences in alcohol and fatal injury: a comparison of data from two county coroners. *Journal of Studies on Alcohol* 57:244–48.

Couzigou, P., C. Coutelle, B. Fleury, and A. Iron. 1994. Alcohol and alcohol dehydrogenase genotypes, alcoholism, and alcohol-related disease. *Alcohol and Alcoholism* 2 (supp.): 21–27.

Dawson, D. A. 1993. Patterns of alcohol consumption: beverage effects on gender differences. *Addiction* 88:133–38.

———. 1996. Temporal drinking patterns and variation in social consequences. *Addiction* 91:1623–36.

Del Rio, C., C. Prada, and F. J. Alvarez. 1995. Beverage effects on patterns of alcohol consumption. *Alcoholism: Clinical and Experimental Research* 19:1583–86.

Edwards, G., et al. 1994. *Alcohol Policy and the Public Good*. Oxford: Oxford University Press.

Eide, A. H., and S. W. Acuda. 1996. Cultural orientation and adolescents' alcohol use in Zimbabwe. *Addiction* 91:807–14

Epstein, E. E., et al. 1995. An empirical classification of drinking patterns among alcoholics: binge, episodic, sporadic, and steady. *Addictive Behaviors* 20:23–41.

Farrell, M. 1989. AUDIT: The Alcohol Use Disorders Identification Test. *British Journal of Addiction* 84:1102–3.

Fillmore, K. M. 1990. Critical explanations—biological, psychological and social—of drinking patterns and problems from the alcohol-related longitudinal literature: critiques and strategies for future analyses on behalf of the World Health Organization. *Research Advances in Alcohol and Drug Problems* 10:15–38.

Fillmore, K. M., et al. 1991. The collaborative alcohol-related longitudinal project: a meta-analysis of life course variation in drinking. *British Journal of Addiction* 86:1221–68.

Fillmore, K. M., and B. M. Johnstone. 1996. The conclusion? Analyses incomplete. *Addiction* 91:1449–53.

Fine, E. W., P. Scoles, and M. J. Mulligan. 1975. Under the influence: characteristics and drinking practices of persons arrested the first time for drunk driving, with treatment implications. *Public Health Reports* 90:424–29.

Forman, S. G., and J. A. Linney. 1991. Increasing the validity of self-report data on effectiveness trials. In *Drug Abuse Prevention Intervention Research: Methodolog-*

ical Issues, ed. C. G. Leukefeld and W. J. Bukoski. Monograph 107. Rockville, Md.: U.S. Department of Health and Human Services.

Fuller, R. K., K. K. Lee, and E. Gordis. 1988. Validity of self-report in alcoholism research: results of a Veterans Administration cooperative study. *Alcoholism: Clinical and Experimental Research* 12:201–5.

Grant, M. 1990. Research priorities for drug and alcohol studies: the next 25 years. *International Journal of the Addictions* 25:201–19.

Greenfield, T. K. 1986. Quantity per occasion and consequences of drinking: a reconsideration and recommendation. *International Journal of the Addictions* 21:1059–79.

Grunewald, P. J., P. R. Mitchell, and A. J. Treno. 1996. Drinking and driving: drinking patterns and drinking problems. *Addiction* 91:1637–50.

Harford, T. C., B. F. Grant, and D. S. Hasin. 1991. The effects of average daily consumption and frequency of intoxication on the occurrence of dependence symptoms and alcohol-related problems. In *Alcohol in America: Drinking Practices and Problems,* ed. W. B. Clark and M. E. Hilton. Albany: State University of New York Press.

Hauge, R., and A. Amundsen. 1994. Innvirker okt tilgjengelighet på bruk av unregistrerte alkoholdrikker? (Does increased availability of licit alcohol influence the use of unrecorded alcoholic beverage?) *Nordisk Alkoholtidskrift* 11:191–99.

Heath, D. B., ed. 1995. *International Handbook on Alcohol and Culture.* Westport, Conn.: Greenwood.

Herd, D., and J. Grube. 1996. Black identity and drinking in the US: a national study. *Addiction* 91:845–57.

Jellinek, E. M. 1960. *The Disease Concept of Alcoholism.* New Haven, Conn.: Hillhouse.

Klatsky, A. L., M. A. Armstrong, and H. Kipp. 1990. Correlates of alcoholic beverage preference: traits of persons who choose wine, liquor, or beer. *British Journal of Addiction* 85:1279–89.

Lemmens, P. H. 1994. The alcohol content of self-report and 'standard' drinks. *Addiction* 89:593–601.

Manning, W. G., L. Blumberg, and L. H. Moulton. 1995. The demand for alcohol: the differential response to price. *Journal of Health Economics* 14:123–48.

Marin, G., and S. F. Posner. 1995. The role of gender and acculturation in determining the consumption of alcoholic beverages among Mexican Americans and Central Americans in the United States. *International Journal of the Addictions* 30:779–94.

Midanik, L. T. 1994. Comparing usual quantity/frequency and graduated quantity/frequency scales to assess yearly consumption: results from the 1990 US National Alcohol Survey. *Addiction* 89:407–12.

Midanik, L. T., and T. C. Harford. 1994. Alcohol consumption measurement: introduction to workshop. *Addiction* 89:393–94.

Midanik, L. T., T. W. Tam, T. K. Greenfield, and R. Caetano. 1996. Risk functions for alcohol-related problems in a 1988 U.S. national sample. *Addiction* 91:1427–37.

Miller, B. A., and M. Windle. 1990. Alcoholism, problem drinking, and driving while impaired. In *Drinking and Driving: Advances in Research and Prevention,* ed. R. J. Wilson and R. E. Mann. New York: Guilford.

Miller, W. R., N. Heather, and W. Hall. 1991. Calculating standard drink units: international comparisons. *British Journal of Addiction* 86:43–47.

National Health and Medical Research Council. 1992. *Is There a Safe Level of Daily Consumption of Alcohol for Men and Women?* Canberra: Australian Government Publishing Service.

Oshodin, O. G. 1995. Nigeria. In *International Handbook on Alcohol and Culture*, ed. D. B. Heath. Westport, Conn.: Greenwood.

Österberg, E. 1981. Alcohol policy measures and the consumption of alcoholic beverages in Finland, 1950–1975. *Drug and Alcohol Dependence* 7:85–97.

———. 1992. Effects of alcohol control measures on alcohol consumption. *International Journal of the Addictions* 27:209–25.

———. 1993. Global status of alcohol control research. *Alcohol Health and Research World* 17:205–11.

Page, J. B., L. Rio, J. Sweeny, and C. McKay. 1985. Alcohol and adaptation to exile in Miami's Cuban population. In *The American Experience with Alcohol: Contrasting Cultural Perspectives,* ed. L. Bennett and G. Ames. New York: Plenum.

Pearl, R. 1926. *Alcohol and Longevity.* New York: Knopf.

Pernanen, K. 1993. Causal attributions in the explanation of alcohol-related accidents. *Addiction* 88:897–906.

Poldrugo, F., P. Salvo, S. Spouza, and D. Bertoluce. 1989. Alcohol-related morbidity in Northern Italy: a comparison with trends in the United States. *Proceedings of the 35th International Congress on Alcoholism and Drug Dependence (ICAA), Oslo, 1988.*

Popham, R. E., W. Schmidt, and S. Israelstam. 1984. Heavy alcohol consumption and physical health problems. *Research Advances in Alcohol and Drug Problems* 8:149–82.

Rehm, J., et al. 1996. On the emerging paradigm of drinking patterns and their social and health consequences. *Addiction* 91:1615–22.

Rimm, E. B., A. Klatsky, D. Grobbee, and M. J. Stampfer. 1996. Review of moderate alcohol consumption and reduced risk of coronary heart disease: is the effect due to wine, beer, or spirits? *British Medical Journal* 312:731–36.

Robb, N. D., and B. G. Smith. 1990. Prevalence of pathological tooth wear in patients with chronic alcoholism. *British Dental Journal* 169:367–69.

Robins, L. N. 1984. Changes in conduct disorder over time. In *Risk in Intellectual and Psychological Development,* ed. D. C. Farran and J. D. McKinney. New York: Academic.

Robins, L. N., et al. 1989. The composite international diagnostic interviean epidemiologic instrument suitable for use in conjunction with different diagnostic systems and in different cultures. *Archives of General Psychiatry* 45:1069–77.

Room, R. 1986. Kettil Bruun, 1924–1985: in appreciation. *Drinking and Drug Practices Surveyor* 21:42–49.

———. 1990a. Measuring alcohol consumption in the United States. *Research Advances in Alcohol and Drug Problems* 1:355–74.

———. 1990b. Recent research on the effects of alcohol policy changes. *Journal of Primary Prevention* 11:83–94.

———. 1996. Drinking patterns and drinking problems: from specifying the relationship to advising the public. *Addiction* 91:1441–43.

Room, R., et al. 1996. WHO cross-cultural applicability research on diagnosis and assessment of substance use disorders: an overview of methods and selected results. *Addiction* 91:199–220.

Rossow, I. 1996. Alcohol-related violence: the impact of drinking pattern and drinking context. *Addiction* 91:1651–62.

Ruhm, C. J. 1995. Economic conditions and alcohol problems. *Journal of Health Economics* 14:583–603.

Saunders, J., et al. 1993. Development of the Alcohol Use Disorders Identification Test (AUDIT): WHO collaborative project on early detection of persons with harmful alcohol consumption. II. *Addiction* 88:791–804.

Schulenberg, J., et al. 1996. Getting drunk and growing up: trajectories of frequent binge drinking during the transition to young adulthood. *Journal of Studies on Alcohol* 57:289–304.

Segal, B. 1996. Cultural issues in cross-cultural research. Paper presented at the Joint Scientific Meeting of the Research Society on Alcoholism and the International Society for Biomedical Research on Alcoholism. Washington, D.C., June 1996.

Simboli, B. J. 1985. Acculturated Italian-American drinking behavior. In *The American Experience with Alcohol: Contrasting Cultural Perspectives,* ed. L. Bennett and G. Ames. New York: Plenum.

Single, E., and S. Wortley. 1993. Drinking in various settings: findings from a national survey in Canada. *Journal of Studies on Alcohol* 54:590–99.

———. 1994. A comparison of alternative measures of alcohol consumption in the Canadian National Survey of alcohol and drug use. *Addiction* 89:395–99.

Smart, R. G. 1996. Behavioral and social consequences related to the consumption of different beverage types. *Journal of Studies on Alcohol* 57:77–84.

Smart, R. G., E. M. Adlaf, and G. W. Walsh. 1996. Procurement of alcohol and underage drinking among adolescents in Ontario. *Journal of Studies on Alcohol* 57:419–424.

Stockwell, T., and J. Stirling. 1989. Estimating the alcohol contents of drinks: common sense errors in applying the unit system. *British Medical Journal* 298:571–72.

Straus, M. A., and G. K. Kantor. 1994. Corporal punishment of adolescents by parents: a risk factor in the epidemiology of depression, suicide, alcohol abuse, child abuse, and wife beating. *Adolescence* 29:543–61.

Straus, R., and S. D. Bacon. 1953. *Drinking in College.* New Haven: Yale University Press.

Takano, T., K. Nakamura, and M. Watanabe. 1996. Increased female drinking in accordance with post-industrial urbanization in Japan. *Alcohol and Alcoholism* 31:41–49.

Temple, M. T., et al. 1988. Collaborative longitudinal research on alcohol problems. *British Journal of Addiction* 83:441–44.

Trotter, R. T. 1981. Folk remedies as indicators of common illnesses: examples from the United States–Mexico border. *Journal of Ethnopharmacology* 4:207–21.

Tu, G.-C., and Y. Israel. 1995. Alcohol consumption by Orientals in North America is predicted largely by a single gene. *Behavioral Genetics* 25:59–65.

Turner, C. 1990. How much alcohol is in a "standard drink"? an analysis of 125 studies. *British Journal of Addiction* 85:1171–75.

U.K. Department of Health and Social Security. 1995. *Sensible Drinking: The Report of an Interdepartmental Working Group.* London: HMSO.

Umezono, T., et al. 1995. Alteration of drinking pattern after the entrance to university. *Japanese Journal of Alcohol and Drug Dependence* 30:435–46.

Wechsler, H., et al. 1994. Health and behavioral consequences of binge drinking in college. *Journal of the American Medical Association* 272:1672–77.

Wechsler, H., G. W. Dowdall, A. Davenport, and S. Castillo. 1995a. Correlates of college student binge drinking. *American Journal of Public Health* 85:921–26.

Wechsler, H., G. W. Dowdall, A. Davenport, and E. B. Rimm. 1995b. A gender-specific measure of binge drinking among college students. *American Journal of Public Health* 85:982–85.

Wechsler, H., et al. 1995c. The adverse impact of heavy episodic drinkers on other college students. *Journal of Studies on Alcohol* 56:628–34.

Weller, S. C., L. M. Pachter, R. T. Trotter, and R. D. Baer. 1993. Empacho in four Latino groups: a study of intra-and inter-cultural variation in beliefs. *Medical Anthropology* 15:109–36.

WHO. 1992. *The ICD-10 Classification of Mental and Behavioural Disorders: Clinical Descriptions and Diagnostic Guidelines*. Geneva: World Health Organization.

———. 1993a. *Composite International Diagnostic Interview, Version 1.1*. Washington, D.C.: American Psychiatric Press.

———. 1993b. *The ICD-10 Classification of Mental and Behavioural Disorders: Diagnostic Criteria for Research*. Geneva: World Health Organization.

Wickramasinghe, S. N., et al. 1995. Ethnic differences in the biological consequence of alcohol abuse: a comparison between South Asian and European males. *Alcohol and Alcoholism* 30:675–80.

Wing, J. K., et al. 1990. SCAN: Schedules for Clinical Assessment in Neuropsychiatry. *Archives of General Psychiatry* 47:589–93.

Wish, E. D., L. N. Robins, M. Hesselbrock, and J. E. Helzer. 1979. The course of alcohol problems in Vietnam veterans. In *Currents in Alcoholism*, ed. M. Galant. Vol. 6. New York: Grune and Stratton.

Wolff, P. H. 1972. Ethnic differences in alcohol sensitivity. *Science* 175:449–50.

Yu, J. 1995. Style, consumption, and problem drinking: a measurement model. *Alcoholism: Clinical and Experimental Research* 19:1192–97.

Yu, J., D. T. Essex, and W. R. Williford. 1992. DWI/DWAI offenders and recidivism by gender in the eighties: a changing trend? *International Journal of the Addictions* 27:637–47.

Yu, J., and W. R. Williford. 1992. Perception, style, and consumption: specifying and testing a structural model on problem drinking. *Journal of Drug Issues* 22:75–90.

Chapter 13

The Implications of Drinking Patterns for Primary Prevention, Education, and Screening

Ann M. Roche and Keith R. Evans

There is one thing more powerful than all the armies of the world, and that is an idea whose time has come.

Victor Hugo

TIME TO "SHIFT OUR GAZE"

The time has now come for us, in the words of the philosopher and social historian Michel Foucault (1975), to "shift our gaze" and to develop a prevention perspective that is more "penetrating." It is argued here that the largely overlooked area of patterns of alcohol consumption should form a major platform for any prevention model and its associated strategies. Without redirecting our gaze in this way we will be condemned to a perpetually limited and limiting view of prevention.

In this chapter, we examine approaches to prevention, education, and screening that are predicated on reducing alcohol-related risks to consumers and to society at large. The approaches supported cover the full spectrum of use from

Ann M. Roche is director of the Queensland Alcohol and Drug Research and Education Centre at the University of Queensland, Brisbane, Australia. Keith R. Evans is state manager of the Alcohol, Tobacco, and Other Drugs Service of Queensland Health, Brisbane, Australia.

abstainers and very occasional drinkers to excessive and dependent drinkers. A framework is proposed that emphasizes patterns of consumption, high-risk prevention strategies, and harm-minimizing strategies. These strategies are contrasted with population-based strategies. Although it is stressed that many population-based approaches are valuable and effective and continue to have a role in a broader alcohol harm-prevention model, special emphasis is also placed on the need to acknowledge different cultural settings and perspectives.

SETTING THE SCENE

Conceptual Shifts

As highlighted in previous chapters, several major conceptual and perceptual shifts have occurred in the alcohol field in recent years. These shifts influence not only our view of problem identification and treatment but also our approach to prevention and education. Outlined below are seven principal conceptual shifts that have recently influenced approaches to the prevention of alcohol-related problems. These and other issues are expanded on in later parts of the chapter.

Rejection of the Single-Distribution Theory For several decades prevention approaches were strongly influenced by the early work of Ledermann (1956), in which he hypothesized that if the mean level of consumption was known for any community then the number of problem drinkers could also be estimated. Further, to reduce the number of problem drinkers it was considered necessary to reduce the amount of alcohol that everyone drank (regardless of current level of consumption). As a consequence, population-based strategies were enthusiastically embraced by various countries around the world.

One of the major conceptual shifts that has occurred in the alcohol field over the past decade has been the recognition (albeit reluctantly in some quarters) of the limitations and inaccuracies inherent within a single-distribution theory of alcohol consumption and all that such a position implies. While it played a valuable part in terms of heightening the profile of prevention issues and fueling debate about them, it nonetheless has done prevention a disservice through the long and protracted effort required to shift the focus of attention away from mean per capita consumption to address more meaningful questions on patterns of consumption, such as occasion of drinking, frequency of episodes of intoxication, drinking setting, and other associated factors.

Resolution of Kreitman's Preventive Paradox Population strategies were further fueled by Kreitman's (1986) depiction of a preventive paradox. A paradox was thought to exist in that it was the individuals who consumed at low-risk levels who incurred the most harm, purely because they were much more numerous than heavy drinkers. Again, this observation was used to bolster population strategies designed to encourage all drinkers to drink less, regardless of current drinking level, with the reasoning that if low-risk consumers (who incurred most of the harm) drank even less, then alcohol-related harms would also be reduced.

Stockwell and colleagues (1996) recently provided a helpful reanalysis of the original work of Kreitman and demonstrated that when attention is focused on patterns of drinking, especially episodes of intoxication, and not just mean consumption levels, the so-called preventive paradox disappears. Thus, it is not overall levels of consumption that provide the best predictor of alcohol-related problems. Rather, it is during specific episodes of at-risk drinking, usually by members of the community who mostly drink at low-to-moderate levels and in low-risk ways, that most alcohol-related problems are incurred. The preventive corollary is that measures of mean consumption, and the subsequently derived control approaches, are less useful than was previously thought to be the case. The conventional wisdom of attempting to get all members of the community to reduce their alcohol consumption, regardless of their current level of consumption, is now seriously questioned.

Alcohol as an Exception to Population Health Control Concepts   Calculation of risk according to a community's mean level of consumption finds its principal protagonists in the public health arguments mounted (successfully and appropriately) for health issues such as salt and hypertension (Rose and Day 1990; Rose 1992). However, the public health population distribution arguments do not fit as comfortably when applied to alcohol because of the nature of the substance, its patterns of use, and its ability to produce dependence (albeit in a limited number of individuals). More importantly, the nature of the substance and its intoxicating potential also place alcohol in a different position from other substances considered under the public health model. In normal circumstances it would indeed be a rare situation in which a specific episode of salt intake was the cause of greater interest and scrutiny compared to the overall mean level of salt consumption. The exact opposite applies with respect to alcohol: it is precisely the specific occasions of use that are of interest from a primary prevention perspective.

The U-Shaped Curve: Alcohol and Health Benefits   The population strategy of aiming for a shift in the alcohol consumption distribution curve to the left was, in part, developed as an alternative to the approach of targeting only those high consumers in the tail of the mean distribution curve. Holman (1995) has offered an additional argument for reconsideration of the population strategy of reducing everyone's consumption level by raising concern that a total reduction in mean consumption level—that is, a shift to the left of the distribution curve—may result in a greater proportion of the community missing out on any of the potential cardiovascular protective effects of low-level alcohol consumption. Mathematical modeling has shown that a greater reduction in excess risk can be achieved through high-risk prevention approaches. Holman recommends a shift in focus from aggregate performance to distributive performance, which would entail the application of high-risk prevention strategies. He maintains that caution must be exercised in our alcohol education and control efforts in order not to reduce intake in those people who are already drinking, through their own choice, at what may in fact be an ideal level. This position is juxtaposed to one that endorses the active promotion of generally low alcohol intake.

A Shift in Focus from At-Risk Drinkers to At-Risk Drinking   The empirical data presented previously in this volume highlight the extent to which much at-risk consumption is of an irregular nature (Stockwell et al. 1996). The notion that at-risk drinkers form a fixed and defined group may be as misleading and unhelpful as the single-distribution model and needs to be closely reexamined. It may be more useful to focus on the drinker who on irregular occasions drinks in a risky manner, particularly as these individuals have been shown to be at elevated risk of a negative consequence of their drinking as a direct effect of its irregular and less frequent nature (Single 1995).

Low-Risk Drinking Guidelines   One of the greater challenges in the alcohol field is to achieve consensus. This axiom has held true for the estimation of safe and sensible drinking guidelines, as countries around the world have made differing recommendations. In establishing guidelines, factors beyond the purely scientific have played a role. Officially sanctioned guidelines need to accord with current practices to have a degree of face validity. Without that validity, seeking acceptance and compliance will be futile.

Until very recently, most drinking guidelines were expressed in terms of weekly consumption and rarely in terms of daily consumption or particular drinking situations (U.K. Department of Health and Social Security 1995). It is now recommended that only daily drinking limits be conveyed to the public, as other less specific guidelines are not meaningful and cannot be scientifically supported (Rehm, Bondy, and Room 1996). From a prevention perspective it is imperative for drinking guidelines to be expressed on the basis of consumption per day (at least), with specific reference and warnings about high-risk situations and circumstances. Until recently, this was not possible in most countries, as such advice (where it existed) tended to be given in mean weekly consumption levels, corresponding to the traditional orientation toward aggregate levels of consumption as opposed to patterns and specific episodes of consumption.

Alcohol and Harm Minimization   Considerable potential exists to apply harm-minimization principles and practices, largely developed for application in the illicit drug area, to reduce harms associated with risky alcohol consumption. Strategies aimed at risk reduction and harm containment have been well received and adopted in a number of settings (witness, for example, the endorsement of harm minimization as the central tenet of Australia's National Drug Strategy by federal and territorial governments). A shift in emphasis away from mean consumption to patterns of consumption provides an opportunity for the application of strategies that have the capacity to reduce the level of alcohol-related harm without necessarily altering the overall alcohol consumption level of an individual, a community, or a society (Heather 1993). Although use reduction, or even total abstinence, may be the most appropriate goal to aim for in many circumstances, it is evident that this is not always desirable, feasible, or necessary.

The apparent contradictions inherent within these two prominent policy positions are infrequently highlighted and warrant closer examination (Roche, Evans, and Stanton in press). One of the principal platforms of harm reduction is the importance of shifting emphasis away from consumption to the consequences of use. When the consequences are negative, then these negative outcomes, and not the act of consuming the substance, constitute the main area of concern. Similarly, when alcohol consumption is viewed from a harm-reduction perspective the focus shifts away from the question of use (regardless of level) to more telling concerns relating to consequences of use.

In our view, minimizing the risks associated with the consumption of alcohol requires the application of a wide array of strategies, including

- appropriate control over access to the product,
- increased knowledge among consumers and health professionals of the risks associated with inappropriate use of the product, and
- minimization of the risk of harms associated with consumption on particular occasions and under particular circumstances.

A Rejection of Public Health Precepts?

Any new approach to prevention does not necessarily entail a rejection of all that has gone before. Many of the traditional public health approaches to the prevention of alcohol-related problems are of great value, including some population-based control strategies. This cannot be stressed too strongly. Similarly, the value of some of the underlying concepts of public health approaches should also be reaffirmed. For instance, notions surrounding the social nature of behavior and the types of phenomena that shape group norms and patterns of behavior, including drinking behavior (Skog 1985), are central to prevention efforts. There is no inherent contradiction in the application of this view of determinants that shape health-related behaviors (and that have driven population control measures) and the application of more targeted measures. In the present context, however, their application is directed toward specific patterns of use rather than global populations and global measures.

CONTEXTUAL ISSUES

The Context of Use

It is necessary, indeed essential, to pay special attention to the context of alcohol use, to situate such use in the beliefs and social practices of particular communities, and to understand the meaning that alcohol has for its users (Good-man, Lovejoy, and Sherratt 1995). Rose (1992), however, as a proponent of population-based control measures, perhaps overinterprets the power of social forces when he states that "social norms rigidly constrain how we live, and individuals who transgress the limits can expect trouble. . . . Social norms set rigid limits on diversity" (p. 56). One is tempted to speculate that this unduly homogenized view of society stems from efforts to adjust a traditionally myopic medical periscope to incorporate more than one individual at a time, thus seeing multiple visions of the same individual simultaneously and believing this to be an accurate reflection of society and social structure.

Clearly, there is great diversity in relation to the use of alcohol within any community or group, which needs to be acknowledged if prevention efforts are to be successful. Rose (1992) warned of impending doom for those wishing to impose minority views on the majority. Curiously, much of what we attempt to achieve in public health involves exactly that, that is, the imposition of minority views on the majority. However, failure at the same time to recognize the vast differences and variations that exist within communities ensures the failure of any intervention.

There is widespread acceptance of the view that it is not necessarily the inherent nature of alcohol, but rather the manner in which it is used, that is of central concern. However, this view has not been sufficiently reflected in either epidemiological studies or prevention efforts. Rehm (1996) is among those who have argued that the field needs to shift its focus to harmful drinking and away from overall volume of consumption: "We need to make fewer value judgments about alcohol as a substance and talk more about the consequences of mixing alcohol use with behaviors—such as workplace tasks, driving a car, or leisure activities—that have an element of danger" (p. 5).

Missing the Meso Level

Our epidemiological and health systems tradition have targeted two levels: the macrolevel, as reflected in population-based surveys of mean consumption levels, and the microlevel, with attention focused on the problems of the chronic long-term user who has come to the attention of treatment services. Prevention and intervention strategies have therefore reflected our knowledge base and overall orientation as shaped by a focus on the macro and micro levels.

What has long been missing, and what has greater meaning and potential from a prevention perspective, is the meso level (see table 13.1). The definition of *meso* found in the Concise Oxford Dictionary is "middle or intermediate." For the purposes of this chapter the term refers to a focus on drinking that is not associated with chronic problems (but that may well be associated with acute or episodic problems). We are particularly interested in exploring the specifics of drinking patterns that contribute to the means recorded in wide-scale databases.

Table 13.1 Characteristics of macro, micro, and meso level perspectives on alcohol use

Perspective	View of alcohol	Epidemiological response	Screening	Prevention
Macro	Inherently toxic substance responsible for major health and social problems.	Collection of data on populations at large, measurement of global mean consumption levels.	Detection of problematic and potentially dependent drinkers.	Limiting access, controlling availability, targeting the whole population.
Meso	Neither inherently benign nor toxic but with the potential to be either or both to the same individual and community depending on the level of use and setting.	Focus on particular episodes of drinking in which individuals or community are harmed or placed at risk; determination of the correlates of such situations.	Screening for episodes and patterns of consumption among all members of the community where there is potential for harm.	Minimizing at-risk and hazardous episodes of consumption; creating environments that facilitate low-risk drinking.
Micro	Inherently benign substance but with capacity to be toxic for those with particular susceptibility (e.g., of genetic origin).	Mapping prevalence of alcoholism in communities.	Detection of "alcoholics" or problems of dependence and associated pathology.	Early intervention for children of alcoholics and those genetically predisposed to dependence.

The failure to observe, record, and interpret these patterns limits our potential to identify and prevent problems specific to particular groups and settings within any community. By the continual use of a wide-frame lens, information is lost that can be of benefit to prevention efforts. It is rather akin to the old saying referring to measures of central tendency: Half the time I am too hot, and half the time I am too cold, but on average I am just right. Clearly, mean consumption approaches, and the control measures derived from them, are not "just right."

From the General to the Specific

While much has been achieved in recent years in broadening the focus of the micro-level orientation through landmark publications such as the U.S. Institute of Medicine's *Broadening the Base of Treatment for Alcohol Problems* (1990), much still needs to be done to bring greater specificity to the macro and meso levels. At present, different patterns of consumption tend to be treated in much the same way. The following scenarios illustrate this point (D. Crosbie, e-mail commentary, 1996):

Scenario A: Between 4:00 P.M. and 6:00 P.M. a man has one predinner drink and then consumes four average glasses of wine over a long dinner. This man will have been drinking relatively slowly and most would say in a responsible fashion. He is unlikely to have experienced any symptoms of intoxication. His blood alcohol content (BAC) will be below 0.03. This one night might be the only night he has had a drink in the last week. Yet this man will have consumed around seven standard drinks in a single day and will therefore be considered to be harming his health. Many guidelines would suggest that he has engaged in binge drinking. *Scenario B:* The same man consumes the same amount of alcohol in two hours without food. His BAC will be significantly higher, and he will probably experience a level of intoxication. Until very recently, most available drinking guidelines treated both the scenarios in the same way.

Growing numbers of recent studies from the United States, Australia, and Canada have found the number of heavy drinking occasions has better predictive power for drinking problems than level of consumption (Stockwell et al. 1996; Single 1994; Room, Bondy, and Ferris 1995). Single (1995) has further highlighted a significant interaction effect whereby the likelihood of experiencing problems is greater for a moderate-level drinker who occasionally drinks immoderately than for a high-level drinker who rarely drinks immoderately.

Appropriate prevention messages here are important. Individuals who would not usually be advised to take harm-minimizing precautions when consuming alcohol should be targeted through prevention efforts to encourage strategies more commonly used by heavier drinkers for those exceptional occasions when they may drink more heavily than usual. For example, emphasis should be placed on maximizing strategies to ensure safe means of transport (e.g., designated drivers) and on training bar staff and hosts to be especially aware of such individuals and their elevated risk status. Prevention efforts from a harm-reduction perspective emphasize environmental controls such as server intervention and a range of other strategies designed to reduce intoxication and consequent harms (Single 1995).

Should Alcohol Be Treated as a Drug?

A curious anomaly exists within the alcohol field in that we frequently hear the cry that alcohol is a drug and should be treated as such. However, most guidelines from esteemed bodies around the world pertaining to low-risk or sensible consumption of alcohol were expressed in terms of weekly consumption and rarely in terms of daily consumption or in relation to a particular drinking situation (U.K. Department of Health and Social Security 1995). Such advice reflects the way countries have, for decades, chosen to collect and shape their epidemiological data. However, it does not reflect how people think of alcohol use in their day-to-day lives. They do not, for example, say to themselves: "Yes, I think I will just stock up on my twenty-one standard units for the week." There are no other medically ratified guidelines pertaining to a substance, commonly agreed to be a drug, that are given in terms of units per week. For example, we are not told: "Yes, Mr. Jones here is your script for penicillin. You will note that I advise that you take no more than forty-two tablets per week," with no other advice or information provided. The shift in focus supported in this chapter is reminiscent of the position posited by Weil and Rosen (1995) with respect to the use of psychoactive drugs generally, in which they maintained that there are no good or bad drugs; rather, there are good or bad relationships with drugs.

Roizen (1993) has argued that alcohol holds a unique position within most cultures in that, in spite of clear evidence of the powerful negative potential of the substance, it is bequeathed a special place of benign innocence, thereby avoiding the need to learn of ways to develop a "good" relationship with it. Under the present model of prevention, the need to learn (either as individuals or collectively as communities) how to use this substance with a minimum of risk takes precedence.

Key Prevention Issues

The prevention and education strategies supported are based on the notion that better outcomes will be achieved for society as a whole if members within the society are encouraged to develop a good and low-risk relationship with alcohol. Special attention is focused on the following key issues with respect to prevention and education about alcohol:

- Drunkenness, intoxication
- Episodes of binge drinking
- Drunk driving (relevant in most countries)

- Drinking by young people
- Special risk situations
- Special risk conditions (both physical and mental)

This approach emphasizes the need for individuals, groups, licensees, parents, police, policy makers, prevention agents, health and human service workers, and the community at large to be acutely aware of:

- High-risk situations
- Contraindications for use
- Sensible means by which to ameliorate any of the potential negative effects of using alcohol
- The dangers inherent in intoxication
- The need to apply safe drinking limits (by occasion and by week)
- The need to stay in control
- The need to avoid consumption in specific settings

This perspective is juxtaposed with a position whereby overall reduced consumption is urged, with no consideration for the way in which alcohol is used or the circumstances surrounding its use. Simplistic public health messages are less useful than those that reflect existing values and forms of behavior and that build on them to allow individuals and communities to foster the development of a good relationship with the drug they consume.

ALCOHOL USE AND RISK

The Concept of Risk

Edwards et al. (1994) have described the "drinker's dilemma," whereby the ability to assess risk associated with any particular drinking episode decreases as alcohol consumption level increases. Assessments of the effects of drinking are described as probabilistic at best, even for the experienced drinker who can predict with some degree of precision what alterations in mood and degree of hangover, for example, might be expected. Rigid individual utilitarian or rational choice models, in which the individual is faced with the impossible burden of balancing the probabilities of risk against pleasure with every sip, were not seen by Edwards and colleagues as an adequate account of actual drinking behavior. Ultimately, however, a determination of risk needs to be made. Rather than opt for an approach that requires lower levels of consumption for all drinkers, one could use the alternative position, which is to maximize the probability of low-risk consumption for all drinkers. This may necessitate changes in drinking environments (of both a physical and cultural nature), better safeguards and mechanisms in place to minimize the possibility of drinkers or their confederates incurring harm, and greater awareness of the need for precautions.

Negotiating Risks

For the vast majority of members in any given community where alcohol is consumed, consumption is considered a recreational activity and is closely associated with leisure activities, if not a leisure activity in and of itself. However, identifying the consumption of alcohol as a largely recreational endeavor does not imply that it is risk free (Hawks 1990).

In much the same way, many other recreational activities have clear risks associated with them (e.g., football, parachuting, skiing, rafting), and sustaining injury as a result of participating in (and sometimes even being a spectator at) such sporting activities is a calculated risk with an estimable probability of incurring a harm. It is recognized that the acceptable level of risk associated with sporting activities differs greatly from that associated with risk in relation to alcohol consumption; sports are generally considered to confer benefits to the participant.

The use of the term *recreational* does not therefore confer or imply a risk-neutral sanction. Where such risks are involved in recreational activities, players, spectators, event sponsors, supporters, and health and other support services organize themselves accordingly. To commence a football game without available ambulance service or first aid facilities would be considered irresponsible in the extreme. Similarly, considerable effort is directed at encouraging athletes to complete appropriate warming up and cooling down exercises to minimize the risk of injury. An alternative could easily be to advise people to engage in less sporting activity to minimize the risk of injury. Indeed, if everyone exercised less, the overall level of sporting injury would be reduced concomitantly.

Similarly, it is useful to think of alcohol consumption as entailing a degree of calculated risk. Responsible use of alcohol by individuals and communities, therefore, calls for the adoption of an array of precautionary measures. With the application of harm-reduction approaches to alcohol use, the introduction of such precautionary measures has become easier. Nonetheless, there is substantially more that could be achieved. Individuals, groups, and communities at large need to be better armed with information about the acute risks associated with alcohol use, not necessarily with the intention of curbing drinking (although in many situations this may be important) but with a view to ensuring that appropriate risk-reduction and risk-management strategies are in place to minimize the likelihood of untoward consequences.

Risky Patterns of Use

In general terms, the overall thrust of this book is predicated on the notion that the risk associated with alcohol use is roughly linear, with a clear dose-response relationship. To wit: low alcohol consumption is associated with negligible short-term health risk and probable long-term health benefits; moderate consumption is associated with possible health benefits and low-level risk; and high alcohol consumption is associated with many health and social problems. While this scenario generally holds true, it remains important to highlight the exceptions to the rule, and these exceptions need to be accommodated within any educational material and prevention approaches while still retaining the essence and clarity of the relationship between alcohol consumption and risk.

For instance, the drinker's age and level of experience with alcohol is a major consideration; novice drinkers may be at great risk of experiencing problems at low levels of consumption. Similarly, moderate drinkers may be at risk of experiencing problems if they drink to intoxication because of low alcohol tolerance level and lack of familiarity with the experience of intoxication. Such people may have fewer safeguarding strategies than those who drink to the point of intoxication more frequently (Single 1995).

The Continua of Risk

Traditional models (see Eliany and Rush 1992 for an example) have correlated the level of risk, based on overall weekly consumption levels, with a treatment continuum: ascending levels of consumption equate with ascending levels of risk and are depicted as corresponding with primary-, secondary-, and tertiary-level interventions. Under this model, high risk parallels a range of measures from treatment and rehabilitation to health recovery and tertiary prevention. That is, levels of risk are depicted as proxy measures for dependence.

An alternative and complementary model, with important implications for prevention efforts, is to construe risk levels as also associated with consequences of both regular use and intoxication in much the same way as Thorley (1985) depicted potential problems associated with alcohol use as falling within three domains: intoxication, dependence, and regular use (see figure 13.1). These three domains, while distinct in pattern and form, also have substantial areas of overlap. Continua of risk also need to incorporate and reflect the risks associated with episodic incidents, for example, intoxication, binge drinking, and situational risk, as depicted schematically in the variable function model of risk (see figure 13.2). Risk level, according to this model, is determined as a function of a range of variables specific to an individual and the context, both social and cultural, in which the drinking occurs.

An important message here for prevention and education workers is that the use of this model makes it more difficult to be definitive or prescriptive about risk. Risk, in terms of this model, has greater variability and fluidity than previously conceptualized and is calculated as a function of a range of issues including

- the amount of alcohol consumed
- the circumstances under which it is consumed
- the individual's susceptibility to the effects of alcohol, and
- temporal issues such as frequency of consumption or length of a drinking occasion.

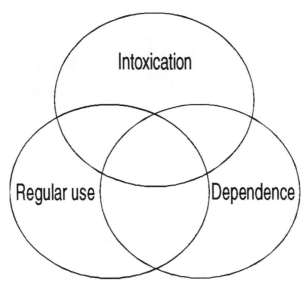

Figure 13.1   The three domains of alcohol use. *Source:* Thorley 1985.

The construct of risk in this model is not necessarily related to dependence; rather, the focus is primarily on acute alcohol problems. Given that this is the area in which the bulk of alcohol-related problems occur (and not within the domain of dependence), it would appear to be more useful to develop our constructs of risk, and subsequent strategies, largely within such a model (see figure 13.3).

The model does, however, require the availability, use, and application of appropriate epidemiological data. An understanding and application of etiological fractions, for example, becomes an increasingly valuable tool for all involved in prevention efforts (English et al. 1995). As noted in previous chapters, such types of appropriate data are not extensively available and have not been consistently obtained. Nonetheless, epidemiological data are increasingly important in the development and implementation of preventive actions of all kinds. Prevention approaches need to be based on the full spectrum of epidemiological and metabolic research, including relevant findings on mortality, morbidity, social consequences, and quality of life (Rehm and Sempos 1995). It is therefore increasingly urgent that appropriate epidemiological tools be used to support the work that needs to be carried out in prevention.

SCREENING

Instruments, Strategies, and Settings

Health programs have placed emphasis on screening as an important primary and secondary prevention tool for several reasons, including the following (U.S. Institute of Medicine 1990):

- LOW RISK...HIGH RISK +

RISK LEVEL

Determinants of variable risk levels

Drug (agent):
Type of alcohol consumed (e.g., concentration by volume of alcohol, whether aerated, e.g., champagne)
Was alcohol taken with food?
Over what time period was alcohol consumed?

Consumer (host):
Age
Sex
Drinking history/experience
Usual pattern of drinking

Environment (setting):
Environmental constraints
Use of non-breakable glass.

Figure 13.2   The variable function model of risk

- Alcohol-related problems are prevalent in many communities around the world
- At-risk alcohol consumption is associated with serious health and social consequences
- Effective forms of intervention are available
- Valid, cost-effective forms of screening are available

Traditionally, the purpose of screening has been defined as detection or case identification (Miller, Westerberg, and Waldron 1995). Cooney, Zweben, and Fleming (1995) have described two conceptual models of screening: the disease detection model and the risk-reduction model. The alcohol screening literature focuses predominantly on disease detection and usually does not address the issue of screening for risk reduction (Cooney, Zweben, and Fleming 1995). Even where efforts have been made to screen for risk reduction, measures have usually been based on an assessment of an individual's regular use of alcohol, using estimates of mean consumption. Little attention has been directed to identification of at-risk episodic drinking through screening.

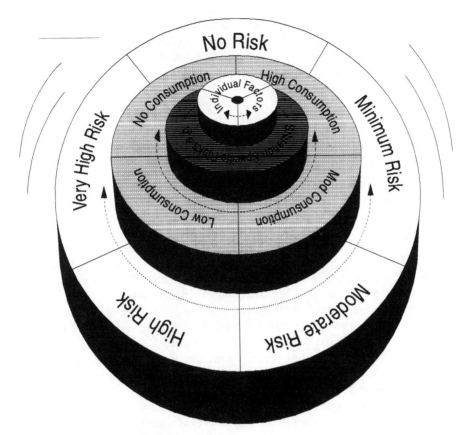

Figure 13.3 Determinants of variable risk

Screening in Context

The value of screening is highly context-specific. In primary-care settings, for example, screening can provide an important evaluation function (Miller, Westerberg, and Waldron 1995). However, its usefulness is highly dependent on the availability of appropriate instruments. Many existing instruments take a "laundry list" approach (e.g., MAST), asking a broad mixture of questions about problems, drinking style, dependence symptoms, perceptions, and help-seeking behavior. Some instruments ask whether these problems have *ever* occurred. Some include lists of problems blended with symptoms of dependence, help-seeking behavior, and self-perception and often provide only a crude general screen (ibid.). The most commonly used screening tools (e.g., the CAGE) do not assess current drinking problems, level of alcohol consumption, or binge drinking and are recommended for use only in conjunction with other sets of questions on quantity, frequency, and binge drinking.

Moreover, most of the screening instruments developed have, until very recently, been validated in clinical populations (Cornel 1994). Similarly, the suitability of existing instruments for groups other than white males is an area of growing concern. There is a paucity of instruments developed within the existing limited conceptual frameworks for use with women, adolescents, the elderly, and the mentally ill or in different cultural settings.

Cooney, Zweben, and Fleming (1995) also noted that an additional disincentive to undertake screening for at-risk drinkers is the potential for detrimental effects on insurability or employment, at least in the North American context. This concern holds true when screening for at-risk drinking is viewed as an extension or component of the disease detection model. If it is seen as something discretely different, such considerations are less likely to arise.

Early Intervention and Screening

A variety of screening instruments designed to detect "alcoholics" or those who are alcohol dependent have been developed since the mid-1970s. More recently, instruments have focused on the detection of drinkers who may be at risk of sustaining harm from their drinking but who are not necessarily dependent on alcohol. Much of the work in relation to early intervention has been of this nature (Babor, Ritson, Hodgson 1986; Roche, Saunders, and Elvy 1992). Indeed, detection of at-risk drinkers has been its principal thrust over the past decade. Engaging health and human services professionals in activities associated with early intervention has been a major area of interest.

The difficulties of involving professionals in these tasks (Roche 1996) stems from their reluctance to label patients or clients as alcoholics. Moreover, there is a general lack of professional knowledge of the levels of risk and health consequences associated with the consumption of alcohol in a nondependent manner. The dominance of the dichotomous paradigm, between diseased and not diseased, allows many health care providers to opt out of involvement with early intervention unless there are clear indicators of alcohol-related morbidity.

One concern about early intervention is the presumption of an inevitable progression to dependence among those identified through a screening procedure. Thus, there was concern that early intervention was intended to arrest the natural progression toward the inexorable decline of the individual into a state of alcohol dependence. While this is clearly not the intention of most early intervention, there is nonetheless a propensity for placing early intervention within the realm of treatment, partly because of the blurred distinction between early and brief intervention and prevention. Indeed, it has been argued that early intervention is not so much secondary prevention as secondary-level treatment.

However, the greatest potential application of early intervention does not lie in the identification of those at risk of developing dependence and the short-circuiting of this process, important as this may be for these (relatively few) individuals. Where early intervention and the underpinning techniques involved in screening, detection, and intervention have shown considerable potency (Babor et al. 1992) is in reducing the consequences of high-risk acute or short-term behaviors such as drinking to intoxication and episodes of binge drinking. This shift in focus is consistent with other major changes that have occurred in the alcohol field over the past decade. It is also consistent with an increased emphasis on early intervention and primary prevention approaches, which are designed to target problematic drinking patterns before more severe problems develop.

The AUDIT

Probably the best-known and most widely applicable screening instrument, in terms of proven suitability for different cultural settings and contexts, is that developed by the World Health Organization during the 1980s called the alcohol use disorders identification test, or AUDIT. This instrument (Babor et al. 1992) was developed from an early intervention perspective and has been tested in trials in numerous countries around the world, including Mexico, Kenya, and Australia. It has also been translated into several languages and used in diverse settings. The psychometric properties of the instrument are sound, with good sensitivity and specificity. The instrument is brief (containing only ten items) and easy to administer, requires a moderate level of literacy or can be administered by a clinician/educator/worker, needs no specific training or qualifications for use, and takes only a few minutes to complete.

Future Developments

The essential components of ideal screening instruments are the ability to detect occasions of drinking and intoxication, because overall consumption levels are less important from a prevention perspective than occasions that represent high-risk situations for the drinker, his or her associates, and the community at large. Screening instruments that assist in this process are sorely needed.

HEALTH BENEFITS OF ALCOHOL CONSUMPTION: AN ADDITIONAL ISSUE FOR PREVENTION

Few areas have been more controversial than the question of the purported health benefits of alcohol. Scientists, public health advocates, the medical profession, and various arms of the alcohol industry have debated this issue over the past few decades, and a consensus has emerged. In sum, when alcohol is consumed at the level of no more than three standard drinks for men and one for women, there is a reduced risk of particular forms of cardiovascular disease and an overall reduction in all-cause mortality (Holman 1995). The caveats are that

- the levels of alcohol in question are relatively modest (the propensity for some to apply the logic that if a small amount is good then a larger amount would be even better must be preempted),
- the effect seems to hold true only for men over the age of forty and women over the age of fifty,
- the same protective benefit could be obtained by other means, for instance, dietary modification or exercise, which may also confer additional health and lifestyle benefits,
- any health benefits from alcohol must also be considered in the wider context of the parallel risks associated with consumption at that level, and
- most alcohol-related problems of an acute nature are experienced by younger age groups, for whom there is no ameliorating effect of low consumption.

The question is whether there is sufficient justification to encourage individuals to drink (Holman 1995). The authors of the United Kingdom's *Sensible Drinking* guidelines argued that there seem to be sufficient grounds to actually recommend increased consumption in certain cases. With regard to nondrinkers in particular, the recommendations state that people who do not drink, or drink very little (less than 1 unit a day) and are in the age groups where there is a significant risk of CHD (men over 40 and postmenopausal women) may, therefore, want to consider the possible health benefit of light drinking. But some will wish to continue to abstain—for very valid reasons—and may instead wish to explore the health benefit of other lifestyle changes which are open to everyone (U.K. Department of Health and Social Security 1995, 35). Whether the question is one of encouraging abstainers to take up drinking or supporting existing drinkers to drink more than they currently do, the issues remain the same. In terms of general public health or public policy messages, there are not sufficient health grounds for promoting the increased consumption of alcohol. Further, any positive cardiovascular health benefit from the moderate consumption of alcohol is only enjoyed by the middle-aged and older members of society. In the light of the newly emerging consensus regarding cardiovascular disease and alcohol consumption, information and education programs already in existence can be reshaped to target populations identified as at risk for developing alcohol-related problems.

The increased debate in the scientific literature has been echoed in the popular media. Hall (1995), for instance, reported that 39 percent of the Australian population in 1994 believed in the cardiovascular benefits of alcohol consumption, compared to 0 percent five years earlier. This belief was also found to be correlated with older age groups, males, the better educated, and the heavier drinkers. What is not known is how well people understand the rationale for the health benefits of moderate alcohol consumption and what they believe to be moderate levels of consumption, at which the protective effect operates. Hall argued that it is important to know how information about the health benefits of alcohol has changed behavior and to what extent it has legitimized existing behavior. Perhaps even more important is the question of whether it acts as an inducement for some to begin to drink or to increase their drinking. These are crucial issues to address if the health benefits associated with alcohol consumption are to be managed in the best public health interests of the community. Consumers have a right to accurate information, but among public health professionals there is a lamentable lack of such information, which leaves consumers on their own. This is not good public health.

PREVENTION: APPROACHES, SETTINGS, AND CULTURES

Aggregate consumption levels of alcohol are no longer considered a sufficiently sensitive and useful gauge by which to measure alcohol-related problems in a community. Similarly, global control measures are no longer considered adequate for prevention efforts. However, there is no need to discard such approaches as alcohol availability measures but to enhance these approaches with sophistication and breadth. What is proposed are strategies to complement existing alcohol control strategies for which there is empirical evidence of effectiveness.

Improved Public Information

The filter through which alcohol-related information has been received in the past has been less than helpful. Programs with the often covert aim of changing people's behavior toward an idealized model of consumption have frequently offered few guidelines. We are not arguing for a return to the old and very much outmoded and ineffective model of drug prevention based on knowledge and attitude change leading to behavior change (Moskowitz 1989). Rather, we suggest that an information base should be developed to inform policies and strategies on alcohol use and to guide consumers, health professionals, and members of the alcohol industry alike. If we speak with a united voice, we can enhance the impact of the health messages being developed and delivered and improve the credibility of all parties concerned.

Only in recent years have safe-drinking guidelines appeared, albeit with regional variations, and only now are precise guidelines on low-risk consumption beginning to emerge. Focusing, for example, on reducing episodes of intoxication and on assisting individuals and communities to achieve this goal is vastly more useful, and plausible, than attempting to persuade all members of the community to consume less alcohol. Such prevention messages can translate into short, sharp, and meaningful public health messages. Similarly, a range of simple policy advice positions can emerge from this platform; an example is advice to schools, parents, publicans, and others concerned with the need for the provision of food in any location where alcoholic beverages are served. Well-researched evidence supports the efficacy of such strategies. However, efforts have been sporadic and isolated. The central and entrenched position occupied by the control-of-distribution theorists has hampered the development of new concepts and strategies and prevented their wide-scale adoption.

Specific Prevention and Education Messages

Future prevention and education messages will be focused increasingly on minimizing the harmful consequences of drinking rather than on drinking per se. Alcohol-impaired behavior is related to several factors, including blood alcohol level, metabolism, age, sex, ethnicity, and history of use. Tailored messages incorporating the relevant factors are required in order to address the major alcohol-related areas of harm. These include motor vehicle accidents (in which major improvements have been achieved over the past two or three decades through targeted messages and such strategies such as random breath testing), falls, drownings, fires and burns, and work-related accidents. In each of these, risk increases incrementally with blood alcohol concentration (BAC) (Naranjo and Bremner 1993). Keeping BAC low, and in particular not drinking to intoxication, will minimize all of the above negative consequences of drinking.

Cross-Cultural Applicability

It is essential that new and emerging models of prevention are cognizant of differing cultural settings while being flexible enough to take account of differences within and between communities. This is a complex issue and needs to be addressed with due consideration for all stakeholders. At the time of writing, the World Health Organization was developing a global substance abuse strategy for indigenous peoples. Early indications suggest that this strategy will address the use and misuse of alcohol within a given community in response to the perceived needs of the community, developed with the active involvement of all members of the community, and implemented by acceptable figures within the community. This approach has much to commend it.

Complex factors influence the likelihood of alcohol-related harm occurring within indigenous communities. A paper referred to in Te Puni Kokiri and Kaunihera Whakatupato Waipiro O Aotearoa (1995, 22) stated that "the best means for minimizing alcohol-related harm in an indigenous community is one which the community develops itself. Such an approach has the key advantage of ownership by the people." Among many indigenous communities, views differ on the approach to take, ranging from total abstention for historical, cultural, or health reasons to low-risk consumption and a view of alcohol as nonproblematic. Recent moves by certain Aboriginal communities in Queensland, Australia, to ban the use of alcohol, in an attempt to address the impact of alcohol abuse on the community, highlight the importance of local decision making.

The dominant models employed in the prevention field have typically tended to have male gender bias and Eurocentricity as their hallmarks. If policy makers, researchers, and program implementers fail to develop prevention strategies that target all at-risk behaviors and individuals, they are doomed to continue to provide advice to those who least need it, while largely ignoring the needs of those whose drinking patterns place them at most risk.

CONCLUSION

It has been pointed out that ''one of the most startling lessons of twentieth-century biology has been the discovery that diversity—genetic, species, and cultural—is a critical part of long-term resilience and survival'' (Suzuki and Oiwa 1996, 6). Similarly, the complex nature of alcohol consumption and alcohol-related problems requires that we in the public health field recognize the diversity of drinking patterns in the community and develop preventive programs that, by their diversity, target the harms we aim to reduce.

In common with population-based control strategists, we hold the view that there is a need to target the entire drinking community, but we approach the question from a different standpoint and with a different endpoint in mind. By redirecting our gaze toward drinking patterns and the problems associated with certain of these patterns, we will be better able to develop, implement, evaluate, refine, and improve those strategies we put in place to prevent the onset of alcohol-related harms. In contrast to the protagonists of reductions in mean consumption, who have argued the need for all to reduce their consumption on the basis of the preventive paradox, we maintain that not all consumers need to reduce consumption in itself but, rather, that we all need to change the consumption patterns that lead to occasions of harm. Our prevention outcomes are to be measured in terms of reduced harms, not reduced consumption.

REFERENCES

Babor, T. F., E. B. Ritson, and R. J. Hodgson. 1986. Alcohol-related problems in the primary health care setting: a review of early intervention strategies. *British Journal of Addiction* 81:23–46.

Babor, T. F., J. R. De la Fuente, J. B. Saunders, and M. Grant. 1992. *The Alcohol Use Disorders Identification Test: Guidelines for Use in Primary Care*. Geneva: World Health Organization.

Cooney, N. J., A. Zweben, and M. F. Fleming. 1995. Screening for alcohol problems and at-risk drinking in health care settings. In *Handbook of Alcoholism Treatment Approaches: Effective Alternatives,* ed. H. K. Reid and W. R. Miller. 2d ed. Boston: Allyn and Bacon.

Cornel, M. 1994. *Detection of Problem Drinkers in General Practice*. Rotterdam: Stichting Verantwoord Alcoholgebruik.

Crosbie, D. 1996. Drinking patterns (E-mail commentary).

Edwards, G., et al. 1994. *Alcohol Policy and the Public Good.* Oxford: Oxford University Press.

Eliany, M., and B. Rush. 1992. *How Effective Are Alcohol and Other Drug Prevention and Treatment Programs? A Review of Evaluation Studies.* Ottawa: Minister of Supply and Services Canada.

English, D., et al. 1995. *The Quantification of Drug-Caused Morbidity and Mortality in Australia, 1995.* Canberra: Commonwealth Department of Human Services and Health.

Foucault, M. 1975. *The Birth of the Clinic: An Archaeology of Medical Perception.* New York: Vintage.

Goodman, J., P. E. Lovejoy, and A. Sherratt, eds. 1995. *Consuming Habits: Drugs in History and Anthropology.* London: Routledge.

Hall, W. 1995. Changes in the public perception of the health benefits of alcohol use, 1989 to 1994. *Australian and New Zealand Journal of Public Health* 20:93–95.

Hawks, D. 1990. Methodological and ethical considerations in ascertaining "recreational" drug use. In *Epidemiology of Illegal Drug Use in Australia, 1990,* ed. G. Wardlaw. Canberra: National Campaign against Drug Abuse.

Heather, N. 1993. Preface to *Psychoactive Drugs and Harm Reduction: From Faith to Science,* ed. N. Heather, A. Wodak, E. Nadelmann, and P. O'Hare. London: Whurr.

Holman, C. D. J. 1995. Analysis, action, and the third creation of public health. Inaugural lecture from the Foundation Chair in Public Health of the University of Western Australia and a McNulty Oration of the Public Health Association of Australia. Queen Elizabeth II Medical Centre, Perth.

Kreitman, N. 1986. Alcohol consumption and the preventive paradox. *British Journal of Addiction* 81:353–64.

Ledermann, S. 1956. *Alcool, alcoolisme, alcoolisation.* Paris: Presses Universitaires de France.

Miller, W. R., V. S. Westerberg, and H. B. Waldron. 1995. Evaluating alcohol problems in adults and adolescents. In *Handbook of Alcoholism Treatment Approaches: Effective Alternatives,* ed. H. K. Reid and W. R. Miller. 2d ed. Boston: Allyn and Bacon.

Moskowitz, J. M. 1989. The primary prevention of alcohol problems: a critical review. *Journal of Studies on Alcohol* 50:54–88.

Naranjo, C. A., and K. E. Bremner. 1993. Behavioural correlates of alcohol intoxication. *Addiction* 88:31–41.

Rehm, J. 1996. Quoted in *Addiction Research Foundation Journal.* Toronto. (May–June).

Rehm, J., S. Bondy, and R. Room. 1996. Towards effective low-risk guidelines on alcohol consumption. *Addiction* 91:31–33.

Rehm, J., and C. T. Sempos. 1995. Alcohol consumption and mortality: questions about causality, confounding, and methodology. *Addiction* 90:493–98.

Roche, A. M. 1996. Increasing primary care providers' willingness to intervene in alcohol- and drug-related problems: a review. *Substance Abuse* 17(4):201–217.

Roche, A. M., K. R. Evans, and W. R. Stanton. 1997. Harm reduction: the roads less travelled to the holy grail. *Addiction.* In press.

Roche, A. M., J. B. Saunders, and G. Elvy. 1992. The role of general practice in the prevention and management of the harm done by alcohol use. Paper presented to the World Health Organization Working Group of the WHO Regional Office for Europe on the Role of General Practice Settings in the Prevention and Management of the Harm Done by Alcohol Use, Vienna.

Roizen, R. 1993. Merging alcohol and illicit drugs: a brief commentary on the search for symbolic middle ground between licit and illicit psychoactive substances. Paper presented at the International Conference on Alcohol and Drug Treatment Systems Research, Toronto, Canada.

Room, R., S. J. Bondy, and J. Ferris. 1995. Risk of harm to oneself from drinking, Canada 1989. *Addiction* 90:499–513.

Rose, G. 1992. *The Strategy of Preventive Medicine*. Oxford: Oxford University Press.

Rose, G., and S. Day. 1990. The population mean predicts the number of deviant individuals. *British Medical Journal* 301:1031–34.

Single, E. 1995. A harm-reduction approach for alcohol: between the lines of *Alcohol Policy and the Public Good*. *Addiction* 90:195–99.

Single, E. W. 1994.Implications of potential health benefits of moderate drinking for specific elements of alcohol policy: Towards a harm reduction approach for alcohol. *Contemporary Drug Problems* 4:273–285.

Skog, O.-J. 1985. The collectivity of drinking cultures: a theory of the distribution of alcohol consumption. *British Journal of Addiction* 80:83–99.

Stockwell, T., D. Hawks, E. Lang, and P. Rydon. 1996. Unravelling the preventive paradox for acute alcohol problems. *Drug and Alcohol Review* 15:7–15.

Suzuki, D., and K. Oiwa. 1996. *The Japan We Never Knew*. Sydney: Allen and Unwin.

Te Puni Kokiri and Kaunihera Whakatupato Waipiro O Aotearoa. 1995. *Te Maori me te Waipiro: Maori and Alcohol*. Wellington: Te Puni Kokiri and Alcohol Advisory Council of New Zealand.

Thorley, A. 1985. The limitations of the alcohol-dependence syndrome in multidisciplinary service development. In *The Misuse of Alcohol: Critical Issues in Dependence, Treatment, and Prevention*, ed. N. Heather, I. Robertson, and P. Davies. London: Croom Helm.

U.K. Department of Health and Social Security. 1995. *Sensible Drinking: The Report of an Interdepartmental Working Group*. London: HMSO.

U.S. Institute of Medicine. 1990. *Broadening the Base of Treatment for Alcohol Problems*. Washington, D.C.: National Academy Press.

Weil, A., and T. Rosen. 1995. *From Chocolate to Morphine*. Boston: Houghton Mifflin.

Chapter 14

Public and Private Partnerships in Prevention and Research

INTRODUCTION

Other chapters have explored the wide range of factors that influence drinking patterns. The diversity of these factors has made clear that any attempt to change hazardous patterns and promote beneficial ones must be broad based and must involve a wide range of partners, all of whom have an interest in health promotion.[1]

Alcohol abuse prevention, health promotion, promotion of only sensible drinking—these strategies require the cooperation of governments, health advocacy organizations, the academic community, and commercial interests. Participants from each sector bring with them values and norms that are based on their individual experiences and that influence their expectations of how the partnerships should function.

Governments are responsible for setting the rules under which policy operates. Therefore, public sector values often center upon equity and inclusion. For governments, the process may become more important than outcomes. The private sector makes and sells goods and services with the expectation of profit. Therefore, private sector values often center upon results and exclusion, and achieving the final objective of the partnership may become more important than the process itself. Voluntary and advocacy organizations are typically problem

1. This introductory section is adapted from text by Barton Alexander.

oriented, with an emphasis on a narrower agenda. In some instances, partnership may seem less virtuous than the process of working to change the system. Finally, the academic community is highly focused on the inquiry process itself and on the charge of pursuing the truth. Working with other interested parties may at times appear to compromise independence, and clear rules of engagement may be required in order to protect this position.

The blending of these unique backgrounds provides a rich ground for addressing partnerships, and the different perspectives can contribute to an attitude of compromise and cooperation. This chapter describes the experience in partnership development in four different environments in which diverse viewpoints, value systems, and cultural backgrounds were brought together in successful models of alcohol abuse prevention.

I. NEW PLAYERS FOR A NEW ERA: HOW UP-TO-DATE IS HEALTH PROMOTION?

Ilona Kickbusch[2]

A couple of months ago a foreign affairs commentary in the *New York Times* took a look at the composition of the G-7 group, which at present includes the US, Britain, France, Japan, Italy, Germany and Canada. It made the point that this composition does not include the key actors that shape the world today and it offered proposals for alternative compositions. One read as follows:

> (1) China; (2) Japan; (3) The US; (4) Germany; (5) Rupert Murdoch, because he is . . . putting together the first truly global telecommunications network and he scares everybody in every market; (6) Bill Gates of Microsoft, because through his software he is building the first truly global marketplace, . . . he is doing more to enlarge the global market for goods and services than any other trade minister; (7) Mother Teresa, because she understands that promoting economic efficiency—a G-7 specialty—is not the same as building a caring society.

Just a couple of months later one might be tempted to change that list of seven yet again, given the rapid developments on the global marketplace. To me, the parallels to health promotion development are obvious: like Alice in Wonderland we had better run fast just to stay where we are, let alone move into new global dimensions.

2. Originally appeared in an article by Ilona Kickbusch: *Health Promotion International,* 26:259–261. Reprinted with permission from Oxford University Press. Ilona Kickbusch is director of the Division of Health Promotion, Education, and Communication, World Health Organization, Geneva, Switzerland.

Revisiting Health Promotion— Widening Our Perspective

In preparation for the 4th International Conference on Health Promotion in Djakarta in July 1997, the World Health Organization (WHO) is in the process of evaluating health promotion achievements and outlining future challenges in the form of health promotion scenarios. This work clearly indicates that we are entering a new phase where public/private partnerships for health promotion increasingly need to complement the healthy public policy initiatives and organizational development approaches. Creativity is called for in responding to global challenges. In preparation for this conference I would like to propose a number of issues that need consideration and pose a number of questions that relate to the cutting-edge role that health promotion should be playing in health development.

Health promotion contributed significantly to moving the health debate— from what we do to eliminate disease—to a paradigm based on the creation and production of health. Investment in health gain is at the core of health promotion, and it has become increasingly clear that the major part of this investment must be undertaken outside of the health sector. Less discussed has been the contribution and responsibility of the private sector in the production of health gain, beyond the critical debate on the alcohol and tobacco industry. Public health action—says the U.S. Institute of Medicine report 1988—must take the form of an organized social response that includes *private organizations, individuals as well as public agencies.* If the health of the public is not just a government concern, implemented by government agencies, but a truly joint societal effort then we need to clarify in more detail where the respective responsibilities lie and what the rules of the game are. We are still far removed from that—in many countries the question is not even being considered.

Who is Promoting Health?

Many insights and strategies that constitute the ''core'' of health promotion are being used successfully in the private marketplace, linking health gain with profit margins. While health promoters still need to argue the case for the importance of self-esteem and social support in the creation of health within a system ruled by a medical paradigm, advertising messages use this knowledge with abundance: self-esteem will for a long time to come be linked with the slogan of a shoe company and every food, soft drink or alcoholic beverage ad shows a social situation—the breakfast table, the party, the pub—if not a situation of seduction. It's all about feeling good (feeling better), being acknowledged, loved and respected. In many parts of the world, health promotion is big business: be it by using health as the added value of an otherwise rather normal product or offering specific products and services that (supposedly) will increase personal or family health. In fact, the health theme has become so dominant that advertising is responding with double messages, e.g., one ad shows a teenager eating breakfast cereal with the parents watching and the voice over advising "just don't tell him it's healthy".

Three industries are particularly active in the health promotion marketplace: the communications industry, the lifestyle and leisure industry and, of course, the health industry itself. I will just highlight a few of the points that I feel need much more analysis, consideration and creative response from the health promotion community.

The Communications Industry

A key player is the media/communications/information industry. It is the mega growth market of the present, it helps create and structure how we live, love, work and play—to paraphrase the Ottawa Charter. This industry will aim to satisfy the publics interests in health matters through massive expansion of its health programmes. Zapping through popular talk shows indicates the prominence of health issues (how did I pick up life again after my stroke, how do I live with a partner who has Alzheimer's, how do I cope with my HIV infection . . . the list is endless and sometimes truly obscure), teenage programmes provide sex education while state agencies are hampered by close scrutiny and problems of language and style, health magazines (fit for fun, men's health) abound and the self-care video market is exploding. A major communications company has just launched a self-care video to be sold through major retail chains: $20 million production costs, $15 million marketing expenses, $19.80 for the consumer. When did a health education authority ever get that amount of money to launch a major campaign? While there is strong resistance from the public to any increase of contributions to health insurance schemes, significant amounts are spent in the private health market—be it for magazines, fitness training, health foods and the like. And the market will continue to expand: 24-hour health channels, interactive health programmes, CD-roms, self-help groups on the worldwide web, health on-line services, etc.

What does this mean in terms of planning and financing health promotion? Where does the personal, where the state responsibility lie? Do we want the market to take over middle-class health while government programs focus on closing the gap? In the developing world interesting projects have been developed that use entertainment—for example soaps and sitcoms—as a way to reach wide populations with key health messages. And, I must say, one of the most impressive portrayals of the dilemma of a girl asked by her boyfriend to sleep with him that I have seen was on the Cosby show. Where does health promotion fit in here? ARE WE WILLING TO ACCEPT THAT THE ABOVE IS HEALTH PROMOTION? If yes, what does it mean for the work of governmental health promotion agencies frequently caught in the political mire and financial squeeze. Will the market take up the controversial issues and will the health education authorities be restricted to the "safe" issues, that do not hurt politicians' feelings or sense of language—and finally miss the target group because of that? Is it good or bad that "the market" is doing a major part of our job? And is doing it rather well? How does that correlate with the fact that there will be 2 billion teenagers worldwide by the year 2001 and that MTV is trying to reach them all.

The Lifestyles and Leisure Industry

The second major health promotion player is the "lifestyles and leisure industry" of products and services (foods, drinks, cigarettes, travel, pop concerts, snacks, entertainment, sports). It of course overlaps strongly with the communications industry and helps finance many of its programmes. These industries will continue to expand into global markets. At the same time, many of these products are produced in the developing world under unacceptable working conditions. A case in point being the shoe company mentioned above. Already today an average of $250 per capita is spent worldwide annually on product packaging and marketing. Advertising is still tax deductible in many countries—meaning that there is a public subsidy of billions of dollars worldwide on the promotion of products, many of which are harmful to health. Should there be a health promotion tax on company expenditure on advertising in general, or an end to tax deductions on advertising for products harmful to health? Or a health promotion levy on advertising and marketing dollars spent? Or an incentive scheme? Such an approach could widen the possibilities of creating health promotion foundations throughout the world, widening the scope from just the tobacco tax levy. It could also open the way to alliances with consumer organizations, responsible companies, sport organizations, arts councils and business representatives as practiced in Australia.

The key question is how can this industry be leveraged for health and healthy products and for healthy work conditions in its own ranks. Ethical issues are beginning to enter the private sector increasingly. An interesting example is the sporting goods industry, whose world federation (representing $100 billion) recently hosted a conference on human rights and child labour, which discussed issues such as fair trade, international standards for social responsibility and the role of business in preventing child labour. Is health promotion leading in these kinds of debates, or lagging behind? How about an alliance between consumer organizations and health promoters to move towards a company health promotion audit in relation to working conditions and goods and services produced. That is not as impossible as it may sound: the UNCTAD recently published a "Benchmark Corporate Environmental Survey" of transnational companies; the World Travel and Tourism Council has identified "sustainable development" as one of its long-term goals, following Agenda 21; and a number of airlines and credit card companies are running the "responsible citizen campaigns". There are groups such as the Washington Business group for Health or the British "Business in the Community".

The Health Care Industry

Finally the health care industry will see health promotion as a market of the future. Hospitals/health service institutions/health maintenance organizations will compete for health gain, quality of care and managed care. They will increasingly enter the area of community health, as is already the case in the USA, where community based projects and assessments allow hospitals to keep a tax free status. Increasingly, areas that were seen to be uniquely the responsibility of the state will be seen to move into the private sector or into public/ private mix. The health care industry will be restructured as totally as the communications industry—meaning the interlinkage of separate functions or "industries" to a new type of service and products—as computer hardware firms buy up software producers, link with telephone and cable companies and go global as "mega media."

The pharmaceutical industry, for example, will redefine its product to be "health" rather than a pill which can be bought at a chemists or in a pharmacy— as IBM buys Lotus, they will get involved in direct health care provision (hospital chains), home order systems (for self-medication) and health advice on-line (interactive television, 24-hour health lines, etc.). A recent ad for an American hospital advertised the totality of its services, including its web home page and the service "Talk to our doctors on the internet": Monday 7 p.m., arthritis; Tuesday 7 p.m., gynecology; Wednesday 7 p.m., heart disease. . . .

Next Steps

Ten years after the Ottawa Charter proclaimed a "new public health" it would seem imperative that "today more than ever public health institutions world wide . . . need to redefine their mission in light of the increasingly complex milieu in which they operate" (Julio Frenk, Mexico).

Our proposal in preparing for the 4th International Conference on Health Promotion is to face up to issues such as the ones raised above, to arrange a series of critical dialogues and think-tanks to move the agenda ahead and clarify our thinking and to explore mechanisms to establish new type or partnerships as well as new tools for health promotion.

Visit our web site soon.

II. EFFECTIVE PARTNERSHIPS BETWEEN THE PUBLIC AND PRIVATE SECTORS

Peter Mitchell[3]

The Concise Oxford English Dictionary defines *partnership* as an understanding between individuals or entities involving "shared risks and profits." This defi-

---

3. Peter Mitchell is with Guinness PLC, London, U.K.

nition has, perhaps, a too narrowly commercial flavor. But the principle is right, capturing the idea of cooperation between different parties (possibly with differing outlooks or motivations) aimed at achieving common gains or benefits. It is this principle that underlies the growing trend especially toward cooperation or partnership between the public and private sectors of the community or, perhaps more precisely, between the public or nonprofit sectors and the private or commercial sectors.

Conceptually, there is little new in this. Commercial patronage of the arts had its origins in medieval Europe and flourished during the Renaissance. The nineteenth century and, even more so, the twentieth have seen considerable and growing patronage or cooperation between the commercial and cultural communities, in Europe and North America particularly. Today, the term often used is sponsorship, an idea most publicly visible in the field of sports, much of which could not survive, at least at the highest levels, without such commercial support. But sponsorship does not only concern sports; the arts are not far behind in their dependence on the commercial world.

This may seem somewhat removed from the area of public-private partnership in matters of public welfare. But the differences are ones of degree; real similarities exist. The distance between, say, an alcoholic drinks company sponsoring a soccer tournament and the same company sponsoring an alcohol misuse project is not so great that experience from one end of the spectrum cannot be valuably transferred to the other.

The lesson most evident from successful public-private partnerships from many fields is the necessity, from the outset, for an understanding between all parties as to their respective motives and objectives. Having a well-defined goal on which all partners agree is vital but is not enough in itself. There needs also to be an appreciation by each partner of why it is involved, what it hopes for, and what are the comparable motivations and expectations of the other partners. Often, these will not be identical. Nor do they need to be for success, provided that each party understands the others and can accept their aims. A public authority may seek private commercial help in providing accommodation for homeless people. The authority's main motivations will be public welfare and, perhaps, a political agenda. The company offering that help may be driven by a mix of humanitarian motives and a desire to be a good corporate citizen. Thus the different aims of each party coincide to the benefit of all.

A good example from the beverage alcohol industry is the cooperative exercise, during 1992 and 1993, between one of the European Commission's directorates (DG5) and the Amsterdam Group (TAG). Among DG5's responsibilities are employment, industrial relations, social affairs, and aspects of public health throughout the European Union. The Amsterdam Group is an industry coalition addressing the social aspects of alcohol in Europe. It comprises fifteen leading companies (Allied Domecq, Bass, Beck and Co., Carlsberg, Guinness PLC, Heineken, IDV Ltd., Interbrew, Kronenbourg, Mahou, Moët Hennessy, Bacardi Martini, Pernod Ricard, Seagram, and Whitbread), representing a major part of European brewing, distilling, and wine making.

To assist its work, DG5 needed an overall, detailed picture of the European drinks industry and its products from an economic, cultural, social, and scientific standpoint. Nothing existed remotely resembling such a comprehensive "map" spanning a fragmented industry across the (then) twelve countries of the EU; nor had it ever been attempted for this industry. DG5 saw that it faced a major task to design such a map. The Amsterdam Group, however, was well placed to do so, even though the need had not previously existed. It had the resources and, more important, the detailed pan-European knowledge of the industry. Thus there was a valuable public-private partnership in the making, as soon became evident in the early dialogue between DG5 and the Amsterdam Group in late 1991.

The definition of a jointly agreed goal was soon clear: the production of a detailed and objective portrait of the EU drinks industry spanning a wide diversity of areas, ranging from economic impact and employment, through cultural influences, to social aspects and health issues. It was to be a report produced with solid academic and scientific authority (a goal achieved by arranging for major work to be conducted, inter alia, through the European Institute of Business Administration in Fontainebleau, France, and the International Life Sciences Institute in Brussels, Belgium).

In this case, the motives of the two partners in this project were different, a fact recognized and accepted by each side. DG5 needed the best possible database, with good academic underpinning, to provide a platform from which any Commission policy recommendations on alcohol issues could be developed. In contrast, TAG wanted on record not simply a balanced picture of the European drinks industry but also an objective study of the economic and social contribution the drinks industry made to Europe, to help the industry represent itself as an important part of the European community. TAG also wanted an analysis that could assist alcohol policy discussions at the national as well as the EU level and even outside of Europe. So the aims of DG5 and TAG had similarities but were far from identical.

Even so, the end result met both parties' needs and the agreed common goal. Far from complicating the project, the acceptance in both DG5 and the Amsterdam Group that each had somewhat different aims helped the complex process of completing it well and quickly (in under eighteen months). Today, four years after publication, it remains a definitive study of its kind (Amsterdam Group 1993).

Of course, the motives of the partners in such ventures will not always be different; sometimes they will be identical. An example from the United States, a major initiative very different in kind from the DG5–Amsterdam Group project, is the Partnership for a Drug-Free America. Starting in the late 1980s, this was an exercise led by private industry, in close cooperation with public health and other agencies, to attack illegal drug use. Initiated and led by the communications and media industry, the Partnership focused on promoting powerful messages on the dangers of illegal drug use, providing considerable television time and print space for the project, as well as making use of the creative talent of the communications industry to ensure that the right messages reached the right audiences. Here the goal of both public and private sectors was simple: to communicate more powerfully and more extensively the dangers of illegal drug use. The motives of both parties were similar: to put more resources into tackling a major and daunting American problem, about which the private sector felt as strongly, as responsible corporate citizens, as did the agencies having professional responsibility for addressing the problem. Enlightened self-interest is probably the best descriptor. It is a powerful motivator.

Most often, in the majority of successful public-private partnerships, the mix of motivations between the partners will be a combination of common aims and aims particular to each partner but always within the framework of an overall, jointly agreed goal. An interesting (and perhaps early) example arose in Europe in the mid-1980s in the collaboration between the World Federation of Advertisers and the European Broadcasting Union, a public body responsible for the conduct of television broadcasting throughout Europe.

The issue was one of reliable measurement of the composition of television audiences, particularly to ensure that sound country-by-country comparisons could be made between the varied broadcasting systems of widely differing European countries. The issue was critical in light of the rapid proliferation of television channels in Europe in the 1980s and the accelerating development of Europe as a single marketplace. The European Broadcasting Union needed common standards of audience measurement to guide its pan-European work. The business community needed them to ensure that dependable comparisons of television audiences could be made between countries for advertising purposes. From these different but overlapping needs emerged a public-private initiative to develop common pan-European standards of audience measurement and to gain acceptance of them by all broadcasters. The end result was a system that now, seven years later, still serves both the interests of TV broadcasting and those of business. Neither sector could have achieved this result alone, but in combination it was possible. Though each sector's needs and aims differed, enough of a common goal existed to make the partnership work. At the time, this initiative was not even thought of as a public-private partnership. In retrospect, it was an early forerunner of what today is increasingly commonplace (European Broadcasting Union 1991).

In the beverage alcohol industry experience is growing fast in the development of productive public-private partnerships to address issues such as improved understanding of the notion of sensible drinking or measures to tackle alcohol misuse. That this is so is hardly surprising, given the explosive growth since the early 1990s of industry-developed social aspects organizations (e.g., the U.K.'s Portman Group, the U.S.'s Century Council, and France's Entreprise et Prevention) dedicated to these issues. At the turn of the decade there were, at best, three such organizations worldwide. In 1997 there are almost thirty, and the numbers are rising. That growth has given increased impetus to constructive cooperation with public health, educational, and other bodies to work toward common ends.

What this experience shows is that there are few if any simple standard models of how such partnerships should be constructed. Country by country, and even project by project, each partnership initiative needs to be developed to address specific goals and the particular thinking of the partners at a given time. Two simple examples make the point, both relating in different ways to the education of young people concerning alcohol. One is the U.S.'s Century Council's new initiative, Promising Practices, which is concerned with establishing the best practice in dealing with problems of alcohol abuse in colleges and universities. Developed in conjunction with Rutgers University and George Mason University, it is now being expanded across the country in close collaboration with university and college administrations and is applied campus by campus in ways that are tailored and adapted to local needs and experience (Century Council 1996). The other example is from the opposite end of the world, Australia's Home Safely project. Developed by a coalition of the Australian drinks industry, it is designed to alert young people to the dangers of drunken driving and to establish agreements between youngsters and parents on how young people can avoid situations that could lead to inappropriate driving behavior. Home Safely, like Promising Practices, was developed in consultation with educational authorities (Home Safely 1986). The underlying goal of both programs is similar, but the form is, appropriately, different.

My own company, Guinness PLC, is in a new partnership with the United Nations Development Programme to help provide clean, safe water supplies across the developing world. The partnership is centered on the development of a water pump that will ensure reliable water supply to impoverished rural communities. The exercise, part of Guinness' wider Water of Life environmental initiative, represents UNDP's first partnership with the corporate world and has called for imagination and lateral thinking from both Guinness PLC and UNDP. But the prize is a public–private partnership that, we believe, will have major benefits for the supply of clean water in the developing world.

III. LESSONS FROM PARTNERSHIPS: THE EXAMPLE OF THE UNITED STATES

Yvonne Lumsden-Dill[4]

Why Form Partnerships?

There are several overarching reasons that public-private partnerships make sense. Despite disparate profit motives, the partners often share an identical

---

4. Yvonne Lumsden-Dill is with Miller Brewing Co., Milwaukee, Wisc., U.S.

social goal: to improve the society in which both function. Examples are a company that allows employees to use work hours to tutor children in inner cities and a company that underwrites a community theater's production. What all have in common is that company officials view such commitments as part of being a good citizen. Benefits to the company may not be directly visible in terms of profits, but they reflect a long-term investment in the community. Partnerships that are increasingly popular are those in which the goals are not identical but are mutual; while both parties acknowledge a direct benefit in working together, expectations may not be the same.

A major factor in bringing the private and public sectors together is the growing shortage of available government funds. Shrinking government budgets are eliminating grant programs, making nonprofit organizations more amenable to public-private partnerships. For generations, nonprofit organizations were wary of joint efforts with for-profit companies. However, as more and more public-private partnerships prove successful, this fear is dissipating. At the same time, companies feel the need to address social issues that affect their employees or their products, and this leads them to partnerships with nonprofit organizations. Companies realize that they cannot pursue profit goals in isolation from social goals and that mutual goals are best achieved through collaboration. They can provide funds and expertise, while public interest organizations provide ideas and committed volunteers.

Early Partnerships in Other Industries

Early partnerships were born out of necessity. Some people trace corporate philanthropy in the United States back to the railroad barons, who were the major underwriters of the Young Men's Christian Association (YMCA), thereby ensuring housing for their train crews. Soon, other companies saw the advantage of philanthropy that directly served the company's interest. In fact, for several decades (up until the 1950s) U.S. corporate law *required* that a company's donations directly benefit its stockholders. That notion made sense, but today's nonprofit organizations criticize a company's philanthropy that is solely in its shareholders' interest. It may be argued that all philanthropy is in a company's ultimate long-term interest. A 1992 *Wall Street Journal* study found that consumers look favorably on companies that are socially responsible.

There are many examples of public-private partnerships. The aerospace industry underwrote aviation research. The petrochemical industry contributed to chemical and environmental research. The pharmaceutical industry continues to fund research for the development of new drugs. Generally, the greatest benefits come from long-term partnerships that may involve a series of projects or a particular program of long duration. Texaco's fifty-five years of sponsoring opera radio broadcasts brought it more than twice its normal market share among car owners who listened to the broadcasts (Steckel and Simons 1992).

Barriers to Alcohol Industry Partnerships

Historically, the alcohol industry in the United States has faced problems that other industries have not had to address. This first delayed and now complicates its forming public-private partnerships. The unique barrier, of course, was a government shutdown of the entire industry. The imposition of prohibition in 1920 and its repeal in 1933 afforded the alcohol industry the distinction of being the only U.S. commercial sector to have its ability to operate or not operate decreed by constitutional amendment. As a closely regulated industry, alcohol has many restrictions on what activities it can undertake. Currently, the Federal Bureau of Alcohol, Tobacco, and Firearms (BATF) supervises all packaging, advertising, and marketing practices of the industry. In addition, each of the fifty states can make its own rules for the industry, including rules that preempt BATF decisions.

Because it operates in an area in which Americans' puritanical values are most often displayed, the industry has voluntarily adopted an advertising code to ensure that its products are used legally and responsibly. Historically, these same puritanical values made members of nonprofit organizations and other observers suspicious of the alcohol companies' motives. Whereas consumers applaud when a company promises to make a donation to a worthy cause every time its credit card is used for a purchase, many are offended if a brewer uses incentives to encourage use of its products. This burden no doubt will plague the industry until the majority of the people accept what the governments of both the United States and the United Kingdom have determined: that moderate consumption of alcohol beverages may improve the health of most people (USDA/USDHHS 1995; U.S. Department of Health and Social Security 1995).

Until recently, even U.S. government actions reinforced suspicions of the alcohol industry. Industry members frequently were not allowed to participate in government meetings dealing with alcohol issues. Worse, for several years "alcohol and other drugs" was the phrase of choice used by the government's Center for Substance Abuse Prevention and recommended in its *Editorial Style Guidelines*. Although the industry vehemently objected to having its products linked with illegal drugs, the policy persisted. In recent years, the Center for Substance Abuse Prevention has revised its editorial guidelines, removing the earlier phrase and using "alcohol and drugs" instead. Though a small step, the decision has opened up a new opportunity for partnerships.

Alcohol Industry Partnerships

When alcohol companies began establishing partnerships with public sector organizations in the mid-1970s, they generally fell into two areas: research and prevention programs. The oldest of the alcohol groups in the United States is the Licensed Beverage Information Council, which was established in 1974 and is funded by all tiers of the industry, including distillers, wine makers and brewers.

LBIC makes grants for educational projects. One well-known project was the long-running Friends Don't Let Friends Drive Drunk billboard campaign carried out in partnership with the Outdoor Advertising Association of America and the U.S. Department of Transportation. LBIC also has partnered with the American Medical Association to fund production of a video to train physicians how better to diagnose the onset of alcoholism.

The track record of the Alcoholic Beverage Medical Research Foundation, founded in 1982, demonstrates the many benefits of research partnerships. ABMRF, with funding from the beer industry in the United States and Canada, supports research to produce new information about alcohol use and disseminates information about the effects of alcohol. It has sponsored scientific meetings on a wide range of topics, such as alcohol and highway safety and the effects of alcohol on the cardiovascular system. An important part in its conference program is played by the International Medical Advisory Conferences held in rotation in member countries Australia, Canada, New Zealand, the United Kingdom, and the United States. The conferences offer scientists in member countries an opportunity to share and discuss new information and research findings. In addition, more than 1,200 scientific reports on their research have been published by ABMRF grantees.

In Scotland, the Alcohol Research Group at the University of Edinburgh was funded originally by the Scotch Whisky Association. The Portman Group now also makes an annual contribution, and the research center obtains government grants for specific projects. In Belgium, the Arnoldus Groep formed a partnership with the Belgium Institute for Road Safety in 1995 to mount a designated driver program, which is supported by posters and television and radio spots. In South Africa, the Industry Association for Responsible Alcohol Use has teamed up with the University of Cape Town Medical School for research into fetal alcohol syndrome.

In the United States, the Miller Brewing Company, in partnership with the Fraternal Order of Police, has provided more than two million copies of a booklet that helps agencies responsible for enforcing alcohol regulations to detect false driver licenses used as identification documents. This booklet has become an integral tool in police training to prevent underage purchases of alcohol beverages. Several members of the U.S. alcohol industry, including Anheuser-Busch, Coors Brewing Company, Heublein, and Miller Brewing Company, underwrite a program to train servers for on-premise, off-premise, and social settings. Primary users of this program, Training in Intervention Procedures by Servers of Alcohol, are alcohol beverage regulators.

The Century Council, which is supported by brewers, vintners, distillers, and wholesalers, has made underage drinking a special target. In one program, Cops in Shops, the council teams up with local alcohol law enforcement agents who pose as clerks in off-premise locations that sell alcohol beverages and, if necessary, make arrests on site. Letting residents know that the Cops in Shops program may be operational any time in a community has a preventive effect on purchases by and for underage drinkers. The Beer Institute, in partnership with the U.S. National Association of Broadcasters, the National Beer Wholesalers Association, and some state liquor control commissions, has for several years distributed television and radio public service announcements to prevent underage drinking and drunk driving. Members of the Beer Institute include all the major brewers, many smaller brewers, and vendors who supply equipment and materials to the industry.

Another unusual U.S. partnership has been struck between the Beer Institute, the National Commission against Drunk Driving, and the National Highway Traffic Safety Administration. This Commission Communities program works with local and state highway safety representatives to prevent drunk-driving fatalities among twenty-one to thirty-four year-olds, the group with the highest percentage of occurrences.

Growth in Public-Private Partnerships

The growth of public-private partnerships in the alcohol industry demonstrates that they work. Some of the reasons are self-evident: the partnerships take advantage of existing efficient information delivery systems, capitalize on the fact that the industry knows its customers best, recognize that the industry is motivated to succeed, and help to bridge the trust gap. But the more companies work in these partnerships, the more it becomes apparent that some of the benefits are subtle. Prevention activities often help to achieve results that regulation cannot and often teach responsibility and awareness of consequences. In addition, companies recognize that their prevention activities can help to demonstrate that sometimes government regulation is unnecessary. Excessive regulation may turn alcoholic beverages into forbidden fruit; this is the case in some efforts to deter underage drinking, such as the fixing of a higher drinking age, which may drive college students to unsupervised, underground venues to drink.

Dr. Morris E. Chafetz, founding director of the U.S. National Institute on Alcohol Abuse and Alcoholism (NIAAA), speaking of the tendency to overregulate alcohol, has written:

> The tendency of experts to describe alcoholism as a problem that is larger-than-life, out of control, and amenable only to the strongest public policy measures, contributes to its bloated perception and to the prevalence of alcohol problems. Public fears about alcohol are used to justify stronger laws to punish offenders and more restrictions on the purchase of alcohol beverages. These very policies, however, victimize alcoholic people, create public policy solutions that don't work, and actually foster alcohol problems. (Chafetz 1996, 48)

As the success record of public-private partnerships in the alcohol industry is being written, it is clear that government in the United States is becoming more positive toward them. In 1991, the state of Arizona passed a law directing the Department of Public Health and Safety to implement drug and alcohol education programs. It specifically instructed the department to assist the regulated industry and interested groups and organizations in contributing to those efforts (Biemesderfer 1992). Idaho and Illinois have similar statutes.

The National Conference of State Legislatures in 1992 published a guide telling members how to build public-private partnerships to deal with abuse of alcohol and drugs. As the introduction explains, as state budgets falter and the health care crisis looms larger, public-private partnerships—programs supported by leaders and funds from both the private and public sectors—have begun to emerge as innovative, practical approaches to preventing substance abuse (Biemesderfer 1992, 2).

In 1994, Elaine Johnson, head of the U.S. Center for Substance Abuse Prevention, called for cooperation between industry and the government in reducing alcohol misuse. She noted that the Clinton administration "understands that the alcohol beverage industry is a legitimate business and acknowledges the contribution to the nation's economy that it makes. . . . It is time to recognize and celebrate together those strategies that simultaneously promote the public health and safety and bottom-line profits" (*Alcohol Issues Insights Newsletter* 1994).

Public-private partnerships, coupled with actions by the government and prevention efforts of other organizations and concerned citizens, have been paying off in significant, measurable results. Thus, from 1986 to 1995, traffic deaths reported as alcohol-related fell from 52.2 percent of the total to 41.0 percent. Teenage drunk-driving fatalities have been reduced by almost 70 percent during the same period, while teenage drinking fell to its lowest level in twenty years. As industry members, governments, and private nonprofit organizations work together to solve common problems, there are indications that the stigma once associated with alcohol products is disappearing, albeit slowly. Respondents in a 1996 Gallup Poll stated that they had become "more aware" of the health benefits of moderate consumption and "more comfortable" with drinking if in moderation.

Initiating New Partnerships in Other Countries

Different countries offer different challenges for those who wish to establish public-private partnerships. But countries that are considering this approach to deal with preventing the misuse of alcohol products have distinct advantages the United States did not have. The first is that dozens of programs have been tested and either modified when necessary or discontinued when they did not produce the expected benefits. Although policies and programs in developing countries, for example, need to be sensitive to cultural differences, there is no wholesale need to reinvent the wheel. Countries now beginning to initiate partnerships can benefit from all this experience. In addition, officials in countries venturing down this path have available to them hundreds of their peers who have trodden the road ahead of them and can readily explain which potholes to avoid.

IV. THE CASE OF THE COLLEGE OF PHARMACY, UNIVERSITY OF CHILE

Hugo Zunino, Jorge Litvak, and Yedy Israel[5]

Chile is a small developing country that aims to increase its national income by applying modern economic policies to open international markets for its products and services. Nevertheless, investment in research and development in Chile is still below 1 percent of the gross national product, indicating a real paucity of basic and technological support to the Chilean industrial system.

Public universities in Chile support almost 90 percent of scientific and technological research programs in the country; private companies still do not consistently invest in research and development. However, a number of corporations are starting to recognize the pressing need to apply quality control to their products and to introduce innovations into their industrial processes and services. Thus, sound linkages between universities and private companies are likely to develop.

The College of Pharmacy of the University of Chile, established in 1883, has been an important center for the development of chemistry and biochemistry in both Chile and Latin America as a whole. At present, the faculty incorporates research projects and teaching in the areas of pure and applied chemistry, pharmacy, biochemistry, and food sciences. In July 1992, fire completely destroyed the faculty's chemistry building, where about 65 percent of all teaching and research activities were located. Thanks to the support of the University of Chile, the Chilean government, and the German government, the building was not only rebuilt but was equipped with state-of-the-art facilities to become one of the most advanced chemistry centers in Chile and in all of Latin America. This fact created an optimum opportunity to enhance the linkage between the faculty and private corporations, especially through the use of modern instrumentation analysis to build appropriate control quality and environmental protection methods.

Among several cooperative projects, one has emerged in the field of alcoholism that illustrates a real public-private partnership in prevention and research. The Faculty of Pharmacy has thus projected a vision for the future, in which highly qualified scientists can interact with private enterprises.

5. Hugo Zunino is the Dean of the Faculty of Chemistry and Pharmaceutical Sciences, University of Chile, Santiago, Chile; Jorge Litvak is with the International University Exchange, Washington, D.C., USA; and Yedy Israel is with Jefferson Medical College, Thomas Jefferson University, Philadelphia, Pa., USA.

Alcohol Abuse in Chile and Its Early Identification

About 20 percent of the adult population of Chile abuses alcohol, resulting in marked morbidity and mortality. In Chile, as in virtually all countries, screening for alcohol abuse and dependence at the primary care level is nonexistent.

Two years ago, during a visit by Dr. Hugo Zunino to the laboratory of Dr. Yedy Israel at Thomas Jefferson University in Philadelphia (U.S.), a recent project on the early identification of alcohol abuse conducted by Dr. Israel was discussed. The project focused on the identification of the problem drinker in the primary-care physician's office followed by the delivery of brief counseling by the physician's nurse. The question was asked, Could not pharmacies also become part of a country's effort to prevent alcoholism in its population? A partnership was forged to test this idea in Chile by involving Farmacias Ahumada, S.A., a major pharmacy chain with over 100 outlets.

Earlier Perceptions

It was generally believed in the past that treatment or interventions for alcoholism were ineffective. Work conducted in this decade has radically changed this perception. Studies have shown that the success of treatment of alcohol abuse and dependence is closely related to the chronicity and severity of the condition. Over a dozen studies have now demonstrated that brief counseling for early problem drinkers and alcohol-dependent individuals is highly effective and efficient.

Identification of the problem drinker in the primary care physician's office, followed by advice from a nurse on how to reduce consumption (allowing for responsible drinking of up to four drinks per day) and the simple handing out of a brochure reduces the problem drinker's alcohol consumption by about 40 percent. Further, when three hours of counseling are provided by the nurse over a period of one year, alcohol consumption by the problem drinker is reduced by 70 percent and alcohol-related morbidity is reduced by 85 percent. This brief counseling also reduces the utilization of medical services by 30 percent.

A second problem inhibiting action by the public health community relates to the lack of nonintrusive methodologies to identify the problem drinker at an early stage. Physicians and other health professionals are concerned about the possibility of offending their patients. Recent work in Canada and the United States shows that traumatic injury is an excellent indicator of recurrent problem drinking (Israel et al. 1996). In studies in a metropolitan area, forty-two physicians asked their patients about previous trauma. Only in cases of reported traumatic injury did the physician ask the patient about his or her alcohol intake. With a total screening of over 15,000 patients and the virtually complete acceptance by both physicians and patients, 70 percent of problem drinkers in the population were identified.

Pharmacists in Alcohol Abuse Prevention at the Community Level

Health care in most countries should be open to any emerging alternatives that promise to improve the health of the population, particularly when those alternatives are low cost and use untapped resources. One such alternative is that of using the pharmacist as an active resource in primary health care and prevention. In recent years, there has been a shift in the role of the pharmacist from one of dispensing to one of active participation in the clinical health team. In many instances, the pharmacist is the first point of contact for the patient and thus also becomes a primary-care counselor for drug abuse, nutrition, hypertension, contraception, pregnancy, and general promotion of healthy lifestyles.

In collaboration with Farmacias Ahumada S.A. in Santiago, the Faculty of Pharmacy has embarked on a project to utilize the pharmacist in his or her potential new role in the prevention of alcohol abuse. This project, currently in progress, has two goals, which are outlined in some detail below.

The first goal is to define the drugs or combination of drugs that are used with greater frequency by the problem drinker than by other pharmacy customers. The literature suggests that alcoholics are more likely than the general population to use certain medications, for example, strong pain killers, antacids, antidepressants, and sedatives. These studies will enable the effectiveness of screening for problem drinking to be compared by (1) medication profiles in the pharmacy; (2) a history of traumatic injuries reported in the same setting, (3) a nonintrusive history of health problems, and (4) the use of the AUDIT questionnaire on alcohol consumption and problem drinking developed by the World Health Organization. It is hypothesized that a combined questionnaire, which includes medicines being purchased or used, reported traumatic injury, and some answers to the AUDIT questionnaire, will be the most sensitive, specific, and acceptable tool for the identification of the problem drinker in the pharmacy.

The second goal of the project is the delivery of cognitive and behavioral lifestyle counseling to identified problem drinkers by the pharmacist in the private pharmacy itself. It is hypothesized (1) that counseling the problem drinker will reduce his or her alcohol consumption to sensible levels, change it to a responsible pattern, and reduce alcohol-related problems; and (2) that pharmacies that become lifestyle centers will be used more often by the consumer, thus having positive financial effects for the owners.

The program is not aimed at reducing the overall consumption of alcohol by the population. Rather, it is aimed at teaching problem drinkers to recognize (cognitive) and avoid (behavioral) the situations that led them to consume alcohol at hazardous levels leading to intoxication. If successful, the program will provide a significant advance in the available knowledge on early identification of alcohol abuse. It will also introduce a new potential role for pharmacists. This new approach will demonstrate the implications for public health that can be derived from the reduction of alcohol abuse in problem drinkers without influencing the consumption in that segment of the population that consumes alcohol in a responsible manner. This will further communicate the notion that health systems should aim at responsible alcohol use, which avoids intoxication and alcohol abuse.

The development of this project has created a positive atmosphere for cooperation between the Faculty of Pharmacy and Farmacias Ahumada and has stimulated other initiatives focusing on common commercial and academic interests. In 1996, Farmacias Ahumada supported an additional pharmaceutical educational program, which allowed for academic activities and exchanges with another academic center in the United States, the College of Pharmacy at Washington State University.

The case presented in this section shows how a specific public-private partnership project has resulted in advantages both to the academic world and to industry in offering greater service to the community without additional cost to the population.

REFERENCES

Alcohol Issues Insights Newsletter. 1994. Vol. 11 (August).

Amsterdam Group. 1993. *Alcoholic Beverages and European Society.* London: Amsterdam Group.

Biemesderfer, S. C. 1992. *Guarding against Drug and Alcohol Abuse in the Nineties: Building Public/Private Partnerships.* Denver: National Conference of State Legislatures.

Century Council. 1996. *Promising Practices: Campus Alcohol Studies.* Los Angeles: Century Council.

Chafetz, M. E. 1996. *The Tyranny of Experts.* Lanham, Md.: Madison.

European Broadcasting Union. 1991. *Development and Harmonisation of TV Audience Measurement Systems in Europe.* Brussels: World Federation of Advertisers.

Home Safely. 1986. *Home Safely.* South Melbourne: Distilled Spirits Industry Council of Australia.

Israel, Y., et al. 1996. Screening for problem drinking and counseling by the primary care physician-nurse team. *Alcoholism: Clinical and Experimental Research* 20:1443–50.

Steckel, R., and R. Simons. 1992. *Doing Best by Doing Good: How to Use Public-Purpose Partnerships to Boost Corporate Profits and Benefit Your Community.* New York: Dutton.

U.K. Department of Health and Social Security. 1995. *Sensible Drinking: The Report of an Interdepartmental Working Group.* London: HMSO.

USDA/USDHHS. 1995. *Nutrition and Your Health: Dietary Guidelines for Americans.* 4th ed. Washington, D.C.: GPO.

Chapter 15

Shifting the Paradigm: Reducing Harm and Promoting Beneficial Patterns

Marcus Grant and Eric Single

TOWARD A NEW APPROACH

In this book, the authors have attempted to provide a strong rationale for a paradigm shift from per capita consumption toward drinking patterns as a more effective basis for measuring and assessing alcohol-related problems and for more effective policy and prevention approaches for dealing with these problems. We have examined current evidence on the relationship between patterns and consequences, acknowledging that in many instances the data are at present insufficient to come to conclusions that are as robust as we would like. We have attempted to relate patterns of drinking to alcohol policy at the individual, community, national, and international levels. And we have begun the process of describing what might be the most appropriate features of a new approach to determining research, program, and policy priorities. This final chapter attempts to summarize, as concisely as possible, where we are today and where we can expect to be tomorrow.

The main purpose of this book is to contribute to the process of establishing and giving objective credibility to the concept of drinking patterns as a basis for alcohol policy. It needs to be acknowledged that the term *drinking pattern* is essentially a metaphor for the sequence of drinking events—many habitual, some

Marcus Grant is with the International Center for Alcohol Policies, Washington, D.C., USA. Eric Single is with the Canadian Center on Substance Abuse, Toronto, Ontario, Canada.

random—that characterize the lives of individuals or groups. In general terms, it is both possible and useful to distinguish between beneficial patterns, which can be promoted as contributing to quality of life, and negative patterns, which are more likely to be associated with health and social problems. Again, in general terms, alcohol policy needs to focus on promoting beneficial patterns and modifying negative ones.

But few patterns are entirely consistent. Even the most negative patterns may contain some positive elements; and the most beneficial patterns may have occasional flaws. Indeed, it is in recognition of these inconsistencies that we attempt in this final chapter to link the concept of drinking patterns to the strategy of harm reduction. One focus for prevention efforts may be to try to eliminate the flaws from the beneficial patterns and to support the positive elements in otherwise negative patterns. Promoting beneficial drinking patterns includes seeking to reduce the harmful effects of alcohol.

It could be argued that this has already begun to happen, at least to a limited extent. A variety of prevention measures have been developed in the recent past that focus less on traditional restrictions over alcohol availability. Instead, they acknowledge, often implicitly, the central thesis of this book, which is that pattern of drinking is a better predictor of both negative and positive consequences than is per capita consumption. Since drinking patterns reveal themselves to a considerable extent in the nature of the drinking occasion or occasions that most typify the patterns, these new prevention measures focus more closely on drinking occasions and seek to find ways of reducing the harm that may arise when drinking takes place.

It is implicit in this approach that much drinking is either entirely or virtually harm free. This assertion is not intended in any way to diminish the seriousness of the harm that can be caused to individuals and communities by inappropriate or reckless drinking. Indeed, the value of an approach based upon drinking patterns is precisely that it throws into sharp focus those negative aspects of drinking behavior most likely to lead to harm to self or others. Equally, such an approach emphasizes that it is not merely the quantity of alcohol consumed that determines the probability of harm but all the components of drinking patterns described in chapter 1 and discussed by other authors throughout this book.

Thus, in choosing to link patterns to harm reduction, we are shifting the focus of policy onto specific risks and negative outcomes, rather than assuming that all drinking is by its nature risky and damaging. Indeed, it is precisely because risky and damaging drinking is the exception rather than the rule that harm reduction is an attractive option to pursue. An analysis of drinking patterns can reveal where the flaws appear in the symmetry of sensible drinking behavior. The challenge is to identify the flaws and deal with them without losing sight of the extent to which the pattern as a whole is fundamentally sound.

This book has presented a variety of examples of interventions aimed at promoting beneficial drinking patterns and at reducing harm associated with drinking. In this concluding chapter, we examine the concept of harm reduction and the relationship between harm reduction and drinking patterns. Included is a look at methods to reduce harmful drinking and promote less-risky drinking behaviors, the importance of both individual and collective responsibility, and implications for the future. We also attempt to reflect issues that have been raised by the independent reviewers to whom a draft of the manuscript of the book was sent.

As with any paradigm shift, we recognize that we are taking steps into the unknown. In acknowledging the need for more and better data, we are challenging both supporters and skeptics to reorient research efforts to yield the information necessary to test the validity and reliability of this promising approach. Also, as with any paradigm shift, our main intention is not to discredit the previous paradigm, although its inadequacies are discussed by several authors, notably in chapters 7 and 8. Rather, we are at pains to point out how the direction in which we propose traveling is a logical extension of the accumulated experience of the past.

Just as it would be erroneous to suggest that there is no empirical relationship between aggregate levels of alcohol consumption and trends in alcohol-related problems, so it would be quixotic to assert that such a relationship should be at the center of policy development. If in the past, there has been a reluctance to translate into practical policy guidelines the accumulating research results on the importance of drinking patterns, then let us hope that this book represents the beginning of a concerted effort to remedy that. Our central contention, so far as the policy implications of this book are concerned, is that increased attention needs to be given to measures that focus on preventing problems associated with drinking rather than on restricting access to alcohol.

HARM REDUCTION

Growing attention has been devoted to harm-reduction measures in a number of public health areas. Harm reduction was developed as an approach to deal with problems associated with illicit drug use, particularly the spread of HIV infection among intravenous drug users. In this context, and in contrast to abstinence-oriented approaches, harm reduction focuses on reducing the consequences of drug use rather than eliminating drug use. It seeks to adopt practical rather than idealized goals. Thus, focus is placed on safer use patterns rather than the deterrence of use per se. Needle exchange programs and other harm-reduction measures have often faced resistance from those who are understandably concerned that such practices may condone or facilitate drug use and thus increase drug problems. But evaluation studies have shown that harm-reduction programs have generally succeeded in reducing the spread of AIDS and other diseases and in helping many dependent users to lead normal lives as productive members of society, without leading to increases in levels of drug use (see, e.g., Donoghoe et al. 1989; Stimson 1989; Buning 1990; Watters et al. 1990; Wodak 1990; Riley

1993). Thus harm reduction has been a very successful movement, both politically and epidemiologically, in the area of HIV prevention.

Harm-reduction measures have expanded to a broad variety of programming aimed not only at reducing the spread of AIDS and other communicable diseases but also at other adverse consequences of drug use (Wodak and Saunders 1995; Single 1995). In the case of illicit drug use, there remains for some the ethical issue of whether harm-reduction approaches condone, or could be perceived to condone, a behavior that is against the law. However, this is clearly not a relevant consideration with respect to alcohol consumption except under some legally defined minimum drinking age or in relation to other behaviors such as driving a motor vehicle.

This is an important distinction. It enables the harm-reduction approach to alcohol problems to be coupled logically with efforts to promote those drinking patterns that maximize benefits, whether expressed in terms of individual health and quality of life or in terms of enhanced socioeconomic functioning. For most drinkers, the vast majority of the time, harm remains distant and improbable. However, as is clear from the discussion of the preventive paradox by several authors in this book, the concept is relevant to all. Thus, as it applies to alcohol, harm reduction refers to policies and programs that focus on reducing the adverse consequences of drinking rather than measures aimed at restricting access to alcohol. As such, it shifts the focus toward those drinking patterns associated with adverse consequences, rather than assuming that all drinking is equally likely to lead to harm. Indeed, it is not assumed that level of drinking is necessarily the most useful distinguishing characteristic.

If less is always better (as the single-distribution approach assumes) then abstinence would logically be best of all. Harm-reduction measures, by contrast, presume that drinking will take place. This does not imply approval or disapproval of drinking; that drinking occurs is simply accepted as a fact that prevention measures must work with. By shifting toward a prevention approach based on pattern of drinking, it is possible to distinguish between safe and hazardous behavior, between responsible and reckless drinking.

Thus, harm-reduction measures are neutral regarding the long-term goals of intervention. They do not exclude the possibility that the eventual goal of intervention might include abstention for individuals who cannot control alcohol intake. Indeed, in some instances, such as when they form part of a tertiary prevention package (see, for example, chapter 13), harm-reduction measures can be a first step toward reducing or even ceasing alcohol use. Harm reduction involves a prioritization of goals, in which immediate and realizable goals take priority when dealing with reckless drinkers who cannot realistically be expected to cease drinking, but it need not conflict with an eventual goal of abstention, when such a goal is appropriate for a particular individual or group. It is, however, incompatible with a view that holds abstention to be the most appropriate goal for society at large, whether or not that goal is seen as attainable. It is simply neutral regarding the long-term goal of interventions, which are pragmatic rather than ideological in their orientation.

Thus, as the term is used in the following discussion, harm reduction refers to those measures that focus on decreasing the risk and severity of adverse consequences arising from alcohol consumption without necessarily decreasing the level of consumption. It is essentially a practical rather than an idealized approach: the standard of success is not some ideal drinking level or situation (abstention or low-risk levels) but whether or not the chances of adverse consequences have been reduced by the introduction of the prevention measure.

It may be helpful at this stage to give some examples of promising approaches to harm reduction in this field. It should be emphasized that this list is intended to be illustrative of the range of potential measures rather than a comprehensive account of available experience. It should also be emphasized that it is frequently by combining measures, particularly at a community level, that results are likely to be most encouraging.

- *Alcohol education.* Although some reviews of alcohol education have suggested that its capacity to initiate and sustain behavior change is less impressive than its proponents would like to suggest, there certainly have been promising examples, such as the French public education campaign (beginning with the *Bonjour les dégâts* television announcements) and the campaigns to reduce drunk driving in Australia and the United Kingdom. Media campaigns are discussed by Galbally and colleagues in chapter 10, which emphasizes that the effectiveness of education is greater when it is perceived as being consistent with other community-level measures. This issue is discussed at greater length in chapter 11 by Heath and Rosovsky, but the potential for clearly focused alcohol education programs to have a positive impact on reckless drinking behavior remains considerable. Education also provides the context for other measures, such as those described below.
- *Responsible hospitality programs.* The development of server intervention programs represents a harm-reduction measure in several respects. Such programs develop house policies to promote moderation, for example, by quality upgrading and by avoiding discounts such as "happy hours" or house specials. Operators are encouraged to monitor entry to prevent underage or intoxicated persons from entering an establishment. Staff are trained to recognize signs of intoxication and gradually to cease service of alcohol to patrons approaching intoxication. Servers are also trained to manage intoxicated patrons appropriately (including the provision of safe transportation home) should these preventive efforts fail. Server intervention programs attempt thereby to reduce problems associated with drinking, particularly impaired driving, without restricting drinking by the majority of drinkers. Evaluation studies have generally shown that establishments that have undergone server intervention programming tend to attract more customers and to be more profitable (Single 1990).
- *Measures to encourage quality control of beverage alcohol.* Although such measures have special relevance for some developing countries, where there

is an urgent need to test for methanol content or to identify toxic contaminants, they are also relevant to special situations in some industrialized countries. An excellent example is provided from Canada by the introduction of special early opening hours for a store of the Alberta Liquor Control Board in downtown Edmonton. The objective of the early opening was to reduce the use of potentially lethal nonbeverage alcohol by skid row inebriates. The measure was not intended to reduce their consumption; indeed, it was expected to increase their consumption of *potable* alcohol. It was focused exclusively on reducing adverse consequences from drinking substances such as shoe polish.

• *Measures designed to ameliorate adverse consequences of intoxication.* Rather than reducing the likelihood that intoxication will occur, these measures reduce the likelihood that serious damage will result. One of the best examples of such measures is the introduction in Scottish pubs of special glassware that crystallizes rather than shatters when broken, resulting in fewer injuries from accidents or if a fight breaks out (Plant, Single, and Stockwell 1997). Other measures include changes in the physical structure of drinking establishments to minimize the risk of accidents or reduce the harm that may result if a fight occurs (e.g., padding of furniture and compartmentalization of space). The *Nez Rouge* (Red Nose) program in Quebec is a community-based service providing two volunteer drivers (one for the drinker and one for his or her vehicle) to anyone who has had too much to drink at a party or licensed establishment. There are also measures not specifically aimed at drinking problems, such as the introduction of seat belts and air bags in cars, which have reduced the risk and severity of adverse consequences from drinking.

• *Early identification and simple interventions.* The evidence that has accumulated on the efficacy and cost-effectiveness of simple screening procedures and brief interventions at the primary-care level is now considerable. Many such programs concentrate upon specific indicators of harm and have as their objective the modification of drinking patterns to avoid the persistence of the occurrence or risk of such harm. The discussion of the role of the pharmacist as a life skills counselor in section IV of chapter 14 is a good illustration of how this approach may be especially relevant in countries where access to medical care may be limited.

• *Controlled drinking programs.* Controlled drinking as a treatment alternative for persons with alcohol-related problems may also be considered a harm-reduction measure. As with other harm-reduction measures, focus is placed on reducing the risk and severity of problems resulting from drinking. Just as harm-reduction measures for illicit drug users do not preclude abstention as a long-term goal, controlled drinking programs do not preclude abstinence as a possible outcome for some drinkers. However, the immediate concern is to reduce the problems associated with drinking. The controversy over controlled drinking is similar in many ways to the acrimonious debate between harm-reduction and zero-tolerance approaches regarding illicit drugs.

As noted above, these examples are intended to be illustrative rather than comprehensive. A recent publication (Plant, Single, and Stockwell 1997) reviews the specifics of harm-reduction approaches to alcohol-related problems in much greater detail. Nor should it be assumed that such measures constitute the totality of a comprehensive approach to the prevention of alcohol-related harm. The population approach to providing a balance between reasonable access and reasonable restrictions obviously creates the broad social context within which harm-reduction measures can be expected to be particularly effective. The difference is that the harm-reduction approach does not presume that the freedom of choice of the majority need be restricted in order to confer some protection, whether real or spurious, on a vulnerable or irresponsible minority.

THE RELATIONSHIP OF HARM REDUCTION TO DRINKING PATTERNS

A draft of the manuscript of this book was sent to a number of independent reviewers. In this section and the section following, we attempt to address some of the most important issues identified by the reviewers.

There is increasing international consensus regarding the validity and utility of drinking patterns as a predictor of social and health consequences (Rehm et al. 1996). The central contention in this book is that their predictive value is sufficiently strong to be able to develop prevention programs, and ultimately public policy, upon this basis. For this to happen, it is necessary to move from the current position, which accepts the potential utility of this hypothesis, to one in which its application in the prevention policy domain is actively explored and promoted. The challenge is to be able to identify which drinking patterns are harmful (and therefore require modification) and which are appropriate (and can therefore be promoted).

Indeed, the most persistent recurring theme in the comments from the independent reviewers was that, although we had convincingly established the reasonableness of our central hypothesis (that patterns of drinking are better predictors of drinking consequences than is per capita consumption), we needed more and better data to be able to describe and classify drinking patterns and to support the design of risk-reduction strategies to supplement or replace the population strategy. In this final chapter, we freely acknowledge the justice of this criticism. In response, we protest that we have gone only as far as current knowledge allows but far enough to demonstrate the urgent need for ourselves and others to go further.

It is beyond the scope of this book, and certainly of this chapter, to propose a new typology of drinking patterns. Some chapters, especially in part 1 of the book, have hinted at possible approaches, but it is likely that epidemiologists, public health advocates, clinicians, and the beverage alcohol industry would all view this issue from somewhat different perspectives. In the first instance, therefore, one might expect to uncover a range of alternative typologies, all of which would have their respective strengths and weaknesses. A challenge for the future is to attempt to bring these together with a view to advancing an overarching typology, which encompasses the various approaches and allows them to coexist harmoniously.

Rehm and colleagues (1996) have called for the development of standardized measures for the various elements encompassed by the term *pattern of drinking* and for more sophisticated methodologies and methods of analysis. Although their demand is an appropriate one and of great importance to the wider acceptance the drinking patterns concept by the scientific community, it falls short of the requirements of those engaged in social policy development, who will certainly be looking for a more accessible way of operationalizing the concept.

At one level, it is relatively straightforward. All things being equal, a pattern of drinking that leads to rapid intoxication is likely to be hazardous, and one that is characterized by moderation is likely to be benign. But all things are seldom equal, and the same level of intake, for example, in different circumstances might have quite different consequences, just as the same drinking style might be judged as more or less appropriate in different cultural contexts. It is also probable that it will prove easier to reach consensus on what constitute harmful drinking patterns than on what constitute benign ones. Nevertheless, the challenge of this approach is to attempt to develop both ends of the typology simultaneously.

An obvious first step is to undertake a secondary analysis of existing data sets that permit some elucidation of different drinking patterns. Arria and Gossop have demonstrated in chapter 4 the richness that may be available from existing sources of information. At the same time, there seems to be sufficient consensus within the scientific community for an examination of the determinants of drinking patterns to become a standard feature of epidemiological and clinical studies. Thus, over time, the inadequacy of existing data on drinking patterns, which is a recurring complaint in almost every chapter in this book, will gradually be remedied. This, in turn, will inform what we expect to be a continuing process of developing a useful and robust typology of drinking patterns.

POLICY IMPLICATIONS

There is a distinct trend toward prevention measures aimed at reducing the harmful consequences of drinking rather than reducing drinking per se. Several factors underlie this shift. One is that there has been a general decline in political support for controls over the availability of alcohol in many countries. Alcohol consumption has been declining in many Western countries since the late 1970s, generating concern for the maintenance of employment in the alcohol production and distribution industries and the hospitality industry and for the maintenance of revenues from the sale of beverage alcohol. At the same time, barriers to trade in beverage alcohol have been eroded by international trade agreements such as the European Economic Community, the North American Free Trade Agreement, and the General Agreement on Tariffs and Trade. It is unlikely that the World Trade Organization will be enthusiastic about measures that could restrict or constrain legitimate trade between countries.

The trend away from controls over alcohol availability is likely to continue as new evidence regarding the benefits of moderate consumption becomes more widely publicized. Indeed, a recent study in Canada has found that the number of lives saved by low-level use of alcohol is actually greater than the number of deaths caused by the immoderate use of alcohol (Single et al. 1996). This finding does not diminish the importance of the number of potential years of life lost and hospitalizations attributed to alcohol misuse, which are shown in the same study to exceed the years of life gained and the number of hospitalizations averted. Nonetheless, the finding that many deaths and hospitalizations are averted by alcohol use is likely to lead to increased attention to prevention measures that focus on reducing alcohol-related morbidity and mortality without necessarily restricting access to alcohol.

In particular, the harm-reduction approach focuses on preventing problems associated with intoxication and heavy drinking occasions. Rather than attempting to persuade light and moderate drinkers to reduce their level of consumption, a harm-reduction approach focuses on measures such as server intervention and preventive education to convince drinkers at all levels of consumption to avoid drinking to intoxication and to take steps to avoid adverse consequences should they overindulge. Furthermore, there is empirical support for focusing on the avoidance of intoxication. Analyses of national surveys in Australia (Stockwell et al. 1994), Canada (Single and Wortley 1993), and the United States (Midanik et al. 1994) have all found that the number of heavy drinking occasions is a stronger predictor of drinking problems than level of consumption. These findings indicate that it may be more efficient to focus on heavy drinking occasions and not the individual's level of consumption per se.

In an analysis of data from a Canadian national survey conducted in 1989 (Single and Wortley 1993), both the level of consumption and the number of times respondents reported consuming five or more drinks on an occasion were related to a series of alcohol problems. It was found that (1) the number of heavy drinking occasions is a stronger predictor of drinking problems than level of consumption and (2) there is an interaction effect regarding the joint impact of the number of heavy drinking occasions and level of consumption, with particularly high rates of alcohol problems among low-level drinkers who occasionally drink immoderately. Similar results have been found using more recent data from the 1993 General Social Survey in Canada on the joint impact of level of consumption and number of heavy drinking occasions on the likelihood of experiencing a drinking problem (Single et al. 1995).

These studies suggest that the likelihood of experiencing drinking problems is greater for a moderate-level drinker who occasionally drinks immoderately than for a high-level consumer who rarely or never drinks immoderately. As indicated in Chapter 1, this finding may be partly due to physical tolerance and it may also reflect the tendency for high-volume drinkers to develop social supports and other mechanisms to minimize adverse consequences of their drinking. There are obviously limits to the extent to which heavy drinkers can control adverse consequences; high-level drinking is associated with an elevated risk of many chronic health consequences, such as cirrhosis. However, for many acute adverse consequences of drinking, such as impaired driving, family dysfunction, and employment problems, relatively low-level consumers who occasionally drink immoderately contribute substantially to problem levels.

Indeed, focusing on drinking patterns makes it possible to understand that it is not necessary to move into the problem-drinking category all those low-level consumers who occasionally experience a problem. Reducing the average consumption of such drinkers would be unlikely to have much impact upon their infrequent and atypical heavier drinking occasions. The patterns approach, coupled with a harm-reduction strategy, enables alcohol policy to be centered on the concept of responsibility, which is a shared commitment involving governments, the beverage alcohol industry, and the individual consumer. What is meant by responsible drinking becomes clearer when it is expressed in terms of avoiding inappropriately heavy drinking occasions. Manifestly, this can be achieved within the context of a wide range of drinking styles, all of which could be deemed responsible.

These recent studies on the impact of patterns of drinking suggest that there may be a great deal to gain by focusing specifically on reducing heavy drinking occasions among all drinkers. This is in contrast to focusing on high-volume consumers or on aggregate level of consumption per se. This is not to say that programs specifically targeted at high-risk drinkers, such as early identification and intervention programs, should not be supported. These would undoubtedly result in reductions in alcohol problems. However, programs focusing on reducing overall levels of alcohol consumption clearly restrict reasonable freedom of choice for the majority whose drinking patterns seldom, if ever, become hazardous.

Thus, while the regulation of beverage alcohol in a general sense provides the context for public policy, it does not in and of itself constitute a coherent approach to the prevention of alcohol-related harm. As we move toward the elaboration of a flexible typology of drinking patterns, which could form the basis for more specific prevention programs, the most conservative and defensible position is probably to focus on heavy drinking occasions. Indeed, the findings above indicate that the most efficient approach may be to target preventive education on the general population but to focus on safe drinking limits and the avoidance of intoxication and other behaviors likely to cause problems rather than on the individual's overall level of consumption.

An essential test for the approach we are advocating is the extent to which it is universally applicable and, in particular, its relevance to countries that, for one reason or another, have not previously been active in the debate on alcohol policy. If sensible drinking (or whatever one chooses to call a drinking pattern based on the acceptance of responsibility for self and others) is to prove a useful concept, then it must have the same validity in parts of the world that do not have well-established drinking customs as it does in those countries in which drinking is integrated into the culture. An appeal to common sense may seem disingenuous, but it is important to recognize that alcohol policies, however good their intentions, have been drifting toward an orthodoxy far removed from the daily experience of most drinkers in the world. Part of the purpose of this book is to widen a debate that has been growing increasingly narrow.

To this end, one of the unique features of the book is that it has brought together contributions from a variety of scientific disciplines, from the public health community, and from the beverage alcohol industry. We are aware that not all speak with a single voice and that there are important differences of emphasis between the points of view expressed in different chapters. But the inclusion of these different points of view within the covers of this book is a demonstration of the conviction that alcohol policy is too important to be left to any one group in society, however wise or well-intentioned the members of that group may be. As we try to operationalize the concept of drinking patterns, as we struggle to find what constitutes sensible drinking for all sorts of people in all sorts of cultural contexts, we need to find a way to include in that process all those who have a legitimate interest in it.

That is what we attempt to do in this book. Its strengths are the strengths of its many authors and reviewers. Indeed, we owe a considerable debt of gratitude to our reviewers for drawing to our attention the areas in which we failed to meet our own ambitious goals. We try, in this chapter at least, to address some of their legitimate concerns, in particular our inability, at this stage, to differentiate modal drinking patterns in terms of their potential for harm and to propose specific measures to modify some patterns, eliminate others, and promote those most closely associated with maximizing benefits. Those tasks remain undone. What we hope to demonstrate is that efforts to do those tasks are already under way, that preliminary results are promising, that there is a broad consensus about the appropriateness of this direction, and finally, that we can expect by this means to contribute significantly to human health and happiness and to the quality of life of the vast majority of humankind.

With the erosion of political support for alcohol control measures and the emergence of new evidence about potential health benefits associated with low and moderate levels of alcohol consumption, it may be expected that alcohol prevention will increasingly focus on the reduction of harmful consequences of reckless drinking rather than on monitoring individual levels of consumption to avoid dependence. A shift from a focus on overall consumption to drinking patterns is therefore not merely of theoretical value. It represents a new prag-matism, which can lead to alcohol policies rooted in the interests of the individuals and communities they are intended to serve.

REFERENCES

Buning, E. 1990. The role of harm reduction programs in curbing the spread of HIV by drug injectors. In *Aids and Drug Misuse*, ed. J. Strang and G. Stimson. London: Routledge.

Donoghoe, M., G. Stimson, K. Dolan, and L. Alldritt. 1989. Changes in HIV risk behaviour in clients of syringe exchange schemes in England and Scotland. *Aids* 3:267–72.

Midanik, L., T. Tam, T. Greenfield, and R. Caetano. 1994. *Risk Functions for Alcohol-Related Problems in a 1988 U.S. National Sample.* Berkeley: California Pacific Medical Center Research Institute, Alcohol Research Group.

Plant, M., E. Single, and T. Stockwell, eds. 1997. *Alcohol: Minimising the Harm.* London: Free Association Books.

Rehm, J., et al. 1996. On the emerging paradigm: drinking patterns and their social and health consequences. *Addiction* 91:1615–21.

Riley, D. 1993. *The Harm-Reduction Model: Pragmatic Approaches to Drug Use from the Area between Intolerance and Neglect.* Ottawa: Canadian Centre on Substance Abuse.

Single, E. 1990. Server intervention: a new approach to the prevention of impaired driving. *Health Education Research* 5:237–45.

———. 1995. Defining harm reduction. *Alcohol and Drug Review* 14:287–91.

Single, E., L. Robson, X. Xie, and J. Rehm. 1996. *The Costs of Substance Abuse in Canada.* Ottawa: Canadian Centre on Substance Abuse.

Single, E., and S. Wortley. 1993. Drinking in various settings: findings from a national survey in Canada. *Journal of Studies on Alcohol* 54:590–99.

Single, E., et al. 1995. The 1993 General Social Survey II: alcohol problems. *Canadian Journal of Public Health* 86:397–401.

Stimson, G. 1989. Syringe exchange programs for injecting drug users. *Aids* 3:253–60.

Stockwell, T., D. Hawks, E. Lang, and P. Rydon. 1994. *Unraveling the Prevention Paradox.* Perth: National Centre for Research into the Prevention of Drug Abuse.

Watters, J., et al. 1990. AIDS prevention for intravenous drug users in the community: street-based education and risk behavior. *American Journal of Community Psychology* 18:587–96.

Wodak, A. 1990. AIDS and injecting drug use in Australia: a case control study in policy development and implementation. In *Aids and Drug Misuse,* ed. J. Strang and G. Stimson. London: Routledge.

Wodak, A., and B. Saunders. 1995. Harm reduction means what I choose it to mean. *Drug and Alcohol Review* 14:269–71.

Principles of Cooperation among the Beverage Alcohol Industry, Governments, Scientific Researchers, and the Public Health Community

Following extensive consultations with individuals and organizations in many countries, a group of experts met in Dublin on 26–28 May 1997 at the invitation of the National College of Industrial Relations and the International Center for Alcohol Policies. At the end of the meeting, in their individual capacities, they adopted by consensus the "Dublin Principles," and expressed the hope that these principles will be generally adopted.

Participants included scientists, industry executives, government officials, public health experts, and individuals from intergovernmental and nongovernmental organizations.

Preamble: The Ethics of Cooperation

The common good of society requires all its members to assume their fair share of social responsibility. In areas related to alcohol consumption, individuals and the societies in which they live need to be able to make informed choices. In order to further public knowledge about alcohol and prevent its misuse, governments, the beverage alcohol industry, scientific researchers, and the public health community have a common responsibility to work together as indicated in these Principles.

I. **Alcohol and Society: Cooperation among Industry, Governments, the Community, and Public Health Advocates**

    A. Governments, nongovernmental organizations, public health professionals, and members of the beverage alcohol industry should base their policies and positions concerning alcohol-related issues on the fullest possible understanding of available scientific evidence.

B. Consistent with the cultural context in which they occur, alcohol policies should reflect a combination of government regulation, industry self-regulation, and individual responsibility.

C. Consumption of alcohol is associated with a variety of beneficial and adverse health and social consequences, both for the individual and for society. Governments, intergovernmental organizations, the public health community, and members of the beverage alcohol industry, individually and in cooperation with others, should take appropriate measures to combat irresponsible drinking and inducements to such drinking. These measures could include research, education, and support of programs addressing alcohol-related problems.

D. Only the legal and responsible consumption of alcohol should be promoted by the beverage alcohol industry and others involved in the production, sale, regulation, and consumption of alcohol.

E. Both government and industry have a responsibility to ensure strict control of product safety.

F. To enable individuals to make informed choices about drinking, all those who provide the public with information about the health and societal impact of alcohol should present such information in an accurate and balanced manner.

- Advertising of beverage alcohol products should be subject to reasonable regulation, and/or industry self-regulation, and should not promote excessive or irresponsible drinking.
- Educational programs should play an important role in providing accurate information about drinking and the risks associated with drinking.

II. Alcohol Research: Cooperation among Industry, Governments, and the Scientific and Academic Communities

A. To increase knowledge about alcohol in all its aspects, the academic and scientific communities should be free to work together with the beverage alcohol industry, governments, and nongovernmental organizations.

B. The beverage alcohol industry, governments, and nongovernmental organizations should support independent scientific research that contributes to a better understanding of the use, misuse, effects, and properties of alcohol and the relationships among alcohol, health, and society.

C. The academic and scientific communities should adhere to the highest professional, scientific, and ethical standards in conducting and reporting on alcohol research, whatever the source of funding for such research.

D. All those concerned in a research undertaking, including funders, should avoid arrangements that might compromise the intellectual integrity and freedom of inquiry fundamental to scientific research and academic institutions.

1. When seeking support, scientific researchers should disclose any personal, economic, or financial interest that might directly and significantly affect the design, conduct, analysis, interpretation, or reporting of any research project.
2. Scientific researchers should acknowledge the source(s) of funding of their research activities in any report of such research.

E. Researchers should be free to disseminate and publish the results of their work. In order to protect proprietary information or trade secrets that do not have public health implications, dissemination and publication may be subjected to reasonable and ethical restrictions agreed in advance.

LIST OF PARTICIPANTS

The following is a list of participants in the Dublin meeting. (Institutional affiliations are provided for information only.)

Dr. Joe Asare, Ministry of Health, Accra, Ghana

Dr. Bernard Le Bourhis, Institut de recherches scientifiques sur les boissons, Paris, France

Mr. Michael B. Crutcher, Brown-Forman Corporation, Louisville, KY, USA

Dr. Ivan Diamond, University of California, San Francisco, CA, USA

Mr. Hans Emblad, International Consortium of Nongovernmental Organizations on Prevention of Substance Abuse, Fribourg, Switzerland

Mr. Marcus Grant, International Center for Alcohol Policies, Washington, DC, USA

Dr. Hurst Hannum, Tufts University, Medford, MA, USA

Dr. David Hawks, Curtin University of Technology, Perth, Australia

Dr. Annette van den Hogen, Heineken N.V., Amsterdam, The Netherlands

Mr. David W. Ichel, Simpson Thacher & Bartlett, New York, NY, USA

Dr. Paul Lemmens, University of Maastricht, Maastricht, The Netherlands

Dr. Jorge Litvak, International University Exchange, Inc., Washington, DC, USA

Dr. Henk van Luijk, Nijenrode University, Breukelen, The Netherlands

Dr. Desmond O'Byrne, World Health Organization, Geneva, Switzerland

Dr. Joyce O'Connor, National College of Industrial Relations, Dublin, Ireland

Ms. Gaye Pedlow, Guinness PLC, London, United Kingdom

Mr. Khee Liang Phoa, Dutch Foundation for the Responsible Use of Alcohol (STIVA), Rotterdam, The Netherlands

Dr. Martin Plant, The University of Edinburgh, Edinburgh, Scotland, United Kingdom

Dr. Flavio Poldrugo, University of Trieste, Trieste, Italy

Dr. Helen Ruddle, The National College of Industrial Relations, Dublin, Ireland

Dr. Norman Sartorius, University Hospital of Geneva, Geneva, Switzerland

Dr. Ronald Simpson, Joseph E. Seagram & Sons Inc., White Plains, NY, USA

Mr. Archer Tongue, International Council on Alcohol and Addictions, Lausanne, Switzerland

Mrs. Takako Tsujisaka, World Health Organization, Geneva, Switzerland

Index

abstainers, 18, 19, 28–29, 49, 70, 75, 79, 108, 115, 144, 156, 175, 244, 247, 260, 289, 290

accidents (*see also* injuries), 18–19, 34, 51, 77, 116, 177–180, 193, 199, 262, 281

Africa, 27, 108

Alcohol Use Disorders Identification Test (AUDIT) (*see also* prevention measures, screening), 233–234, 259, 259, 284

alcoholism (*see also* dependence), 18, 34, 45–51, 130–132, 135, 146, 211, 222, 223, 258, 282–283

Argentina, 16

Asia, 27, 31, 105

Australia, 12, 29, 36, 91, 97, 145, 162, 193–195, 226, 246, 250, 259, 261, 263, 279, 291, 294

Austria, 12, 16, 27, 36

Belgium, 12, 36, 279

beer (*see also* beverage type), 11, 27, 96, 99–100, 117, 144, 157, 223, 279

beverage type (*see also* beer, wine, distilled spirits), 7, 8, 9, 11–12, 15, 25, 28–29, 70–71, 72, 95, 105, 108, 116–118, 223

binge, 8, 17, 18, 19, 65, 69, 72–73, 75, 76, 94–95, 222, 224, 250, 251, 254, 259

biomedical factors (*see also* health benefits, health risks), 29, 45–52, 63–84, 91, 105–106, 109, 110, 142–143, 231

blood alcohol content (BAC) / blood alcohol level, 73, 134, 145, 161–162, 179

brief intervention (*see also* prevention measures), 21, 144–145, 256–259, 282–285, 292

Bulgaria, 16

Canada, 11, 14, 17, 20, 26, 27, 29, 30, 31, 34, 36, 58, 97, 160–161, 224, 250, 268, 278, 279, 292, 294

cardiovascular disease (CHD) (*see also* biomedical factors, health benefits, health risks), 3, 19, 29, 64, 67, 69–71, 73–76, 78–79, 82, 142–143, 156, 230–231

Chile, 115, 281–285

China, 16

control of consumption (*see also* control measures, Ledermann, single distribution theory), 1, 2, 129, 133–134, 138, 145, 153–155

control measures, 3, 8, 32, 205–216, 234–236, 294
  advertising, 8, 33, 143, 158–159, 209, 300
  availability, 33, 136, 143–144, 163, 235
  legal drinking age, 8, 161, 279, 290
  licensing hours, 8, 159
  outlet density, 159–160, 209
  price, 32, 33, 136, 147, 157–158, 171, 208, 235
  prohibition, 109–110, 143, 160–161, 208, 212, 277
  rationing, 143, 160
  taxation, 8, 157–159, 176, 193
  zoning, 8, 33
  (*see also* control of consumption,
    Ledermann, single distribution theory)
cross-cultural research, 8, 91–92, 103–123, 223, 226, 230, 232–234, 262, 263, 294, 300
Cuba, 16, 27, 37
Czechoslovakia, 17, 35, 37
Czech Republic, 16
Cyprus, 16

Denmark, 16, 17, 27, 37
dependence (*see also* alcoholism), 13, 34, 93, 222, 245, 254, 258, 289, 297
developing countries, 12, 27, 195, 212, 232–234
distilled spirits (*see also* beverage type), 11, 27, 95, 96, 99–100, 118, 157, 223, 226, 279
drink driving (*see also* control measures, prevention measures), 8, 9, 20, 34, 116, 134, 145, 161–163, 179, 228, 251, 278, 281, 290
drinking culture, 7, 10, 12, 95, 96–97, 104, 109, 110, 112–114, 117, 118–119
drinking guidelines, 104, 145, 161–163, 226, 246, 251, 260, 246, 262, 296
drinking occasion, 3, 7, 9, 10, 20–21, 91–92, 103, 123, 115–116, 117, 215, 216, 244, 250, 288, 295–297
drunkenness (*see also* intoxication), 18, 93–94, 96, 97, 108, 110, 244, 251

economic factors (*see also* control measures, external costs), 32, 107, 157–158, 169–186, 191, 195, 196, 235, 294
Europe, 27, 28, 29, 30, 32, 108

external costs (*see also* control measures, economic factors), 169–185, 190–192, 196, 197

Fiji, 91, 92, 95–96
Finland, 17, 27, 28, 29, 37, 73, 118, 135, 144, 160, 163
France, 12, 14, 16, 27, 28–29, 34, 36, 114, 143, 158, 163, 268, 291

Germany, 12, 16, 27, 37, 158, 268
Ghana, 91
Greece, 16
Guatemala, 92, 97

harm minimization (*see also* prevention measures), 3, 145–146, 194–195, 244, 246–247, 250, 253, 262–263, 288–293, 294–297
health promotion, 198, 267–272
health risks (*see also* biomedical factors, liver disease), 2, 3, 51–52, 66–68, 69, 71–78, 142, 156, 170–171, 181–182, 229–230, 300
health benefits (*see also* biomedical factors, cardiovascular disease), 1, 3, 67–68, 69–71, 74–75, 97–100, 142–143, 156, 245–246, 260–261, 295, 297, 300
HIV/AIDS, 195, 197, 289–290
Hungary, 16, 27, 35, 36

Iceland, 27, 29, 32, 35, 37, 92, 96, 108, 117, 160
injuries (*see also* accidents), 52, 64, 65, 66, 77, 229, 253
intoxication (*see also* drunkenness), 19, 21, 30, 31, 49, 73, 143, 145, 244, 245, 254, 259, 291
Ireland, 16, 17, 26, 27, 29, 35, 37, 299
Israel, 16, 37
Italy, 16, 27, 28, 36, 158, 163, 222, 268

Japan, 27, 29, 224, 226, 228, 268

Kenya, 259

Latin America, 10, 12, 27, 209, 234, 282
Ledermann (*see also* control of consumption, single distribution theory), 13–14, 90, 92–93, 129–130, 131, 132–138, 145, 147, 153–155, 244

liver disease (*see also* biomedical factors, health risks), 20, 34, 35, 71–73, 120, 134, 143, 144, 222, 296
Luxembourg, 16, 37

Malaysia, 16
measurement
  drink size, 8, 141, 225–226
  consumption level, 7, 8, 15, 17, 19, 94, 141, 221, 222, 223–224, 225–228, 294, 295, 297
  drinking context, 10–11, 222, 223–224
  effectiveness research, 143–144, 145, 234–236
  frequency, 78, 116, 139, 222, 225–228
  per capita consumption, 3, 15–19, 25–27, 63, 94, 132–136, 143, 235, 288, 296
  problems, 15–19, 48–51, 52–56, 65–66, 93–97, 138–140, 228–230, 245, 250, 253–256
  self-report, 30, 66, 226–228
  temporal variations, 7, 10, 20, 21, 224, 232, 255
  validity, 230–232, 233–234
Mexico, 16, 105, 109, 209, 259
Micronesia, 94, 160
Morocco, 16
mortality, 66–68, 70, 74, 132, 142–143, 145–146, 172–174, 182, 191–192

Netherlands, 12, 37, 144, 158
New Zealand, 17, 37, 279
Nigeria, 92, 226
Norway, 14, 16, 17, 27, 29, 37, 73, 118, 159, 160, 163
Nordic Countries, 10, 11, 12, 25, 135

Peru, 16, 37
Poland, 16, 27, 37, 163
Portugal, 16, 28, 36
preventive paradox, 9, 116, 131, 138–140, 155, 244–245, 263, 290
prevention measures
  breath testing, 145, 162–163
  designated drivers, 250, 278, 291, 292

education, 34, 44, 46, 56, 57, 144, 193–195, 197, 199, 200, 212, 213, 235–236, 246–247, 251, 261–262, 278–280, 283–285, 291, 296, 300 (*see also* harm minimization)
psychosocial factors, 43–45, 52–59, 78–79, 90–94, 110–115, 131, 222, 223, 231–232

quality of life, 2, 4, 97–100, 256, 290, 297

Romania, 35, 36
Russia, 16

screening (*see also* Alcohol Use Disorders Identification Test, prevention measures), 56–59, 141, 243, 251–252, 256–260
Singapore, 16
single distribution theory (*see also* control of consumption, Ledermann), 8, 12, 132–138, 146–148, 153–155, 244, 246, 290
Slovakia, 16
Spain, 16, 28, 36, 158, 163, 223
Sweden, 17, 27, 31, 37, 75, 114, 144, 160, 163
Switzerland, 16, 27, 29, 35, 36

Thailand, 16
treatment, 34, 254, 292
Tunisia, 16
Turkey, 16
Truk, 94, 160

Ukraine, 16
United Kingdom, 12, 17, 27, 37, 158, 159, 162, 226, 246, 251, 268, 279, 291, 292
USA, 12, 17, 19, 25, 27, 29, 30, 31, 32, 35, 37, 108, 113, 143–144, 160–161, 222, 224, 228, 250, 268, 277–281, 295

Venezuela, 16
violence, 95, 96, 116, 143, 180–181, 292

wine (*see also* beverage type), 12, 27, 99–100, 117–118, 144, 157,233, 226, 279

Yugoslavia, 35, 36